Contemporary Marriage

Structure, Dynamics, and Therapy

Contemporary Marriage

Structure, Dynamics, and Therapy

Edited by

Henry Grunebaum, M.D.

Associate Clinical Professor of Psychiatry, Harvard Medical School, Boston, Massachusetts; Senior Psychiatrist, Massachusetts Mental Health Center, Boston, Massachusetts, and Cambridge City Hospital, Cambridge, Massachusetts

Jacob Christ, M.D.

Associate Clinical Professor, Department of Psychiatry, Emory University School of Medicine, Atlanta, Georgia; Visiting Lecturer, Medical University of South Carolina, Charleston, South Carolina; Staff Psychiatrist, Northside Community Mental Health Center, Atlanta, Georgia

Little, Brown and Company
Boston

To
Michael
Eric
Daniel
Frans
Charlotte
Martin
Cathy
and
their
generation

Preface

Our experiences as clinicians and teachers have convinced us that what the therapist most requires in his or her work is an understanding of the basic forces that impinge on and determine the course and quality of married life. Some of these forces stem from the historically evolving problems and values of our society, some from the basic biological differences between the sexes, and still others derive from psychological factors, often subconscious, molded by past experiences and by the vicissitudes inherent in an intensely intimate relationship. The book is divided into three major parts: the first discusses the social forces that impinge on marriage; the second describes the course and psychology of the marital relationship; and the third deals with the diagnosis and treatment of couples with marital difficulties.

It is hoped that with an understanding of the interplay of social, psychological, and biological forces, the clinician will be better equipped to evolve a therapeutic approach shaped to the unique needs of the particular couple seeking aid and counsel. Further, it is our hope that this book will be useful to students of psychology, marriage and the family, social work, pastoral counseling, and psychiatry and ultimately useful to married couples in their quest for rewarding marital relationships.

We are indebted to Judith Grunebaum and Kathy O'Brien for their critical readings and helpful suggestions and to Justin Weiss for his help in selecting a title for this book.

H. G.
J. C.

Contents

xi Contents

Contributing Authors

Virginia D. Abernethy, Ph.D.

Assistant Professor in Psychiatry (Anthropology), Vanderbilt University School of Medicine, Nashville, Tennessee

Gwen J. Broude, Ph.D.

Research Associate, Department of Psychology and Social Relations, Harvard University, Cambridge, Massachusetts

Jacob Christ, M.D.

Associate Clinical Professor, Department of Psychiatry, Emory University School of Medicine, Atlanta, Georgia; Visiting Lecturer, Medical University of South Carolina, Charleston, South Carolina; Staff Psychiatrist, Northside Community Mental Health Center, Atlanta, Georgia

Joan M. Constantine, Dipl. Family Therapy

Family Therapist (private practice), Acton, Massachusetts

Larry L. Constantine, Dipl. Family Therapy

Clinical Instructor in Psychiatry, Tufts University School of Medicine, Boston, Massachusetts; Instructor in Psychiatry, Center for Training in Family Therapy, Boston State Hospital, Dorchester, Massachusetts

John Demos

Professor of History, Brandeis University, Waltham, Massachusetts

Ellsworth A. Fersch, Jr., Ph.D., J.D.

Lecturer, Department of Psychology and Social Relations, Harvard University, Cambridge, Massachusetts; Chief Psychologist, Community Mental Health Services, Massachusetts Mental Health Center, Boston, Massachusetts

Warren J. Gadpaille, M.D.

Adjunct Professor, Department of Psychology, Counseling and Guidance, University of Northern Colorado, Greeley, Colorado; Psychiatrist, Porter Memorial Hospital, Denver, Colorado

Janet Zollinger Giele, Ph.D.

Senior Fellow, Radcliffe Institute, Radcliffe College; Research Associate, Department of Sociology, Harvard University, Cambridge, Massachusetts

George W. Goethals, Ed.D.

Lecturer on the Psychology of Personality, Harvard University; Consultant in Psychology, Harvard University Health Services, Cambridge, Massachusetts

Henry Grunebaum, M.D.

Associate Clinical Professor of Psychiatry, Harvard Medical School, Boston, Massachusetts; Senior Psychiatrist, Massachusetts Mental Health Center, Boston, Massachusetts, and Cambridge City Hospital, Cambridge, Massachusetts

E. James Lieberman, M.D., M.P.H.

Clinical Assistant Professor of Psychiatry, Howard University College of Medicine, Washington, D.C.

**David Maddison,
F.R.A.C.P., F.A.N.Z.C.P.**

Foundation Dean, University of Newcastle Medical School, Newcastle, Australia. Formerly, Professor of Psychiatry, University of Sydney, Sydney, Australia, and Head, Department of Psychiatry, Royal Prince Alfred Hospital, Camperdown, Australia

Bernard I. Murstein, B.S.S., M.S., Ph.D.

Professor of Psychology, Connecticut College, New London, Connecticut

Norman A. Neiberg, Ph.D.

Assistant Director, Division of Legal Medicine, Massachusetts Department of Mental Health; Assistant Psychologist, Department of Psychiatry, Massachusetts General Hospital, Boston, Massachusetts

Avodah K. Offit, M.D.

Clinical Instructor in Psychiatry, Cornell University Medical College; Consulting Psychiatrist in Sexual Treatment and Study Program and Outpatient Psychiatrist, Payne Whitney Psychiatric Clinic, The New York Hospital; Coordinator, Sexual Therapy and Consultation Center, and Adjunct Assistant Psychiatrist, Lenox Hill Hospital, New York, New York

Beverley Raphael, M.B. B.S. D.P.M., M.A.N.Z.C.P., M.R.C. Psych.

Associate Professor in Psychiatry, University of Sydney; Honorary Psychiatrist, Royal Prince Alfred Hospital, Sydney, Australia

Rhona Rapoport, Ph.D.

Co-Director, Institute of Family and Environmental Research, London, England

Robert N. Rapoport, Ph.D.

Director, Institute of Family and Environmental Research, London, England

Constantina Safilios-Rothschild, Ph.D.

Professor of Sociology and Director, Family Research Center, Wayne State University, Detroit, Michigan

James W. Smith, Ph.D.

Coordinator of Clinical Services, Boston Institute for Psychotherapies, Boston, Massachusetts; Psychologist (private practice), Boston and Brockton, Massachusetts

Robert S. Steele, Ph.D.

Assistant Professor of Psychology, Wesleyan University, Middletown, Connecticut

John A. Vering III, B.A.

Student and Member of Law Review, University of Virginia Law School, Charlottesville, Virginia

Lynn Parker Wahle, M.A.

Visiting Lecturer, Continuing Education Program, Jane Addams School of Social Work, University of Illinois; Faculty, Family Institute of Chicago/Center for Family Studies, Institute of Psychiatry, Northwestern University Medical School and Northwestern Memorial Hospital, Chicago, Illinois

Jurg Willi, M.D.

Assistant Professor of Psychiatry, University of Zurich; Clinical Associate Psychiatric Outpatient Clinic, University of Zurich, Zurich, Switzerland

John Zinner, M.D.

Clinical Associate Professor of Psychiatry and Behavioral Sciences, The George Washington School of Medicine and Health Sciences, Washington, D.C.

I
Marriage and Society

Changes in social values and obvious vicissitudes in marriage notwith-standing, the institution of marriage is still very much with us. This is true despite the fact that in many modern societies, and increasingly in our own, the satisfaction of sexual needs often takes place without the sanction of a marriage ceremony. People may marry somewhat later in life on the average than they did 20 years ago, but they still marry in overwhelming numbers, and they marry again and again. It is not the act of marrying that is changing, but rather the reasons individuals have for marrying and how they define a good marriage.

There are those who believe that monogamous marriage is on its way out and that alternative forms of marriage will ultimately take its place. These theories are discussed in the chapter by Giele, who suggests that the alternatives to marriage are at least as difficult to cope with psycho-logically. The Constantines, while advocating a freer and more open view of marriage, make clear in their chapter that group marriage is at best a complicated undertaking. For ourselves, we are impressed that the desire for roots and historical continuity is an essential human attribute, perhaps deriving from man's millenia of evolution from ancestors who lived in small groups or clans. So, marriage, while changing, will probably continue as a major alternative for many.

However, new meanings of the marriage bond have evolved as the sacred nature of that bond has eroded in our increasingly secular society. In the words "before God and this company," "God" no longer carries the weight He used to. "This company," however, continues to be important, although influenced by the greater mobility of our society. The economic assumptions underlying marriage are changing as women attain equal rights and increased earning power. Sexual mores and attitudes about the relationship between the sexes have changed, and the necessity for and ability to engage in effective family planning have led to control of fertility and smaller families.

It appears that the nature of marriage and the age at which people marry are changing due to the development of contraception and its increasing acceptance. This has led to the separation into three stages what was formerly accomplished simultaneously by the act of marrying. Until recently marriage meant the commitment to live with another adult, the opportunity for an active sexual life, and the decision to have children. However, increasingly, marriage is no longer believed to be necessary for sexual activity, and cohabitation of an unmarried adult man and woman is becoming acceptable.

A most useful concept is the idea that at any given time in history some individuals are living their lives in the manner viewed as usual for the time, while others are conducting themselves in ways which are somewhat old-fashioned, and still others are vanguards of the future. In the light of this perspective, it seems apparent that clinicians will today encounter couples who live according to the norms of the past and others who are conducting themselves in ways which the society has yet to accept as appropriate. In particular, it is our belief that much of what is described in this book applies not only to married couples, but to couples in general. There are certain overriding psychological implications of any adult pairing which involve long-term commitment and intimacy (particularly sexual intimacy).

Divorce statistics are always quoted in the context of the changing patterns of marriage. The number of divorces seems to be steadily increasing in the United States and most Western societies. Adherents of traditional, religious views of marriage see divorce as highly undesirable or even sacriligious. Yet, Italy, a predominantly Catholic country, voted in 1974 to retain its new liberal divorce laws. In the United States, for some time, a fairly liberal, humanistic view has prevailed; that is, that people should not be forced to live together in an unhappy marriage and divorce is increasingly accepted. Divorce is thought of in a variety of ways: as a release from bondage, as a neurotic search for novelty, or as the natural growing apart of individuals. One of the reasons for this change in attitude may be the increased longevity of life due to advances in science and medicine. "Til death do us part" now may span a period that in the past may have been two lifetimes. Two lifetimes with one person may wear thin even the most ideal relationships.

But regardless of how outsiders view divorce, it is rarely experienced as other than tragic and painful by the participants. As at the beginning of marriage, the impact of society and its laws on the process of divorce is critical, as discussed in the chapter by Fersch and Vering. The present legal system often fosters an adversary situation in which one of the partners must be found guilty. However, there is a growing trend toward no-fault divorce, whereby two people may dissolve their marriage simply by mutual consent. This is a reflection of modern society's tendency toward freeing the individual from bondage while offering him the pain of choice. Divorce permits either life as a single person or re-marriage with a renewed chance for happiness, freeing people from the long-held view of marriage as the only route to successful adaptation and happiness.

Happiness is clearly a major goal of most individuals who marry, yet the extent to which it can be directly achieved as a goal rather than as a by-product of other activities must be questioned. Marriage has always served the biological and economic needs of individuals and the need of the species to perpetuate itself through protection of the young. In her chapter, Abernethy discusses recent changes in society and the effects on marriage of the fact that it is becoming less essential as an economic union necessary for survival of the couple. Increasingly, marriage is a union, bound by emotional ties between individuals in a society whose values are in flux.

The traditional expectations of a marital partner are loyalty, mutual respect (honor), and mutual caring. Recently, newer expectations have been added to these, such as companionship, sexual satisfaction, and support in solving personal psychological problems. To be a best friend, a favored bed-companion, and a "therapist" are difficult tasks, especially "through sickness and health, for richer and poorer, for better and worse."

The responsibilities of marriage have not only increased in number, but the criteria of success are less well-defined and more likely to be inherently contradictory. Being a "good provider" or a "good housekeeper" is a well-defined task, while being a good companion is more vague, as it may require silence at one time and conversation at another. The more the demands on a marriage are clear-cut and concrete, such as earning a living, procreating, and caring for the other person in times of illness, the more clearly can the success or failure be assessed. However, sexual gratification, psychological assistance to another person, and friendship are far more subtle, indefinite, and sophisticated in their requirements, the more so as individuals evolve and change over time. In addition, the fulfillments sought for in marriage are often contradictory in their requirements. Stability, loyalty, and dependability are qualities which do not easily coexist with stimulation, excitement, and variety. Synthesis will be hard won, requiring much from each partner if they are to achieve it.

Similarly, higher expectations now are demanded of the married couple as parents. In contrast to the situation in the underdeveloped countries and in the not-too-distant past of the more affluent countries, most children born today in modern Western societies will survive childhood rather than die at an early age. Each child is more important, and it is no longer considered sufficient to rear up moral, hardworking offspring whose deviations may be explained as innate deficiencies, the influence of evil companions, or obstinancy. Now, parents expect, with the help of experts, to rear children free of psychological problems, well-liked by all, and moral and hardworking to boot. The responsibility for deviations from this ideal are attributed to the parents both by themselves, by professionals in the field of child psychotherapy, and by therapists. A generation of adults who have grown up in a Freudian world, insightful into the influence of their parents' personalities on their own lives, may well expect that their children will have much to blame them for.

The sheer limitations of time and energy force on couples painful choices and recurrent conflicts. The role of parent and the role of spouse will recurrently conflict. One cannot diaper a baby or help a child with his or her homework and at the same time have a heart-to-heart talk with one's husband or wife or even a chat over a dry martini. The blithe assumption that a good marriage will automatically produce happy children must seriously be questioned. "Spousehood" is hard work, and the same is true of parenthood; the resolution of conflicts and loyalties between these two roles can at times be strenuous. The same is true of the demands on time and energy of work, hobbies, relatives and friends, or simply the desire to be alone. Yet, even though these contradictory demands require resolution and mutual cooperation by the marital partners, a marriage will be overburdened and impoverished without the support and stimulation of friends, relatives, work, and the outside world. Intimacy is a highly valued experience, but too much dependence on a spouse alone to satisfy emotional needs may place too great a burden on a marriage.

We have been impressed by how few studies have been done on the effects of children on marriage. The effects of children on marital happiness have, however, been investigated to some extent; marital happiness appears to decline as children increase in number and as they become older, rising gradually again to its pre-child level as they graduate from school and leave home. Children have a major impact on the life of a couple as all parents with a colicky baby know. In fact, from our observations it seems at least as likely that "good" babies make happy parents as that happy parents make "good" babies.

The traditional view was that a young man must first be economically independent and must be able to support a wife and children before he contracted a marriage. He was to be the breadwinner and the wife was to be the housekeeper and mother of his children. What is more, it was almost certainly the case that her parents either selected him or had a veto power over her selection. For instance, the great-grandmother of one of the authors is said to have told her father (this was remembered and passed down because it was regarded as a revolutionary statement) that while she would never marry a man of whom he disapproved, she would never marry a man she did not love.

Changes in the means of production have had a powerful influence on our views of marriage. Industrialization brought with it the separation of home and work and separate roles for the female and male. But technology has advanced so far that most factory work requires little physical strength, thereby opening up this job market to women. In addition, the majority of jobs in our current economy are in the service professions, and thus, can be performed equally well by men and women.

The increasing economic equality of women in the job market, in business, and in the professions has also blurred the rigid separation of roles for the sexes, as discussed by the Rapoports in their chapter. Concomittantly, marriage is no longer viewed as a partnership in which life's tasks are divided according to custom. Rather, it is now often a voluntary association of two equals, both increasingly capable of sustaining themselves and of performing many or most of the necessary tasks, the division of which is determined by cooperative decision-making.

There is reason to believe that the urbanization of our society has also had major consequences for marriage, although it is difficult to separate myth from fact, as Demos discusses in his chapter. We have grown up with values from an earlier age which we see only dimly, often mistaking our wish to idealize the past for fact. We tend to envisage the nineteenth-century rural American family living happily together on a farm, with grandparents present and other relatives not far away. Our myth suggests that the extended family provided ample support for any individual in need, a scene of idyllic bliss without conflict. Yet the shorter life expectancy and the difficulties of travel in the past were hardships which alone make this picture an unlikely reality. Clearly, the family life was far from idyllic for the multitudes of immigrants or slaves who came to this country, leaving behind many of their relations, friends, jobs, and cultural roots, or for those who went West to the frontier in search of land to farm or their fortune. Nonetheless, it is our myth, and we compare our present rootless state to that era. This nostalgic idealism existed even in Greek times and Egyptian papyrus states, "Times are no longer what they used to be and children do not obey their parents."

This complicated mixture of myth and reality influences our current expectations of marriage. Today the married couple is thought to live in relatively greater isolation from the origins of either spouse. Usually there are only two generations living in the house — the parents and the children. The spouses in this nuclear family are thought to be economically and emotionally far more dependent on each than was the case in the past and the ties of young adults to their parents are often spoken of as dependence. Clearly this is a pejorative label when compared with its opposite, independence. Bowlby, among others, has maintained the essential humanness of our need for attachments to each other, and the search for rootedness, tradition, and heritage are powerful forces as the persistence of ethnic groups and styles demonstrates. In the recent American past the efforts of individuals were directed more to freeing themselves and leaving behind their roots. But now we see an increasing awareness of community, continuity, and ethnicity as a counterweight to existential loneliness and anomie.

Insofar as couples are isolated from their families they tend to depend on outsiders for advice or help in times of conflict and crises. Clergymen, counselors, social workers, psychologists, and psychiatrists are increasingly involved in the rebalancing of marriages that are in dysequilibrium. But it is sheer speculation to maintain that a society in which the extended family existed was more conducive to the mental health of the marriage. And it would clearly be misleading and unfounded to say that our grandparents had fewer marital problems; perhaps their problems were experienced differently or simply ignored due to the presence of other problems. What is vital today is not that the professionals have a solution to marital problems, but that they help couples toward a clearer perception of just what is troubling them, opening the way to the possibility of greater mastery. The therapist will be assisted in this task if he apprehends the dynamic complexity of the social context within which the struggles of intimacy take place.

1
Myths and Realities in the History of American Family-Life

John Demos

To study the history of the American family is to conduct a rescue mission into the dreamland of our national self-concept. No subject is more closely bound up with our sense of a difficult present — and our nostalgia for a happier past. How often, in reference to contemporary problems, does the diagnostic finger point in the direction of family life. Significantly, this emphasis comes from both the right and the left. Conservatives detect a loosening of the bonds of family, a poisonous infiltration of permissiveness. Time was, they contend, when domestic life established sound patterns of authority that served to guarantee an orderly society. On the other side, counterculture spokesmen decry a damaging trend toward rigid — and alienating — "nuclear" households. It is their aim to recapture the spirit, if not the exact forms, of an "extended family" system allegedly typical of the premodern era. These perspectives differ greatly as to substance, but there is a common pejorative thrust. In both cases the story of the family through time is a story of decline and decay.

But the *reality* of family life in the past is something else again. To capture that reality is an extraordinarily difficult task. Source materials are scattered and fragmentary. The pertinent methodologies are

9

highly complex. And, in truth, professional historians have only recently become concerned with such seemingly private and personal subjects. For precisely the same reasons, however, the field presents a fascinating challenge to scholars. Moreover, since there is such an overlay of myth and misconception here, the outcome may have some sociological importance. If the family in contemporary America warrants special consideration — perhaps even a major overhaul — then this must be based insofar as possible on an accurate understanding of the previous history of the American family.

The first Americans were, of course, post-Elizabethan Englishmen and heirs of a traditional culture with roots far back in the medieval past. This culture was imported whole when they crossed the ocean to begin the settlement of a "new world." Prominent among their mental baggage were deeply held beliefs and values about family life — its proper shape and substance and its place in that larger scheme of things that has sometimes been characterized as the "great chain of being."

There was, to begin with, the unquestioned assumption of a tight link between the family and the community at large. The individual household was the basic unit of everyday living, the irreducible cell from which all human society was fashioned. It formed, indeed, the model for every larger structure of authority; as one seventeenth-century author declared, "a family is a little church, and a little commonwealth . . . a school, wherein the first principles and grounds of government and subjection are learned, whereby men are fitted to greater matters in church or commonwealth." Or — to reverse the metaphor — religious and political communities were only families writ large. The head of the family, normally the father, was also an agent of the state. In fact, the principle of fatherhood lay right at the heart of most political thinking in this period. The higher ranks of men — gentry, noblemen, bishops — were all pictured as fathers to those who fell within their various jurisdictions. The king was simply the grandest and most powerful of these patriarchal figures. Of course, the Puritans — prominent among the colonial settlers — came to exclude the king from their scheme of authority, but this was a substantive, not a structural, difference. Like all men of their time, they assumed the fusion of family and community in the preservation of order.

But what did this mean in detail? It meant, first of all, that a man was not free to do entirely as he pleased within his own family. The larger community — the state — felt concerned in all his behavior toward his wife and children, and acted accordingly. Thus, for example, a disobedient child was not only punished with a thrashing at the hands of his father; he was also liable to action by the courts. Or — another example — colonial magistrates might remove a child from the care of "unseemly" parents and place him in some other family. Or, again, a local court could order the reunion of a husband and wife who had decided to live apart. Occasionally, this obliged a man (or a woman) to leave the colonies altogether, in order to search for a long-lost spouse in England. In general, individuals who lived by themselves were regarded as potential sources of disorder, and court records are full of directives to such people to find a family in which to locate themselves. In all these ways the state might interfere in the sphere of family life. The word *interfere* expresses, of course, our own view of the matter, and the point is that people in the seventeenth century felt quite differently. They regarded such activity as a natural and vital prerogative of the state.

This pattern seemed appropriate because the premodern family performed a wide range of practical functions, both for its own members and for society at large. The household was, for example, the primary unit of economic production and exchange. The vast majority of the American colonists were farmers, and, as in most agricultural communities, there was ample work for everyone, right down to the very young. These families possessed an occupational cohesion not even approximated in our own day. Moreover, the family was also the chief agent of education in colonial America. Schools were limited both in their number and in the character of their facilities, and colleges were for the wealthy few. It was, therefore, from parents that most children learned what they knew of the three Rs. And it was parents (or parental surrogates) who transmitted the vocational skills that would be essential to adult life, whether in farming or (less often) in some one of the skilled trades. In this connection the apprenticeship system precisely epitomized the larger significance of family life.

The family also provided a variety of social services, which now pertain to other institutions. It was the usual place of recourse for sick persons and the elderly. (Old people no longer able to care for themselves would sometimes move in with the family of a grown son, in exchange for a gift of money or land.) Orphans and the indigent were "placed," by local magistrates, in particular households. Even criminals were occasionally handled in this way — implying the effectiveness of the family both as an agency of restraint and as a setting for personal reform.

This range of activity and function, so different from that which obtains today, has fostered the belief that the colonial family was different in its *composition* as well. Scholars have long thought that premodern society was organized into "extended households" — large kin-groups, including several conjugal pairs, and spanning three or four generations. A corollary assumption has connected our own "nuclear" pattern with the coming of the Industrial Revolution little more than a century ago. But recent demographic research has shown these notions to be quite unfounded. It is now clear that nuclear households have been the norm in America since the time of the first settlements, and in England for as far back as evidence survives. The fundamental unit, then as now, was husband, wife, and their natural children. Occasionally, to be sure, this group was modified through the temporary residence of an elderly grandparent (as mentioned previously), or of an apprentice, or of some charge on the community; but such arrangements were of limited impact overall.

The most compelling evidence of this nuclear orientation relates to the process of marriage-making. It was the firm expectation of all concerned that a newly wed couple would establish their own separate *ménage.* The families of both bride and groom joined together to provide the necessary means, contributing land, housing, money, and personal effects in amounts stipulated by formal "deeds of gift." Usually such agreements involved painstaking discussion — and often some rather tough bargaining. The fathers of the intended exercised a powerful hand here, by virtue of their control over property; but it should not be thought that these were arranged marriages in some total sense. Affection took precedence — in the literal sense of coming first in time — and practical considerations followed. Life in these communities presented regular opportunities for courtship and some for sexual dalliance (witness the long sequence of "fornication" cases in the court records).

In practice, the range of potential partners was limited by factors of geography and social class. Most colonial settlements were small (less than

100 families), and there was little chance for courting between towns.
Moreover, it was expected that a man and woman planning marriage would
evince an overall equality of material — and spiritual — estate. But love
must be present, to begin with, and would hopefully remain strong as the
couple waxed in years. The letters of John and Margaret Winthrop are a
moving testimony to marital devotion ("I kiss my sweet wife, and think
of thee long. Farewell, thy John."), and it seems reasonable to infer
similar feelings among humbler folk who did not leave written records
behind.

As in all societies, however, some marriages worked less well than
others. In a few cases, a *very* few, the local courts might sanction
divorce. The acceptable grounds were limited to desertion (for a period
of no less than seven years), adultery, and impotence. (The third of
these grounds reflects the important assumption that marriage should
provide sexual companionship and yield children.) Incompatibility was
recognized as a significant problem — an occasion sometimes for outside
intervention, but not for divorce. Legal records reveal a variety of domestic troubles in frequently pungent detail: a man punished for "abusing
his wife by kicking her off from a stool into the fire"; a woman charged
with "beating and reviling her husband, and egging her children to help
her, bidding them knock him in the head, and wishing his victuals might
choke him"; a couple "severely reproved for their most ungodly living in
contention with the other." In all such cases the courts stood ready to
declare their interest and to exert their authority.

For the colonists, as for people everywhere, family life was influenced
by profound beliefs as to differences of age and gender. Concerning
women, the thinking of this period was clear enough: in virtually every
important respect theirs was the weaker, the inferior, sex. Their position
in marriage was distinctly subordinate, their chief duty being "obedience"
to their husbands. Their mental and moral capacities were rated well below those of men. Governor Winthrop's journal records the sad tale of a
lady who went insane "by giving herself largely to reading and writing";
in short, intellectual activities were simply unsuited to women's character.
There is one other element in the colonial view of women that is hard to
specify and even harder to analyze: an implicit, but unmistakable, under-
current of suspicion and fear. Femininity was linked to deep and mysterious dangers — an inherent potential for evil and corruption. There was a

sense that women were less than trustworthy. Thus one finds in legal and personal documents a comment like the following: "If you would believe a woman, believe me . . . " It also seems significant that witchcraft was attributed far more often to women than to men. (There are cultures where the reverse is true.) Still, one must not overemphasize these alleged sex differences. Colonial women were never truly set apart. Women's lives, and characters, overlapped with men's at many points; a whole world of thought and feeling and practical circumstance was effectively shared. Their experience from day to day was too similar, their partnership too profound, to support the more radical forms of sex-typing that would develop in a later era.

And what of the young in colonial America? There remain from the period various books and essays on the proper deportment of children, which convey some impression at least of what was expected. A central theme in these works — especially, but not exclusively, in the writings of the Puritans — is the need to impose strict discipline on the child virtually from the beginning of life. Here is the advice of Reverend John Robinson, a leading preacher among the Pilgrims just prior to their departure for America: "Surely there is in all children . . . a stubbornness and stoutness of mind arising from natural pride which must in the first place be broken and beaten down, that so the foundation of their education being laid in humility and tractableness, other virtues may in their time be built thereon." The key terms are *broken* and *beaten down*. The child was regarded as coming into the world with an inherently corrupt and selfish nature, and this created *the* central problem for parents. Another urgent concern was the inculcation of religious principles — again, from an extremely early age. Cotton Mather's diary contains the following description of a conference with his 4-year-old daughter:

I took my little daughter Katy into my study and then I told my child I am to die shortly and she must, when I am dead, remember everything I now said unto her. I set before her the sinful condition of her nature, and charged her to pray in secret places every day that God for the sake of Jesus Christ would give her a new heart. I gave her to understand that when I am taken from her she must look to meet with more humbling afflictions than she does now [that] she has a tender father to care for her.

A tender father indeed! This passage startles us; the calculated appeal to fear affronts our sense of the needs and sensibilities of children. But there is a vital issue of context here. *Colonial society barely recognized childhood as we know and understand it today.* Consider, for example, the matter of dress: in virtually all seventeenth-century portraiture, children appear in the same sort of clothing that was normal for adults. In fact, this accords nicely with what we know of other aspects of the child's life. His work, much of his recreation, and his closest personal contacts were encompassed within the world of adults. From the age of 6 or 7 he was set to a regular round of tasks about the house or farm (or, in the case of a craftsman's family, the shop or store). When the family went to church, or when they went visiting, he went along. In short, from his earliest years he was expected to be — or to try to be — a miniature adult.

The above description has blurred somewhat the distinction between theory and practice, between norms and actual behavior, in the settlers' approach to family life. It is necessary, therefore, to consider more directly the ways in which their ideals and expectations were modified, and in some cases transformed, by various factors inherent in the American environment.

There was, first of all, the simple factor of space. Most of the colonists assumed that the proper way to live was in compact, little village-communities, such as their forbears in England had known for centuries. But in the New World, of course, the ecological context was wildly different. Out beyond the fringes of settlement there was land for the taking — seemingly limitless in extent and empty of "civilized" use or habitation. (Thus was the presence of Indians discounted.) For many people this presented an overpowering temptation — to move, and to live for and by oneself. Thus, by the early eighteenth century, the typical pattern of settlement was not a checkerboard of well-spaced villages, but rather a straggling, jumbled mosaic with houses strung out willy-nilly into the wilderness.

But the lure of empty land fragmented not only villages; families, too, were significantly affected. Movement away from the older centers of settlement was often accomplished in terms of successive generations. Young people, as they approached adulthood, began to consider the possibilities of settling new land near the frontier. The usual alternative was to accept a "portion" in their home village, that would come from their parents on the occasion of marriage, but often this portion was simply much *less* than what they could hope to gain for themselves elsewhere. And so they would leave. There is a passage in William Bradford's famous history of Plymouth that vividly lays bare this dimension of colonial experience. Bradford deplored the process whereby settlers moved steadily away from Plymouth to take up new lands elsewhere, leaving the original site "like an ancient mother grown old and forsaken of her children, though not in their affections, yet in regard of their bodily presence and personal helpfulness; her ancient members being most of them worn away by death, and she like a widow left only to trust in God." The metaphor is poignant enough in its own right, but it must have rung doubly true for many of Bradford's readers. For it was part of the New World experience that families should be continually divided and that at least some elderly people should be left behind to fend for themselves after their children had moved on.

This altered balance between men and their environment would, in the long run, affect authority relations within the family. There are many scraps of evidence to suggest that the position of the young was measurably strengthened. If a child — an older child — felt unduly constrained by his family situation, he could simply leave. Better still, he could use the threat of leaving as leverage in struggles or quarrels that might arise with his parents. There was also the fact that younger persons were often the most flexible and resourceful in meeting the challenges of the new land. Here, indeed, is the start of a central theme in the lives of immigrant families through the whole course of American history: parental authority is progressively undermined as the child discovers that he is more *effective* in the new setting than his foreign-born father and mother.

It also seems evident that the American environment worked to improve significantly the status of women. We can trace this process most easily with respect to a woman's legal standing: her right to hold property, for instance, was extended well beyond the traditional limits of the Old World. Moreover, by the eighteenth century many women were active in business and professional pursuits. They ran inns and taverns; they managed a wide variety of stores and shops; and, at least occasionally, they worked in careers like publishing, journalism, and medicine. More broadly, they seem to have interacted easily and informally with men, in all sorts of everyday encounters. There are, in the records of colonial America, no grounds for inferring a pervasive system of deference based on sex.

And what accounts for this rise in woman's status? First, there was her sheer functional necessity given the special circumstances of colonial life. Her area of responsibility included those basic domestic chores with which we are still familiar today, and much, much more. The average household was also a miniature factory — producing clothing, furniture, bedding, candles, and other such accessories — and in all this the woman's role was central. There were also some occasions when she joined the menfolk for work in the fields. Finally, it was very much to her advantage that she was relatively scarce. Recent studies suggest that men outnumbered women by a ratio of roughly three-to-two during most of the colonial period.

One more topic, highly germane to family life, deserves special mention here — namely, the prevalent attitudes and behavior in regard to sexuality. The traditional view is tediously familiar: Puritans were nothing if not puritannical; thus colonial culture was characterized by sexual repressiveness of an extreme kind, and the trend ever since has been slowly but steadily in the direction of greater "freedom." But this picture is seriously misleading, for the reason (among others) that it obscures important changes even within the colonial period. It is true enough that the earliest settlers, especially in New England, maintained a firm moral code, which proscribed all sexual contacts outside of marriage. However, this code was directly violated by at least some individuals from the very start, and in the eighteenth century it was widely compromised. Gradually fornication ceased to be a crime that was taken into court; instead legal dockets became filled with cases of "bastardy." In short, there was a growing tolerance for premarital sexual experience; the main problem was the disposition of those illegitimate children brought into the world as a result of this tolerance. There is other evidence bearing out the same trends. It is possible, for example, to obtain rates of bridal pregnancy by comparing the dates on which given couples were married with the dates of birth of their first children. (A "positive" case is recorded whenever the interval is eight months or less.) The results for colonial America are most interesting. Positive cases appear only rarely until the very end of the seventeenth century. In the early eighteenth century, however, the rate rises markedly. And by 1750 as many as one-third to one-half of the brides in some communities were going to the altar pregnant.

By the end of the eighteenth century it was clear that American family-life had been considerably transformed. Some elements of the transformation have been sketched in the preceding pages: the break in the tight web of connections between the family and the larger community; the dispersion of the household group, with the young increasingly inclined to seek their fortune in a new setting; the improvement in the status of wo-men; the erosion of parental authority; and a growing permissiveness in the area of sex. These changes were experienced by many people at the time as a kind of decline, and there is a nonpejorative sense, too, in which they represented a loosening of old commitments and standards. It is im-portant to see the tendency whole, because the early nineteenth century marks a crucial transition point in the history of American family-life, which, to some extent, entailed an effort to turn back the clock. This does not mean that the pattern of the settlement era was revived in any specific terms, but, broadly speaking, some of the trends discussed above were now reversed. Thus, for example, women's status began to decline again in certain respects; new attempts were made to subject children to stern discipline; and sexual mores swung back into a more restrictive mold. Above all, there developed a powerful movement to endow the family as such with new and deeper meaning.

The process was evident, first of all, in the growth after 1800 of a new literary genre, extolling the blessings of home and hearth in rapturous detail. Books of "domestic advice" fairly gushed from the presses, and their readership expanded dramatically. Trite and sentimental as they seem today, one can hardly doubt their salience for their own time. Their simple message, endlessly repeated, was the transcendant importance of family life as the fount of all the tender virtues in life. Love, kindliness, altruism, self-sacrifice, peace, harmony, good order: all reposed here be-hind the "sacred portals" of home. Here, and nowhere else — for it was widely agreed that the same virtues were severely threatened in the world at large. Indeed, if the home should give way, human life would be re-duced to the level of the jungle. We should note well this assumed disjunc-tion between home and the life of the individual family on the one hand, and the "outside world" on the other, for it was truly fundamental to many aspects of nineteenth-century culture. Hitherto perceived as com-plementary to one another, the two spheres were increasingly presented in the light of adversaries.

All this was related to a new, anxious, and dichotomous view of the present quality and future prospects of American society. There was a

mood of expansiveness abroad in the country, a sense of unlimited opportunities for individual enterprise, an impatience with institutions, a readiness to challenge all forms of traditional restraint. Americans of every
sort believed that they were carrying out a uniquely wonderful experiment
in human improvement, which would one day yield perfectionist — not to
say, millennial — results. But there was also a darker side. Careful analysis
of the popular culture of this period reveals deep undercurrents of fear, a
sense that all meaningful bearings were slipping away.

Right here the family would play a pivotal role. The vision of worldly
gain, the cultivation of the "go-ahead" spirit (a favorite period phrase)
was enormously invigorating, to be sure; but it also raised a specter of
chaos, of individual men devouring each other in the struggle for success.
Somewhere, the old values — especially the *social* values — had to be safely
enshrined. One needed some traditional moorings, some emblem of soft-
ness and selflessness to counter the intense thrust of personal striving that
characterized the age. There had to be a place to come in out of the storm
occasionally, a place that assured both repose and renewal. That place,
lavishly affirmed from all sides, was Home.

Rooted at the center of Home stood the highly sentimentalized figure
of Woman. It was she who represented and maintained the tender virtues.
Men, of course, had to be out in the world, getting their hands dirty in all
sorts of ways; indeed it was precisely because of this that their women
must remain free of contamination. The literature of the time shows a
consistent preoccupation with the career of the well-meaning but sorely
pressed male, deeply involved in the work of the world, but holding ever
before his eyes the saintly image of the lady in his life. It was she, to quote
from a popular sermon, "who, like a guardian angel, watches over his
interests, warns him against dangers, comforts him under trial; and by her
pious, assiduous, and attractive deportment, constantly endeavors to render him more virtuous, more useful, more honourable, and more happy."
Such a creature was "a pearl beyond price," a fit centerpiece in what has
been called "the cult of True Womanhood."

This posture of admiration — almost of reverence — contrasts sharply
with the imputations of deviousness and inconstancy found in some earlier
assessments of women. But it would be quite erroneous to infer from
such flattering rhetoric any genuine improvement in women's status. In

fact, the nineteenth-century American woman, when compared to her grandmothers in colonial times, had given up a great deal. For example, women could no longer be permitted to work outside the home (except among the poorest classes, where the issue was simple survival). Their position in life was defined in terms of a purity that was directly opposed to everything characteristic of the larger world. Thus the domestic hearth was both their altar and, from another perspective, their prison. As one scholar has aptly written, nineteenth-century American woman was "a hostage to the old values held so dear and treated so lightly . . . the hostage in the home." And, like all hostages, she was not free to come and go as she pleased.

But there is more still. Even within the home her influence was sharply circumscribed. A husband's authority was supposed to be absolute in all major family decisions. By contrast, a wife's authority was exerted entirely by way of symbolism. Indeed her great virtue was submissiveness and obedience to the will of her spouse, and her central role was that of comforter. (Here is a random sampling of titles of contemporary essays on the subject: "Woman, Man's Best Friend," "Woman, the Greatest Social Benefit," "Woman, a Being to Come Home To," "The Wife, Source of Comfort and Spring of Joy.") In all this, one absolutely basic assumption seems clear: women would not live for themselves. Their function was to provide moral uplift for everyone else with whom they came in contact — chiefly their husbands and children. Meanwhile no one wished to consider what they might do on their own account and for their own reasons.

There was a single exception to the rule that women must not be active outside their homes. The churches of this era had launched a vast program of humanitarian reforms, and looked to their female membership for day-to-day support. Few people could object when women involved themselves in distributing Bibles, or encouraging missionary work, or planning orphanages and almshouses, for here was a plausible extension of their inherent *moral* role and influence. But problems arose when they crossed a critical boundary line and began to participate in more patently political reform.

It was one thing for women to go about their neighborhoods raising money to send clergymen to convert the heathens in India or Africa; it was quite another thing to have them making speeches before antislavery conventions. The latter was too much a public activity; it verged on the "outside world" which could only sully a woman's purity. Yet for some women the lines drawn between these various forms of humanitarian work did not seem altogether clear. And, for at least a few of them, there were disturbing parallels between the slavery of the Negro and the position of their own sex. It was no coincidence that the first important advocates for women's rights were closely associated with abolitionism.

In its beginnings, organized feminism was very much a nineteenth-century phenomenon; its end, of course, is not yet in sight. This complex and important movement cannot be described here; but certain of its general characteristics deserve at least brief notice. It was not, at first, primarily about the right to vote; it was much more centrally about the right of women to work outside the home. The early feminists despised all the adoring rhetoric about woman-in-the-home; they sought to expose this myth of domesticity for what it really was. But so entrenched was the pattern against which they fought that it was many years before they could make significant headway. Thus the early phases of feminism are best seen not as a sign of improving status for women, but rather as a cry of protest against intolerable confinement. It is a striking symbol of all this that the so-called bloomer fashion was a matter of some importance in the eyes of the first feminists. Their attempt to free women from the literally suffocating network of stays, corsets, and hoop skirts that formed the conventional dress of the time directly paralleled their attack on the figuratively suffocating environment of Home.

And yet the relation of feminism to the cult of true womanhood was not entirely antipodal. In fact, in some ways cultural stereotypes nourished the growth of the movement. The idea of feminine purity was distinctly two-edged; in the hands of conventional moralists, it helped to rationalize the confinement of women to a domestic role, but it could also serve an opposite purpose. If women were inherently more virtuous than men, should they not use their influence to purify politics, business, the world of public affairs? This question was resolved, for particular individuals, on a variety of different grounds; much depended on one's view of politics, reform, religion, and history. Here lay the origins of a dilemma that has pervaded the growth of feminism ever since. Are women to have equal status because they are similar to men (in all essential particulars), or because they are generically different (and in some ways superior)? Is their full participation in public life to be justified on the basis of a humanity shared with men, or of some sex-defined "specialness" (that might enable them to contribute to society in distinctive ways)? Many of the early feminists were logically tied to the former position, but emotionally inclined toward the latter. To this extent, one can regard them as True Women — dressed in bloomers.

The True Woman of the nineteenth century was only one-half of the most thoroughgoing system of sex-role differentiation ever seen in American history. Men, too, were typed to the point of caricature. As previously mentioned, they belonged preeminently to the world of affairs. And if this was their sphere, it called forth an appropriate character, which included strength, cunning, inventiveness, endurance — a whole range of traits henceforth defined as exclusively masculine. The impact of these definitions on family life was truly profound. The man-of-the-family had now become the breadwinner in a special sense. Each day he went away to work; each night he returned. His place of work no longer bore any relation to his home environment. What he did at work was something of which other family members knew little or nothing. His position as husband and father had been altered, if not compromised; he was now a more distant, less nurturant figure, but he had special authority, too, because he performed those mysterious activities that maintained the entire household.

Among their other attributes, American men of the nineteenth century were saddled with a heavy burden of libido. Sexual desire was regarded as an exclusively male, and mostly unfortunate, phenomenon. Women, in their purity, were supposed to be passionless — not merely chaste, but literally devoid of sexual feelings. This complex of ideas was an invention of the age, with massive behavioral consequences.

The whole subject of sex was enveloped in a pervasive hush, which remained virtually unbroken until our own century. Polite conversation was protected from "stain" by the use of well-chosen euphemisms; legs, for example, now became "limbs," and pregnancy itself was mentioned only as "a delicate condition." Clothing was designed to cover all parts of the body except the face and hands; and even statues in museums were discreetly draped if their sculptors had failed to provide for "decent attire." Women were examined by male doctors — indeed babies were delivered — behind sheets and blankets, which, by totally excluding eye contact, ensured virtue but impeded sound medicine. Coitus was sanctioned only within marriage, and only for the purpose of procreation; even then it was viewed as a necessary evil. (Marriage manuals advised that frequent "congress" might lead to poor health and recommended once a month as a reasonable standard.) Masturbation became *the* phobia of the times; to practice this "secret sin" was to risk intemperance, insanity, and death. Adolescent boys went to sleep strapped in elaborate devices intended to prevent even *involuntary* desire, and dozens of patent medicines offered a similar promise of "relief."

Still, there was general agreement that male sexuality was finally irrepressible. Although everywhere resisted by polite society, it would continue to flourish in a thousand dark corners. And so it did — witness the growth, in the middle of the nineteenth century, of a vast industry of prostitution. (Regrettable as this was, it preserved certain fundamental distinctions: men indulged their lowest instincts with women from the lowest social class.) For many women, of every status, the situation was more tortured still. Recent research on the history of gynecology has uncovered a demand, in an astonishing number of cases, for the surgical procedure of clitoridectomy. Evidently this was the last resort of women who, contrary to expectation, found themselves afflicted with sensual wishes.

Given all these conventions, it is hard to imagine that many married couples were gratified in their most intimate relations. But sex was merely an extreme case of a pattern that affected every sort of contact between men and women. When their appropriate spheres were so rigorously separated, when character itself appeared to be so gender-specific, what was the likelihood of meaningful communication? Gone was that sense of instinctive sharing, that implicit sexual symmetry, which had suffused the full range of experience in premodern society. Instead there was a new mode of partnership — formal, self-conscious, contrived. Men and women came together from opposite directions, as uncertain allies. Understandably, many of the alliances so formed did not survive. Divorce rates, which rose steadily after mid-century, barely hinted at the true dimensions of the problem. For every marriage that was ended in court, unrecorded others dissolved through tacit agreement between the parties themselves or through simple desertion of one by the other. It is worth noticing, in this connection, the development of the notorious "tramp" phenomenon. Demoralized and destitute wanderers, their numbers mounting into the hundreds of thousands, tramps can be fairly characterized as men who had run away from their wives. (They had, of course, run away from much else besides.) Their presence was mute testimony to the strains that tugged at the very core of American family life.

Many observers noted that the tramps had created a virtual society of their own, based on a principle of single-sex companionship. But in this they followed an important trend in the culture at large. The early decades of the nineteenth century witnessed an extraordinary proliferation of "voluntary" associations — clubs, lodges, unions, circles, and the like. Men and women, even boys and girls, joined with groups of their peers for reasons that ran a wide gamut from frivolity, to self-improvement, to social reform. In a great many instances, membership was restricted to one sex or the other. The Elks, the Mothers' Association, the volunteer firemen, the Women's Christian Temperance Union, all shared this same characteristic: quite apart from their specific activities, they offered companionship with one's own (sexual) kind. Increasingly, such companionship seemed preferable to what could be found at home. The growth of these organizations was, then, another sign of a deficit in family life, and particularly in the relations of men and women.

Sex-role differentiation was paralleled by an increasing sensitivity to differences of age. And of all such differences those pertaining to childhood received the greatest attention. Now, for the first time in Western history, the child stood out as a creature inherently different from adults — someone with his own needs, talents, and character. This did not, of course, happen all at once, but from a long view the change was unmistakable. Around 1800, for example, children began to appear in clothing that was distinctively their own. They were also spending more and more time at play among groups of their peers. Of similar import was the development, toward mid-century, of a system of Sunday schools. This was explicit recognition that the religious needs of the child were special and different, and that it was quite inappropriate to have him sit through regular church services with his parents.

But perhaps the most telling evidence of this trend was the astonishing growth, and distinctive content, of popular literature on childrearing. To be sure, there had always been some books of this type in circulation, but they were mostly imports from England or France, and were decidedly casual in tone. Their chief concern was manners — how children should behave in a variety of social situations. The nineteenth-century literature, by contrast, dealt with the development of the child's character in a much deeper sense. Moreover, it was an exclusively native production; foreign models no longer seemed appropriate to the American scene. In part, this expressed a new spirit of truculent nationalism, but it was something else as well. For one feels in these works a note of extreme urgency — a reflection, presumably, of the fright and puzzlement of many parents faced with the task of raising children in the brave new world of nineteenth-century America.

What was it that gave to childhood both a more distinctive and a more worrisome aspect than for several generations before? There was, first of all, the factor of massive social and economic change. The nineteenth century spanned the transition from an agrarian, small-town social order to one that was characterized by large-scale industrialism and urbanization. But the view of the child that made him virtually a miniature adult was particularly appropriate — perhaps *only* appropriate — in an agrarian setting. On the farm he could, and did, take part in the work of the place from his earliest years. Most likely, too, he grew up to be a farmer himself. In short, it made sense to regard him as a scaled-down version of his father. Consider, by way of contrast, the position of a city child in the mid-nineteenth century. His father worked in an office or factory on the other side of town; the child himself knew hardly any of the details. He had no economic function in the household whatsoever. Moreover, his own future course, including his adult vocation, was shrouded in uncertainty. The diversified economy of the city opened up many possibilities. There was no reason to assume that what he would eventually do, would bear any relation at all to what his father was doing. In short, circumstances seemed to isolate the child in a profound way and to create a gulf between the generations that had not been there before.

But there were other reasons, too, for the heightened concern with childrearing. The weakening of traditional institutions appeared to leave the individual family very much on its own. If people failed in their duty as parents, there would be no one else to do the job for them. Everything depends on the child's home environment: this was the message of all the authorities on the subject. Yet on so much else these authorities spoke with a divided voice. What, for example, should be the long-range goals of childrearing? What type of character would a model home foster? Cer-

tainly there was much concern with the development of qualities like
independence and resourcefulness — a readiness to assert one's own claims
and interests. Because America had become an egalitarian society, open to
talent, the child should be encouraged in a certain style of expressiveness,
which would help him to realize his inner potentialities. It was this that
led foreign visitors to regard nineteenth-century American families as unduly child-centered. There was, however, another side. The same writers
on childrearing gave great emphasis to the values of order, discipline, control. Children must be imbued with moral precept from an early age and
must learn implicit obedience to legitimate authority. Thus, and only
thus, would they develop the sound conscience and steadfast principles so
necessary to ensure a straight course in the face of all the pitfalls they
would encounter in later life. These two main criteria of development —
expressiveness and control — were logically at odds with one another, and
attempts to apply them simultaneously were bound to end in confusion.

This was, moreover, a time of widespread reassessment of the moral
standing of children. To some extent old notions of infant depravity were
revived, and parents were once again urged to concentrate on "breaking
the will" of the very young. But such views never regained overall dominance, and by the middle of the century various countertrends were
plainly in evidence. At one extreme was a new and highly idealized picture of childish innocence and inborn purity — as with Little Eva in
Uncle Tom's Cabin. But while many people would have recognized Little
Eva as at least a symbolic possibility, their expectations for their own offspring were considerably more modest. Increasingly, the child was viewed
as a *neutral* quantity — with potentialities for either good or evil.

If there was one outcome toward which all of the above trends seemed
to point, it was a deep intensification of the parent-child bond or — to be
more precise — of the mother-child bond. The careful rearing of children
was, after all, the most important activity of the True Woman. From
virtuous homes came preachers, philanthropists, presidents ("All I am I owe
to my angel mother" [a favorite period cliché]); from disorderly ones came
thieves and drunkards. There was no doubting either the impressionable
nature of the young or the decisive impact of the domestic environment.
Yet if children were so deeply subject to the influence of their parents,
there was also an opposite effect. A familiar character in novels from the
period was the errant or ungrateful child. Though raised by solicitous

parents in a morally scrupulous home, he yielded in later life to worldly temptation, and filled his days with crime and debauchery. When reports of his conduct filtered back, his parents were stricken with grief, and one (or both) took ill and died. This plot-line lays bare an innermost nerve of family life in nineteenth-century America. Father, mother, and children were locked in a circle of mutual responsibility, and the stakes were literally life-and-death.

Anxiety reached a peak at the moment when a child left home to make his way in the outside world. Here was a test both of his personal integrity and of the family in which he had grown up. Most young men took this momentous step in their late teens or early twenties; for women of about the same age there was a comparable shift — into marriage. Increasingly, as time passed, these events were joined to significant psychological changes, involving nothing less than the shape of the developmental process. Indeed, one can ascribe to this period the addition of a generically new stage of development between childhood and maturity — the stage known ever since as adolescence. Before the nineteenth-century adolescence was not recognized, and, from all indications, was rarely experienced in the forms so familiar today. By 1850 shrewd observers detected new patterns of behavior, and special problems, among some of the nation's youth; by 1900 these were so widespread as to command an organized social response. (It was only then that the term *adolescence* entered into common discourse.)

The sources of this change were variable and complex, but much depended on the widening gap between the generations. When childhood and adulthood had been defined in such sharply different ways, it was harder to move from one to the other. Growth itself came to seem disjunctive and problematic — no longer a smooth ascent gradually accomplished, but a jolting succession of leaps and bumps. Adolescent behavior expressed the reluctance and doubt of young people about to undertake that last and longest leap of all, into adult life and responsibility. From an intrapsychic standpoint, the critical issue was (and remains) identity. Always, in premodern society, youth had received an adult identity in the natural course of things. The decisive change, in more recent times, has been the presence of so many *alternatives* — of career, of life-style, of moral and philosophical belief. In ever-growing numbers young people have faced demanding choices, which greatly complicate the preadult years. Thus, as one scholar has written, adolescence is "like a waiting period . . . a temporary stopover in which one can muster strength for the next harrowing stage of the trip."

It was the plan of this chapter to carry the story of American family life forward to about the year 1900. There is no space here to deal with our own century, and perhaps that is better left to other branches of social science anyway. Obviously we have witnessed striking changes even within the last two or three decades: the renewed activity of the women's movement and the so-called sexual revolution come readily to mind. At the same time there are profound continuities. Much of what we expect from family life bears the stamp of an earlier time — repose, comfort, a place of refuge from the rigors of the wider social environment. But all this is beyond the scope of the present inquiry.

So, too, are many earlier events and trends which, while highly interesting in themselves, lie outside the historical middle. From the early nineteenth century onward, immigrants have flowed in a vast tide to America from all parts of Europe. Differing widely in language, religion, and custom, these groups have also presented special variants of family life. (For example, immigrant families have tended toward more frequent "extension" than native American ones.) Blacks have played an equally significant role. Black families have, of course, been subject to the most extraordinary pressures, first, of slavery and later, of massive social prejudice and exploitation. (Recent studies have uncovered evidence of great resiliency in the response to these pressures, far more than the fashionable myth of black matriarchy would suggest.) Still another area of special interest is the long and variegated history of utopian communities. Most of these have proposed radical alterations in family structure, ranging from the celibacy of the Shakers, to the polygamy of the early Mormons, to the "complex marriage" of the Oneida Community. (Americans have long believed that the preservation of social order depends on sound family life; the utopians simply stood this idea on its head.)

Immigrants, blacks, reformers: here are major sources of the diversity that has attended American life for the past two centuries. Yet there is, after all, a powerful mainstream tradition. The chief minority groups have themselves acknowledged as much, by gradually approximating the cultural norm with the passage of succeeding generations. The alternative models of the utopians have been either forcibly suppressed by government fiat (as in the case of the Mormons) or fatally weakened by attrition (for example, the Shakers). Thus a scholar may still claim to speak of "American family-life" in general, as if such a thing has actually existed!

The same type of intellectual license is needed to underwrite a set of conclusions about the meaning of the past for the current and future course of the American family. History never provides clear-cut lessons, except for those who must have them at any price (including truth), but it does lay down the boundaries within which events are likely to develop. Perhaps this is particularly true in the present case, since the family is such a deeply conservative institution — so slow to change, so powerfully interwoven in our personal and collective roots.

First, and definitely foremost: there is no Golden Age of the family gleaming at us from far back in the historical past. And there is no good reason to construe recent trends in terms of decline and decay. To every point alleged as an adverse reflection on modern family life, one can offer a direct rejoinder. Consider, for example, the matter of divorce. We all know that the rate of legal divorce has been rising enormously in recent years. (In fact, the trend is more than a century old.) But what does this tell us about marital failure? In earlier times countless marriages were ended by simple, and legally unrecognized, desertion. Hence the figures in question are partly an artifact of legal history — a more general access to the courts, and so forth. Even without this effect, troublesome problems of interpretation would remain. Perhaps we seek more from marriage than did our forebears — more intimacy, more openness, more deep-down emotional support.

But surely these comparative judgments, which purport to make one period better than another, are beside the point anyway. Far more important is the effort to understand how family life relates to larger historical processes. For the family continually interacts with other cultural institutions and, more especially, with the variable circumstances of its membership. There is a sense in which every historical era gets the family system it needs and deserves. Thus, in colonial America, the norm was a stable "peasant" household, gradually evolving toward looser internal forms to permit full exploitation of a novel environment. Thus, too, the nineteenth-century family experienced a wrenching transformation under the multiple impact of industrialization, urban growth, egalitarian ideology, and demographic change. It is hard, in fact, to avoid seeing the nineteenth century as a time of troubles — not to say tragedy — in the history of the family. Sex-role typing, the generation gap, a guilt-laden sense of domestic responsibility, tortured attitudes toward sexuality — the total situation was hardly a benevolent one. And yet we should remember that massive social change always exacts a high price in human suffering. The period from about 1820 to 1920 encompassed a veritable revolution in American life and culture, and the pressures on the family were necessarily extreme. Surely the vast majority of people who experienced all this found something immensely valuable in their domestic life. Perhaps, indeed, it was Home that kept the toll of misery from rising far higher. Who can say that any alternative pattern would have worked better?

But this, in turn, raises further questions. Is the notion of "alternatives" meaningful in any sense? Is the family amenable to planned social intervention? In short, can we hope to influence the shape of our domestic life — let alone to change it? Surely, in individual cases, the answer may be affirmative; but what about larger schemes, for redesigning the family *system*? On this, history enters a caution. As noted previously, Americans have always assigned a primary causal role to family life: good homes will create a good society (or, from the standpoint of reform, change the family, and you will change everything else). To be sure, there is a certain logical plausibility here. But, in practice, it is much easier to trace those processes that move the other way — that is, *from* the society at large, *to* the family in particular. On the checkerboard of social institutions, the family seems to display a markedly reactive character. Time and again it receives influences from without, rebuffs them, modifies them, adapts to them. There are dynamic and reciprocal aspects in all this, but even so, the openings presented to human agents bent on "social engineering" are extremely small.

Can we, then, realistically expect a widespread trend toward extended families, as advocated by some critics of contemporary society? Impossible! For nothing has been more durable in the long history of Western family life than its nuclear character. Will we see a new era of restrictive childrearing, in protest against cultural permissiveness? Most unlikely, for developmental norms depend on much else besides household structure. Careful study on these and related points may suggest the limits within which the family is likely to develop. For the most part, they are modest limits — some will say, confining ones. But this need not be received as a counsel of despair. For if the current patterns of family life are the only ones we have, they are nonetheless variable enough and flexible enough to yield many different outcomes in immediate human terms. *The* family, considered as a species, is molded by history and thus lies beyond our power to control. Not so those *particular* families to which we personally belong. The past lives in us always; but what we make of it, individually, is up to ourselves.

2

American Marriage in Cross-Cultural Perspective

Virginia D. Abernethy

Marriage is one of the few institutions that exists in all human societies. The recognition of marriage as an institution implies that it is a culturally patterned adaptation of individual and group needs within the context of particular environments and technologies. The orderliness of society and the security of the individual are enhanced to the degree that a culture recognizes the legitimacy of some form of social organization that clarifies the sexual and economic rights and obligations of men and women, and, through reproduction, provides for the continuity of the social group. The universality of marriage is thus perceived in the cluster of functions that it performs for persons and societies.

Specifically, marriage regulates and stabilizes sexual relationships within a society: unlike other primates, no human group allows sexual access to depend principally on male dominance hierarchies. Secondly, marriage is a solution to the problem of replacement or recruitment in society: it legitimizes children born to a woman and, in so doing, tries to ensure that responsible adults will provide for the care and socialization of the young. Lastly, the rules governing marriage organize division of labor between sexes, which is the most rudimentary and the only universal form of occupational specialization: although cross-culturally, few tasks are consistently assigned either to male or female, marriage as an economic arrangement capitalizes on the ability to learn complementary skills that are then stereotyped as sex roles.[1]

Shifting to the permutations of these functions as seen from the perspective of an individual in a particular society, one may again ask, What is marriage for? What are the objectives of this legal contract that binds principals alone or the principals and their relatives to a bundle of reciprocal rights, duties, obligations, and privileges? Is marriage for the purpose of having children? For the mutual happiness of the man and woman who marry? Is marriage a way of cementing alliances between groups? Does marriage provide an economic and social framework that is a springboard to other activities?

Cultures vary in the emphasis accorded each objective, and in some societies one or more objectives may be absent altogether. The manifestations and range of cultural attitudes to the "goods" of marriage can illuminate some strains intrinsic to marriage in particular societies, and therefore it is to a study of societies that we now turn. A review will locate modern Western marriage along the continua of emphasis on (1) individual happiness, (2) alliances between politicofamilial units, or (3) means of access to socioeconomic benefits. A detailed discussion of children as a goal of marriage follows.

AMERICAN MARRIAGE IN PERSPECTIVE

Cross-cultural comparison suggests that the normative pattern for marriage in the United States is unusual in the degree to which it emphasizes happiness as an individual "right" and equates this state with emotional attachment between spouses and in conceptualizing the conjugal relationship exclusively as a contract between consenting individuals, rather than a politicoeconomic alliance between families.

---

[1] Recent anthropological writing suggests that a dichotomy based on having or not having child-rearing responsibilities is more accurate than the male-female distinction in predicting what other activities will be performed by a member of a society. That is, childless females and males tend to follow pursuits that are similar to each other's but distinct from those of individuals charged with childcare. This analysis of human societies is consistent with observations of feeding and traveling groups of chimpanzees [60].

Marriage for Happiness

Reviewing research on marriage in the United States during the 1960s, Hicks and Platt conclude that, "In our society marriages are assessed by two norms: happiness and stability" [26].

It will undoubtedly be granted that the criterion of happiness employed by professional students of the family is consistent with the pervasive lay ideals of romantic love as prerequisite to marriage and continuing conjugal affection as its major goal. This respect for — indeed enshrinement of — the emotions, is a comparatively recent development and distinguishes present marriage norms from nineteenth-century dictates of rationality, which stressed good health, strong character, and similarity of religion as reliable guides to mate selection [23].

Barring a national crisis, there is little ground for anticipating a return to traditional criteria and expectations. The earlier standards were based on a pressing need of spouses for each other as working partners in agricultural or home-centered enterprises. Whereas at agrarian and hunter-gatherer levels of technology, husbands and wives are often nonreplaceable by other personnel and make complementary contributions to subsistence, the economy of more developed societies allows most goods and services to be obtained in other ways — in markets, restaurants, and laundries, from electricians, gardeners, housekeepers, and so on. Given that money is in adequate supply, both specialization of labor and the impersonality and transferability of money and services are factors that make dissolution of marriage in our society easier.

Thus, it is by default of subsistence pressure as a stabilizing force that the burden of binding marriage partners comes to rest on personal and emotional attachment. In wealthy industrial nations this fragile bond of conjugal emotion is invoked and supported through the romanticism of the mass media, the cosmetic industry, marriage counseling and psychotherapy directed toward improved communications and interpersonal relationships.

Ironically, the crisis of modern marriage is intrinsic to its main support: great expectations for emotional fulfillment in marriage lay the groundwork for later disappointment and are related to the high divorce rates of the nation. One may also presuppose a reservoir of discontent and feelings of having been cheated in marriage that do not find legal expression [17, 35].

Marriage As a Political or Economic Alliance

When the extended family has corporate functions in ownership of land or business, marriage partners are frequently co-opted as representatives (or even de facto hostages) for their respective kinship units. For instance, the bride and groom may be scions of banking houses, trading partners, or adjoining farms or kingdoms, with the marriage becoming a vehicle for consolidating wealth or confirming politicoeconomic arrangements. Such interlocking of kinship with economic and political relationships is most common in preindustrial societies where the economy is dominated by agrarian or relatively small-scale financial and manufacturing enterprises. In the circumstances described, where marriage may be an instrument of family strategy in its external power relationships, the stability of the conjugal tie becomes a vital family concern.

By contrast, there are few instances in modern Western society of the marriage alliance's being economically or politically significant to the families of the couple. In the United States, for example, ownership in major productive enterprises is distributed through large sectors of the population, and rarely would a marriage forge a controlling interest in a big company or divorce dissolve such. In the political domain, the rare marriages between offspring of prominent families occur amidst great publicity and could, through informal channels, be advantageous; however, in a democratic system of elected officials, only machine politics can provide the continuity to give extended family alliances long-term impact. Within the military establishment, marriage may consolidate the influence of families that for generations have been "Army" or "Navy"; but again the network is informal and in no sense rigid. Consequently, even in these cases, the threat to vested interests posed by marital dissolution is limited, and, although relatives may counsel against divorce as disruptive to individual careers and emotions, seldom are sufficient forces mobilized to overwhelm the couple's inclinations.

An outstanding exception in the modern Western world is the British royal family, whose aversion to divorce is well known. Insofar as the monarchy has survived and justifies continuing privilege in terms of a symbolic contribution to British identity, instability within royal marriage could undermine its remaining function. Thus, it is not surprising that in recent times pressure from royalist interests has reportedly been sufficient to prevent marriage between royalty and divorced persons and to remove an offender from line of access to the throne [19].

The atypical examples cited serve principally to illustrate the comparative isolation of kinship from politicoeconomic spheres in the postindustrial period; no material benefits to the natal families are expected to accrue from their childrens' marriages. It is a functional correlate that, far from representing alliances between corporate family units, Western marriage tends to be a contract between individuals only. The families of the bride and groom may not meet until the engagement party or wedding. They hope to like each other, but are themselves as far from feeling party to a contract as they are unlikely to have vested interests in the alliance. It is enough, for example, that a daughter is marrying a fine-looking boy who has a promising future. If and when marital dissolution appears imminent, the parents may weep (for their grandchildren?), but they are unlikely to rave or threaten. Only rarely in modern Western society are the extended families of a couple bound by the latter's marriage or do they feel themselves so threatened by its demise that significant forces will be mobilized to forestall the event.[2]

In conclusion to this section, it may be noted that some currents of writing on the contemporary family stress that, although particular marriages lack continuity or stability, remarriage of divorced persons is common; and therefore marriage is shown to retain its importance as the preferred basis for household formation. However, in focusing on trends, the present analysis suggests not only that the extended family has ceased to function as a stabilizing agent for particular alliances but also that pressure exerted by the family should diminish for *any* marriage as values catch up with the reality that kinship is no longer a major instrument of politicoeconomic strategy. In short, this politicoeconomic function of marriage is not important in postindustrial societies, and thus is not available to sustain marriage as a dominant institution of the society.

Marriage As a Springboard to Society

To some extent all societies regard marriage as a preferred framework within which, or from which, individuals conduct other activities. The American

---

[2]This freedom of principals to a marriage contract from accountability to their natal families is observed in many hunter-gatherer as well as in highly industrialized societies. Despite the disparity in technological level, a common denominator is minimal investment by the family, qua family unit, in the factors of production.

norm in this respect is unremarkable in being approximately intermediate between (1) the rigid prescription of the Muslim culture, in which, essentially, a woman must marry to be respectable [33], and most hunter-gatherer groups, whose subsistence technology makes it virtually impossible for either a male or female to live alone and (2) the opposite extreme, as illustrated in Ireland, of institutionalized alternate life-styles featuring very late marriage or celibacy [16].

Until recently,[3] wedlock was the undisputedly preferred, as well as the statistically normative, state for American women. All periods between 1880 and 1969 have seen over 75 percent of the female population 14 years of age and over married, widowed, or divorced. In 1969, almost 90 percent of women 18 years old and over were or had been married [57, 58]. The value placed on marriage for women is integrally related to other societal patterns, such as the banning of females from many occupations [51, 52], and lone (unmarried or otherwise) women from public places and from social participation [21, 51].

Not only American women, but also American men, have traditionally considered marriage to be a helpful framework for the conduct of a full life. Apart from providing domestic comfort and a ready partner for social and sexual activity, marriage enhances a man's attractiveness to employers who value settled reliability. Marriage may also increase upward mobility if business is conducted through the skillful entertaining of clients or associates; and it is commonly believed to enhance the political profile of candidates for public office.

Thus, there is small doubt that, for society at large, marriage presently retains its preeminence as a springboard to other activities. However, close scrutiny suggests that these secondary benefits of marriage derive to some extent from the value placed on marriage: a married status facilitates movement through countless social, economic, and political domains only because it is commonly acknowledged that it is good to be married. The circularity here is apparent, and suggests the query, "If the value placed on an institution lacks foundation in real adaptive advantage, will it persist?"

Presently, heterosexual marriage is under attack by diverse interest groups that include hippies, communes, the Gay Liberation Movement,

---

[3]Statistics from the U.S. Bureau of the Census show nearly one-half of women aged 21 in 1970 to be single, compared to approximately one-third in 1960.

and the Women's Liberation Movement. Their advocacy of alternate life-
styles appears to be having an impact that varies with region and socioeconomic level [55, 61]. At the least, the rhetoric of Women's Lib is
likely to support the decision of a number of young women to delay, redefine the terms of, or forgo marriage in favor of other commitments.
Slowly emerging patterns that are conducive to a reduction of pressure on
women to marry include a newfound social freedom for "singles," the
companionship offered by communal living styles, and community tolerance of heterosexual cohabitation without adherence to legal formalities
[61].

The foregoing discussion has touched on the intrinsic weakness of
modern Western marriage as related to its primary dependence on the emotional attachment between spouses (instead of on subsistence needs). It
has also suggested the relative unimportance of marriage in the politicoeconomic realm, with the consequent diminution of stabilizing pressure
on a marriage alliance exerted by families protecting vested interests.
Moreover, the benefits conferred by marriage as a framework for other
life pursuits seem partially, at best, to depend on the positive valuation of
marriage; but a value unsupported by real adaptive advantage is a fragile
foundation for any behavior pattern. There remains to examine the adaptive significance of marriage in the one aspect of social life it monopolizes,
namely, legitimate reproduction.

Marriage and Children

On no other objective of marriage is there greater consensus the world
over: children are a desired outcome of marriage, and everywhere marriage
legitimizes the children born to a woman [24]. The positive valuation of
children can be inferred both from most informants' statements and from
the rules governing disposition of children in the event that the usual family structure is disrupted, as by divorce or death. The issue typically turns
on who has "rights" to children.

Cross-cultural study of marital dissolution reveals that rights over children are assigned across a wide range of possibilities that are independent
of the legal status of partners within the marriage. For instance, bride-
price is often, but not necessarily, conceptualized as the purchase of the woman's procreative powers and thus predictive that rights to children are

retained by the male parent or his relatives or both. Place of residence after marriage is also a good, but by no means invariable, clue to the disposition of children after death or divorce. The following examples suggest that a society's attitudes toward children may be viewed on a continuum, having as its logical endpoint the preeminence of maternal or paternal rights in regard to progeny.

Among the Hopi Indians of the southwestern United States, a child's economic, legal, and residential affiliation stays unalterably with the mother's family, although the child remains bound to the father's family by strong emotional ties. This society traces descent (relationship by birth as opposed to relationship by marriage) through the female line. Marriage is usually between a man and a woman of the same village (or *mesa*); there is neither bride-price nor dowry; and residence after marriage is with the wife's family. The husband works his wife's family's fields, but he is in no sense an authority figure in the household. Rather, this position is held by the wife's brother or wife's mother's brother, although both of these men actually live elsewhere, namely, with their wives' families! Divorce among the Hopi is frequent. About 40 percent of Hopi marriages end in divorce. Perhaps because it entails few economic dislocations, a man ceases to till his divorced wife's fields, but she and her children continue to live with and be provided for by her extended family. The parents' marital status notwithstanding, affectionate, nonauthoritarian relationships between father and children also are expected to persist, and a network of continuing ritual privileges and obligations bind children to other members of the father's family [56].

The Tlingit of the northwest Canadian coast illustrate a second variant of the children's belonging to the mother's family. In this society, descent and inheritance are traced through the female line, but residence after marriage is with or near the husband's family. In case of divorce, the wife and children return to her family's village, which, because of the conjunction of matrilineal descent and virilocal residence, will be her brother's home [40].

Legal rights to children are also unequivocally retained by the mother and her kin among the Kai of New Guinea. This arrangement is somewhat unusual in its association with both patrilocal residence after marriage and institutionalized bride-price, payable by the groom's family to the woman's father, brothers, and maternal uncles. Observation of marital dissolutions, however, reveals that bride-price confers only exclusive sexual rights over the wife and that this is distinct from rights over her procreative powers. Thus, in an ordinary divorce (one in which fault cannot be clearly assigned), a man does not retain rights to his children's labor, nor can he claim jurisdiction over them, nor is he entitled to return of the bride-price. However, the bride-price would be forfeited by the woman's family if the divorce was precipitated by her elopement or adultery [40].

Proceeding along the continuum, one finds that in a large segment of the world the rule of rights over children is flexible, allowing such factors as age of the child, ability of a parent to care for the child, and sex of the child to influence outcomes. The common denominators of societies making do with ad hoc arrangements of this order are the related circumstances that (1) there is little reliance on children's contribution to subsistence, and (2) the economy is not "labor intensive." Most hunter-gatherer groups, as well as the technologically advanced nations, meet these criteria: many hunter-gatherers appear to amply satisfy their limited wants with a leisurely work style involving only adults in their prime, and the highly productive, automated industries of modern nations similarly have minimal use for (unskilled) child labor. Moreover, in technology-oriented societies, individual productivity is delayed until after the long period required to learn the specialized skills and occupational roles required for mobility within the economy.

The latter constellation is familiar in the United States, where children remain an economic liability, rather than an asset, well past adolescence. Inevitably, the issue of rights over children assumes a different flavor when children are unable to contribute to the family economically or when such a contribution could undermine the parents' self-esteem. Under conditions of divorce or separation, the father's *rights* over children frequently are transformed into the father's *obligation* to continue financial support. The physical care of younger children is most often entrusted to the mother, and in this sense she has rights, which are rarely waived. So long as the children must be supported by their father, she gains a measure of financial security by caring for them. The usual disposition of children to the mother reflects both (1) the imperative that the father earn enough to support them, which typically entails work away from home and (2) the cultural emphasis on preserving emotional bonds: the mother's presumably greater affective involvement with children is felt to justify her claim to priority in regard to their physical custody.

Continuing with a cross-cultural overview, one discovers the parochial nature of the Western assumption that a mother's emotional commitment to the child confers a legitimate legal claim. On the contrary, a great number of societies recognize the strong affectional mother-child ties but do not find in them a basis for granting a woman prior rights to her children. There is considerable variation, however, in the flexibility of those rules or customs that reserve legitimate claims to children to the father and his family.

For instance, among the Kwaio a widow must usually relinquish her children if she chooses to leave a deceased husband's village to return to her natal home. Exceptions do occur, however, when the husband's relatives who contributed to her bride-price are also deceased or otherwise unavailable to assert their claims, or if the mother's family offers to repay a portion of the bride-price, thus buying back rights over the offspring. This is an example of bride-price explicitly securing rights to procreative powers [28].

A similar emphasis on transference of the women's procreative powers through bride-price is seen among the Thonga of South Africa. In this society, a woman's offspring belong to her family only in the rare case that the bride-price remains unpaid. Normally, her issue belongs unequivocally to the father's family, and should she die childless, her family would be obliged to return the bride-price [40].

In extreme cases of the preeminence of father rights, there are no exceptions or institutionalized arrangements whereby the mother's family can reassert rights to children. Exemplifying this extreme are the Guari Katchin of Burma, where, in the unusual event of divorce, the woman returns to her natal village, while the children remain with the father. A nursing infant goes with its mother, but this necessity is clearly time limited, and after weaning, the child returns to the paternal domicile [32].

Cross-culturally, then, children are a primary objective and desired outcome of marriage. Children of one or both sexes may be valued for their contributions to the work force. In addition, males add to the fighting strength of the society, and females may be prized as sources of income (bride-price) or, by fathers, as tradable assets in securing a wife for oneself or a son. However, rights and responsibilities in regard to children are differentially assigned to spouses and their relatives, and, as a corollary, the importance of children to the several parties in a marriage contract may vary considerably.

Weighing the importance of factors that account for the positive valuation of children, one finds that in agricultural societies even very young children contribute substantially to subsistence, whereas the general pattern in a technology-oriented society is that immature offspring are not an economic asset but are valued primarily because they are love objects [38]. This phenomenon can be logically related to the impersonality of the communities in which a large proportion of the population lives. A technological orientation is frequently associated with social and geographic mobility. Under conditions of great mobility there are impediments to the continuity of friendships; except in crisis situations, relatives outside the nuclear family tend to be unavailable as sources or objects of nurturance and support.[4] Therefore the small family unit turns inward to satisfy emotional needs and the adding of children to this elementary family grouping assumes urgent proportions.

However, an additional and more subtle motive may be a factor when parenthood as a rewarding emotional experience is emphasized. Perhaps a frequently verbalized and insistent positive valuation of the young represents denial or a rationalization of the reality that, rather than being an asset, children are a financial and, occasionally, even an emotional, liability. Since children cost so much — they must be good.

Indeed, in mature industrialized societies the dominant culture goes to the extreme of asserting that children should not be an economic asset: child labor is forbidden, and the old person who becomes financially dependent on an adult son or daughter may be stigmatized. The reality that many old people are at least partially dependent on children in no way contravenes the value placed on independence or the shame associated with becoming a burden[8]. The covert wish that children function as old-age security no doubt exists at some level, but it is a culturally illegitimate expectation in Western society that can be articulated only by "undesirables" such as the cockney renegade in *My Fair Lady:* "I'm getting married in the morning . . . I'll be supported by my children . . . and never have to work again" [37].

---

[4]Although mother-daughter visiting is reportedly frequent in some classes, [14] it appears to be diminished by social mobility [3]. Moreover, kinship ties become increasingly vulnerable to mobility as genealogical distance increases, and beyond primary relatives, visiting, may lapse altogether as one family rises or falls on the social status ladder [3].

The refusal of economic contributions from children should not be equated with an absence of other demands made on children. The demands unmistakably exist, but they are attuned to psychological, rather than material, goods. The constricted opportunities for reciprocal giving and receiving in an industrial, market-oriented, and migratory society leave a void into which the expected gratifications of marriage and parenthood are thrust. When the marital relationship is unsatisfactory, the emphasis on children as the major or only satisfaction in marriage appears to increase [41]. To a degree which is often unrealistic, children are expected to satisfy a woman's emotional cravings, affirm, if not create, her identity, give meaning to her life, and cement a marriage [21]. A man's social identity depends on children to a lesser degree, and meaning for him may hinge on giving children more than he had when he grew up or on having heirs to benefit from his achievements. Self-recognition and evidence of prepotency are added factors in the chip-off-the-old-block boast.

Insofar as children are valued as objects of affection, it follows that they will be expected to reciprocate love as they mature. Mother's Day and Father's Day are institutionalized opportunities for children to express appreciation for all that has been done for them.[5] It is thus a consistent and culturally legitimate expectation that children should forebear from distancing themselves and should provide emotional security for their aged parents [54].

However, it is recognized, and is a source of conflict for many an insightful parent, that parents' demands for closeness from their children may be self-defeating. Indeed, the isolation of old people, as well as the present demand for (and conditions in) nursing homes,[6] suggests that, paradoxically, a generation dedicated to making life easier or better for their young is not receiving the hoped-for spontaneous warmth from the beneficiaries of the hard work and self-denial. Even when they are old and growing feeble, there is the attitude that parents ought not complain. Lifetime values and obligations persist, and the ethos that children should not be burdened supports the old person in behavior that shields the son or daughter from responsibility and guilt [8, 54].

---

[5] But LeMasters and Riesman conclude that children are rarely appreciative [36, 49].
[6] In a paper presented in 1971 at the Harvard Center for Population Studies, Dr. Rashi Fein noted that in 1969 the United States spent $3.3 billion on nursing home care [20].

Given these conditions, some of today's adolescents and young married couples can hardly fail to conclude that one benefit supposedly accruing to parenthood is evanescent: the much publicized failure of communication between generations and the unwillingness and inability of mobile families to care for an old person must, inevitably, shake the belief that children are rewarding in the long run.

Moreover, the circumstances under which many present-day mothers must raise their children often lead to disillusionment with the maternal role itself. There is evidence that some of the frustration produced in women by childrearing responsibilities derives from geographic mobility and the consequent disruption of intimate and close-knit relationships within the community. Women who maintain relationships with old friends despite a move are usually restricted to rare visits because of physical distance; and the lesser level of intimacy and trust inherent to new friendships in a new community is less supportive or emotionally rewarding. Also, friends will not infrequently favor different childrearing objectives, techniques, and values. The mobile mother is thus exposed to numerous variants in childrearing theory and practice. This may be confusing to a parent and, if conflicting strategies are utilized, also to the child. The mother's initial uncertainty and the predictable fractiousness from a confused child interact to reduce confidence and competence in implementing any approach, and thus lead directly to maternal frustration [1].

In regard to childrearing, the contrast of our society with traditional, more stable societies is marked. In other cultures, the sharing of an experience within an intimate circle leads to a common interpretation and thus to a consensus on meaning and appropriate action. Although such closure of the communications network, or parochialism, entails a reduction in information and alternatives, it also fosters certainty. In childrearing this means that a woman is sure of objectives for herself and for the child and has confidence in the techniques for achieving her goals [1].

Cooperation in exchanging childcare responsibilities becomes practical only when mothers share values and utilize them similarly. Children of women in tightly-knit, traditional networks are accustomed to similar demands and constraints and thus do not challenge or disrupt the modus operandi of the household they visit. Under these circumstances, it is not difficult to care for a friend's or a relative's child. On the other hand, children's expectations about permissible deportment or entertainment are unlikely to be similar if their mothers have different models for child-rearing. Faced with caring for a child who has been taught by other standards, a mother has the alternatives of constant policing or of ignoring a breach of discipline while her own child's behavior is "corrupted"[1].

As numbers of women follow ambitious, job-oriented husbands into new communities and attempt to raise children in unfamiliar, if not alien, surroundings, the crisis of motherhood will mount. It can be expected that mothering will increasingly be characterized by uncertainty, rigidity, bookishness, and frustration in place of spontaneity and a sense of responding to the child's developmental needs.

The effect of the first child on the conjugal relationship is a further factor that will be assayed in the ongoing cultural valuation of children. Intimacy and affection between spouses is a highly valued objective in modern marriage, but recent studies tend, with increasing consistency, to the conclusion that parenthood is negatively related to this desired state of man-woman bliss [30,31]. Family life-cycle literature consistently shows high initial satisfaction in marriage, which is followed by decreased satisfaction that coincides with the advent of children and which is most pronounced during the preschool years. The literature shows, finally, a gradual resurgency of satisfaction in the "empty-nest" phase of the marriage [6, 34, 50, 53]. The fluctuations in satisfaction appear to be more pronounced for wives than husbands [31]. Case studies also suggest that parenthood threatens communication, intimacy, and mutuality in marriage [22], that husbands may anticipate parenthood with ambivalence [42], and that immature wives regress into pathological states under the stress of motherhood [13]. These findings are consistent with survey data from a large, representative sample in which childless couples report higher marital satisfaction than do parents [48].

However, an earlier study suggests that satisfaction in marriage is not related to the presence or absence of children [11], a finding that may be explained by independent data showing childless couples at either extreme of marital satisfaction, whereas parents tend to be average on this dimension [29]. Satisfaction aside, stability of a marriage appears to be increased by the presence of children [41, 48]. Definitive research is not available, but such a study might compare parent couples at various stages in the family life-cycle with childless couples matched on age, years married, and socioeconomic variables; moreover, the relatively greater ease of divorce for childless couples, which theoretically could eliminate most dissatisfied childless couples from any currently married sample, should be controlled by incorporating into the research design estimated divorce rates for childless and parent couples after a designated number of years of marriage.

Nonetheless, if only the feeling content of marriage is considered as a variable, the weight of evidence thus far suggests that, given the present circumstance of great emotional demands on the marital bond, a choice for children is frequently a choice against the marriage.

Trends in Parenting
The feelings engendered by the nonexistent economic benefits of children and the waning emotional rewards of parenting appear to be making a natural alliance, in our society, with the demographic warning that we face a population crisis. The author suspects that the recent spate of liberalization in abortion and contraceptive legislation and judicial decision could not have occurred without impetus from both sources: the disillusionment with parenthood and the Malthusian threat of overpopulation.

The impact of these developments on marriage has yet to be widely felt. However, a vision of the future may exist in the ethos of couples who live together, put off childbearing, and deny the need of entanglement through marriage. When a child is desired, such couples will usually enter into the formality of a marriage contract. It now appears that the viability of a male-female coalition independent of marriage should be considered [41a]; the highly valued emotional core of modern marriage can apparently exist without the formalities of the institution [31]. Marriage proper, with its defining function of legitimizing and guaranteeing to the society the responsible rearing of children, will be relevant only to those couples desiring children.

An underlying assumption has been that the decision to have children can be brought under rational control through contraception. The soundness of this premise may be questioned, however, in view of the Bumpass and Westoff estimate that one-fifth of all births between 1960 and 1965 were unwanted [9]. This pattern appears to be changing [15], perhaps as a result of improved contraceptives and postconception technology (the morning-after pill), but nonetheless one may take note of unconscious motivations that appear to impel a woman or couple toward parenthood. It is thought that such traits as an exaggerated dependency need, a passive-aggressive mode of relating to others, and denial as a defense mechanism are related to ineffective birth control despite an avowed intention to avoid pregnancy [2].

The generality of such unconscious motivations in the population at large is unknown. There exists the probability that a need to give nurturance is innate, rather than a pathological expression of dependency needs. In this event, a block on reproduction, a major outlet for nurturance, could persist in a healthy individual only in conjunction with learned sublimations; these might range from work in the helping professions (e.g., medicine, teaching) to gardening, animal husbandry, or simply keeping a pet.

Summary

Cross-culturally, marriage is defined by its functions. The point discussed in this chapter is the extent to which marriage is losing functions, losing its adaptive advantage as a way of life in our society. Marriage has much diminished in significance both for organizing labor to meet basic subsistence needs and as an adjunct to politicoeconomic strategy. Only the great human longing for others with whom to share and enjoy is still met for the majority by the spouse and children of nuclear-family marriage. Nonetheless, the danger inherent in investing a great part of oneself in these narrowly circumscribed and possibly antagonistic relationships is increasingly recognized and finds voice in fringe groups of protesters and social innovators. The decrease in the functions of marriage and the emotional demands placed on the heterosexual-pair relationship should perhaps be considered as significant and nonreversible factors in the twentieth century. Together, they lend impetus to today's search for alternative modes of living and loving.

REFERENCES

1. Abernethy, V. Husband, Mother, and Social Network in Relation to the Maternal Response. Ph.D. dissertation, Harvard University, 1969.
2. Abernethy, V., and Grunebaum, H. Psychological interference with fertility control. Unpublished, 1970.
3. Aldous, J. Inter-generational visiting patterns: Variations in boundary maintenance as explanation. *Family Process* 6:235, 1967.

4. Benedeck, T.   Parenthood as developmental phase. *Journal of the American Psychoanalytical Association* 7:389, 1959.
5. Benson, L.   *Fatherhood.* New York: Random House, 1968.
6. Blood, R., Jr., and Wolfe, C.   *Husbands and Wives: The Dynamics of Married Living.* New York: Free Press, 1960.
7. Bronfenbrenner, U.   Interview. *Time,* Dec. 28, 1970. P. 37.
8. Brown, R.   Family structure and social isolation of older persons. *Journal of Gerontology* 15:170, 1969.
9. Bumpass, L., and Westoff, C.   The perfect contraceptive population. *Science* 169:1177, 1970.
10. Burgess, E., and Cottrell, L. *Predicting Success or Failure in Marriage.* New York: Prentice Hall, 1939.
11. Burgess, E., and Wallin, P. *Engagement and Marriage.* Philadelphia: Lippincott, 1953.
12. Burr, W.   Satisfaction with various aspects of marriage over the life cycle: A random middle-class sample. *Journal of Marriage and the Family* 32:29, 1970.
13. Cohen, M.   Personal identity and sexual identity. *Psychiatry* 29:1, 1966.
14. Cohler, B.   Mothers and grandmothers: Personality and child care in two generations. Unpublished, 1970.
15. Commission on Population Growth and the American Future, An Interim Report. Washington, D.C.: U. S. Government Printing Office, 1971.
16. Connel, H.   Marriage in Ireland after the famine: The diffusion of the match. *Journal of Statistical and Social Inquiry Society of Ireland* 19:82, 1955-56.
17. Cuber, J., and Harroff, P. *The Significant Americans.* New York: Appleton-Century-Crofts, 1965.
18. Dyer, E.   Parenthood as crisis: A re-study. *Marriage and Family Living* 25:196, 1963.
19. Edward VIII. *A King's Story.* New York: Putnam's, 1951.
20. Fein, R.   Paying for medical care in the United States. Unpublished, 1971.
21. Friedan, B. *The Feminine Mystique.* New York: Norton, 1963.
22. Gavron, H. *The Captive Wife: Conflicts of Housebound Mothers.* New York: Humanities Press, 1966.
23. Gordon, M., and Bernstein, M.   Mate choice and domestic life in the nineteenth-century marriage manual. *Journal of Marriage and the Family* 32:665, 1970.
24. Gough, E.   The Nayars and the Definition of Marriage. In P. Bohaman (Ed.), *Marriage, Family and Residence.* Garden City, N.Y.: Natural History Press, 1968.
25. Grunebaum, H., Neiberg, N., and Christ, J.   Diagnosis and treatment planning for couples. *International Journal of Group Psychotherapy* 19:185, 1969.
26. Hicks, M., and Platt, M.   Marital happiness and stability: A review of the research in the sixties. *Journal of Marriage and the Family* 32:553, 1970.
27. Hobbs, D., Sr.   Parenthood as crisis: A third study. *Journal of Marriage and the Family* 27:367, 1965.
28. Keesing, R.   Kwaio fosterage. *American Anthropology* 72:991, 1970.

29. Landis, J., and Landis, M. *Building a Successful Marriage.* Englewood Cliffs, N.J.: Prentice-Hall, 1963.
30. Laws, J. Parenthood as crisis. *Marriage and Family Living* 19:352, 1957.
31. Laws, J. A feminist review of marital adjustment literature: The rape of the locke. *Journal of Marriage and the Family* 33:483, 1971.
32. Leach, E. Aspects of bridewealth and marriage stability among the Katchin and Lakner. *Man* 57:50, 1957.
33. Lee, L. Law and family planning: A publication of the population council. *Studies in Family Planning* 2(4):81, 1971.
34. LeMasters, E. Parenthood as crisis. *Journal of Marriage and the Family* 19:352, 1967.
35. LeMasters, E. Holy deadlock: A study of unsuccessful marriages. *Sociological Quarterly* 21:86, 1959.
36. LeMasters, E. *Parents in Modern America.* Homeward, Ill.: Dorsey Press, 1970.
37. Lerner, A., and Loew, F. "Get me to the church on time" (song). *My Fair Lady.* New York: Schappel, 1956.
38. Lerner, M. *America As a Civilization.* New York: Simon & Schuster, 1957.
39. Lopata, H. *Occupation Housewife.* New York: Oxford University Press, 1971.
40. Lowie, R. *Primitive Society.* New York: Horace Liveright, 1920.
41. Luckey, E., and Bain, J. Children: A factor in marital satisfaction. *Journal of Marriage and the Family* 32:43, 1970.
41a.Mead, M., and Heyman, K. *Family.* New York: Macmillan, 1965.
42. Meyerowitz, J. Satisfaction during pregnancy. *Journal of Marriage and the Family* 32:38, 1970.
43. *New York Times.* "Population Growth in the U.S. Found Sharply Off." Nov. 5, 1971. P. 1.
44. O'Neill, W. *Divorce in the Progressive Era.* New Haven, Conn.: Yale University Press, 1967.
45. Orden, S., and Bradburn, N. Dimensions of marriage happiness. *American Journal of Sociology* 73:715, 1968.
46. Poloma, M., and Garland, T. The married professional woman: A study in the tolerance of domestication. *Journal of Marriage and the Family* 33:531, 1971.
47. Rapoport, R., and Rapoport, R. N. The dual-career family: A variant pattern and social change. *Human Relations* 22:3, 1969.
48. Renne, K. Correlates of dissatisfaction in marriage. *Journal of Marriage and the Family* 32:54, 1970.
49. Riesman, D. *The Lonely Crowd.* New Haven, Conn.: Yale University Press, 1961.
50. Rollins, B., and Feldman, H. Marital satisfaction over the family life cycle. *Journal of Marriage and the Family* 32:20, 1970.
51. Rossi, A. Equality between the sexes. *Daedalus,* Spring, 1964.
52. Rossi, A. Barriers to the career choice of engineering, medicine or science among American women. In J. Mattfield and C. VanAken (Eds.), *Women and the Scientific Professions: The MIT Symposium on American Women in Science and Engineering.* Cambridge, Mass.: MIT Press, 1965.

53. Rossi, A. Transition to parenthood. *Journal of Marriage and the Family* 30:26, 1968.

54. Streib, G. Intergenerational relations: Perspectives of the two generations on the older parent. *Journal of Marriage and the Family* 27:469, 1965.

55. *Time* Essay. The American family: Future uncertain. *Time*, Dec. 28, 1970. Pp. 34–39.

56. Titeiv, M. Old Oraibi: A study of the Hopi indians of Third Mesa. Cambridge Papers of the Peabody Museum of American Archaeology and Ethnology, Vol. 22, No. 1, 1944.

57. U.S. Bureau of the Census. *Historical Statistics of the United States, Colonial Times to 1957.* Washington, D.C.: U.S. Government Printing Office, 1960.

58. U.S. Bureau of the Census. *Statistical Abstract of the United States:* 1970 (91st ed.). Washington, D.C.: U.S. Government Printing Office, 1970.

59. Walters, J., and Stinnett, N. Parent-child relationships: A decade review of research. *Journal of Marriage and the Family* 33:70, 1971.

60. Williams, S. The limitation of the male-female activity distinction among primates. *American Anthropology* 73:805, 1971.

61. Winch, R. Permanence and change in the history of the American family and some speculations as to its future. *Journal of Marriage and the Family* 32:6, 1970.

3

Marital Alternatives: Extended Groups in Modern Society

Larry L. Constantine
Joan M. Constantine

Modern American society has long maintained a myth of monolithic monogamy, a myth that belies the evidence that there has always been substantial variation within family structure, marital goals, and marital functioning. Unfortunately, the assumption that marriage means one specific thing, a constant for all people and for all time, is so imbedded in our culture as to have affected the attitudes of family professionals, the structures of their theories, and the course of treatment they employ. Events that fall somewhat outside the mythological marriage model tend to be seen in even more absolute terms as annoying exceptions, pathologies, or problems to be solved without honest examination of the social, personal, and interpersonal contexts in which deviations from the norm are imbedded.

In recent years this attitude has been changing somewhat for the better. Both researchers and therapists are recognizing, for example, that extramarital sex is not necessarily a symptom nor a disease. Society, however, is not waiting for therapeutic models to catch up to the actual variances in marriage. Such popular slogans as "Different strokes for different folks" and "Do your own thing" are evidence of pluralistic attitudes in the cultural milieu. The therapist is now called on to modify and expand his view of marital health and normality even if his models and theories fail.

In various ways, the family is being extended beyond its traditional boundaries (indeed, the boundaries may be blurring altogether). Extended groups resulting from changes in family structure are arising in many quarters. Those who treat marital problems have an obligation to understand these innovations and to be able to approach them nonperjoratively. A family structure is not a problem to be treated, but rather a context in which problems may be imbedded. The unconventional family structure may or may not be related to the problems a family manifests.

FORCES EXTENDING THE FAMILY

Family boundary diffusion and expansion must be understood in the context of both broad social forces and common human propensities. Too often, normal human responses to an exceptional environment (liberating, alienating, oppressing) are seen as problems of the individual or of the marital dyad.

What We Do

The number of extended family versus nuclear family groups in our culture's past is unknown, and debate rages even concerning the present. The nuclear family is known to be a class-related phenomenon but one not limited to middle-class Caucasians [1, 19]. The isolated nuclear family, whatever its statistical extent, is a pervasive presence at the very least in the minds of most Americans. And perceived isolation is real isolation. To the extent that people see their family as insular, its functions increasingly arrogated by external institutions, they will focus on its affectional and supportive functions. This same focus is an expected reaction to the stresses of a fast-paced and alienating world. But high expectations may exacerbate internal stress, lowering the family's ability to deliver and contributing to a spiral of stress on the family and its boundaries. Under such conditions, increasing interest in sodalities and extended groups of all kinds, including group marriages, family networks, encounter groups, and communes, is a functional adaptation.

At the same time, tolerance for deviant and variant life-styles is growing in most segments of society, even if the law lags. The prognosis for this pluralism may be uncertain, but its present state of health is vigorous. And beneath the cultural pluralism is an emphasis on individualism in matters of life-style, sex, work, politics, and so on. There now exist overt sexual variations that were not possible a decade or so ago, except on an isolated, surreptitious basis. The pattern in sexual liberalization has been for vocal liberty to precede and exceed liberal activity. Expanded family forms involving sexual variance are no exception, and popular utopian novelists like Robert Rimmer[1] anticipated and stimulated today's experimentation through intellectual appeal.

What We Are

Any analysis of society, present or future, must reckon with the importance of the drive for self-realization in shaping social history. This growing interest in actualizing one's potentials is both a social and a psychological process. The technologically advanced state of our society makes it possible for increasing numbers of individuals to advance up Maslow's ladder [14], while the hierarchical nature of needs in the psychic makeup assures that, given the opportunity, people will shift in motivation and behavior. As greater numbers of people are involved, self-realization becomes a social force, even to the extent of institutionalization (as in "growth centers") and cultural identity (the "encounterculture"). Many things suggest that this interest is self-accelerating: even negative forces such as dissatisfaction with family life move people and social structures into focusing on self-realization if the mechanics and economics of the society are of a scale to support deemphasis on production and consumption.

Rather than pretending to have a comprehensive theory of the psychosexual nature of humans, we would like to focus attention on two factors in sexual attraction and involvement that are often neglected but are especially germane to the present discussion.

Sexual attraction is modulated primarily by two factors — novelty and intimacy. People sexually desire those who are new and those with whom they have become otherwise interpersonally involved. Incest taboos and

---

[1] Author of *The Harrad Experiment*, which described a college with coed rooms, and *Proposition 31*, about a group-marriage tetrad. Rimmer's *ex officio* status as guru of new multiperson sexualstyles is manifest in his two collections of letters; *The Harrad Letters to Robert H. Rimmer* (Signet, 1969) and *You and I Searching for Tomorrow* (Signet, 1971).

similar normative restrictions on sexual actualization with the "intimate in-group" are evidence for the interpersonal intimacy factor rather than against it. The conflict between intimacy needs and novelty needs is precisely the dilemma on which man's conflict-ridden traditional marital-sexual social structures are hung. Thus, monogamy is almost without exception (on a worldwide ethnographic basis) coexistent with structured provision for a variety of sexual partners. In the rare culture that insists on unrelieved monogamy (e.g., ours) the result is that infidelity is the statistical norm even though the moral norm is fidelity. In terms of overall sexual drive, response to novel potential partners, and sexual actualization of interpersonal intimacy, the more recent (nonsexist, amoral) research does not support innate male-female differences. Previous assertions of innate gender differences in these areas are fully explainable as male myths, since males have historically been in the ascendency and thus able to assert their own need for novelty while denying it in their partners, except during seduction, when it served their ends to maintain the converse.

In short, when people do get involved, they are apt to get sexually involved, unless substantial social forces intervene; and these are becoming ever more insubstantial. Moreover, given the opportunity, people will seek a variety of sexual partners. Since there are obvious trade-offs (in time if not also in other dimensions) between variety and intimacy, many alternative marital-sexual styles are possible with varying emphasis on each, reflecting the varying individual importance of variety and intimacy. For convenience, these ideas can be called the *two-factor theory* of human sexuality. If this theory is accurate, much that follows is easily understood; if it is not, what follows remains valid, though less easily explained.

The previous emphasis on sexual psychology reflects the structure of current extensions of the family. While not all new variants involve non-monogamous sex, it is in the realm of peer involvement in the conjugal unit that expansion is taking place, while agglomeration through acquisition of children and older generations is distinctly passé. In many cases, potential for sexual expression with other members of the expanded family, even if unconscious or unactualized, may play a role in motivation and has often emerged, sometimes to the surprise of participants.

DIMENSIONS OF EXTENSIONS TO THE FAMILY

Changes in marriage and family structure may be thought of as occurring in several distinct dimensions. In general, we find families, especially young families, becoming characterized by loosening boundaries [13]. Close friends may function as, and appear to be, members of the family for periods of time. Interpersonal intimacy beyond the basic dyad is often part of a total ethos that does not draw sharp distinctions between who is inside and who is outside. This is often most evident in communes, both urban and rural. The family may thus become extended in the interpersonal dimension through relationships with quasi-familial members. The level of interpersonal involvement with quasi-familial members may be comparable to that within couples. Networks of families based on such bonds crossing loose family boundaries are apt to become more common. Stoller's proposal of the "intimate network" represents an anticipation of this as a significant social phenomenon [20].

With or without interpersonal intimacy, families may band together for shared economic, practical, or philosophical reasons into expanded living groups. Co-residence is a second dimension in which many families are expanding and in which many more may be expected to expand; agrarian communes are the more publicized manifestation of this process, although urban communes with more or less conventional economic bases (often professional) are more numerous but less visible. A telephone survey in early 1972 identified over 200 urban communes in the greater Boston area alone.

The most widespread extensions of the contemporary family are taking place in the sexual dimension. It requires little specialized knowledge to anticipate a sexual element in extended families based on interpersonal intimacy, or common residence, or both. The two-factor theory also predicts this. However, sexual elements of intimate networks or joint residences may not be actualized for numerous reasons: religion or personal ethics, possessiveness, extreme jealousy, or inability to recognize the sexual element. It has been our experience that this dimension is almost always present beneath the surface, and generally it will be found that at least one member of any group has a conscious awareness of the sexual undercurrents.

The novelty aspect of the two-factor theory anticipates exclusively or largely sexual extensions such as exchange of sexual partners ("swinging" or "mate-swapping"). To the extent that intimacy needs are not met, a participant in mate-swapping may be motivated to establish an interpersonal adjunct to the primarily sexual basis of swinging, but the lack of opportunity for developing interpersonal intimacy in the typical swinging encounter tends to maintain a status quo in which the extension is reserved to the sexual dimension. Since individual variations in novelty and intimacy needs are to be expected, some swingers may be expected to move in the direction of intimate networks of sexually involved friends (intimacy needs predominating or unmet), while others might stay within a hard core of strictly social, strictly physical sexual encounters. Both patterns are known.[2] It appears that some individuals may successfully compartmentalize their need satisfaction and maintain long-term participation in isolated short-term sexual encounters devoid of other interpersonal content, although these individuals are a minority.

The presence or absence of interpersonal, residential, and sexual dimensions in extended-family groups influences both the degree of difficulty in formation and maintenance of the extended form and the therapeutic problems of working with those extended groups that seek professional assistance.

EXTENDED GROUPS AND DEVIANCE: AN OVERVIEW

By deviance, we mean the degree to which a life-style departs from societal norms that are themselves arbitrary and changing. We reiterate that deviance is not pathology, although participants in unconventional family styles may experience no less stress or difficulty in functioning than anyone else. While extended groups are as varied as the people who comprise them, some patterns are common enough to have been labeled. There is some value in exploring these patterns for their implication for treatment of marital problems.

Minor Deviance: Swinging

Social mate-swapping — "swinging" as it is known to most of its adherents,

[2]Bartell [3] studied primarily novelty-motivated swingers; Palson and Palson [18] have focused on those that have made a transition in the direction of intimacy. Typologies of swingers have been proposed by Symonds [21], Varni [22], and Denfeld [10].

group sex to the sensation-minded media — is a family extension essentially limited to the sexual dimension. Swinging couples are often conventional in every respect except their involvement in social occasions when sexual partners are exchanged. Bartell [2] and Denfeld and Gordon [11] have even formulated an interpretation of research that suggests that over-conventionalization of other aspects of the marriage might be a response to breaking the boundary in the sexual sphere. The extension may even be limited to physical sexual encounters under restricted structured circumstances, such as swinging parties. Dating, even casual social meeting outside that context, may be prohibited and heavily censured if it occurs. Couples thus reduce the number of life-style departures with which they must cope. Strong sanctions against relating (other than sexually) maintain the stability of the marriage.

Swinging of this sort is obviously a minor deviance, though it may seem to depart radically from usual family patterns. Swinging parties may simply replace television, bowling, or other recreation.

Intermediate Deviance: Open-Ended Marriage

An open-ended marriage[3] is one in which both partners share an ethos that values the contribution of alternate interpersonal involvements without setting limits on the nature or depth of involvement. It is open-ended in that it includes any number of alternate relationships or any degree of intimacy and expression, including sexual involvement. The life-style of such a couple is much more likely to deviate significantly from the conventional, though it need not be radical. By definition, an open-ended marriage implies fairly loose family boundaries. The underlying ethos values interpersonal intimacy. Intimate mutual friends may be intricately involved in family functioning for varying periods of time. Sexual involvement is neither precluded nor essential, though in the two-factor view, most of the adjunct relationships in the open-ended marriage can be expected to lead to sexual intimacy. These partially extended families contrast dramatically with both swingers and the conventional pattern of extramarital affairs. A wife's lover may also be the husband's close friend, and all three may share many activities. New involvements, rather than being feared or merely tolerated by the spouse, are likely to be encouraged. Such couples feel positively about the spouse's alternate involvements in

[3] A term first used in this context by Reverend Ronald Mazur in a plenary address at the 1970 annual meeting for the National Council on Family Relations [16].

proportion to the spouse's satisfaction in the relationship or to the extent that the relationship contributes to the spouse's personal growth.

Some people do in fact find this ethos congruent at the deepest level. Couples who successfully establish this extended marital life-style may be uncommonly secure in their primary dyadic relationship. They tend in general to reject notions of exclusivity and possessiveness and other scarcity, commodity-oriented or zero-sum approaches to affection and interpersonal relations.

Major Deviance: Group Marriage

A group, or multilateral, marriage [5] incorporates extra partners into the conjugal unit within a common residence. With each member perceiving himself or herself as having a marital commitment with at least two other members, the structure can be simultaneously cohesive, complex, and difficult. Living together on a day-to-day basis adds to the difficulty of maintaining more than one intimate relationship at a time. Probably for this reason, actual multilateral marriages tend to be small, involving three, four, five, or at most six, conjugal partners. Multilateral marriage constitutes a major commitment to an almost total life-style. The whole of family life is affected rather than just certain aspects or time-bounded segments.

At the same time, the group marriage may offer special advantages where growth in self-realization is the goal. Its power is exactly that of the group in other growth-oriented contexts: encounter groups, sensitivity training, and group therapy. An ethos of personal growth is a common theme among group-marriage participants [4].

Indeterminate Deviance: Communes

The term *commune* has been indiscriminately applied to many groupings that are better described in other words. The commune is quintessentially a community, a group extended by residence. Frequently, but not always, families in communes are extended by significantly exceptional interpersonal bonds as well. There is great variance in the sexual (and also marital) structure within communes. Popular notions virtually equate communes with group marriage, free sex, and orgies. There are no adequate survey data, but it appears that within communes a free (or freer) sex ethic is common but no more common than monogamous patterns. Even supposedly free-sex communes may be observed to follow a pattern of serial monogamy rather than multiple simultaneous involvements [7]. Group marriages within communes are known but are much less frequent than the press, popular mythology, and misnomers suggest.

The life-style in a commune can be comparatively conventional, as in a monogamous, urban commune of professionals, or radical in numerous ways, for example, in being agrarian, in espousing a free-sex ethic, in practicing communal childrearing, or in rejecting any monetary structure.

CLINICAL SIGNIFICANCE OF EXTENDED GROUPS

We see the emerging styles of extended-family groups as, basically, manifestations of intrinsic, normal human propensities. The emergence of these propensities into behavior and social patterns is made possible and probable by the contemporary social milieu. Clinical labels such as *acting out* and *immature* serve no purpose but obfuscation. Working with new styles of marriages requires a clear, openly negotiated "therapeutic con- tract" that incorporates what a person or family wants to accomplish with what the therapist can bring to facilitate the sought-after changes. Hidden agenda on either side are likely to be exceptionally destructive. It is the therapist's responsibility to examine his own motivations to make sure that his religion (mystical or scientific, from church or from medical school) does not lead him to try covertly to change his clients' life-styles without their permission.

Coping and Jealousy

The boundary of the nuclear family cannot simply be modified without compensatory adaptation in various parts of the system. The family, but especially the marital dyad, develops coping attitudes and behavior. It is likely that many clients will primarily desire help in adjusting to their chosen life-style. This is already especially true of couples with styles involving comarital-extramarital sexual involvement.

To some observers, the central clinical problem in the new life-styles is jealousy. But jealousy is merely the response to a situation in a given life- style context. What is unique about the extended-group context under discussion is that it does not assume exclusivity. The participants must cope not so much with jealousy as with the absence of exclusive sexual access (or other types of access). The absence of exclusiveness carries with it the threat of loss and of interpersonal insecurity, which may be even more central.

Various coping responses can be identified, including some not specific to sexual boundary modifications. The choice of coping adaptation will, of course, be a function of the clients' as well as of the therapist's prejudices. We do favor those approaches that promote personality integration rather than segmentation. Though both approaches are equally effective in the short-term, integrative approaches appear to have fewer long-term problems; certainly they are more consistent with accepted holistic models of the fully functioning person.

In one method of coping with jealousy, permeability of the family boundary in certain exchanges is restricted to specific interpersonal modalities. For example, outside intellectual companionship may be acceptable but not "emotional" sharing. This may be termed *isolation of modality*. In conventional marriages, only nonsexual modalities (and not all of these) are permitted. Denfeld and Gordon's interpretation [11], is that this conventional strategy is inverted by swingers. Thus exclusiveness is lost only in the sexual area, avoiding a threat of loss of the whole person. The dyad is preserved.

Individual relationships may be compartmentalized in such a way that the participant's life is divided into distinct nonoverlapping, noncompeting areas. This concept is championed by Neubeck and beautifully illustrated in his fictional account of what is really a cyclic form of monogyny [17]. Compartmentalization can be taught; it is an exercise in excluding from consciousness whatever is not immediately present. It is ill-suited to multiple relationships involving co-residence or frequently shared contact.

Both isolation and compartmentalization may too easily permit maintenance of conditions that are basically personality dystonic, that is, experienced as conflicting with the self. The Palsons [18] argue that most long-term swingers eventually adopt a mode of coping they call *individuation*. Individuation stresses that each person, hence each relationship, is unique. An alternate sexual involvement or friendship cannot threaten the dyad because it cannot supply the person with the same things. To contrast, isolation implies that alternate involvements are nonthreatening because they can supply only certain things; compartmentalization implies they are nonthreatening because they are time bounded. Individuation can cope with both multimodality and time overlap.

Individuation is a zero-sum approach in that it recognizes replacement as a possibility; only the fact that the equivalence of relationships is imperfect bars replacement by another. It is overly simple in that it fails to take into account that a new relationship might represent an overall gain even if it is not the equivalent of an old one in all dimensions.

In a non-zero-sum approach, gain to one spouse through alternate involvement does not imply loss to the other nor the threat of replacement. One approach is through integration of alternate involvements into the dyad such that relationships are inextricable. This is the reverse of compartmentalization and changes the usual "It's either her or me" to "It's either us or neither." Mutual participation in almost all aspects of a relationship serves the same purpose by directly providing both spouses with the same benefits. Either of these integrative means can be oversimplified. A relationship inseparable from the prior dyadic one may simply be forced, while shared participation may only aggravate potential competition or jealousy.

In all cases, the essential matter is the mental set of the coping partners. If a couple or group truly believes that individuation guarantees the continuance of established relationships, this is a successful method.

Our own research has led to the formulation of an integrative model of jealousy [5] in which the individual's mode of perceiving and organizing reality emerges as central in affecting the probability that a given interpersonal situation will trigger jealous behavior. *Synergic perception* refers to a particular world view in which conceptual opposites are seen as integral and interdependent rather than polar and mutually exclusive [15]. A person who perceives reality synergically would be likely to see deviance and normality as processes dependent on each other for definition and continuation, for example.

Our model of jealousy and the evidence to date suggest that the more synergically a person organizes his reality, the fewer his problems with jealousy. Synergic perception of a relationship transcends the dichotomy of self and other. What is gain to the other is also gain to the self. Shoes on the feet of one make the other's feet feel good. Seen synergically, situations which might otherwise pose the threat of personal loss, thus leading to jealous behavior, instead provide satisfaction.

Synergic perception has been established as an element of psychological health. Extensive clinical work and experience in the conduct of workshops on jealousy demonstrates that people can learn to perceive situations more synergically through role playing, exercises, and other kinds of "designed experiences" which focus on synergic and non-zero-sum aspects of human relations and provide relatively safe opportunities to practice looking at relationships from this viewpoint. For example, a couple may be asked to share with each other positive things each feels he has gained from the other's experiences outside the marriage, including work, school, friendships, and the like.

Communication Problems

Problems in communication are hardly unique to extended family groups, but their context and pattern may be unique. Many distinct conjugal dyads may have to be dealt with. Communication via third parties (which sometimes involves the children in conventional families) may be a common group response to blocked communication in any one dyad. As in the usual therapy situations, fostering effective communication may be the therapist's most important function in enabling clients to resolve their own problems. But this may be more difficult because of the complexities involved in extended family interactions. It may be difficult to involve all participants in the therapy process.

The unit of treatment depends on the contract. If the therapist's function involves a responsibility to the group ("Keep us together" or "Keep me in it"), then probably the whole group or network must be brought into the process, certainly as allies and preferably as active participants. This involves the therapist in situations that include quasi-familial members, neighbors, or lovers — people normally regarded as outsiders. Mixed therapeutic patterns that involve individuals, particular dyads, or other subgroups in specific processes are also effective.[4]

Sexual Problems

The multiple sexual involvement found in some extended groups is not itself a significant source of problems. Sexual interchange across traditional boundaries does often supply the setting for revelation of other problems. (Jealous behavior is more apt to be a response to a sexual transgression than to other boundary violations [8].)

In on-going groups with common residence, the choice of immediate sexual partners becomes a prime focus. Highly structured solutions (such as rotation) appear to bring temporary symptomatic relief. Spontaneous

[4]Grunebaum [12] may be a useful guide to therapeutic approaches. Counseling of extended family groups is dealt with in more detail by Constantine, Constantine, and Edelman [9].

pairing consumes energy and leaves open the potential for someone's remaining unchosen. In a functioning group of secure adults this need not be a blow to self-esteem, but in other circumstances essential insecurity or fear of inadequacy may be brought to the surface by such rejection.

Group sexual activity is an alternative. This too has its pitfalls in triggering release of latent problems. Though at extreme variance with tradition in society and psychiatry, group sex appears to be a harmless but highly enjoyable form of multiple intimacy for many people and for some even a peak experience [8].

Other Problems

Probably the most ubiquitous presenting problem that the therapist deals with is generalized anxiety from clients operating under conditions of low information. The interpersonal tensions and pressures that are inevitable concommitants of intimate group formation are equally important factors in the client's early history. Second thoughts over commitment to a radical family life-style, concern that there might be hidden long-term consequences (frequently relating to children), and feelings of isolation from the mainstream of society are common. Seeking therapeutic help may be part of broader searching behavior, which includes attempts to contact other participants in the client's particular family life-style, efforts to identify legal and other resources, and literature searches for personal accounts and formal studies.

The therapist may find it sufficient to reassure and alleviate anxiety in order to mobilize the client's own coping resources.

Other special problems in extended family groups in which the therapist may play a facilitative role include decision-making, excessive pressures on individuals to grow, conflicts in private versus group time and activities, and structure-building processes in general [5, 9].

PROBLEMS AS REASONS

A minority of participants in extended groups are undoubtedly motivated by or are seeking resolution of personal or interpersonal problems. For group marrieds as a class, significant psychopathology can be ruled out [5], and though data are not available for communitarians and swingers, the same is likely to be true of them. If boredom is considered to be a marital problem, then a marital problem may be the motivation for a substantial proportion of people who engage in swinging [3].

Two possible patterns of deficit motivation for seeking extended involvement can be illustrated by two cases.

CASE 1   Though she was not the prime mover, Anne permitted the formation of a group marriage by not exercising her veto at a critical juncture. A young mother of one preschool child, Anne primarily sought security. She did not feel her relationship with her husband was really primary with him, and she saw two partially committed husbands as better than one. With the right people, larger groups may better fulfill security needs, but Anne's insecurity was heightened by her husband's deep involvement with her co-wife and her own lack of involvement with the other man.

CASE 2   A young couple sought resolution of sexual inadequacy through intimate involvement with a couple they saw as more sexually sophisticated. Premature ejaculation was their presenting problem. Interestingly, the husband found that the other woman's faster responses enabled him to bring her to climax, while the wife found the other man's slower responses permitted her to reach orgasm. This did not, however, help their dyadic problem, and it led to mutual blaming. After limited counseling, the couple concluded they did not and had not really loved each other and that the sexual inadequacy was merely a symptom. They subsequently separated.[5]

Both cases share a common factor with numerous more successful and less problem-motivated attempts at extended marriage — the wives ultimately made major personality gains, growing significantly in autonomy and sense of self-worth.

Dyadic Discord

Extended-family groups have a way of revealing or exacerbating existing dyadic problems. Often relationship problems surface that might have remained indefinitely subclinical. Feedback and perspective from intimates beyond the dyad help to counteract dyadic "scripts," "games," and hidden agenda yet may supply little in the way of constructive input. This input the therapist can do admirably, serving not only the extended group but also the dyad, should it later separate from the extended relationship.

[5]The group dissolution process is analyzed in more detail in Constantine and Constantine [6].

LOOKING FORWARD

In the immediate future the therapist may be called on to deal with many more existing deviant family forms. A more distant version may be envisioned in which part of the counselor-therapist's function will be to assist individuals and groups in finding or creating a marital-family life-style tailored to their unique personalities and capabilities. The coming of that exciting day when we design holes to fit pegs will depend not only on general social change, but also on personal change by individual counselors and therapists.

REFERENCES

1. Auerswald, E. H. Interdisciplinary vs. ecological approach. *Family Process* 7:202, 1968.
2. Bartell, G. Group sex among the mid-Americans. *Journal of Sex Research* 6:113, 1970.
3. Bartell, G. *Group Sex: A Scientist's Eyewitness Report on the American Way of Swinging.* New York: Peter H. Wyden, 1971.
4. Constantine, L. Personal growth in multiperson marriages. *Radical Therapist* 2:1, 1971.
5. Constantine, L., and Constantine, J. *Group Marriage: A Study of Contemporary Multilateral Marriage.* New York: Macmillan, 1973.
6. Constantine, L., and Constantine, J. Dissolution of marriage in a nonconventional context. *Family Coordinator* 21(4):457, 1972.
7. Constantine, L., and Constantine, J. Group and multilateral marriage: Definitional notes, glossary, and annotated bibliography. *Family Process* 10:157, 1971.
8. Constantine, L., and Constantine, J. Sexual aspects of multilateral relations. *Journal of Sex Research* 7:204, 1971.
9. Constantine, L., Constantine, J., and Edelman, S. Counseling implications of comarital and multilateral relations. *Family Coordinator* 21(3):267, 1972.
10. Denfeld, D. Towards a typology of swinging: The trophy hunters. Paper presented at the Groves Conference on Marriage and Family, San Juan, Puerto Rico, May 8, 1971.
11. Denfeld, D., and Gordon, M. The sociology of mate-swapping: Or the family that swings together clings together. *Journal of Sex Research* 6:85, 1970.
12. Grunebaum, H., Christ, J., and Neiberg, N. Diagnosis and treatment planning for couples. *International Journal of Group Psychotherapy* 19:185, 1969.
13. Kafka, J., and Ryder, R. Notes on marriage in the counterculture. *Journal of Applied Behavioral Science* 9(2,3):321, 1973.
14. Maslow, A. *Toward a Psychology of Being.* Princeton, N.J.: Van Nostrand Reinhold, 1962.

15. Maslow, A. *Eupsychian Management.* Homeward, Ill.: Irwin, 1965.
16. Mazur, R. *The New Intimacy: Open-Ended Marriage and Alternative Lifestyles.* Boston: Beacon Press, 1973.
17. Neubeck, G. Polyandry and Polygymy — Viable Today? In H. Otto (Ed.), *The Family in Search of a Future.* New York: Appleton-Century-Crofts, 1970.
18. Palson, C., and Palson, R. Swinging in wedlock. *Society* 9(4):28, 1972.
19. Scheflen, A., and Ferber, A. Critique of a Sacred Cow — The Nuclear Family. In A. Ferber, M. Mendelsohn, and A. Napier (Eds.), *The Book of Family Therapy.* New York: Science House, 1972.
20. Stoller, F. H. The Intimate Network of Families. In H. Otto (Ed.), *The Family in Search of a Future.* New York: Appleton-Century-Crofts, 1970.
21. Symonds, C. The utopian aspects of sexual mate swapping: In theory and practice. Unpublished, 1970.
22. Varni, C. Contexts of Conversion: The Case of Swinging. In R. Libby and R. Whitehurst (Eds.), *Renovating Marriage.* Danville, Calif.: Consensus Publishers, 1973.

4

Changing Sex Roles and the Future of Marriage*

Janet Zollinger Giele

In their book, *Symmetrical Families*, based on research carried out in England in 1970, Michael Young and Peter Willmott [31] state that relationships of women and men have changed from patriarchal to egalitarian. Where once it was the husband who went out to work and the wife who stayed at home, both now are more likely to work, and both are free to pursue leisure at home. Family life flourishes because the household is the primary unit of consumption and leisure. As a result the roles of men and women both as producers and consumers are becoming symmetrical.

Examination of family ideology in the United States over the last 50 years [8] reveals that such symmetrical trends are apparent not only in the economic realms of production and consumption, but also in the moral arena, where women have gained premarital sexual freedom once thought appropriate only to men. *Fathering* and *parenting* are terms that have emerged alongside *mothering* in the literature of child psychology. Income support for fathers of indigent families has been discussed as a possible supplement to the programs of aid to dependent children aimed primarily at mothers.

Much of the current literature on the future of marriage, however, says little of the trend toward symmetry. It focuses instead on marital

*This paper is based on a lecture sponsored by the Department of Sociology and Anthropology at Wellesley College, February, 1973.

experiments that appear unconventional and even bizarre in comparison with Young and Willmott's blue-collar symmetrical families or with the professional dual-career families in England described by Rhona and Robert Rapoport [20]; many American family sociologists and therapists [6, 17, 26, 27] are fascinated by urban communes, group marriages, and open-ended relationships that feature nonexclusive sexual access between partners as a cornerstone.

What shall one make of these two streams of commentary on the nature of contemporary and future marriage? Perhaps English observers are biased to describing only "respectable" marriages. Or, perhaps, radical experiments simply occur more frequently in America. My purpose in this chapter is to set forth a larger theoretical framework that can encompass both perspectives. Then it should be possible, by comparing both perspectives against a standard, to identify the major assumptions, emphases, and omissions that each exhibits.

SYMMETRICAL MONOGAMOUS MARRIAGE

Generally, research [7, 10, 18, 20, 31] that describes "shared-role" marriage is striking for its preoccupation with work and obligation. In this research husbands and wives are asked how they manage their dual responsibilities to both work and leisure. They report [20] how they involve their children in helping at home, how they schedule activities, and how they take turns performing household duties. Reports of family life on the kibbutz [28] similarly revolve around division of labor between the sexes and the shifting nature of contractual obligations as each collective became wealthier and had more children.

Implicit in these writings is a strong Puritan ethic in the families observed, with high priority on work, dedication to democratic principles, and social responsibility. Social contract is emphasized at the expense of attention to hedonism or egoistic concerns. Emotional feelings, sexuality, and conflict, divorce, and disruption are submerged in relation to production and mutual obligation, which are the priorities. When sex is mentioned, as in Benjamin Schlesinger's account [25] of premarital relations in the early Israeli kibbutz, it is to point out that sexuality between the young, unmarried people was largely controlled and disciplined. After marriage, extramarital sexual relations and divorce were exceptionally rare, if not virtually unknown. Dual-career families seem similarly devoid of concern with sex, emotions of love or hate, or the ever-present fear of disruption and break-down that appears in reports about sexually nonconventional marriage experiments.

NONEXCLUSIVE MARRIAGE

Dual-career families have innovative work patterns and sexual arrangements that are conservative. By contrast, descriptions of sexually nonexclusive marital experiments appear to give much less attention to work patterns and far more to innovation in the expressive dimension of life. These mar-ital experiments range from the multilateral marriages among several couples who share mates [4] to *ménages à trois* (frequently made up of two females and one male) or urban communes where sexual relations may occur between successive partners [22].

Many descriptions of the nonmonogamous marital forms reveal perva-sive concern for stability of the relationship, thereby suggesting its fragility. Participants in the experiments appear to feel that the threat in convention-al marriage is the confinement and stifling of growth. They emphasize self-realization and personal growth through expansion of marital boun-daries. Nonexclusive access to sexual partners is held out as a means to growth. In the symmetrical family, equal opportunities for working and consuming are principal avenues to satisfaction. In the sexually radical experiment, it is the expression of personal feelings primarily through sex-ual activity that is the central theme.

Compare the central themes in the following quotations. Young and Willmott's projection for the future of marriage centers around jobs [31]:

In this century wives have been doing a job outside the home that they did not greatly care for and the husbands a minor job inside the home that they did not greatly care for either — each therefore showing signs of the bonds that held them to the past as well as their partial recognition of the new order which they have been helping to bring into being. By the next century — with the pioneers of 1970 already at the front of the column — society will have moved from (a) one demanding job for the wife and one for the husband, through (b) two demanding jobs for the wife and one for the husband, to (c) two demanding jobs for the wife and two for the husband. The sym-metry will be complete. Instead of two jobs there will be four . . . .
Such a new relationship to the world outside the home will affect all that goes on in it, and vice versa. "If we have children," more wives will say, "will you look after them as much as I?" And, "If my career requires a move of house, will that count as much as yours?" [p. 278].

On the other hand, Rustum and Della Roy [23] articulate a different norm developing among avant-garde family counselors and therapists. They project the future of marriage as follows:

With the engagement-including-sex, we have broken the pre-marital half of monogamy's monopoly on sex. It is our judgment that for the health of the institution it will become necessary in America in the next decade to break the second half also — post-marital sexual expression. (Recall that our theory demands that we seek to maximize the number of deep relationships and to develop marriages to fit in with a framework of community.) To do this we are certain that the monopolistic tendencies of relationships must be broken, and hence the question of sexual relations cannot be bypassed. We believe that in the coming generation a spectrum of sexual expression with persons other than the spouse are certain to occur for at least the large majority, and possibly most persons. If monogamy is tied inextricably with post-marital restriction of all sexual expression to the spouse, it will ultimately be monogamy which suffers. Instead monogamy should be tied to the much more basic concepts of fidelity, honesty, and openness, which are concomitants of love of the spouse, but which do not necessarily exclude deep relationships and possibly including various degrees of sexual intimacy with others. In the studies and counseling experience of many, including ourselves, there is no evidence that all extramarital sexual experience is destructive of the marriage. Indeed more and more persons testify that creative co-marital relationships and sexual experience can and do exist. [pp. 344-345]

EVALUATION AGAINST THEORETICAL CONSTRAINTS

On the basis of these examples, it appears that two different kinds of change are occurring in contemporary marriage. The first touches the structural division of labor. The second grapples with the form by which the marriage of the future can express love and commitment. Furthermore, change in the one is somehow connected with change in the other. As John Scanzoni states [24]:

The husband exchanges the status and economic benefits he provides to his wife for expressive rewards, deference, and conjugal solidarity. If, in the future, he is no longer able to provide these resources in a *unique* fashion, *what are the basic processes which then account for feelings of solidarity, cohesion, and which lead to marital stability?* May we therefore expect more marital instability among the better educated, owing not only to negative conflict over wife's achievements, but also because they are less bound together — less interdependent — than were the partners in marriages based on role-specialization? [p. 139]

It seems now that the future division of labor between the sexes is clear, though not fully realized. The literature on symmetrical families indicates that there will be more overlap in the duties that each sex performs. Old boundaries will be blurred. Though women still may have primary responsibility in the kitchen, and men in full-time paid work outside the home, the extent to which each sex can enter and feel at home in the domain of the other will probably continue to increase. In certain classes and occupational groups both husband and wife will cook and both husband and wife will hold paid jobs. This will probably not happen in all segments of society. A lumberjack and his wife may maintain a fairly traditional division of labor by sex. A husband-and-wife team of physicians may both work and rely on household help to perform the traditional tasks of the wife. A faculty couple who both teach and work close to home may, on the other hand, come close to realizing the ideal of merged sex roles. Despite pluralism, the overall trend seems nonetheless clear.

In the realm of love and commitment, however, the form of change is not yet clear. The recent literature suggests drastic and various revisions of the exclusive monogamous relationship. Some change seems inevitable, but what it will be is not settled. The people involved are themselves hardly describing battles already won, as are the dual-career people who describe their solutions and satisfactions. Experiments in group marriage and intimate network relationships sound more tenuous and fragile; doubts about the success of these experiments seem justified, considering the jealousies and dissolutions that appear to be frequent.

In the face of a situation that is still changing, the purpose of this chapter is to examine the constraints that theoretically limit any intimate social structure such as marriage. Against those constraints it should be possible to evaluate the two major marital innovations — symmetry of marital roles and expansion of the marital boundaries.

Symmetrical families seem to have solved a number of major problems. They appear likely to survive and be duplicated in large segments of the population. By contrast, nonexclusive sex experiments in marriages, or expanded marriages, have so far been short-lived and remain confined to small segments of the population. The O'Neills, who interviewed some 400 couples in 1970-1971, made the following observation [16]:

While some benefits were noted from extra-marital sexual experiments, it was observed that by and large these experiences did not occur in a context where the marital partners were developing their primary marriage relationship sufficiently for their activity to count as a growth experience. [p. 407]

The relative success of the dual-career family and the rather more tenuous survival of the nonexclusive sexual experiments are probably the result of the respective ability of each form to solve certain basic structural
problems set by the nature of human personalities and social organizations.
These problems must be attacked at the level of biological needs, the personality, social institutions, and culture. Specifically:

1. Marriage must live within certain biological constraints and satisfy cer-
    tain physical needs. Any form of marriage that is successful must ad-
    dress itself to sexual drives and take into account the different sexual
    natures of male and female.
2. Marriage must support individual personalities. Intimate in nature, it
    must cope with some of the most private emotional needs of the partners.
3. As one of many social groups, marriage must be compatible with the
    social fabric in which it finds itself. Marriage relates the individual to
    the larger family unit and to other social entities such as the economy
    and the political and residential communities.
4. Finally, marriage through its religious or ethical foundations is related to
    the cultural values of the larger society. It expresses given traditions; it
    also generates new normative standards that sustain and renew the
    larger moral community and are in part communicated through the
    socialization of children.

To what extent is each of the two major marriage innovations capable
of bearing the biological, emotional, social, and cultural demands placed
upon it? In general, the expanded marriage appears to offer some very
real sexual satisfactions. However, its capacity to deal with emotional
strain and social conflict is problematic. The sexual satisfactions of dual-
career or symmetrical families are, in contrast, almost unknown and may,
in fact, be precarious or nonexistent; but these families are highly aware of
the way they relate to the surrounding society. While they face difficulties,
they appear, by and large, to have surmounted them. An analysis of the
relative success of each marriage innovation in meeting the four fundamental requisites follows.

Biological Constraints and Sexual Functioning
It is hard to make a judgment for either expanded marriage or sexually

conservative symmetrical marriage on the basis of erotic satisfaction alone. If sexual satisfaction thrives on both novelty and intimacy, nonexclusive marriage may do more to ensure against boredom, but monogamous symmetry may better assure stability, and thus intimacy, in the long run.

From biologist Trivers [29] come data on differences between male and female sexuality in a number of species. Generally, males are more promiscuous, females more selective, in choice of sexual partners. Trivers explains this phenomenon by referring to natural selection. Because a male has less invested in each sperm (measured by percent of body weight) than a female has invested in each egg, the male gets more reproductive payoff from many copulations than from a few. It is to the female's reproductive advantage, however, to be more selective of the partner who fertilizes the egg because she has relatively more invested in each one.

The human analogy in an earlier day would have been obvious. The double standard permitted men to sow wild oats but enjoined women to guard their chastity. In this day of effective contraception female risk of pregnancy is lower, and with it, seemingly, has come a decreased male and female interest in sexually exclusive relationships. There no longer seems to be a biological basis for either a double standard or the standard of exclusive monogamy. Both sexes are free to roam; one need not even be constrained out of a sense of fairness to the other. In fact, it is argued by some that both sexes may benefit from expansion of the marital boundaries, and young people, especially, find it difficult to justify monogamy intellectually [15].

The work of Masters and Johnson on human sexual inadequacy [2, 13] might cause some doubt. Their work reveals that many sexual problems are social in nature rather than purely physical. The common male dysfunction, premature ejaculation, frequently arises from fleeting and guilt-ridden sexual contacts. Therapy, following the Masters and Johnson formula, which is "you have to give to get," implies an intimate and loving relationship between partners who treat each other as equals. Thus both prevention and treatment of sexual dysfunction imply long-term commitment and devotion to the partner without the threat of one's partner's seeking satisfaction elsewhere.

Accounts of actual sexual experience within an ideology of freedom raise further questions about the viability of sexually nonexclusive arrangements. Thomas Cottle [5] has described young women's doubts, sense of sadness, and lack of fulfillment that accompany premarital sexual inter-course when there is no deep affection or sense of commitment. Kathleen Kinkade [11] in her account of life in Twin Oaks, a rural commune in Virginia, notes the sense of desertion and emotional insecurity that befell young women after they became pregnant and their primary partners either left the commune or found other women. Perhaps it is no accident that both these examples deal with the dissatisfaction of women when their male partners are not monogamous. There may be real differences between men and women in the degree to which they prefer monogamous sexual relationships, and the differences may result from natural selection, much as Trivers argued in the case of other species.

In the last analysis, however, the decision for or against one marital innovation or another does not rest on biological criteria alone. Because sexual functioning is colored by social context, the sexual benefits of a particular marital innovation are not in and of themselves sufficient grounds for evaluating the whole structure. Emotional, practical, and symbolic consequences of each model must also be taken into account.

Emotional Constraints: The Problem of Differential Investment

Marriage is a great deal more than a socially accepted locus for sexual inter-action. Traditional Western marriage vows include a promise of the part-ners to remain faithful to each other for better or for worse, in sickness or in health, until one of the partners dies. In that promise is implied possible future costs that may not be easy or pleasant to pay, as well as present returns that are evident at the time of marriage. Traditional marriage fore-sees a partnership throughout the whole life span — through bearing children and raising them in the early years of the marriage and continuing until old age and perhaps through infirmity at the end.

Part of the stability of traditional marriage may have been due to demo-graphic causes; people died young and the average marriage probably did not last more than 20 years [3]. But there were structural features as well that promoted permanence. Households were units of production as well as of consumption. The loss of one's partner was the loss not just of a companion but of a co-worker, a loss that jeopardized independence and survival itself. Of the two major new marriage innovations, symmetry in work roles appears to provide a structure that ensures somewhat more stability and permanence than expansion of marital boundaries. Why is this so?

The answer can be couched in the language of investment [1] or be given in the sociological context of functional interdependence. In brief, the partners in dual-career or symmetrical marriages seem much more highly interdependent than those in multilateral arrangements. The bonds are firmer, the mutual investment in each other greater than in a three-or-four-person network, where less utility is derived from any single pair-bond. Therefore, to the extent that partnership with a single person maximizes the utilities to be gained from marriage, there will be equilibrium or stability in that relationship. That relationship may become unstable if the satisfactions decline sharply or are greatly below what can be found elsewhere, which is frequently the case. Thus, even in the case of symmetrical marriage, Young and Willmott predict that there will be a continuing increase in the divorce rate but that divorce will usually be followed by another monogamous pair-bond [31].

Strains will be inescapable. There will inevitably be more divorces because people will be seeking a more multi-faceted adjustment to each other, with the two outside jobs clicking with the two inside ones; and because the task will be harder, there will be more failures. Chester, reviewing the evidence about recent trends in divorce and other kinds of marital failure, concluded that in total "breakdown is probably increasing in volume among contemporary marriages. On the basis of speculative estimates . . . perhaps one sixth to one quarter of contemporary marriages may ultimately experience some form of breakdown." The trend is not necessarily disastrous. The people we interviewed who had married more than once did not appear any less content than others. [pp. 278-279]

By contrast the instability of the multilateral network is of a different order. Some observers have noted that it is rare to find a group marriage that has been in existence for more than two years [19]. This impermanence stems from the structure of interchange. When decline occurs in satisfaction with one partner, it is probably relatively easy to substitute another pair-bond that maximizes specific utilities. It is probably harder to substitute a more complex pair-bond of the symmetrical type that satisfies many different needs in one relationship.

In sum, less total reliance on the marital unit as a source of satisfaction subjects it to greater likelihood of termination by one or both parties. The urban family is less dependent than the rural family on the household unit to satisfy all its needs and therefore is subject to more frequent separation and divorce. So also, participants in multilateral marriages are usually less dependent on a single pair-bond to satisfy all their needs and are therefore more likely to change partners or break up and form new units.

The multilateral framework may in some instances facilitate mobility and freedom of choice and change, but it threatens the position of the weak. Such persons are unable to provide the company and gratification they once promised. The monogamous vow "for better or worse" promises security to these unfortunates. No alternative partners are built into the system.

Is it necessary to make any judgments in favor of one alternative or the other? Perhaps one day it will be clear what the emotional benefits of freedom are as compared with those of security. For the moment it is possible only to make a judgment about what is best for the deserted, the ill, and the children. When the stronger or healthier partner leaves, society has an interest in what becomes of those left behind.

Perhaps something should be said here about love. Saint-Exupéry's Little Prince [23a] loved his rose because he had watered it, shaded it, and humored it. He thought it was unique, and he was sad when he discovered a whole field of roses. Love is the expression whereby two partners communicate their strong affection and attachment for each other and their willingness to sacrifice because of it. Saint-Exupéry depicted love as, in part, a result of investment in the other. Love, like all forms of social interaction, is an exchange. But it is different from other forms of exchange in its inclusiveness. It accepts the other, warts and all, so to speak. It also gives to the other without selfish regard for payment or return.

Does one of these marital innovations better express love and therefore promise sacrificial giving if the need arises? In the long run the dual-career family perhaps expresses love better, but in the short run the dual-career structure may be so tightly closed and demanding that it offers no succour to the "lonely wanderer." The intimate network may offer a chance to express love better, albeit at a more superficial level. Having found support and intimacy, the wanderer may then be ready to enter a long-term bond again.

The two types of relationships may thus both be viable for the same person by serving different needs at different times in his or her life. If each is to be effective, however, it must dovetail with the larger social fabric in which the individual operates. This is the next criterion against which marriage forms must be measured.

Social Context and Capacity for Mobility

The marital group must be compatible with the larger society to the degree that it supports, or at least does not interfere with, work, on the one hand, and reproduction and childrearing, on the other. The extended family of agrarian China, Europe, and Russia and the nuclear family of modern-day technologically advanced societies appear to have emerged and thrived because each in its respective form was compatible with the means of production and the demographic needs that predominated in each period. While the extended family provided a large work force and many ties of mutual support that were necessary for agriculture, the nuclear family of today is adapted to the mobility and individuation required by an industrial society [9].

Which marital innovation — role symmetry or boundary expansion — appears most adaptive to the society of the future? In the other-directed society that relies on peer pressure and peer support, it may be that each will have its place, depending on the phase in the life cycle of the individual and the vagaries of the economy. For the moment, the dual-career pattern seems more generalizable than group marriage, because its bonding has the enormous advantage of strength and simplicity. The emotional bookkeeping of satisfaction is confined to one major peer relationship, that is, with the marital partner, rather than with a number of partners. Furthermore, the dual tie permits mobility and adaptation to change without breaking the relationship, because it is not so dependent on residence in a particular community. A partnership of two people can move more easily than can a relationship of more than two.

Another issue is support of personal growth and self-realization. Advocates of expanded marriages put this value first. The avenue they recommend is expanded sexual activity; yet it should be noted that the value of self-realization is also acknowledged in the dual-career family, though less explicitly advocated. Self-realization in the dual-career family is, however, tied to achievement in work and to enjoyment of a family life that may include children. Can it be said with assurance that one of these marital forms fosters self-realization more than the other?

From society's point of view, a marriage that fosters work-orientation and childrearing makes a somewhat more direct and identifiable contribution than a marriage that promises only greater self-realization and sexual satisfaction. Therefore from a societal perspective, the dual-career model seems to go farther in realizing the age-old human value placed on work and procreation.

There may still, however, be a time and place for both types of marital innovation. The symmetrical model seems more appropriate to the child-rearing years and middle age; the expanded relationship may work well for people not yet entering that phase and for people who are widowed, separated, divorced, or in unstable family situations. The expanded form may have inherent appeal to persons in transition. It may serve single persons newly located in a community. It may give that sexual gratification and opportunity for experiment that precedes achievement of personal identity and the mature capacity to love, reproduce, and work.

There is also the possibility that expansion of sexual boundaries will become only one of the modes of expansion. A pair-bond could expand itself synthetically by the addition of friends, not relatives, who might share meal preparation, childrearing responsibilities, housing costs, and recreation. Such regrouping, based on instrumental needs, might turn out to be adaptive in the cases of shortages, financial recessions, and loneliness.

No matter what the marital form, however, the question of length and depth of commitment is significant. To remain in an adaptive, flexible position, persons may choose an intimate network that does not imply lifelong commitment. Or, on the other hand, if persons decide to have children or commit themselves to a partnership that they hope will be permanent, they may officially marry. The meaning of commitment itself has several interpretations, depending on the circumstances.

Moral Constraints: Commitment, Freedom, and Fairness

Commitment to any relationship implies the acceptance of a social contract that binds together the members in a web of obligations and rights. John Rawls [21] lists three ideals for any social contract — that it recognize liberty, equality, and fraternity.

The ideal of liberty in marriage is explained by Anne Morrow Lindbergh in dance imagery [12]:

There is no holding a relationship to a single form. . . . A good relationship has a pattern like a dance and is built on some of the same rules. The partners do not need to hold on tightly, because they move confidently in the same pattern, intricate, but gay and swift and free, like a country dance of Mozart's. . . . The dancers who are perfectly in time never destroy "the wingéd life" in each other or in themselves. [p. 104]

Equality is also implied in her metaphor. Each partner must have the freedom to go on choosing and loving the other. Each partner must take the risk entailed by not having control over the other.

But fraternity is a concept of a different order. It operates when there is a difference between partners. Justice, says Rawls, requires that the strong help the weak, for if any person had to choose ahead of time (ignorant of his own position in the system) what should be the obligation of the strong, the answer would be the same: justice is fairness. When people differently endowed are bound together in a mutual exchange, the strong should help the weak [21].

What has fairness to do with the marriage contract? Marriage innovations discussed here have made it clear that the contract can be understood differently, depending on the circumstances. The Rawls criteria hold out the possibility of judging each marriage according to the fairness standard. Standards of fairness are operating in each marriage type, but the ways in which the fairness standard particularly applies vary according to circumstance. In the symmetrical family, the contract calls for equal opportunity to work. Fairness there not only demands alteration of the traditional sex-role division of labor but also apparently dictates a relatively chaste standard of sexual conduct. Sexual relationships outside the marriage give the active partner gratifications that are not balanced by professional or household gratification to the inactive spouse. The code of equal sharing and fairness in a symmetrical marriage is thereby understood as monogamous in the sexual arena. In expanded marital forms, however, the fairness doctrine is primarily realized through the principle of honesty and openness. Sexual activity with a person other than the primary partner is presumably fair if everyone is open about it. Openness provides opportunity for the inactive partner to protest or withdraw.

Surprisingly, marital sexuality, which we have already treated in connection with biological needs, is intertwined with abstract moral and ethical issues of commitment. The reason is that sexual activity is symbolic of that commitment, but the symbolism varies according to different marital subcultures. On the one hand, the body may be viewed as the most important thing the person has to give, and sexual intercourse therefore becomes the symbol of the deepest and most far-reaching commitment, which is to be strictly limited to one pair-bond. On the other hand, participants may define sexual activity as merely a physical expression that,

since it does not importantly envelop the whole personality nor commit
the pair beyond the pleasures of the moment, may be regulated more permissively.

There appears to be no simple relationship between symbolic definition
and marital form. Proponents of multilateral marriages argue that intimate
feelings should find expression in sexual activity. In addition, they advocate openness and honesty about feelings, yet they do not link intimacy
and expression of the full personality to exclusivity nor to a long time-
frame. On the other hand, symmetrical marriages do not advocate sexual
expansion, yet by their emphasis on work and role-sharing as essential
values, they perhaps relegate sexual activity to the realm of the merely
physical. One suspects that if sexual activity occurs outside the dual-
career dyad, it does so sub-rosa. Does this mean that in symmetrical marriages sexual activity does in fact symbolize, though not necessarily reflect,
depth of commitment and that it is therefore threatening to the marriage
itself when it occurs outside it?

Perhaps the only pattern that can be discerned in this confusion of
possibilities is that the symbolism of sexuality does vary for the participants according to the kind of social contracts they have drawn. Rules
and regulations surrounding sexual expression are symbolic of the type
of commitment made between partners. In the case of the expanded
marriage, nonmonogamous sexual activity is not so threatening because
the participants themselves have defined the situation as being experimental, transitional, or therapeutic. In the dual-career or symmetrical marriage,
however, the effort in forging a new division of labor between the sexes is
so demanding that it seems to exclude the possibility of other intimate
attachments. In that context sexual activity that is more than fleeting,
superficial, or purely physical is a threat to the primary relationship itself
and therefore must be denied as a valid or important expression of personal
growth or self-realization.

CONCLUSION

In 1966 Margaret Mead [14] envisioned a future in which each person would
have two marriages, one for procreation and the other for companionship
in the later years. Perhaps a more accurate projection is that in the future
several types of marriage will be available to each individual. They will

include (1) traditional marriage, (2) the symmetrical shared-role pattern for persons who have settled into a long-term pair-bond, and (3) the intimate network, or multilateral, marriage for persons who are in transition between youth and adulthood or between married adulthood and single status. Each of the two major innovations solves sexual, emotional, and practical social needs, but the nature of each solution is different, and the life situations of persons who choose them are probably also different.

In the future there may well be a differentiated marriage and family system that provides alternative models appropriate to the length and degree of commitment that each person feels capable of making. Through processes of transition, such as living together, marriage, separation, divorce, and death of the partner, an individual will be able to move from one living arrangement to another. Robert Weiss [30] has recently said that 60 percent of all marriages undergo some form of voluntary separation. At each voluntary separation or at the death of the partner, it is possible to choose among single status, traditional monogamy, symmetrical marriage, or the intimate network. The choice reveals not only the type of commitment a person makes, but it also determines what meaning others should attach to his or her sexual activities, emotional attachments, and capacity for social mobility.

Perhaps most important of all is that the participants understand the strengths and limitations of each marital form and not confuse the rules of one with another. Then individuals can choose accordingly and measure the adequacy of the particular role bargain they enter against expectations appropriate to that form.

ACKNOWLEDGMENTS

The author wishes to acknowledge the helpful critical comments on an earlier version of the paper that were made by Pauline Bart, David Giele, Henry Grunebaum, Hilda and Merton Kahne, and Robert Weiss.

REFERENCES

1. Becker, G. S. A theory of marriage: Part I. *Journal of Political Economy* 81:813, 1973.
2. Belliveau, F., and Richter, L. *Understanding Human Sexual Inadequacy.* Boston: Little, Brown, 1970.

3. Bernard, J. *The Future of Marriage.* New York: World, 1972.
4. Constantine, L., and Constantine, J. Where is marriage going? *The Futurist* 4:44, 1970.
5. Cottle, T. J. The sexual revolution and the young: Four studies. *New York Times Magazine*, Nov. 26, 1972. P. 36.
6. Dreitzel, H. P. *Family, Marriage, and the Struggle of the Sexes.* New York: Macmillan, 1972.
7. Fogarty, M. P., Rapoport, R., and Rapoport, R. N. *Sex, Career and Family.* London: Allen & Unwin, 1971.
8. Giele, J. Z. Changes in the modern family: Their impact on sex roles. *American Journal of Orthopsychiatry* 41:757, 1971.
9. Goode, W. F. *World Revolution and Family Patterns.* New York: Free Press, 1963.
10. Holmstrom, L. L. *The Two-Career Family.* Cambridge, Mass.: Schenkman, 1972.
11. Kinkade, K. Commune: A Walden-Two experiment that succeeds because it deals with cussedness where it is. *Psychology Today* 6:75, 1973.
12. Lindbergh, A. M. *Gift from the Sea.* New York: Watts, 1956.
13. Masters, W. H., and Johnson, V. E. *Human Sexual Inadequacy.* Boston: Little, Brown, 1970.
14. Mead, M. Marriage in two stages. *Redbook Magazine*, July, 1966. Reprinted in H. A. Otto (Ed.), *The Family in Search of a Future.* New York: Appleton-Century-Crofts, 1970.
15. Nemy, E. "Fidelity: Is it Nothing More Than an Old-Fashioned Concept?" *New York Times*, March 26, 1973. P. 50.
16. O'Neill, N., and O'Neill, G. Open marriage: A synergic model. *The Family Coordinator* 21:375, 1972.
17. Otto, H. A. *The Family in Search of a Future: Alternate Models for Moderns.* New York: Appleton-Century-Crofts, 1970.
18. Parnes, H. S., Shea, J. R., and Spitz, R. S. *Dual Careers: A Longitudinal Study of Labor Market Experience of Women*, Manpower Research Monograph, no. 21. Washington, D.C.: U.S. Department of Labor, 1970.
19. Polk, B. B., Stein, R. B., and Polk, L. The potential of the urban commune for changing sex roles. Unpublished.
20. Rapoport, R., and Rapoport, R. *Dual-Career Families.* London: Penguin, 1971.
21. Rawls, J. *A Theory of Justice.* Cambridge, Mass.: Belknap Press, 1971.
22. Rogers, C. R. *Becoming Partners: Marriage and Its Alternatives.* New York: Delacorte, 1972.
23. Roy, R., and Roy, D. Is Monogamy Outdated? In H. P. Dreitzel (Ed.), *Family, Marriage, and the Struggle of the Sexes.* New York: Macmillan, 1972.
23a. Saint-Exupéry, A. *The Little Prince.* New York: Reynal & Hitchcock, 1943.
24. Scanzoni, J. *Sexual Bargaining, Power Politics in the American Marriage.* Englewood Cliffs, N.J.: Prentice-Hall, 1972.
25. Schlesinger, B. Family Life in the Kibbutz of Israel: Utopia Gained or Paradise Lost? In H. P. Dreitzel (Ed.), *Family, Marriage, and the Struggle of the Sexes.* New York: Macmillan, 1972.

26. Smith, J. R., and Smith, L. G. Co-marital sex and the sexual freedom movement. *Journal of Sex Research* 6:131, 1970.

27. Sussman, M. B., and Cogswell, B. E. The meaning of variant and experimental marriage styles and family forms in the 1970's. *Family Coordinator* 21:375, 1972.

28. Talmon, Y. *Family and Community in the Kibbutz.* Cambridge, Mass.: Harvard University Press, 1972.

29. Trivers, R. L. Parental Investment and Sexual Selection. In B. Campbell (Ed.), *Sexual Selection and the Descent of Man 1871-1971.* Chicago: Aldine, 1972.

30. Weiss, R. S. Marital separation: Incidence and effects. Unpublished, 1973.

31. Young, M., and Willmott, P. *The Symmetrical Family.* New York: Pantheon, 1973.

5

Marriage
and Career

Rhona Rapoport
Robert N. Rapoport

This chapter is concerned with marriage and work — two spheres of social
activity in which men and women have been involved in very different ways
in the past, but in which the nature and meaning of their involvements are
currently undergoing changes. The changes are proceeding at different
rates for different parts of the population, and there is considerable variation in the patterns of personal involvements. Different occupational
situations have different impacts on the nonwork aspects of life. Families
in which the father is absent for extended periods, for example, experience
considerable stress. Different points in the life cycle present different focal
issues, and resources are different for handling them. Young couples are
more likely to plan for deferred gratification, for example, than are older
couples at retirement, though the two phases have some elements in
common.

We shall provide only a general account of the trends in marriage and
career and will not attempt to touch on all the qualifications, contingen-
cies, and variations that are known to exist. The aim is to give a perspective on some salient patterns now emerging and to discuss their implications, particularly for those in the mental health professions. We shall
concentrate on the "established" phase of family life-cycle and work-cycles,

giving less attention to the earlier and later phases.

HISTORICAL PERSPECTIVES

Work life and family life, now highly segregated both physically and conceptually from one another, were not always so. In most preindustrial societies, work and family life were more highly interconnected. Many kinds of work enterprises were coterminous with the family, or manned by family members, e.g., farming, running a bakery, restaurant, small factory; all mingled work and family activities in such a way as to create a single fabric of life. When there was a sharp sex differentiation, it was usually, though not always, called for by manifest physical differences. The men tended to work at the heavier tasks of farming, hunting and fishing, mining, and fighting, particularly prior to mechanization, while the women worked closer to the domestic base, particularly before the use of effective birth control techniques.

The physically greater strength of men did not always mean that they did the hardest work. Women often did work requiring considerable stamina, such as in agriculture or herding. A Victorian English traveler is said to have been shocked when he saw men in Anatolia allowing their women to carry the heaviest loads. He was told apologetically that the men realized mules were better for carrying loads, but that the people in that region of Anatolia were too poor to afford mules.

Part of the separation of work and family life that has endured to the present day is a result of the enlightened wish to protect women and children from physical exploitation, which was prevalent even in industrial England in the sweatshops of the towns and in the mines. However, the most powerful impetus for the segregation of work and family came from the development of rationality in cost accounting, part of what Weber termed *the spirit of capitalism*[19]. The spirit of capitalism encouraged the deliberate, rational pursuit of material gain. The fact that it was reinforced by the religious ethic of the Reformation made it possible to achieve merit in the afterworld through worldly accomplishments in this world. A chain of financial, organizational, and technological developments stemmed from this sacred legitimation.

The key concept of rationality brought about changes in the nature of the workplace and the rise of large organizations. If a manufacturing industry, for example, was to be competitive with others in the field, under the ethic of achievement and rationality it had to operate according to principles quite different from those governing family life. In a business's fiscal affairs, for example, there had to be a strict accounting for investments and profits if efficient strategies were to be developed. This required the separation of domestic accounts from those of the enterprise. In personnel selection, one had to choose the one most skilled for the job, regardless of kin obligations or other nonrational criteria. Thus, the logic of separating the family from work and from the workplace was reinforced by the pressures of industrial and commercial competition.

From these trends came the set of social and psychological rationalizations for segregating the two worlds of work and family. Work became almost entirely the man's world: tough-minded, ruthless, competitive, aggressive — no place for a woman except in a sheltered supportive role (e.g., as a clerk or secretary). The home, in contrast, became the domain of the "gentler" sex, particularly for the middle classes. It was thought of as both a haven, where an atmosphere of love and support was provided to the breadwinner, and as a place for the socialization of the young. Along with this notion of the two spheres, each ruled by a different set of norms, there developed a set of stereotypes about sex differences that supported the structural segregation. Women were seen as being not very clever in business affairs. Men were seen as biologically unattuned to children. The culmination of this was in Victorian England, when these conventional models governing work-family relationships were at their most vigorous. Tennyson, in *The Princess*, put it thus:

Man for the field and woman for the hearth;
Man for the sword and for the needle she;
Man with the head and woman with the heart;
Man to command and woman to obey;
All else confusion.

Educational practices supported these views, and aside from the early feminists, who concentrated on the vote for women, and a few dissident philosophers, such as John Stuart Mill, the cultural belief and value systems of Western society reinforced the pattern and have continued to reinforce it until recently. In the Victorian England of Florence Nightingale, the average age of girls leaving school was much lower than that of boys, and when women did go on to any sort of higher education, they studied "women's" subjects — those geared to domesticity. When a family had several children of both sexes and there were only limited educational opportunities, a boy was selected for further schooling; he was an automatic and natural choice over a girl.

Sociological theory reflected conventional practice, conceptualizing men as "instrumental" leaders in family groups and women as "expressive" leaders. Thus, in the formulations of Parsons and Bales [9] the family was thought of as an institutionalized example of the more general tendency of small human groups to produce two kinds of leaders. Some, however, believe it indicates that this is the natural order of things and that normal women instinctively enact expressive roles and normal men instinctively enact instrumental roles. Even in psychiatry and clinical psychology, the conventional system has been taken to be "normal." Women who deviated from the conventional sex-typed norms of conduct (e.g., by choosing a career in favor of marriage and a family) were likely to be seen as masculine, competitive with men, and as having problems expressing their more natural maternal or female sexual wishes.[1] This line of analysis is still fairly prevalent, although sophisticated clinicians are now more likely to explore alternative lines of interpretation.

CONTEMPORARY TRENDS

Of the many modern trends in work and family life, four are mentioned here.

1. There is greater equality of educational opportunities and therefore increasing similarity of life interests between men and women. This trend is reflected in the growth of female participation in the labor force.
2. There are changes both in the nature of work and the meaning assigned to work that make it more possible for men and women to participate on equal terms.

[1] For some reason the idea that career-orientation only characterized deviant women was rarely raised by such successful female followers of Freud as Helene Deutsch and Anna Freud in reference to themselves but only in reference to other women. It is only now being critically reexamined by such psychoanalytic writers as Jean Miller and Roy Schaefer [8, 17].

3. There are changes in the home and in the quality of domestic life that have affected both women and men. Women find it less demanding to run a house, given the technological aids available, and, paradoxically, less possible to attain fulfillment exclusively in the home. At the same time, men are becoming more home-oriented.
4. There is improved family planning. Biomedical technology now makes it possible to fix both the size of family and timing of pregnancies, so that having children can be made to dovetail with the couple's situation and aspirations to a degree never before possible. This planning is now accepted on a more widespread basis; it is a societal norm.

These trends, it is argued, make it necessary to view any particular arrangement for combining marriage and work in a different light from previously. Cultural norms that were dominant in the past gave rise to a set of perceptions and evaluations (clinical and social) that made any arrangement other than the conventional one appear to be deviant or pathological. A new set of assumptions is appropriate. Consider the implications of the following trends outlined.

Trend Toward More Equal Educational Opportunity

The statistics concerning this trend differ from country to country, and there are fluctuations resulting from sex imbalances created by wars. However, by and large, the gap in educational achievement between males and females has been closing everywhere, but especially in the United States, Britain, France, Sweden, and in the Eastern European countries. At the beginning of the century, women constituted one-fifth or less of the total population receiving higher education; now they constitute nearly half. In contrast to the past trend of women's being channeled almost exclusively into "women's fields" — primary school teaching, nursing, social work, and, at a lower level of skill, receptionist, secretarial, clerical, and domestic work — women are increasingly found in almost all fields. The trend is most marked in the industrialized countries that have the strongest egalitarian ideologies, notably, the Scandinavian countries, the Eastern European countries, and Israel [20]. The differences from country to country are partly accounted for by differences in societies' sex role definitions and the level of qualifications required for specific occupations. For example, the differences in percentages of Soviet, as compared with

American, women doctors is affected by these factors. In Russia 75 percent of all doctors are women; in the United States under 10 percent are women. But there are other factors specific to the national cultures. This is seen in the fact that 70 percent of Denmark's dentists are women, compared with 7 percent of Great Britain's dentists. In this case, the differences in standards of training and job definition are negligible; it is a matter of educational precedents and other such historical factors.

Economic elements do play a part in the American-Russian contrasts. The amount of money needed by both the student and the institution to train a doctor in the United States is so great that medical educators generally are loath to train women on the assumption that they are likely to follow the conventional pattern of dropping out. If the state is making the investment and needs the manpower resources, it may, as is the case in Denmark and Russia, find a way to facilitate the training and follow-through.

It is only the most recalcitrant sexist who today would claim that women's innate abilities bar them from "mind" careers. Medicine, dentistry, law, and business are defined as "masculine" in some countries, but in other countries the same fields, with no appreciable difference in qualifications required, have a more neutral definition, and these definitions can change as conditions allow. In the United States the percentage of women lawyers rose from 1 percent to 3.5 percent between 1910 and 1960. In the Soviet Union the percentage of women lawyers rose from 15 percent in 1941 to 32 percent in 1964 [3].

These and other statistics point in the same direction. The increase in educational opportunity produces, to a large extent, an increase in equal participation in high status occupational roles. But the pace of change and the degree of effect on occupational choice produced by education are uneven. The ideologies of equality that are available, the access to institutions are all relevant. And, everywhere there has tended to be a leveling-off of, and in some cases even a slight drop in, percentages of women in prestigious and remunerative occupations at a point below the percentage of men. This is variously ascribed to (1) hard-core, last-ditch male defense of the strongholds of power, (2) lags in female motivation to make the extra effort to rise to the top in the more competitive fields, (3) a cultural lag in the redistribution of domestic responsibilities between the husband and wife, and (4) a new general deemphasis on work-achievement as a cardinal value, in which women are *leading* the field rather than lagging behind, as it superficially appears.

Trends Related to the Nature and Importance of Work in Contemporary Life

The Protestant ethic brought with it a dedication to work that was religious in its fervor. In the early days of the Industrial Revolution, it was necessary to restrain enthusiastic capitalist entrepreneurs from making exploitive use of child and female labor. As a consequence, the removal of women from the workplace became a mark of gentility and a measure of civilization, as well as a practical matter in the separation of family finances from those of the enterprise.

However, more recently the general nature of work in society has shifted its balance from predominantly heavy, dirty, and potentially dangerous jobs to predominantly light, clean, safe jobs. Rather than a strong back and a weak mind, the modern worker in an advanced technological job or a skilled job in any large bureaucratic organization or service industry, is likely to require a quick mind and dexterous fingers. Personal traits, such as reliability, good judgment, ability to get along harmoniously with others, are likely to be important. Sex differences indicated in test results of such measurable traits as aggression and visual-spatial capacity, aside from their questionable validity as factors in assessing biological potential, today are not considered as relevant to job placement. The archetypical ruthless, hard-driving businessman may have reached the top in the past, but the successful modern managing director is perhaps more likely to have arrived at the top because of his intuitive judgment, logic, memory, and financial acumen, traits that are no longer thought of as preeminently masculine. As Wilensky puts it, ". . . what happens when the hunter is an executive of an automated meat-packing firm and the warrior an expert in guidance systems? Male superiority in speed and strength cannot count here" [20].

Furthermore, it is suggested by many men, as well as by women, that the single-minded dedication to the requirements of a competitive career are neither necessary to the economy of the more developed countries nor desirable from the point of view of human values. The one-dimensional man, as described by Marcuse, is the product of the heroic dedication to work and career that has provided the "steam" for the organizational and professional advances that followed the Industrial Revolution [6]. The contemporary trend, although incompletely and variably expressed, is toward a more varied and balanced set of personal involvements. However, it is noteworthy that in many countries where radical changes have occurred in the economy and where ideology favors equality, e.g., the Eastern European countries, sex differences persist.

In the Western countries the persistence of sex-linked contrasts in the pattern of work and family relations is even greater. In our study of the orientations of 1960 graduates of British universities eight years after they left college, both men and women showed an increase in familial involvement as they moved from being single to being married and becoming parents, but the women's increase was much greater (Table 1).

Table 1 Family As the Source of Greatest Life Satisfaction Among 1960 British University Graduates (percentages)[a]

	Single	Married with No Children	Married with Children
Men	11	42	59
Women	14	58	82

[a]Our survey work was based on Alice Rossi's NORC Study of Women Graduates. We are indebted to her for many of the ideas tested in this work, although she is not responsible for what has emerged.
SOURCE: Adapted from Fogarty, Rapoport, and Rapoport [3].

This pattern reflects the tendency for women to withdraw, at least temporarily, from career involvements during the period their children are small. The same critical event in the family life-cycle — the arrival of children — affects men in an opposite way. For men, there is likely to be a spurring of ambition in the occupational sphere, partly to provide for their increased family responsibilities. For women, there is a tendency to defer, lower, modify, or give up their occupational aspirations. Our studies of level of aspiration at different points in the life cycle show a relatively small discrepancy in percentages of boys and girls with high career aspirations in secondary school: 34 percent of men and 28 percent of women want to get to the top or hold a high position. The great divergence comes by the end of college: 57 percent of men and 21 percent of women want to get to the top or hold a high position. Occupational opportunities are by this time being assessed in a more calculative way and are "realistically" adjusted to, perhaps with the guidance of conventional counselors, parents, and teachers.

The most decisive cleavage between the sexes emerges with the arrival of children. About 14 percent of women college graduates with children, as compared with 69 percent of men with children, aspire to high positions in their occupations. The greatest percentage of women in this group maintaining high aspirations is found among those who want to try to work continuously, even though they also wish to be wives and mothers. A continuous work orientation is now found in over one-third of college-educated women; and when it is coupled with a strong career orientation, it tends to be characterized by a set of circumstances, about which there is consistent information both from survey data and from intensive case studies of dual-career families [11, 13].

An analysis of British dual-career couples as compared with a sample of more conventional couples yields several conclusions. First, the career-oriented women differ more from conventional wives than do the two sets of husbands from each other. The contrasts that we observed, moreover, provided a different line of interpretation than we might have evolved had our studies taken place in a clinical setting. The women in dual-career families tend to be only or first-born children; they are from a somewhat higher social class than are their husbands and they had mothers who worked and liked working (or, if their mothers did not work, they tended to dislike their exclusively domestic roles). The parental families of many of the dual-career wives were likely to have had a history of tension in some of the key family relationships, possibly countering the conventional idealization of family life. While the husbands of these career-oriented wives were not conspicuously different in social background from husbands from conventional families, they did differ in terms of how they related to their wives. They were less threatened by the idea of women having strong, independent roles, and they seemed to feel it desirable, or at least understandable that they should facilitate their wives' aspirations. The differences seem in part to relate to their greater empathy with members of the opposite sex, based on their earlier family relationships, particularly warm and understanding relationships with their mothers [12].

We have defined the different ways in which one family member facilitates another's efforts to achieve his or her aspirations in the face of various constraints and have termed them *enabling processes* [14]. Enabling processes consist of several elements. One important element is attitudinal. The husband's belief that women should have equal career opportunities is of great importance; and when this attitude is present, there is an increased tendency for the wife to be career-oriented. When the husband backs up his ideological conviction with increased participation in the domestic tasks — shopping, cleaning, cooking, childcare — the structural impediments to a full career participation are eased. In fact, with the decrease in the availability of paid domestic help, the husband's participation in some household tasks is necessary for all but the most amazon of housewives.

Trend Toward Restructuring Domestic Roles

The restructuring of domestic roles is still evolving. There are, of course, many variables governing the degree of male participation. One crucial variable is the acceptance by men of joint participation of husband and wife in domestic tasks. As Pleck [10] and others are showing, this is a very far-reaching process with implications for our society and value system.

Other variables are standards of household upkeep, age and number of children, flexibility of the two sets of work commitments, and so on. There are also important distinctions between helpful participation and real responsibility. Men are increasingly lending a hand with "feminine" tasks, such as dishwashing and shopping, as well as keeping modern household utilities working. A middle-class American household may depend on the functioning of dozens of machines, so this may provide considerable involvement. But it is much rarer to find men who take full responsibility for a whole domestic sector, such as the food sector — planning meals, shopping, cooking, and serving.

According to the responses of British university graduates, the *preferred* pattern of division of labor for both men and women is that the wife retain responsibility for the cooking and childcare, while the cleaning and other more chorelike tasks are given to domestic help when possible. The other areas in which both prefer males to take charge are in minor repair jobs. Gardening is an area in which both men and women see some kind of joint participation as desirable. There are some widely found divergences. The women would, for example, like joint activity in regard to home decorating, whereas the men would prefer decorating to be done by an outside party.

When one examines actual division of labor (as distinct from preferences), the young family is only rarely able to hire sufficient outside help to whom it can delegate the less attractive chores; usually the wife does them. The husband also does minor repairs more frequently than he would like, and the couple retain gardening and shopping for major items as joint activities. There are interesting cultural differences in this, though by and large the picture is similar [15, 16]. In England gardening is much more likely to be seen as a domestic activity in which husbands are involved, along with decorating and minor repairs. Americans are slightly more likely to see gardening as a chore and to want to delegate it. In England childcare is more likely to be linked to the chore aspects of domestic work, along with cleaning and washing. In America, childcare is more likely to be linked to the feeding and cooking sector. These differences are only suggestive. There are many variations, and the whole area of cultural differences in sex-role conceptions and the domestic division of labor merits further research [3].

Thus, many men do support the general idea of women's having careers, though by no means do *all* men. Male involvement in the day-to-day responsibilities of running the household — accompanied by stabilized role — is far less prevalent than is the supportive attitude. Special circumstances do exist that make it easier to institute such changes as, for example, when the husband works at home as a writer or sculptor. But even this sort of situation does not assure the kind of structural social change that will facilitate the wife's outside domestic employment, and in some cases it even sets in motion a male reaction against domestic involvement.

Experiments with cooperative living, as in the Swedish service houses or the communes, provide other alternatives. Perhaps the most promising possibility for structural rearrangement lies with the tendency toward job restructuring, providing more flexibility and more part-time job options for men as well as women. It is more likely under these circumstances that husbands will entertain role changes in the family both because they are better able to, as their career arrangements become more flexible, and because they will see that it is more in their own interests and in their family's interests to do so. Ours is a time of fundamental reassessment of family organization, both internally and in relation to external networks and organizations [18].

SUMMARY AND IMPLICATIONS

A family structure in which both spouses are active in the occupational sphere as well as in the marriage is likely to be more widespread. The conventional family structure — father as only breadwinner, mother as exclusively housewife — has already given way, both statistically and normatively, to a new pattern. In this pattern, the wife interrupts her career for a time when she has small children but intends to return to it at some point — the point varying according to various facilitative elements in her situation, her own motivation, and the opportunity structure.

This trend will be accelerated to the extent that men see it to be of value to them as husbands and as employers. The changes in the employment situation require overcoming stereotypes and making structural alterations to accommodate women. These changes also depend on their producing discernible gains in the domestic situation. Higher income, greater satisfaction for the wife, becoming a more interesting mother and wife, and sharing the insecurities and strains of economic provision are some of the more frequently expressed overall benefits. These benefits have to be weighed against the costs, which are likely to include overload and strain because of the present situation of inadequate support institutions, such as day-care. The greatest immediate toll is likely to be in the area of leisure activities and on interpersonal relationships, the two being interrelated to some extent. Marriage, like any other relationship, becomes more complex when it is organized as a partnership rather than as a hierarchy of leader and follower. Decision-making becomes a more important *family* task, taking more time and energy because there are more conflicts to resolve. However, with the broader base of participation, the quality of decisions may be improved. The outcome, of course, is affected by the capacity of the family to manage the tasks posed by the new complexities in their lives.

In considering the problems raised by these trends, a good deal of attention has been given to policy and planning issues, e.g., conditions of employment, housing and childcare, and educational programs and practices. There are also theoretical and practical implications for the mental health professions. In considering the issues of changing sex roles and of the relationships between work and family life, it is apparent that, broadly speaking, thought and practice in the mental health field have tended to be conservative. Though many clinicians writing theoretically about such phenomena as creativity or pioneering innovation and neurosis, the observations do not touch very close to the lives of ordinary people. But now, when we are involved in a widespread social movement and when, at the same time, many clinicians are expressing their views through mass media and as policy consultants to government and organizations as well as in clinical settings, it is more important that they "get with" the changes underway.

The three main focuses of attention that seem to require revision are (1) those associated with occupational identifications, choice and performance, (2) those associated with marital choice and relationships, and (3) those associated with individual personality factors, such as sexual identity. These are, of course, interrelated, but they are often dealt with separately and, depending on the type of psychological theory and practice, are thought of as separate problem areas.

In the area of work, it is increasingly likely to be taken as a matter of course that men and women are potentially interested in the whole range of occupations. As redistributions occur, it will be seen as less strange for a man to want to become a nurse and a woman to want to become an engineer. Conventional clinical frames of reference that interpret these interests as psychopathological tendencies will have to be replaced by a more neutral framework capable of taking into account the "de-sex-typing" of work roles. In the realignment process and in the cultivation of interests traditionally associated with the opposite sex, individuals are likely to benefit as much from help in coping with others' irrationalities as well as their own problems of doubt and anxiety. Clinicians have hitherto tended to align themselves, interpretively, with the conventional view, though there are, of course, exceptions.

In marital relationships, there has been a similar conservatism of viewpoint, and a challenge similar to that presented in the workplace is at hand. The conventional view, as represented, for example, in Lidz's work, suggests that when there are marital tensions in a family in which both partners work, the onus is likely to be placed on an investigation of the reasons why the wife rejects her maternal role [5]. At the other extreme, the socialist view as applied to psychiatry, e.g., in the work of the Knoblochs [4], suggests an inquiry into why the husband cannot tolerate his wife's working when confronted by marital tensions in a family in which both partners work.

In both cases the new approach that we suggest assesses the marital difficulty bifocally, so to speak, with both the husband's and the wife's difficulties being taken into account.

In the area of individual functioning, the redefinition of sex roles and changing concepts of sex types is likely to result in a period during which there will be considerable concern about sex identity. The danger in mental-health work is that of imposing a conventional view — sometimes but not always associated with a generation gap — on people who are not necessarily being socialized with the same ideas of what constitutes masculinity and femininity as prevailed a generation ago. There is sometimes an assumption that reduction of contrasts in the definition of sex roles will result in personal confusion, with symptoms of inadequacy and the other symptoms that accompany it. Older people who see unisex couples walking down the street wearing pants and both with long, flowing hair often say that they are confused and cannot tell which is which. The crucial issue for personality development of the individuals concerned is not, however, whether their elders are confused, but whether they themselves are confused. There are a number of focuses for confusion among the young today, but sexual identity is not conspicuous among them. This is an area that merits further investigation.

There is likely to be a period of fairly widespread experimentation with alternative forms of marriage and career — communes, dual-career families, families that are involved in new arrangements of role-swapping, job-sharing, and the like. During this period there will very likely be problems to be worked through, since roles that are being assumed have no traditional models according to which behavior can be patterned. The new experimentation is likely to involve a good deal of doubt and uncertainty. The resolution of interpersonal problems arising in these new situations should be approached with an awareness of the social context of change and of the processes of conflict resolution intrinsic in such change.

Many of the issues of interpretation, management, and dissemination of clinical and social research findings are still subject to debate. To some extent, the problems of changing sex roles can be understood in the context of changing power relations, comparable to the problems generally experienced in minority-majority group relations. Lessons can be applied that are generic to processes of resolution of conflicts between socially dominant and socially disadvantaged persons [7]. There will be self-hate, guilt, excessive sensitivity, and distrust until new definitions of self and other can be worked out that will allow new structures and norms to become established. But the issues of sex-role identity, of family and work, of love and aggression are even more in the bailiwick of those in the mental health professions than are the other varieties of intergroup tensions and changes. Therefore, the challenge before those in the caring professions is a particularly poignant one: can they work out ways of thought and action, theory and practice that will implement their traditional goals of healing and adjustment while at the same time using their skills and expertise to facilitate the change process.

REFERENCES

1. Bailyn, L. Career and family orientations of husbands and wives in relation to marital happiness. *Human Relations* 23(2):97, 1970.
2. Bernard, J. *The Future of Marriage.* New York: World, 1972.
3. Fogarty, M., Rapoport, R., and Rapoport, R. N. *Sex, Career and Family.* Beverly Hills, Calif.: Sage Publications, 1971.
4. Knoblochova, J., and Knobloch, F. *Family Psychotherapy.* Public Health Papers, No. 28. Geneva: World Health Organization, 1965.
5. Lidz, T. *The Person.* New York, Basic Books, 1968.
6. Marcuse, H. *One-Dimensional Men.* Boston: Beacon Press, 1964.
7. Miller, J. Psychological consequences of sexual inequality. *American Journal of Orthopsychiatry* 41(5):767, 1971.
8. Miller, J. *Psychoanalysis and Women: Contributions to New Theory and Therapy.* New York: Brunner/Mazel, 1973.
9. Parsons, T., and Bales, R. F. *Family, Socialization and Interaction Process.* London: Routledge and Kegan Paul, 1956.
10. Pleck, J., and Sawyer, J. *Men and Masculinity.* Englewood Cliffs, N.J.: Prentice-Hall, 1974.
11. Rapoport, R., and Rapoport, R. N. *Dual-Career Families.* Baltimore: Penguin, 1971.
12. Rapoport, R., and Rapoport, R. N. Early and late experiences and adult behavior. *British Journal of Sociology* 22(1):16, 1971.
13. Rapoport, R., and Rapoport, R. N. Further considerations on dual-career families. *Human Relations* 24(6):519, 1971.
14. Rapoport, R., and Rapoport, R. N. Family Enabling Functions: The facilitating husband in the dual-career family. In R. Goslin (Ed.), *Support, Innovation and Autonomy.* London: Tavistock, 1973.
15. Rossi, A. Equality between the sexes: An immodest proposal. *Daedalus,* Spring 1964.
16. Rossi, A. Transition to parenthood. *Journal of Marriage and the Family* 30, 1968.
17. Schafer, R. Problems in Freud's psychology of women. *Journal of the American Psychoanalytic Association* 22(3):459, 1974.

18. Sussman, M. Family, Kinship and Bureaucracy. In A. Campbell and P. Converse (Eds.), *The Human Meaning of Social Change.* New York: Russell Sage Foundation, 1972.

19. Weber, M. *The Theory of Social and Economic Organization*, translated by A. M. Henderson and T. Parsons. London: Oxford University Press, 1947.

20. Wilensky, H. Women's work: Economic growth, ideology, structure. *Industrial Relations* 7(3):235, 1968.

6

Divorce:
Legal Requirements v.
Psychological Realities

Ellsworth A. Fersch, Jr.
John A. Vering III

Laws affecting unhappily married persons and the role of lawyers in implementing the laws are generally opposed to what mental health professionals consider to be in the best therapeutic interests of those persons. The legal requirements concerning divorce, custody of children, alimony, and support are so often opposed to psychological realities that persons seeking resolution of marital conflict may be required to lie to satisfy legal requirements, while, at the same time, they may be encouraged to be honest in an attempt to face psychological realities. Lawyers representing such persons and mental health professionals treating them often find their roles antagonistic rather than complementary. A sample case will illustrate how legal and psychological concerns often conflict in matters surrounding divorce, making even more difficult what is at best a difficult problem.

CASE EXAMPLE

Frank and Joan had been married for 10 years and had three children. For the last few years their marriage had been troubled by increasing arguments and general unhappiness but without physical abuse. Both had sensed a growing estrangement, and each had

103

attempted to enlist the children in the frequent conflicts. They both talked about divorce but were not clear on what it involved. Both had heard stories from friends who had been divorced, and they hoped to avoid similar difficulties. Finally, Joan, who was somewhat reluctant to get divorced, went to see a psychiatrist; Frank, determined to be divorced, went to a lawyer.

The psychiatrist encouraged Joan to talk about her situation, explored her feelings about herself, her husband, and the marriage, and suggested conjoint family therapy. He felt that the marriage was in trouble but that it could be saved and the partners helped through therapy. He felt it was important for both partners to be in therapy, and he offered to see each one separately for a few meetings and then to see them together. He said that each would have to try to be honest in exploring why the marriage had been falling apart and that the therapy would be difficult but rewarding. He told Joan what the fee would be.

The lawyer asked Frank briefly about his marriage and then outlined for him the Massachusetts laws on divorce [26, 28]. He explained that Massachusetts statutes list a limited number of grounds for divorce and he enumerated them: adultery, impotency, utter desertion for at least one year, nonsupport, cruel and abusive treatment, gross and confirmed intoxication by liquor or drugs, a prison sentence for five years or more. He stated that while none of these grounds fit Frank's case exactly, the general category of cruel and abusive treatment came the closest. He explained that while proof of physical violence by one spouse to the other was not required, words, to be sufficient grounds, must create a reasonable fear of personal violence. He suggested that violence was a stronger ground and said that while acts must not always be corroborated, it was up to the judge to decide whether a witness was necessary. He said that the law required one party in a divorce to be guilty and that the guilty party was usually the husband. He said that the wife would generally get custody of the children and one-half of the husband's net income for alimony and child support payments. He pointed out that it would require three months, at least, to complete an uncontested divorce action and that the decree of divorce would not be final until six months after the action was heard by the court. He warned Frank that, if Joan were to contest the divorce, he might not be able to secure it and that in return for not contesting it Joan might demand a higher percentage of his net income and less favorable visiting rights for him with the children. Finally, the lawyer explained alternatives to an in-state Massachusetts divorce, such as claiming residence in another state or a foreign country, and suggested that Frank could not afford such a possibility nor could the travel and time away be undertaken. The lawyer said he would do all he could as an advocate for Frank, that Joan would have to have her own lawyer, and that he wanted neither to meet nor talk with Joan. He said he would talk with her lawyer. He told Frank what the fee would be.

Joan returned from her talk with the psychiatrist encouraged that there might be some way to save the marriage; Frank returned from his talk with the lawyer discouraged at the legal problems involved in securing a divorce. Frank refused to see the psychiatrist, saying that it was too expensive, would accomplish nothing, and that he felt he could not afford a psychiatrist and the two lawyers that would be required should they eventually seek a divorce, as he was sure they would.

Frank subsequently moved out. Joan refused to agree to a divorce and contacted a lawyer of her own. Finally, through a process of bargaining between the two lawyers, she settled for an agreement that gave her 70 percent of Frank's net income for child support (with each child's support terminating as the child reached majority) and for alimony (until she remarried or died) and that limited visiting privileges for him with the children. It was further agreed that she would file for the divorce, thus making Frank the guilty party.

When the trial took place, a year later, Joan brought with her a friend who testified that physical fights had taken place between Frank and Joan. The judge, after a hearing taking six and a half minutes, granted the decree. Six months later the divorce became final [29]. Joan had, in the interim, considered seeing a social worker at a nearby clinic but instead joined Parents without Partners. Frank wanted to remarry a year later, but the woman in question felt he was financially incapable of supporting both her and his former wife and children.

As this case illustrates, the law in respect to the malfunctioning marriage does not reinforce the marriage but instead encourages the malfunctioning. The law, as it impinges upon persons in the midst of marital conflict, generally encourages a lack of real communication between them and among professionals who might help, mandates dishonesty on their part, and, at least indirectly, dishonesty on the part of their counsel, and increases disrespect for the law among all who participate in the proceedings — all at the time it is supposedly upholding both marriage as a social institution and law as a socially acceptable means of resolving conflict. The law seems to reflect society's desire to punish married persons in an unhappy and malfunctioning marriage as a way, perhaps, of repairing the marriage or at least as a way of maintaining an illusory view of marriage. Along the way, the law also seems to punish lawyers and mental health professionals.

HISTORICAL BACKGROUND OF DIVORCE

To understand the divergence between the legal requirements for divorce and the psychological realities, we must detail the historical background and the legal requirements of divorce, together with their lack of psychological underpinning. Then we can discuss the impact of laws and of lawyers on unhappily married persons, the proposals for reform, their impact, and the means for implementing them.

Historically, there have been a number of changes in the divorce laws. In Ancient Rome, divorce was readily obtainable, and the state concerned itself primarily with the property rights, not the separation, of the couple. With the rise of Christianity, however, there was a reversal of this interest. In England, for example, from the twelfth century through 1857, divorce was allowed only by a special vote of Parliament. Needless to say, only a few very wealthy, very determined individuals were granted divorces. But there were alternate paths that an unhappy couple could take: annulments were common and could be purchased from the ecclesiastical courts for a suitable fee; divorce from bed and board — separation — was allowed by the ecclesiastical courts on a fault basis; and the poor who were unhappily married could desert.

After 1857, the ecclesiastical courts lost their power over divorce to the civil courts, which began granting absolute divorces on the ground of adultery [5]. Gradually the fault grounds were expanded to include extreme physical cruelty. The United States adopted the English divorce laws, and these laws continued to evolve in this country [43].

PRESENT-DAY GROUNDS FOR DIVORCE

Today the legal grounds for divorce vary from state to state [10, 11]. Almost all the grounds are based on the concept of fault, whereby one party, who is guilty, injures the other party, who is innocent. In most American jurisdictions, as in the case example previously presented, the guilty party in the divorce proceeding is the husband and the innocent party the wife [8].

The Fault Concept

To understand how the law operates we must examine the assumptions behind the fault concept as it applies to divorce. Among the major assumptions are these: (1) marital breakdown is caused by one guilty party, (2) stringent divorce laws maintain family solidarity, (3) children benefit from a public policy that makes it difficult for their parents to be divorced, and (4) greater crime, suicide, instability, and related disorders result from high divorce rates.

Each of these assumptions has been challenged as invalid. First, the commonsense notion that it takes two to tangle reflects the psychological reality that both partners are involved in the breakdown of a marriage. Even one of the most serious of the legal grounds for divorce, adultery, can better be viewed as a symptom or a result of, rather than the cause of, marital breakdown. Second, the solidarity that may be attained through failure to obtain a divorce may be illusory, or worse, if it is built on a foundation of bitterness and hate. Third, psychological and sociological evidence tends to show that children in conflicted homes suffer more than do children in divorced homes [2, 15, 32, 38]. Furthermore, most divorced people remarry, and over 50 percent of these second marriages are as successful as ordinary first marriages [1]. The available evidence would indicate that divorce laws designed to benefit children should be liberalized to permit a child to grow up, not in a conflicted family, but in a happier family with a new parent. Fourth, there is no evidence showing that the correlation between divorce and crime results from easy divorce laws. A comparison of the crime rates of New York which has traditionally had strict divorce laws, with those of New Mexico, which has traditionally had liberal divorce laws, reveals that in 1972 the robbery rate in New York was almost four times as great as the robbery rate in New Mexico [39]. These statistics suggest that easy divorce laws are not a significant cause of crime. Both divorce [25] and crime [40] are more common among people from the lower socioeconomic class, but this suggests that poverty breeds crime and divorce, not that divorce breeds crime and poverty. Similarly, the higher suicide rate among divorced men and women [20] does not prove that divorce leads to suicide. It is more reasonable to assume that individuals who are psychologically troubled tend to choose their mates unwisely, tend to get divorced more often, and are more likely to commit suicide than are less troubled, more stable individuals.

Even though these assumptions behind the fault concept have been challenged as invalid, the grounds for divorce in most jurisdictions reflect the fault orientation. A comparison of the difference between the legal reasons for divorce and the real reasons emphasizes the divergence between legal requirements and psychological realities.

Legal Reasons and Real Reasons
Of the legal grounds alleged as grounds for divorce and annulment in 13 states in 1958, cruelty accounted for 60 percent and desertion for 25 percent of the cases [42]. Yet, as indicated by a study made about the same time, the opinions of lawyers in cne state as to *real* causes of divorce gave a different picture, with finances and nonsupport, adultery, drunkenness, and incompatibility each accounting for approximately 20 percent of the cases [18]. A somewhat different picture was presented in a study of divorcees in Detroit who gave as the main causes of their divorces finances

(and nonsupport) in 20 percent of the cases and authority clashes, drinking, gambling, personality clashes, and no real home life each in approximately 10 percent of the cases [16]. Finally, a list compiled almost a decade later in another study indicated the views of domestic-relations judges on the causes of divorce. In order of decreasing importance, they were: drinking, financial problems, infidelity, unsatisfactory sexual relations, desertion, and in-law problems [34]. A comparison of these studies [8] with the legal grounds for divorce shows the wide discrepancy between the grounds for which divorces are legally permitted and the real reasons for divorce.

This discrepancy is also reflected in the gap between what the law states and how divorces are actually granted. In practice, less than 10 percent of divorces are contested [24], and most of those are contested on the issues of who will be the guilty party, of how much will be paid in alimony and child support, and of the awarding of child custody [43]. In the vast majority of cases, no defense is raised to the divorce action, and the court accepts whatever evidence the party in court offers [24]. In practice, cruelty is the alleged ground in almost two-thirds of all divorce actions; wives are granted divorces in about two-thirds of all divorce actions [8]; children are awarded to the mother in most actions [12]; and the actual divorce proceeding takes only 10 to 15 minutes [21].

What the law requires, of course, is not that the couple examine its marriage and report honestly to the court its failure; rather, the law requires that the couple fit its problem into a restricted legal framework. What the couple does, therefore, is look for the easiest possible ground for divorce, which is usually cruelty. If easy grounds are not available, an unhappily married couple — given resources, skilled counsel, and some patience — can find ways to achieve its goal. New York, prior to 1967 when its divorce law was liberalized to include grounds other than adultery, provided a good picture of how unhappily married couples who could not obtain New York divorces found ways to terminate their relationships: annulments were common; out-of-state divorces, often in Nevada or Mexico, were popular; and desertion was common among the poor. It was necessary for the partners to balance the convenience, timeliness, and repercussions of the various grounds for divorce and to plan their divorce action accordingly.

Given the ingenuity of people and the accepted ways of maneuvering around the required grounds for divorce, the impact of the statutes would be troublesome for all, and perhaps especially burdensome for the poor, but of major consequence for few were it not for the attendant consequences of the fictions that are maintained. For when legal requirements diverge from psychological realities, those requirements affect areas broader than the narrow one of obtaining a divorce, and they tend to perpetuate more fictions that are less easily circumvented or exposed.

Thus, for example, the fault requirement, that a party (usually the husband) be designated as guilty, usually affects the amount of alimony awarded to the innocent party (generally the wife). A declaration that a wife is guilty may preclude her receiving adequate alimony, even though she may be in desperate need of financial support. Similarly, fault-finding based on a single act of adultery may prevent a fit parent from being given custody of the children. Or a parent (usually the father) who is furnishing support to the children may be prevented from taking part in supervising the proper distribution of the funds, as in money expressly to be set aside for higher education. Or the parent not awarded custody of the children (usually the father) may feel powerless, and may indeed be powerless, to influence the course of the children's lives because of the way the divorce law operates.

The facts presented thus far document the divergence between legal requirements and psychological realities. To bring the two into closer agreement, efforts at reform have been made. The central proposal for reform rests on the overall concept of no fault [13, 35, 37, 44].

NO-FAULT DIVORCE

No fault, as a general concept, has been widely discussed in a variety of areas. In automobile insurance, for example, until recently all states followed a fault orientation. When an automobile accident occurred, an attempt was made to determine which driver was at fault. Through his insurance company that driver was responsible for the damage done in the accident; he received nothing, however, for the damage to his own car or person. Naturally, in the confused picture that is often today's driving, it was difficult to determine fault. Consequently, a large body composed of trial lawyers, adjusters, insurance companies, expert witnesses, and others grew up around the litigation of automobile insurance cases. Not surprisingly, among those most opposed to no-fault auto insurance have been those members of the bar who litigate such cases and whose economic status depends on the work generated by an attempt to fix blame. Nevertheless, some states, such as Massachusetts, have recently passed no-fault legislation, and other states are debating its merits. No fault, as a concept, has been extended to other areas of the law. Among them is divorce.

No-fault divorce involves a recognition that it takes two to destroy a marriage and that when the marriage has all but legally ended, those two can bring about its dissolution more effectively and more justly without the sham of a fault-finding inquiry by focusing on custody, support, and alimony in a way that tries to protect both partners. Since 90 percent of the divorces granted are uncontested anyway, no fault to some extent only legitimizes what has been the prevailing situation and does it in a way that seeks to bring legal requirements into line with psychological realities.

Currently, a few states employ only the no-fault concept in their divorce law. A larger number of states have merely added the no-fault ground of irretrievable breakdown of the marriage to their fault grounds for divorce. And some states employ one or both of the two exceptions to the fault concept: (1) incompatibility and (2) living separate and apart for a given period of time [10,11]. Incompatibility is an alternative to fault divorce and is a popular ground for divorce in the states that have adopted it. Proving incompatibility, however, can sometimes be difficult, for if the law is strictly applied, the incompatibility must be serious and not a mere difference of opinion. Also, fault grounds can be used to prove that the couple is incompatible, thereby defeating the goal of keeping fault grounds out of the courtroom [24].

The other exception, living separate and apart from the spouse for a given period of time, is a no-fault ground for divorce that applies in more than half the states. The law, in this instance, recognizes the psychological reality that spouses who live apart for an extended period of time have in fact terminated their marriage. A serious problem with the living separate and apart doctrine is that there are great variations in the time required for separation before the marriage can be legally terminated. In Vermont, for example, a divorce can be granted if the couple has lived separate and apart for 6 months [41], whereas in Rhode Island a couple must wait 5 years, an unnecessarily long time [36].

Defenses in Fault-Based Divorce

Proponents of no-fault divorce point to another clear sign that the fault-oriented laws are out of touch with psychological realities: the nature of defenses in divorce actions. Because an innocent party is suing a guilty party, the latter may raise defenses to show that the innocent party is indeed at least partially guilty. Given that information, the judge may refuse to grant the divorce to either party. Among the most discussed of such defenses are recrimination, collusion, connivance, and condonation.

Recrimination is the doctrine that the court may deny a divorce if both parties are guilty of marital fault even though both parties want a divorce [30]. Recrimination is based on the "unclean hands" doctrine, which prohibits the granting of relief to a litigant who has acted illegally in the matter before the court. Thus, courts have sometimes refused to grant a divorce to a couple when both have been guilty of adultery. The rationale often used is that both partners should suffer for their mutual wrongdoing. Massachusetts, in an effort at some reform, eliminated recrimination as a defense in 1973 [27].

Collusion can be a defense to a divorce action if either party commits a marital offense in order to get a divorce, or introduces false evidence of an offense not committed, or suppresses a valid defense [31]. Although the legal requirement is clear, the psychological reality is quite different. Since divorce is available in most states only on fault grounds, collusion is a common practice. Most judges and lawyers, therefore, ignore the law concerning collusion, increasing disrespect for law but permitting the divorce laws to operate. The problem arises for the couple when the law is not ignored.

Connivance, a less common defense against fault-based divorce, exists if one spouse consents to the partner's commission of an offense, as where a couple voluntarily engage in mate swapping [31]. The couple cannot obtain a divorce on the grounds of adultery if they consented to the acts.

Condonation is a more common and more serious bar to fault-based divorce. That doctrine states that if a spouse is forgiven for a marital offense, a divorce cannot be granted because of that offense [30]. To illustrate, a husband's action for divorce against his wife on grounds of cruelty can be denied because the couple had engaged in sexual intercourse (evidence of condonation) after the alleged cruel act.

Attitude of Some Lawyers

These defenses, together with almost a dozen other rarely used ones, demonstrate the divergence between legal requirements and psychological realities. Although no-fault divorce attempts to close the gap, it has met stiff oppo-

sition from lawyers who work within the fault system. In 1972 the House
of Delegates of the American Bar Association (A.B.A.) overwhelmingly defeated a proposal for no-fault divorce. A report [17] of the rejection sum-
marizes a no-fault divorce proposal and the major economic, moral, and
practical objections to it:

[The proposal] had been drafted by the National Conference of Commissioners on
Uniform State Laws, a group of 250 judges, lawyers and law professors from the 50
states that tries to reduce disparities among state laws.

The no-fault divorce proposal would have established "irretrievable breakdown" of
a marriage as the sole grounds for divorce. California, Colorado, Michigan, and North
Dakota have recently passed laws adopting this concept, but in most other states
divorces are granted only if one party is found guilty of such grounds as adultery,
cruelty, or abandonment.

On the issue of no-fault divorce, the association's section on domestic relations law
objected. Some lawyers believed that the measure would drastically reduce domestic
relations law practices.

[The] acting chairman of the section on family law, posed the issue as "whether
the family itself in this country will go down the drain" because divorce would become
too quick and easy.

The proposed law sets up a minimum 30 day cooling off period after the filing of a
divorce action and requires a divorce hearing within 30 days.

[The] president of the Michigan Bar Association assailed the "unseemly speed" of
divorce under the new no-fault law in Michigan. He said the common experience of
divorce lawyers was that reconciliations often occurred during the year or more required to obtain divorces in most states.

The statute would also reduce the legal age to marry to 18 years without parental
consent and 16 with it. In many states the age is 21 without consent. It would also
divide each couple's property evenly rather than require judges to decide the amount
of alimony on a case by case basis.

The National Association of Women Lawyers and the A.B.A.'s young lawyers' section
also opposed the uniform act. It was rejected by a 170-72 vote.

The action of the American Bar Association was additionally significant
because it was the first time in the history of the relationship between the
association and the National Conference of Commissioners on Uniform
State Laws that the A.B.A. had refused to approve an act drafted by the
commissioners [6]. In the same year, the Massachusetts House of Representatives killed all 10 of the divorce reform bills brought up before it [22].

THE LAWYER'S ROLE

As these items suggest, one cannot properly speak of the impact of laws
on unhappily married persons without speaking of the influence of lawyers

on those persons, for it is through lawyers that the divorce laws are translated into action. In fact, most persons contemplating divorce are quite ignorant of the law. What they are aware of is the breakdown in their own particular marriage. When one of the married partners does go to a lawyer, he or she generally goes in search of the means of ending the marriage. What the partner finds is that not all lawyers will handle divorces and not all lawyers who handle divorces treat the matter similarly. Generally speaking, lawyers are trained as advocates. They represent one side of a dispute and argue their client's case. Thus, the lawyer helps the person fit the factual situation within the legal framework. As in the case example given previously, the lawyer may explain the legal grounds for divorce and the details of the process. The lawyer will need to question the client about the marital situation in order to make out a cause of action for divorce. He will need to know the expectations of the client concerning custody, alimony, and support. He will discuss the situation with the client, indicating the probable successes of different courses of action.

The lawyer also sets the adversary process in motion by acting as counsel for that partner. The other partner, if the couple is to go through with the divorce, must secure his or her own lawyer to act as an adversary in the proceeding. Since a divorce action culminates in a trial, the lawyer will act as advocate for his party. Those who argue most strongly for their clients fulfill their role as traditional lawyers.

But there is another type of lawyer who handles divorce cases. Admittedly, in the minority — and perhaps more a result of current social service orientations in law schools and among young practitioners than an outgrowth of legal tradition — is the lawyer who sees his role as one of counseling the client or couple, who tries to effect a reconciliation, or who acts as a conduit to professional mental health workers for partners in marital difficulty, especially in the prelitigation stages. But the professional role of a lawyer, his being consulted often as a last resort, the reluctance of most clients to pay if a reconciliation is effected (since that is not seen as lawyers' work), and his focus on legal as opposed to psychological matters in his training and his associations strongly favor his being an advocate.

The problem for the divorce lawyer is that legal rules and psychological realities diverge. His training has taught him to work within the laws, to effect problem-solving, to fit the facts of the case within the rules, and to argue for his client's interests. But his common sense, his human awareness, and his personal views about marriage, and family life, and divorce make the advocate's role much different in divorce matters. Since most people seeking divorce do not have difficulties that fit within the neat categories the legislature has defined, the lawyer is caught in the further dilemma of whether or not to encourage the client to distort the truth or to lie outright in order to secure a divorce. Some lawyers ask few questions of the client, so that the client will not have an opportunity to lie to them; at the same time these lawyers give the client a lot of information so that the client can invent on his own. Some lawyers refuse a case in which they know there are lies. And some lawyers accept the inevitability of lies and distortions because of the difficulties with the divorce laws. Given the many variables, finding a suitable divorce lawyer can be a difficult task. Being one is as difficult.

THE MENTAL HEALTH WORKER

The mental health professional, interviewing the lawyer's client or the client's spouse, might focus on different elements of the situation; he is not constrained by a need to prove certain elements to make a cause of action for divorce. The lawyer and the mental health worker have different functions, but their work ought to be complementary rather than antagonistic. Nevertheless, the fault concept renders their work antagonistic [44].

The lawyer, while deciding to what extent other professionals would be of help, must also respect the couple's desire to be dealt with only within the legal system and not to have the mental health system thrust on them. He must decide the extent to which he will encourage them to consult a mental health specialist.

PROBLEMS FOR LAWYERS

Whether or not the couple consults a mental health specialist, the lawyer may be faced with a difficult situation as he discovers more about the family or as he gets the assistance of other professionals. As an example, suppose that the lawyer representing the wife in the divorce action in the case example presented previously in this paper conferred, with her permission, with the wife's psychiatrist. The wife wanted custody of the minor children. The lawyer knew that courts generally give custody to the wife. What, then, if the lawyer learned that the psychiatrist felt strongly that the wife was not the suitable person to have custody of the children? What, then, would have been the lawyer's role? As advocate for his client he would argue for her interests as she saw them; as a gatherer of diverse opinions on the situation in dispute, he might agree that the husband should have custody of the children.

Assume that the lawyer argued strongly for his client but that the court awarded custody to the father. In a manner of speaking, the lawyer has had the best of both possible worlds: he has fulfilled his traditional role as advocate, but the child has been given to the more suitable parent. Assume, on the other hand, that the lawyer argued strongly for his client and his client won, despite the lawyer's and others' better judgments. What responsibility, if any, does the lawyer have once his role as advocate has ended?

Lawyers generally reserve for themselves a smaller, less responsible role for subsequent developments and events than social workers, psychiatrists, and others would assign them. The lawyer generally sees himself as a part of an adversary system of justice. Proposals of no-fault divorce may involve other aspects, such as family courts and greater interdisciplinary cooperation, that would challenge this view of the lawyer's role and the legal system. Although some lawyers and writers are calling on lawyers to fulfill larger roles, fundamental changes in the lawyer's role will not come quickly.

In general, then, a person consulting a divorce lawyer will find that the lawyer's focus is on the requirements of the law rather than the psychological realities. Lawyers feel more comfortable dispensing legal advice than psychological advice, though they often give their commonsense views. The issue of the role of the lawyer in divorce matters is an important one, for, unless there is proper implementation of the reform proposal, no-fault divorce could be as empty of psychological reality as fault divorce generally is, and as damaging. At least lawyers now know how to work within the fault framework. What guidelines would there be should no-fault divorce be adopted in many states?

CALIFORNIA'S NO-FAULT DIVORCE LAWS

The experience of California puts this issue in perspective. California has revised its statutes: divorces are no longer obtainable in California; marriages are simply dissolved upon a finding of irreconcilable differences or incurable insanity [3]. Irreconcilable differences, according to one writer, "are defined tautologically as those factors which make it appear that the marriage should be dissolved" [16]. Separations are also based on irreconcilable differences. In effect, the law allows divorce or separation on demand.

In California, specific acts of marital misconduct are not admissible, except when they bear on the issue of child custody or when the court finds them necessary to establish the existence of irreconcilable differences [16]. This does raise the possibility that one spouse may force the other into accepting lower support payments in order to avoid having evidence of misconduct, such as adultery, introduced into the child custody hearing.

Overall, the California statute is an effort to bring legal requirements into line with psychological realities. The concept of guilt, which can almost never be assigned only to one marriage partner, has been virtually eliminated from the courtroom. At least the adversarial bitterness has been removed from the proceedings. Even the petition has been redesigned: the former adversary petition *Jones v. Jones* has been replaced by a neutral petition, *In re marriage of Jones and Jones* [3]. The atmosphere of the proceeding terminating the marriage has changed; the theory, and it seems also to be the practice, is that the two partners can then better set about the tasks of property division, alimony, child custody, and support.

With regard to property division and alimony, California has made a significant change in its laws. As a community property state, California has assumed in general that almost all property accumulated by a couple after their marriage belongs half to the wife and half to the husband. Upon divorce, California divides the community property on a 50-50 basis unless the couple decides to divide it differently. Previously, the innocent party received the bulk of the community property if the divorce was awarded on grounds of extreme cruelty, adultery, or incurable insanity. Since 96 percent of California's divorces were based on extreme cruelty, the law worked hardship through its unfairness [17].

California has also changed its laws concerning alimony. Now California bases alimony on the "needs and circumstances of the parties, the duration of their marriage, and the ability of the supported spouse to engage in gainful employment without interfering with the interests of the children in his or her custody" [3]. Previously, alimony had been a punishment for marital fault, and payments had often been a great burden.

California has changed its laws concerning child custody only slightly. Custody decisions are based on the best interests of the child. Young children usually go to the mother. If there is a contest between a parent and a nonparent, the nonparent wins only if a parental award would be detrimental to the child and if the award to a nonparent is required to serve the best interests of the child. Previously, the nonparent could win custody by showing that the parent was somehow unfit, as when the parent had committed one act of adultery, even though the parental award would not have been detrimental to the child [16].

Critics of the new California law point to two defects. First, the law has retained the interlocutory period of six months between the first decree of dissolution and the final judgment. They feel that, to prevent the hardening of attitudes after the first decree is issued, this period should come between the filing of the petition of dissolution and the first dissolution decree. Second, California failed to enact the recommendation of the Governor's Commission on the Family that a family court be established. This court was to have jurisdiction over family matters, allowing for centralization of records and for cooperation among members of different professions and services[16].

While such courts are rare, there appears to be interest, at least in an experimental way in a university setting, in such a project. The Harvard Family Law Project, for example, an experiment in interdisciplinary cooperation, brings together teams of lawyers, social workers, psychiatrists, clinical psychologists, and others to "provide more effective service in the family law area." Its training program for student lawyers focuses on case referrals, weekly case conferences, human relations training, referrals to other agencies, and legal "grand rounds" [9]. Perhaps California will implement such a proposal.

California's new statute took effect on January 1, 1970. An appraisal of its operation during 1970 suggested the following: although California's divorce rate increased by 18 percent, Nevada's declined by 15 percent and Mexico's by 20 percent, part of which must be attributable to the California experience; furthermore, the filing rate for annulments in California was down 17 percent, for legal separations down 40 percent [4]. Overall, the new California legislation seemed to have had no effect upon the rate of marriage breakdowns. Its effect on divorces seemed to be that Californians were staying at home to get them.

California, then, has tried to remove the unreality and bitterness from

the divorce proceedings: the fiction of innocent and guilty parties has
been cast aside; perjury, collusion, and the wholesale mockery of the
divorce laws have been eliminated; respect for the law has been restored.
Proponents of divorce law reform have seen a growing number of states
follow California's lead by passing no-fault divorce laws [10, 11].

DIRECTIONS FOR THE FUTURE

In closing, five directions for the future should be pointed out. First, the
increasing interest in no-fault divorce will certainly meet opposition from
lawyers and moralists, but the trend toward no-fault is clear. As of mid-
1974, 28 states permitted divorce upon a showing of irretrievable breakdown of the marriage or incompatibility [11]. Another indication of the
growing acceptability of no fault is the American Bar Association's approval, at the organization's February, 1974 meeting of a proposal permitting
divorce upon a showing that the marriage is irretrievably broken [34].
This action was a sharp reversal of the A.B.A.'s overwhelming rejection
of no-fault divorce in 1972.

   Among other directions for the future, there may be increased interest
in preventing ill-considered marriages, perhaps through a longer waiting
period, through counseling, or related means. Third, there may be more
attempts to educate persons before they are married as to the rights and
responsibilities of marriage and divorce. Fourth, there are efforts to re-
think policies for child placement in contested cases of adoption, foster
care, and the like. Two psychiatrists and a lawyer have suggested that
psychological parenthood is more important to a child than biological or
current legal parenthood and that child placement decisions must go "beyond the best interests of the child": the child's needs must be paramount
and there must be minimum state intervention once a decision is made
[14]. Such rethinking will continue and probably be applied to custody
decisions in divorces as well.

   Finally, and perhaps most important, it may be that one law will
change divorce proceedings more than anything we have previously mentioned. The Equal Rights Amendment to the United States Constitution
[7, 23], if ratified by 38 states, could eliminate all legal distinctions based
on sex. Its effect on unhappily married persons would not be known for
some time, but within a few years the amendment might drastically
change the notions of divorce by removing the woman's presumed rights

to alimony, support, and custody; or it might have no real effect on these. Even now, the interest in and controversy over equal rights have resulted in some reassessments of the relations between the partners in an unhappy marriage.

CONCLUSION

Meanwhile, despite the great variability in states' laws that concern persons who are seeking divorces, they generally have one characteristic in common: present legal requirements, for the most part, contravene psychological realities. So long as this remains true, unhappily married persons and their lawyers will continue to say what is necessary to conform to law, will deal as best they can with psychological realities even while they are distorted by the law, and will realize to their distress that the law dispenses with psychological considerations at a time when they might be most helpful.

REFERENCES

1. Bernard, J. No News But New Ideas. In P. Bohannon (Ed.), *Divorce and After.* New York: Doubleday, 1970. P. 12.
2. Burnichal, L. G. Characteristics of adolescents from unbroken, broken, and re-constituted families. *Journal of Marriage and the Family* 26:44, 1964.
3. California Civil Code, §4500 *et seq.*, 1974.
4. Cannell, J. D. Abolish fault-oriented divorce in Ohio — as a service to society and to restore dignity to the domestic relations courts. *Akron Law Review* 4:110, 1971.
5. Dicey, A. V. *Lectures on the Relation between Law and Public Opinion in England* (2nd ed.), London: Macmillan, 1914. P. 347.
6. Divorce, uniform laws style. *American Bar Association Journal* 58:484, 1972.
7. Equal Rights Amendment: Proposed twenty-seventh amendment to the United States Constitution. United States Code, Supplement III to the 1970 Edition, 1973. P. xxxi.
8. Foote, C., Levy, R. F., and Sander, F. E. A. *Cases and Materials on Family Law.* Boston: Little, Brown, 1966. Pp. 637-640.
9. Ford, M. The Harvard family law project: An experiment in interdisciplinary cooperation. *Harvard Law School Bulletin* 23:18, 1972.
10. Freed, D. J. Grounds for divorce in the American jurisdictions. *Family Law Quarterly* 6:179, 1972.
11. Freed, D. J. Grounds for divorce in the American jurisdictions: Changes in grounds and corrections in chart. *Family Law Newsletter* 13:1, March 1973; 14:8, June 1973; 14:18, Fall 1973; 14:13, Spring 1974.
12. Freed, D. J., and Foster, H. H. Divorce American style. *The Annals of the American Academy of Political and Social Science* 383:84, 1969.

13. Gaylord, C. L. Something is loose in the marital woods. *American Bar Association Journal* 59:1306, 1973.
14. Goldstein, J., Freud, A., and Solnit, A. *Beyond the Best Interests of the Child.* New York: Free Press, 1973.
15. Goode, W. J. *After Divorce.* New York: Free Press, 1956.
16. Gough, A. R. California shows how: Divorce without squalor. *Nation* 210:18, 1970.
17. Graham, F. P. Bar group backs equal abortion but it rejects a uniform no fault divorce law. *New York Times,* Feb. 8, 1972: P. 37.
18. Harmsworth, H. C., and Minnis, M. S. Non-statutory causes of divorce: The lawyer's point of view. *Marriage and Family Living* 17:316, 320, 1955.
19. High cost of divorce in money and emotions. *Business Week*, Feb. 10, 1975. P. 83.
20. Hunt, M. *World of the Formerly Married.* New York: McGraw-Hill, 1966. P. 144.
21. Kay, H. H. A family court: The California proposal. *California Law Review* 56:1205, 1968.
22. Kenney, M. All 10 divorce reform bills strike out in house. *Boston Globe,* May 3, 1972. P. 24.
23. Kneeland, D. E. The Equal Rights Amendment. *New York Times*, Feb. 7, 1975. P. 37.
24. Levy, R. J. Uniform marriage and divorce legislation: A preliminary analysis prepared for the special committee on divorce of the National Conference of Commissioners on Uniform State Laws. Unpublished, 1967.
25. Marriage game: Findings of the Bureau of the Census survey. *Time*, Oct. 25, 1971. P. 51.
26. Massachusetts Bar Association. *You, Your Marriage, and the Law.* Boston, n. d.
27. Massachusetts General Laws, Chapter 740 of the Acts of 1973. Codified at Massachusetts General Laws Annotated, Chapter 208, § 1, 1974.
28. Massachusetts General Laws Annotated, Chapter 208, § 1 *et seq.*, 1974.
29. Massachusetts General Laws Annotated, Chapter 208, § 21, 1974.
30. Mayer, M. F. *Divorce and Annulment in the 50 States.* New York: Arco, 1967, Pp. 45-47, 53-54.
31. Moore, M. M. Analysis of collusion and connivance bars to divorce. *The University of Kansas Law Review* 36:194, 1968.
32. Nye, F. I. Child adjustment in broken and unhappy homes. *Marriage and Family Living* 19:356, 1957.
33. Paulsen, M. S., and Wadlington, W. *Statutory Materials on Family Law.* Mineola, N.Y.: The Foundation Press, 1974. P. 34.
34. Quenstedt, U. R., and Winkler, C. E. What are our domestic relations judges thinking? Monograph no. 1, *American Bar Association Section of Family Law*, July 1965. P. 1.
35. Rheinstein, M. *Marriage Stability, Divorce, and the Law.* Chicago: University of Chicago Press, 1972.
36. Rhode Island General Laws Annotated, § 15,5,3, 1974.

37. Sheresky, N., and Mannes, M. *Uncoupling: The Art of Coming Apart.* New York: Viking, 1972.
38. Society for Promoting Christian Knowledge. *Putting Asunder: A divorce law for contemporary society.* London, 1966, Appendix D, §7, 15.
39. U.S. Bureau of the Census. *Statistical Abstract of the United States: 1973* (94th edition). Washington, D.C., 1973. P. 147.
40. U.S. Government Printing Office. The challenge of crime in a free society: A report by the President's commission on law enforcement and administration of justice. Washington, 1967. P. 44.
41. Vermont Statutes Annotated, Title 15 §551, 1974.
42. Vital Statistics of the United States 1: 2-26, Table 2-X, 1958.
43. Walker, T. B. Beyond fault: An examination of patterns of behavior in response to present divorce laws. *Journal of Family Law* 10:271, 1970.
44. Zuckman, H. L., and Fox, W. F. The ferment in divorce legislation. *Journal of Family Law* 12:515, 1972.

II

The Structure and Dynamics of Marriage

In Part II we have endeavored to clarify the course and nature of the marital relationship. Increasingly it has become clear that intensely intimate relationships are not to be understood only, or even principally, in terms of drive satisfaction. Marriages do not inevitably prosper when drives are gratified, nor does divorce inevitably occur when gratification is limited.

Sexual expression is an important aspect of most marriages, and yet it is difficult to explain the decision of two people to marry and stay married as the outcome of sexual gratification, since many do so even when sexual pleasure is largely lacking. What appears to be more significant is that the human relationship itself is what is important. Having someone to talk to who will attempt to understand and affirm the other person's uniqueness as an individual is of prime importance. When mutual affirmation exists in the context of closeness and intimacy, one can feel truly known.

123

As Goethals describes, individuals develop, from childhood on, familiarity with certain modes of relating to others and seek out in adult life people who will fit into these familiar modes. All of us have known people who after a divorce have either married someone similar in character to their previous spouse or someone diametrically opposed, so that the difficulties inherent in their first marriage are either repeated or reversed. Thus, what remains unchanged is the mode or style of the relationship.

Increasingly, it has become clear that a psychology of intimate relationships involving intense feelings is central to an understanding of marriage. A psychology of individuals is a necessary but insufficient basis for marital or family therapy. In an intensely intimate relationship such as marriage, there appears to be a basic psychological tendency to experience the other person as embodying both certain loved and hated characteristics of the self and to treat them accordingly. Potential partners who are unwilling or unable to comply with these projections may seem too alien to be suitable. These expectations are discussed by Zinner in his chapter as "projective identifications," and Ronald Liang, in particular, has focused attention on the need and power of individuals to force others to comply with them.

The fundamental basis for the traditional marital relationship lies in the differences between the sexes and their need for each other. Procreation and continuation of the species are no longer viewed as primary motives. At the present time there is much discussion, often heated, about the impact of socialization on biological givens and vice versa, in terms of their effects on the ultimate expression of sexual characteristics. It is an obstacle to the furtherance of knowledge that the professionals who are most expert in the study of the effects of the social environment are little acquainted with the biological basis of human behavior, while biologists, by and large, are equally unfamiliar with the influences of socialization. In his chapter Gadpaille has summarized what is known about the biological givens and their behavioral concomittants. Since the material presented may be unfamiliar and even difficult for nonmedical therapists, it merits careful reading.

Marriages extend over a continuum of time, with the beginning and the end being the two most dramatic points. Two chapters in Part II are devoted to the beginning and ending of the marriage relationship. The frames of reference used by Murstein in his chapter and by Maddison and Raphael in their chapter are quite different, and yet each chapter emphasizes the importance of these nodal points as processes which are important for the understanding of the marriage relationship. Clinicians know that how a couple met, what attracted them to each other, and what they thought required changing "tomorrow" are matters well worth exploring. It may also be fruitful to bring a troubled couple to consider what life would be like without the other partner and to realistically assess the meaning and values inherent in their marriage. The effects of a spouse's death on the surviving partner are pervasive and profound, as Maddison and Raphael document in their chapter; they go beyond the loss of sex drive satisfaction and the need to assume previously shared role functions. A vital source of self-affirmation is lost and life's meaning and purpose is diminished without someone who knows that one lives and cares that one lives. The death of a spouse, of course, has varying consequences, depending on the age of the couple. The importance of the fear of loneliness as a motive for marrying and staying together is illuminated in this chapter.

Safilios-Rothschild has endeavored to clarify certain aspects of married life relating to the way decisions are made. Couples like to think that they act out of love, but it is clear that they also act out of fear, sometimes the fear of the other's greater power. Murstein has indicated that even during courtship the value an individual places on himself or herself affects the course of the courtship. This is true during the marriage as well, but cruder forms of power such as physical force, economic power, and verbal ability can also be important. Clinicians are familiar with the situation in which the spouse who cares less is able to control the other who cares more about the relationship and who is more willing to compromise. Sometimes this leads to the curious, but common, marriage in which the overtly more disturbed individual determines major decisions, while the healthier spouse gives in for the sake of peace. Psychological studies of marital power relationship and clinical understanding of troubled couples can be mutually enriching. While marital decision-making is often discussed as though rationality prevailed, we know that to attempt to understand family-planning decision-making rationally is, in a way, a paradox — clinical investigations of "planning" deal with what is often experienced by the participants as an unplanned happening, often an "unexpected" happening. Yet only through such attempts at description can we arrive at an understanding of how couples come to do the things they do.

7

Research on the Physiology of Maleness and Femaleness

Warren J. Gadpaille

There still remains a wealth of ignorance in the scientific understanding of masculinity and femininity. In view of the obvious fact that the human race has always been divided into two sexes, it is chastening to admit that there is not even general agreement on their differences, much less on the etiology of such differences. In this chapter, the interest focuses primarily on the origin and development of innate masculine-feminine differences that may be independent of environmental and cultural influences, and specifically on the contributions made by biological and physiological research to their further understanding.

The basic anatomical, adult hormonal, and reproductive differences need no further explication — they are properly conceived to be distinctions of maleness and femaleness. But the sex-specific emotional and psychological characteristics of males and females are not clearly understood. The personality traits commonly ascribed particularly to men or women are often perceived simply as learned behavior. This perception, however, presupposes no innate distinguishing characteristics. A more precise definition of masculinity or femininity is those sex-linked psychological and behavioral manifestations, including social behavior, not directly related to copulation and reproduction. Are there any such differences that are inborn? If so, what roles do such factors as evolution, embryology, and physiology play? Does the simple fact that men and women have different bodies cause them also to have different emotions and attitudes?

These considerations are only recently beginning to be adequately researched. Psychological theories and popular assumptions about masculinity and femininity have too often been accepted as proven fact. As a kind of reactionary backlash, some insist that all distinctions are cultural artifacts, perpetuated through the centuries by males in the service of their continued dominant role. Clearly, the issue merits objective evaluation. It is most unlikely that any innate differences, could they be demonstrated, would result in one sex's being inferior to the other. It is hoped that biological research may illuminate some of the controversial and obscure issues of masculine-feminine differences.

NEUROENDOCRINE AND NEUROANATOMICAL STUDIES

Within the past two decades, experimental studies have established beyond question that certain anterior portions of the hypothalamus govern and regulate not only the physiological aspects of reproductive function, but sexual behavior as well. Harris [36, 38] has reviewed the literature and reported his own experiments demonstrating that neurohumoral substances elaborated in the anterior hypothalamus are carried by portal vessels in the pituitary stalk and in turn regulate the release of anterior hypophyseal gonadotropins. Lesion experiments [89, 90], stereotactic implantation of sex hormones [54, 55, 60], stimulation experiments [20], and autoradiographic studies of cerebral uptake of tagged sex hormones [60, 85] reveal a focus of sex-regulatory behavior in the hypothalamus, anterior midline, and preoptic areas. An additional element was introduced by experiments [19] that demonstrated not only that the hypothalamus controls cyclic ovulation in rats but also that neurohumoral stimulation of the pituitary occurs regularly and predictably under certain light-conditions related to the time of day, thus opening the way for tying sexual behavior and function in with environmental conditions and stimuli.

Neuroanatomical investigations have explored other central nervous system connections and associations with the hypothalamus that are involved in sexual response. In a long series of experiments with squirrel monkeys, MacLean [56, 57] not only has located a nodal point for penile erection in the medial part of the medial dorsal thalamic nucleus and mapped areas of genital stimulation in the septum and in the major projections of the median forebrain bundle, but also has called attention to some interesting proximities between sexual and other functions. The limbic lobe is bent around upon itself, bringing into close anatomical juxtaposition areas relating to oral, olfactory, and anogenital functions. This is not mere physical proximity; carefully located points of electrical stimulation demonstrate that both oral and genital activity can be elicited together in identical discrete loci and that "excitation in a region involved in oral mechanisms readily spills over into others concerned with genital function" [56, p. 206]. The identical close anatomical and neural associations exist between loci, mediating aggressive and sexual expression. It is thus clear that there is a functional neuroanatomical substrate for the frequent blending of oral and sexual activity and for the association of sex and aggressive attack.

HORMONAL STUDIES

There is obviously an overlap between this section and the previous one, since hormones were used in many of the subject studies. A distinction is made, however, because in those studies already reviewed, hormones served as tools in the primary purpose of elucidating anatomical structure and function. In this section, interest is focused on the actions and effects of the hormones themselves and their influence on sexual dimorphism and the differentiation of males and females, both biologically and psychologically.

It might be expected that the lower a species on the phylogenetic scale, and therefore the less complex its central nervous system and reproductive structure and function, the more widespread the effects might be of sharply altering its hormonal environment. It is perhaps surprising, even so, that in some species a total reversal of both phenotype and genotype is possible. In the small killfish (*Orizeas latipes*), Yamamoto [107] treated genetic male (XY) larvae with female hormone, and, instead of differentiating as fertile males, they differentiated as fertile XY females capable of breeding and reproducing as females. In like fashion, functionally fertile XX males, YY females, and YY males were produced, their reproductive function and differentiation being determined entirely by the hormone to which the larvae were exposed and not at all by their genes. In an interesting behavioral correlate, the YY males have been found to be strongly dominant over XY males in shared tanks, both in aggression and in frequency of fertile matings [30]. The investigators refer to YY's as *supermales* and infer that the intensified male behavior is due to the extra Y chromosome.

In the lower mammals (most work has utilized rats, rabbits, and guinea pigs), one may easily study the paradigm of morphological sexual differentiation. In early embryonic life, the tissue anlagen of both sets of internal reproductory organs are laid down in each fetus. The primordial gonad consists of a rind that is capable of differentiating into the ovary and of a core that can become a testis; the Müllerian ducts differentiate into tubes, uterus, and vagina, and the Wolffian ducts into epididymus, vas deferens, and seminal vesicles. In normal embryological development, one set degenerates and becomes vestigial, while the other becomes functional. The external morphology of the two sexes differentiates from the same embryonic anlage. The genital tubercle becomes either penis or clitoris; the same skin becomes either clitoral hood or skin covering penis and urethra; and the labioscrotal tissue either fuses over the urogenital groove to become the scrotum or remains separated as the labia.

The time sequence and mediation of this physical dimorphism will be significant for future discussion. The genetic code of either XX or XY apparently determines only the differentiation of ovary or testis, after which fetal hormones from either gonad take over further differentiation. If the embryo is to be male (XY), the testes differentiate earlier than would the ovary in XX. The fetal testes secrete both androgen and a separate Müllerian-inhibiting substance, the latter producing regression of the Müllerian duct system and the androgen producing development of the Wolffian structures and differentiation of the external tissue as normal male genitalia. (Of incidental interest is the fact that the separate Müllerian-inhibiting substance appears to be local in action, in that unilateral removal or implant of fetal testis permits or inhibits Müllerian structure development only on the side affected [46].) Since the XX genetic code does not stimulate testicular tissue, it subsequently causes the ovary to proliferate from the primordial gonadal rind. Thus, the ovary differentiates in the absence of androgenic hormones. And, while the fetal ovaries secrete female sex-hormone substances, it is essentially in the absence of androgens (see beyond), rather than due to the action of estrogens, that Müllerian structures develop and external genitalia become morphologically female, while Wolffian ducts disappear.

The fact that such a rigid time sequence exists, specific for each species, suggests the concept of a critical period — a limited time span in or before which some form of interference in sexual dimorphism may take place, but after which the "die is cast" for that particular structure or function. Many experiments have demonstrated this critical period and have shown that it may be extremely short. Jost [46] has shown that if a male (XY) rabbit fetus is castrated in utero by day 19, all internal and external differentiation is female, with no evidence even of Wolffian remnants, whereas by day 24 it is too late to prevent total male differentiation of all structures, with no remnants of the Müllerian system.

Another principle, amply verified in further studies to be discussed, is suggested by Jost's work: that is, that nature's prime disposition is to produce females; maleness only results from something added — androgens. In the absence of androgens, whether the fetus is of XX or XY genotype, differentiation will proceed as female, although in the genotype XY, in mammalian species at least, ovaries will not differentiate. The converse is not true; the absence of ovaries, and thus of estrogenic and progestinic substances, does not interfere with female internal and external sex structure development, though such individuals will naturally be infertile. This specific influence of fetal hormones on sexual dimorphism has been demonstrated via several different approaches. Genetic (XX) female guinea pigs have been masculinized in utero by maternal injection of androgenic substances during the critical period [36, 38, 39]. Depending on the amounts of hormone and the accuracy of the timing, these experimental animals differentiated as morphological males, though their gonads were ovaries. Parallel experiments have been accomplished by the feminization of genetic males. In addition to Jost's fetal-castration experiments, castration of the male neonate rat (the critical period for sexually dimorphic differentiation in the rat is prior to the fifth neonatal day) permits the retention of the female pattern of cyclic release of gonadotropins [37].

More dramatic is the use of the antiandrogen cyproterone acetate, a substance that blocks the androgens from the fetal testes. When this substance is injected into pregnant rats, the genetic male offspring have external genitalia identical to those of females [82, 83]. Thus, in the absence of androgen, morphology develops according to female pattern without regard to the genotype of the animal.

Sexually dimorphic physiological function, too, is differentiated by the

same principle, and the important site on which the presence or absence
of androgens acts, and in turn permanently differentiates its regulatory
function, is the hypothalamus. Neonatal testosterone administered to
female rats produced an acyclic (male-type) pituitary release of gonadotropins resulting in anovulatory, sterile ovaries. Both the pituitaries and the
ovaries of such treated animals resumed normal cyclic and ovulatory
function when transplanted to untreated (hypophysectomized or
ovariectomized) females [38]. The pituitaries, however, would function
only if placed in anatomical contact with the hypothalamus [92].
Cross-sex pituitary transplants in normal rats result in the gonadotropin-
release pattern of the host animal, indicating no sex differences in the
pituitary [38]. The level of physiological maturity of the ovary or the
hypophysis is shown to exert no influence upon its capacity to function,
by the finding that either organ will assume mature function when removed from immature rats and implanted in sexually mature animals in
whom the corresponding organ had been removed [36]. Thus, it is the
sexual differentiation of the central nervous system, more particularly
the hypothalamus, that is determinative.

The most exciting finding in all the experiments thus far discussed is
that there is also a differentiating effect on mating and other sex-related
behavior that exactly parallels that of the physiological dimorphism. The
testosterone-masculinized female guinea pigs [86] showed absent or
markedly diminished female sex responses to normal males, and, when
ovariectomized, were unresponsive to exogenous estrogens. They displayed sexual behavior more typical of males, and exogenous androgens made
them sexually responsive in male fashion. None of these reactions occurred
in ovariectomized, untreated females. Analogous findings were reported
in similarly testosterone-treated female rats [3, 38, 39].

Male rats castrated at birth displayed female behavior to normal males
when under the influence of exogenous estrogens, whereas castration after
day 10 did not promote the display of such behavior. Exogenous testosterone in such rats had only a slight effect in producing male behavior
[37, 39]. Fetal males treated with cyproterone, if prevented from having a
masculinizing puberty by castration, and subsequently given female hormone replacement, developed female responses to normal males; the normal males responded to them as to females and did not distinguish them
from normal females [83].

It is apparent, then, that fetal hormones have an inductive or organizing effect on the hypothalamus and on any ancillary neural tissue that subsequently determines sexual behavior. Some ambiguous and contradictory evidence leads to some difference of interpretation as to whether the same brain structure is organized to release both anatomical-physiological dimorphism and behavioral sexual differentiation, or whether separate hypothalamic centers are inductively acted on by the presence or absence of androgens at the critical period [25, 104]. (There is some evidence that in the rat, neonatal testicular androgen appears to have an organizational influence at the spinal level on neural tissue mediating sexual reflexes [40]. The *absence of androgenic effect* at the particular critical period for a given species — whether absent normally as in the genetic female or artificially through castration or antiandrogen treatment — results in a brain organized to produce morphological females, to function cyclically in the mediation of pituitary gonadotropin release (female pattern), and to release male sexual behavior and response under conditions of mating and the introduction of female sex hormones. Male behavior is minimal or abolished whether genotypic males or females are observed, and regardless of the introduction of androgens after puberty. The *presence of androgenic effect* at the critical period — whether normally from fetal testes or artificially through introduction of exogenous androgens into a genetic female — suppresses female morphological differentiation in favor of male morphology and organizes the hypothalamus to function acyclically (male pattern) in the mediation of pituitary gonadotropin release and to produce male sexual behavior in mating situations and in response to exogenous androgens; female sexual behavior is diminished or absent whether or not the subject animal is a genotypic female or male and regardless of exogenous female sex-hormone administration. In other words, there is (at least at these phyletic levels) unequivocally a male brain and a female brain, demonstrably distinct from one another, mediating sex-specific physiology and mating behavior. Harris [38] suggests that in the mammalian species studies there are two definite functional differences between male and female brains: (1) the hypothalamus of the female regulates the secretion of gonadotropins cyclically, whereas that of the male induces steady secretion and (2) the two types of brain induce different sex-behavior patterns, in that it is easier to evoke sexual response to the opposite sex than to the same sex in the normal animal. Harris's observations also suggest two additional differences possibly related to the different sex of the brains: (1) there is a greater aggressiveness in animals with either normally or artificially masculinized brains and (2) there is a consistently increased growth rate in animals with masculinized brains and a decreased growth rate in animals with feminized brains; these disparate rates are those characteristic for normal males and females.

Out of this bewildering plethora of material can be summarized four principles: (1) the principle of a critical period for influencing sex differentiation, (2) the principle of nature's primary intent to differentiate females, with the complication of something (androgens) having to be added to produce a male, (3) the principle of distinctly different male and female brain structures, and (4) the principle of differentiation of neural (hypothalamic) tissue to produce male or female sex behavior. Quoting from Phoenix et al. [86, p. 379], "The embryonic and fetal periods are periods of differentiation (of the neural tissues mediating mating behavior) in the direction of masculinization or feminization. Adulthood, when gonadal hormones are being secreted, is a period of activation; neural tissues are the target organs and mating behavior is brought to expression. Like the genital tracts (at adulthood), the neural tissues mediating mating behavior respond to androgens or to estrogens depending on the sex of the individual . . . ." In support of the separate times of influence of hormones on the hypothalamus (organizing or activating), Harris [38] mentions two "generations" of Leydig cells, one fetal (perhaps functioning at induction phase) and another maturing at puberty.

The biological studies of primates have been scant thus far. The very difficult job of devising an androgen treatment compatible with maintenance of pregnancy has greatly impaired the size of study population, but a few such subjects have been studied. Genetically female rhesus monkeys bred from mothers androgenized during the critical fetal period, were morphologically indistinct from normal males.

The special value of studying primates is that they display considerable sex-related behavior that is not directly linked to mating — behavior that has been defined as masculine or feminine. Based on field and captivity observations of young rhesus monkeys, it has been determined that there are sexually dimorphic differences in social behavior. The males threaten, initiate play, engage in rough-and-tumble play, and attempt mounting with much greater frequency than females, and they withdraw less

often from threats or approach by other monkeys. The masculinized
female (XY) monkeys display sex behavior much more typical of normal males than of normal females [108]. According to recent reports,
these monkeys are not old enough for residual behavior effects in adulthood to be studied; however a few are well into puberty and approaching
adulthood, and there is evidence of some diminution of the marked brain-
determined cross-sex behavior as they get older.

ANIMAL BEHAVIOR STUDIES

Most of the studies previously discussed share the observation that behavior is integral to the study of hormonal effects and quite uniformly reveal the capacity of cross-sex hormones, administered at critical periods, to
alter sexual behavior toward that of the opposite sex. A few other types of
experiments, especially with primates, shed light on related areas. Beach [5]
has reviewed much of this material and reports that it is typical for extran-
eous, nonsexual stimuli to inhibit copulatory behavior in males more
readily than in females, that previous experience may alter the male's
responsiveness more, and that in chimpanzees sexually inexperienced females are more capable of copulation than sexually inexperienced males.
Moreover, in the primates studied, ablation of the cerebral cortex destroyed
the males' capacity to copulate but not that of the females. In line with
the implications inherent in the principle that something — androgen —
must be added to the basic biological recipe to produce male sex differentiation (thus by definition making maleness more complex), these observations lend strength to the idea that maleness and masculinity are more
difficult to achieve and more vulnerable to disruption.

The Harlows's famous studies [33, 34, 35] of the consequences of
rearing conditions on rhesus monkeys has uniformly demonstrated that
inadequate mothering and lack of peer-group social contact and sex play
during childhood produced adult monkeys that totally lacked the capacity
for adult sex behavior, successful copulation, and conception. What surprised behavioral scientists most was the clear evidence that peer-group
social and sexual play was more important than mothering; lack of
mothering could be overcome by peer experience, but lack of peer experience left ineradicable incapacities. While none of the males has been reported to have recovered, a few of the females have been gradually

induced by patient and experienced males to become sexually receptive, to conceive, and to give birth, although they are totally rejecting mothers. This lends further support to the theory of greater resistance to sexual dysfunction in females.

Studies of chimpanzees reared in isolation yield interesting data. One report [87] indicates that they suffer the same sexual incapacities initially as do rhesus monkeys, but that most of them are subsequently able to learn to copulate. In research at the Aeromedical Research Laboratory [51], the animals reared in isolation past maturity showed the same ineptness of adult sexual responses. This indicates that the critical period for learning adult sexuality is between puberty and early adulthood. Again, it was shown that females could overcome this ineptness and reluctance with the help of experienced males, but that male inabilities cannot be overcome. Data on chimpanzees are further evidence that males are more susceptible to disruption of sexual function than are females. These data correlate with other primate data to indicate the increasing importance of the cerebral cortex and of learning as the phylogenetic scale is ascended.

HUMAN STUDIES: ANOMALIES

Since it is unthinkable that such experiments as those discussed be conducted on humans, other means of study must be utilized. Unfortunately for the afflicted persons, but fortunately for medical science, nature has provided almost entirely analogous human conditions — results of various chromosomal anomalies, developmental disorders, and iatrogenic conditions. By far the most integrated and intense research into these human conditions has for many years been conducted under the direction of Dr. John Money at the Psychohormonal Research Unit of The Johns Hopkins University School of Medicine. Money has enumerated seven variables of sexual differentiation in the human [75]. Under normal developmental conditions, all the variables are integrated consonantly as male or female. In the anomalous and disordered conditions to be discussed, it will be seen that they may vary independently of one another within the same individual, with striking and illuminating consequences. These variables are (1) chromosomal sex, (2) gonadal sex, (3) hormonal sex, (4) internal accessory reproductive structures, (5) external genital morphology, (6) sex of assignment and rearing, and (7) gender role and orientation established while growing up.

Androgen-Insensitivity Syndrome

Analogous to the antiandrogen effects of cyproterone and to fetal castration before the critical period in the male, is the human condition known as the endrogen-insensitivity syndrome, or the testicular-feminizing syndrome [65, 67, 68]. In this condition, the embryo forms as a genetic XY male, and the genetic code differentiates fetal testes; but due presumably to an inherited defect in cellular enzymes, the cells of the body (including the brain) are unresponsive to androgen effect from the fetal testes. The Müllerian-inhibiting substance of the testes typically reduces the Müllerian structures to vestiges, but because the cellular defect causes the fetus to develop as though no androgen were present, external genitalia differentiate as female, testes descend no farther than the groin, and the child is born as a perfectly normal-looking girl. She is reared as a girl, and the disorder usually comes to light only after puberty, when she has failed to menstruate. Even though in the typical case the testes are producing normal amounts of male hormonal substances, her body responds only to the small amount of estrogenic material normally produced in the testes and adrenal cortex, and external physical development at puberty proceeds in female fashion with typical female habitus and fat distribution and with breast formation. When her amenorrhea is investigated, it is discovered that her vagina is a short blind pouch, her uterus and tubes are vestigial, and her gonads, which may be palpated in the groin, are testes. Cytological studies show the absence of sex chromatin (Barr body) and the typical male XY genotype.

The gender identity, as well as the gender of assignment and rearing, of these people is unequivocally feminine. Their interests are typically feminine [58, 74]. They are not tomboys, and they function quite successfully as women, wives, and adoptive mothers when appropriate corrective genital surgery and estrogen administration are accomplished. This syndrome demonstrates again the principle that nature will differentiate a female in the absence of effective fetal androgen and that chromosomal, hormonal, and gonadal sex is regularly overridden by this female-first principle and by gender of assignment and rearing.

Turner's Syndrome

In this genetically transmitted chromosomal anomaly, typically the conceptus lacks one of the normal complement of sex chromosomes — the Y — , resulting in a 44-X chromosome pattern, or a sex chromosome pattern referred to as XO. This defective genetic code is incapable of differentiating either ovaries or testes, with the result that neither fetal androgens nor estrogens are elaborated, and internal reproductive structures do not develop. Again, in accordance with the principle of preferential female differentiation, external genitalia at birth are those of a normal female, although other physical stigmata classically accompany this syndrome, including short stature, webbed neck, cubitus valgus, and low posterior hairline. Because of gonadal aplasia, physical puberty does not take place unless and until estrogen replacement is undertaken; obviously, these women are sterile [44]. Mean intelligence is average, but verbal IQ is significantly higher than performance IQ [73, 93] because these women suffer from a specific type of space-form perceptual deficiency [63, 93].

Of special interest is the fact that the gender identity of these women is female in every sense; indeed, XO girls and women scored more feminine than did normal girls and women on psychological tests that reliably differentiate masculine from feminine attitudes in this culture [17, 93]. These people are very maternal and make good adoptive mothers. Despite their many handicaps, emotional and psychosexual disturbance and instability are absent [79]. Thus, it is again demonstrated that neither the second X chromosome nor fetal estrogens are necessary for the differentiation of female morphology and gender identity. Since ovaries produce small amounts of androgenic substances, it may be hypothesized that the almost hyperfeminine development of these women may be due to the total lack of androgens during the critical period of hypothalamic organization for differentiation of sexual behavior.

Both of the conditions previously described parallel the feminizing experiments involving critical-period castration or antiandrogen treatment with male animals. There are also human disorders that parallel the masculinization experiments with animals.

Adrenogenital Syndrome

Adrenogenital syndrome (hyperadrenocorticism due to congenital adrenal hyperplasia [45]) is a hereditary condition resulting from a recessive gene. The gene produces a metabolic error that inhibits the normal production of cortisone, thus leading to excessive production of adrenal androgenic (and estrogenic) hormones. The condition may occur in genetic males or females.

In females, congenital adrenal hyperplasia produces pseudohermaphroditism, with varying degrees of masculinization of the external genitalia (depending upon the amount of androgen and the age of the fetus when the effect begins), ranging from an enlarged clitoris to completely fused labioscrotal folds and normal appearing penis with penile urethra. Gonads are ovaries, and Müllerian duct structures differentiate more or less normally, the vagina usually opening into the urethra. Evidence that this condition often begins in early fetal life is indicated by Wilkins's finding that excessive androgen must be present before the twelfth fetal week for there to be any fusion of the labioscrotal folds [105]. Postnatally, growth is abnormally rapid, but early closure of epiphyses results in short stature with stocky limbs in proportion to trunk. Virilization begins early, with pubic hair often appearing by two years of age. Development appears precociously masculine, with facial hair, deepening of voice, and failure of breast development; menstruation does not occur and ovaries are anovulatory.

The study of such female hermaphrodites has elucidated psychosexual differentiation in several areas. Treatment that effectively reverses masculinization and permits emergence of female appearance and function (in conjunction with corrective surgery) has existed only since 1950 [106]. It has therefore been possible both to study women who have been treated with cortisone, only after having grown to adulthood with all the effects of virilization, and women treated since infancy and thus spared the physical virilization. In the behavioral studies, the cases of those treated early are of particular importance, because these women did not grow up with the psychological burden of ambiguous sexual appearance and disfiguring virilization and their potentially adverse effects on psychosexual orientation, body image, and ambivalent parental and cultural interaction.

When reared as girls, even the late-treated group had virtually no disturbance of core gender identity in spite of their masculine appearance. But both early- and late-treated groups of female hermaphrodites displayed statistically significant deviation in the direction of masculine attitudes, as measured by the criteria of sexually dimorphic behavior developed at the Psychohormonal Research Unit at Johns Hopkins [71]. Compared with normal controls, both early- and late-treated adrenogenital women had, as children, been much more frequently known to themselves and others as tomboys; had overwhelmingly preferred boys' toys and play to girls'; had been much less interested in infants, infant care, and doll play; had preferred boys' clothes and had been much less interested in cosmetics, hairdos, and jewelry; had been much less satisfied with the female role; had been much more active in sports and outdoor activities; had phantasized less about romance and marriage; and had generally expressed preference for career over marriage [15, 53]. It is likely that this behavior pattern is related to the effect of androgens in the fetal period because of the negligible difference between early- and late-treated women. There is increased psychosexual pathology and typical masculine response in the late-treated women. They exhibit increased homosexual activity and inclination; the majority respond with genitopelvic arousal to visual and narrative erotic stimuli (statistically more characteristic of males [50]) as well as to tactile stimuli (female characteristic); and most have very high (to the point of being a problem) levels of sex drive and gratification [16]. Another finding of interest is that women with hyperadrenocorticism have significantly high IQs [61, 73, 77].

Progestin-Induced Hermaphroditism

An iatrogenic form of female hermaphroditism (which is induced by the administration of progestins during early pregnancy in the effort to prevent threatened abortion but which administration, in certain cases, exerts endrogenic effects [105]) offers a further check on the conclusions drawn from the naturally occurring cases. As a known consequence of such medication, some girl infants may be born with any of the same degree of masculinized external genitalia, but without, of course, subsequent virilization. In spite of the condition's being recognized and surgically corrected from birth and the children reared as girls, on follow-up these progestin-induced hermaphrodites had firm female core gender identities but had similarly more masculine than feminine psychosexual identities in exactly the same ways as did the adrenocortical females; they had even higher IQs [18, 73]. When both types of female hermaphrodites are compared with females with Turner's syndrome, the distinctions are thrown into sharp perspective. The two hermaphroditic types are almost identical in behavioral masculinization and clearly distinct from the totally feminine Turner's syndrome patients [73]. High IQ has also been demonstrated in children of mothers treated prenatally with progesterone where there was no fetal masculinization, and the degree of IQ elevation was shown to be correlated both with increased dosage and an earlier administration [11]. The indication that these various sexually dimorphic patterns are induced by the presence or absence of androgens in the fetal period is consistently evidenced by the fact that the same behavioral differentiations are found regardless of the postnatal conditions in the subjects.

There are complementary findings from the study of male patients with congenital adrenal hyperplasia. In such patients, it is the fetal hypothalamus of a male that is subjected to early and excessive androgen. If untreated, these boys show clinically precocious puberty. The psychosexual development of such boys, including those with idiopathic precocious puberty [72], reveals a much increased energy expenditure, especially in infancy, early occurrence of the capacity for frankly sexual imagery and erotic dreams, and early establishment of the capacity for sexual arousal by erotic visual imagery. With one exception noted in the literature [97], capacity for arousal by homosexual stimuli is entirely absent. These boys generally cannot imagine themselves being aroused by such thoughts or acts. Other forms of deviant sexuality were also notably absent in act or reported fantasy. This and other studies [77, 78] have revealed the same statistically high IQ in these hyperandrogen cases. Once more, androgen effect upon neural organizers of sexually dimorphic behavior at the critical fetal period must be postulated, because early- and late-treated persons showed no significant differences.

The male analogue to the progestin-induced female hermaphrodites is uncertain. Money [70] cites a *Medical Tribune* article of December 26, 1968, about a group of boys in Jerusalem who were exposed to high doses of progesterone (100 mg. or more) in utero, and who were reported by A. Russell as showing more than usual sexual interests and play in childhood. These boys, also showed an elevation in IQ.

In the interest of completeness, two other sex-chromosome anomalies will briefly be mentioned because of the possible influence of the chromosomal defect upon behavior.

Klinefelter's Syndrome

People with Klinefelter's syndrome have a genotype of 44 + XXY, or one extra X chromosome. They differentiate as morphological males; genitalia are normal but at puberty may fail to enlarge normally; testes are small and usually azoospermic. There is a tendency toward eunuchoid body build; many develop breasts; and sex drive and frequency of male sexual activity is generally low. Some degree of mental deficiency is found with high frequency, and males with Klinefelter's are unusually prone to emotional instability and psychosexual disturbance, including homosexuality and transvestism [65, 80]. Consistent with all the accumulated evidence, it may be speculated that the additional X chromosome not only disorders physical dimorphic specificity, but also in some way interferes in utero with appropriate neural organization of sexual behavior.

XYY Syndrome
This little-understood syndrome is not yet incontrovertibly linked with predictable behavior deviations. There is provisional evidence that such males may tend to impulsivity and lack of appropriate regulation of behavior in regard not only to aggression and violence, but also to sex characteristics somewhat reminiscent of the XY supermale killfish [68].

Other Hormonal Psychosexual-Differentiating Factors
Two additional hormonally differentiated attributes are of interest. One is the finding that postpubertal women have a greater sensitivity to odors than do men. This has been demonstrated to be due to the presence of estrogen; it is lost with estrogen deprivation or androgen administration and regained with replacement of estrogen [91].

The other is that it now appears to be thoroughly documented that androgen is the hormone that regulates the intensity of sexual drive in both men and women. The evidence derives from many sources, some of which are reviewed by Money [62, 65]. Libido increases in both sexes due to exogenous androgen administration and congenital adrenal hyperplasia; there is a lessening of libido in androgen-deprived women but no lessening if only estrogens are lacking. The use of androgen-depleting substances (cyproterone acetate, methyloestrenolone, and medroxyprogesterone) has been proved to decrease sex drive in male sex criminal [69]. An intriguing new concept that has recently been advanced [14] suggests further that the erotic and affectional components of sexual relations in women (men have not yet been studied) may be separately mediated, based upon differential loss of erotic or affectionate feelings, depending upon whether androgens or estrogens, respectively, are eliminated.

We must return to the consideration of female pseudohermaphrodites of the adrenal hyperplasia type to describe the most important principle of psychosexual differentiation evidenced by the studies of the various human disorders. Because of the range of genital masculinization possible, many such genotypic females were misidentified at birth as boys and were reared as boys. Many studies and review articles [18, 31, 32, 61, 65, 76] have demonstrated convincingly that gender of assignment at birth and gender of rearing override all other determinants of sexual dimorphism and determine with virtual immutability the core gender identity and gender of orientation of the individual. There have been many instances of children with identical genotypes, hormones, gonads, and internal accessory structures, some of whom were reared as boys and others as girls. In almost every instance the child came to regard himself or herself as male or female according to the way he or she was reared and remained that way permanently, even in the face of contradictory pubertal changes. Most dramatic are those instances in which even the external genitalia are more like or even typical of that of the sex opposite to the one the child was assigned and in which he was reared. Even in these instances, gender identity is and remains a consequence of assignment and rearing. It is thus clear that gender of assignment and of rearing predictably overrides all contradictory determinants such as chromosomes, hormones, gonads, internal and external sexual morphology, and secondary pubertal changes.

Other types of hermaphrodites demonstrate this same principle, though often not as dramatically. The genotypic male with androgen insensitivity is uncompromisingly feminine, although in this instance external morphology does not contradict gender identity. The same dominance of gender of assignment and rearing is demonstrated in microphallic boys misassigned as girls.

An ancillary finding of major importance in these studies is the early age at which gender of assignment and rearing exercise an indelible effect. The studies indicate that the critical period for formation of core gender identity may be between 12 and 18 months and that after about 2 to 2 ½ years of age, shift of core gender identity is almost impossible to accomplish, even when *all* sexual determinants are those of the other sex. Thus far in the literature there are relatively few reported cases of successful shift after that age; there are, on the other hand, numerous reports of psychological havoc and tragedy brought about by efforts to effect or enforce such a shift after the critical period.

It would almost appear that this principle of the transcendence of gender of assignment and rearing negates the significance of all the studies discussed — all the carefully assembled evidence for the existence of male and female brain structures. But although the exceptions may be few, there are enough to be worth noting. Some exceptions are to be expected. When a newborn has anomalous genitalia, the parents are at times quite uncertain of gender, and they express that uncertainty in confused gender-rearing practices. When parents are given conflicting diagnoses of their infant's sex by different physicians at different times, the same confusion in rearing may result. This is unfortunate for the child since he or she is never really sure of his or her sex; they form no genuine core gender identity, and they usually suffer severe emotional disturbances as a consequence.

But more interesting are the few in whom consistent gender of assignment and rearing does *not* determine core gender identity. One study [32] reports five individuals whose gender orientation was ambiguous or deviant from that of rearing. Another study [1] reported six persons whose sex appeared unambiguous at birth and who were unambiguously reared, but who from earliest childhood had believed they were of the opposite sex and at puberty developed into the opposite sex. Of the six, one was genotypically opposite to external appearance, three were persons with Klinefelter's syndrome who were reared as girls, one had testicular atrophy of unknown etiology, and one had abnormal amounts of follicle-stimulating hormone and pregnanediol despite the presence of male gonads. Stoller [99] describes another exception. Zuger [110] has researched the literature and collected a considerable number of cases in which he considers core gender identity to be dissonant with gender of assignment and rearing. The most complete compilation of exceptions to the principle of the primacy of gender of assignment and rearing, and the most carefully documented and reasoned opposing view, is that of Diamond [13].

It is helpful to summarize additional conclusions relating to psycho-sexual differentiation that have emerged from the study of disorders of human differentiation. The most important one is that of the prime importance of gender of assignment and rearing — its transcendence over all other determinants. The second major conclusion is that, in humans as well as in lower animals, there is fetal organization of neural structures (essentially, the hypothalamus) into essentially male or female brain structures that not only mediate different hormonal and reproductive functions, but also predictably affect behavior. From this principle, the Psychohormonal Research Unit at Johns Hopkins has evolved a number of criteria that reliably (by statistical analysis) distinguish normal boys and men from girls and women, in this culture at least [32, 65, 66]:

1. *Energy-expenditure level* (higher in boys).
2. *Play, toy, and sports preference.* Boys initiate more play, indulge in and withdraw less from body-contact and rough play, prefer guns and quasi-aggressive play, and prefer competitive sports. Girls generally have opposite preferences and enjoy doll and "house" play.
3. *Clothing preference.* Boys prefer shirts, trousers, or jeans and have little interest in jewelry or cosmetics. Girls prefer dresses and frilly things, are interested in jewelry and cosmetics, and are concerned with hairdos.
4. *Maternalism.* Girls are interested in dolls and doll play and are fascinated by infants and infant care. Boys are usually not.
5. *Career ambition.* Girls predictably rate interest in marriage and family above career, while boys show the opposite preference.
6. *Body image.* Each sex conceptualizes itself, for example, in drawings, consonant with gender orientation.
7. *Perceptual erotic arousal patterns.* Males experience genitopelvic arousal from visual and narrative erotic stimuli. Females usually require tactile stimuli for genitopelvic arousal.

Lest it immediately be protested that many of these criteria may be cultural artifacts, it is admitted that some may be. Indeed, there is recent evidence for greater genitopelvic arousal in women by visual stimuli than had been thought [96]. However, the evidence has demonstrated a consistency in the shift toward the cross-sex preferential pattern even in persons unambiguously reared in one sex but fetally influenced by the cross-sex neural organizing mechanisms. If all the listed preferences were totally cultural, one must expect that such persons would accept the culturally prescribed attitudes of their sex of assignment and rearing in the same statistical ratios as for normal persons. There is interesting corroboration for regarding maternalism, for example, as being more than culturally determined in a comparison of completely feminized male transsexuals with a group of persons with the complete syndrome of testicular feminization [74]. In the latter, the neural organization in the fetal critical period is female; in the transsexuals, all had had normal fetal testes and fetal androgen, and all had a soma that could and did respond to prenatal and postnatal androgens. Those with androgen insensitivity (who had female brains) showed typical interest in infants and infant care. The transsexuals (who had male brains), though identified in every other way with what they perceived as feminine traits, lacked the interest in infants and infant care; they definitely preferred and were more comfortable with toddlers and children.

EPIDEMIOLOGICAL STUDIES

It is a well-known fact that there is a higher mortality among males than among females; this is true for all ages of life [64]. It is probably less well known how nearly total is this increased male vulnerability to disorder and death or the manifold ways in which it expresses itself. The phenomenon is by no means limited to humans. Ciocco [7] reviews the literature showing consistent findings in other species. The higher male mortality ratio is much more striking when the stillborn ratio is considered. Prior to accurate sex determination by the presence or absence of the sex-chromatin body, fetal mortality was variously estimated as 57.1 percent male [7] to 120:100 male over female [2]; it was generally considered that the ratio of male-to-female fetal mortality was higher in those abortions occurring early in gestation. Recently, better methods of determining the sex of the abortus suggest much higher ratios of male concepti: 122:100 in one study [100] and 160:100 in another [102]. The most widely accepted figure currently for birth ratios is 106 males to 100 females. By teleological reasoning, one might suspect that nature is trying to offset the consistently greater loss of males.

The mortality for males is also higher in infancy and early childhood. Bakwin's early study [2] indicated that there were from 130 to 134 deaths in white males compared to 100 in females in the United States birth-registration area from 1915 to 1924. During this time, infant mortality was declining, and the ratio of male-to-female deaths increased as the overall mortality fell. The ratio was highest neonatally, and decreased with age through early childhood. Of all diseases recorded, female infants had higher death rates only for pertussis and erysipelas. Ciocco [7] found disorders of the endocrine system to be the only postnatal conditions (in all ages) in which female mortality predominated.

With the burgeoning of scientific knowledge in genetics, more recent studies have sought the reasons for such disparity. In a massive tabulation of literature and hospital admissions focusing on bacterial septicemia and bacterial meningitis in infancy [103], it was found that males were more susceptible to infections, considerably more likely to die of them, and that the disparity was even greater for infections caused by gram-negative organisms. After the advent of antibiotics, mortality greatly decreased, but the mortality ratio of males to females was still much higher, suggesting that antibiotics help most those who are least vulnerable (echoing Bakwin's findings). Childs [6] reviews the literature and current knowledge and elucidates what is known about the genetic etiology of this and other increased male susceptibilities. Even though certain mechanisms (such as dosage compensation) tend in part to reduce the female's great quantitative chromosomal superiority by largely inactivating the second X chromosome (it becomes the Barr body), the female still has a chromosomal mass that is 4 to 5 percent greater than the male's, since a Y is essentially one-half the size of an X. One type of advantage conferred is by virtue of the probable existence on the X chromosome of one or more genes having a role in the formation of immunoglobulins. This may express itself as a greater or faster female postnatal antibody response and adaptation (there is no susceptibility disparity in utero or immediately after birth, while there are circulating maternal antibodies), and the critical sex difference may be in the formation of the specific antibodies against gram-negative organisms (γ_1-globulins).

A second major female advantage is the capacity for heterozygosity, with all the known survival benefits inherent in that condition; random inactivation of one or the other X chromosome from cell to cell still allows metabolic differences traceable to heterozygosity. Isoalleles may mask or reduce the effect of a deleterious mutant of the same allele when paired with it — an impossibility for the homozygous male. The known X-linked diseases are vitamin D-resistant rickets, nephrogenic diabetes insipidus, a number of drug-induced anemias, immunoglobulin deficiency, clotting disorders, and hypoparathyroid deficiency. Females may escape such conditions or have them in mild forms because of the protective isoallele, whereas in males they exist exclusively or in full-blown form; when protection is a matter of degree and can be measured (as it is in nephrogenic diabetes insipidus), the female's double dose of the normal gene provides twice the measure of protection of that found in the male. This genetic disparity leaves females more prone to one kind of disorder; the autoimmune diseases (such as lupus erythematosis and rheumatoid arthritis) are possibly related to a double dose of the allele mediating the structure or formation rate of immunoglobulins. The problems inherent in female cyclic hormone production, to be discussed later, may predispose females to a second class of disorders.

Male vulnerability is not limited to physical disorders. There is a known higher incidence of paraphilias among males. The investigations of the Institute for Sex Research have reviewed the sex-linked incidences of many of these disorders of psychosexual development [48, 49]. While statistical data on illegal and taboo activities are prone to inaccuracy, few clinicians or behavioral scientists would deny that homosexuality is more prevalent among men than among women. The disparity is even higher in the bizarre paraphilias, such as fetishism, sadism, masochism, and bestiality, and there are paraphilias that are to be found only in males, (necrophilia, for example). On the simple level of normal sexual function, females are capable of more frequent orgasmic response [59]. Further, a female may submit to coitus with minimal participation and in the face of multifarious sexual fears and conflicts and yet conceive and fulfill her reproductive function, whereas a male can perform his reproductive function only under complex and emotionally supportive conditions in which it is possible for him to attain an erection, maintain it adequately for intromission, and ejaculate; the inhibitors to male sexual functioning are legion.

Studies are also being made of sex-specific behavioral differences in newborns, before the likely intervention of rearing influences. One such investigation [98] indicates that the amount of activity displayed by male infants depends upon the amount and nature of maternal handling, whereas in females activity develops independently — yet another example of the greater contingency of normal male development. Another study has found that newborn males raise their heads higher than do newborn females [28], which is perhaps a correlate of the observed increased energy expenditure in males.

All of the observations and disparities previously discussed have a familiar ring. Throughout the animal studies reviewed previously in this chapter runs the theme of the greater difficulty in differentiating the male organism and male sexual behavior, the greater difficulty in achieving masculine behavior, and the greater ease with which maleness may be interfered with, distorted, or abolished. It has also been shown that males are considerably more prone to physical disease and that both the physical and psychosexual disadvantages of maleness apply inescapably to mankind. Thus, from the data can be evolved one more principle of sexual differentiation: the human male is more vulnerable to physical and psychosexual disorders of development than is the human female.

ADULT HORMONAL STUDIES

Earlier in this chapter some of the apparent effects of hormones and their disturbances on the early genesis of masculine-feminine distinctions were discussed. The normal cyclic-acyclic sex differences in adult life may also have some bearing upon emotional function and behavior.

Dalton has documented the remarkable concentration of female dysfunction during the premenstruum-menstruum phase of the menstrual cycle. She estimates that this phase cumulatively constitutes approximately 25 percent of a woman's life during her reproductive years. Yet during this 25 percent of each month occur 49 percent of all crimes committed by female prisoners [9], 45 percent of punishments meted out to school girls [8], 53 percent of suicides [10], and 46 percent of admissions to mental hospitals [10]. The rate at which female students pass advanced examinations is 13 percent lower during this phase [12]. According to a study by the British Road Research Laboratory, 60 percent of women's traffic accidents occur during this 25 percent of their lives that constitutes the premenstruum-menstruum phase [101].

The psychophysiological reasons for this clustering of female dysfunctions are not clear. Shainess [94] found that in a group of 103 women, significant premenstrual distress and behavioral disorders were suffered only by those women who had demonstrable conflict with their mothers and who had not been well prepared for menarche by their mothers. These emotional factors impaired their ability to welcome and value their womanhood. They were thus conditioned to respond with fear and depression to menstruation. This was an important study, and it would be useful both to see the study replicated and to see the results of similar studies in other cultures.

The complex and subtle endocrine correlates of the so-called premenstrual syndrome are far from clearly understood and are currently the subject of rather intense research. There is considerable evidence that the sudden decrease in circulating progesterone, which commonly occurs 24 to 48 hours before the menses begin, may trigger the distressing symptoms [29]. This explanation would fit appropriately with the physiology of the postpartum period, a time when women experience their most sudden and massive decrease in circulating progesterone and when they are similarly prone to severe emotional disorder.

The emotional effects of progesterone, however, are confusing and contradictory. In some studies, the premenstrual distress becomes significant at the height of the luteal, or progesterone-producing, phase [41], and other studies have linked depression and loss of libido with the use of oral progesterones [26]. On the other hand, progesterone is often used successfully to treat premenstrual tension and postpartum disturbance [10]. The preponderance of evidence would seem to indicate that progesterone has a calming and antidepressant effect [27], perhaps through its antagonizing actions on such active adrenocortical hormones as aldosterone [42]. However, this reasoning leaves the depressant effect of progestinic oral contraceptives unexplained. Janowsky et al. [43] have recently reviewed much of the related research, citing data that suggest that ovarian hormone psychopathology, like affective disorders in general, may be associated with alterations in brain monoamines.

These data leave many questions unanswered. Does every woman who displays premenstrual emotional lability have a history of emotional trauma connected with menarche? While such a proposition appears exaggerated, it is nonetheless true that the physiological correlates do not account for the many women who usually have no premenstrual emotional disturbance. Perhaps there are genetically determined variations in ovarian hormone metabolism that help account for individual differences in response. Such physiological mechanisms and variations, however, can function in any woman only in concert with her emotional and developmental states. But regardless of emotional factors, the physiological mechanisms are probably normal phenomena that, through interactions not yet understood, can disrupt the emotional balance of women who, for whatever reason, are susceptible. When these physiological changes occur, they are specifically and innately female disturbances and are reflected in feminine social behavior. Even if Shainess's findings [94], linking premenstrual disturbance with premenarchial trauma, were to have pan-human validity, the female cyclic hormonal pattern poses developmental and coping tasks unique to females. As we have seen, this is one of the remarkably few physiological disadvantages that are exclusively female.

PSYCHOLOGICAL CONSEQUENCES OF BIOLOGICAL DIFFERENCES

Since this chapter focuses specifically on research in physiology, psychological correlates will be mentioned only briefly. (For a fuller discussion, see Gadpaille [23] and Rossi [88].) One must have some cognizance of those emotional and psychological aspects of male-female dimorphic development that have their origin in biological differences. The most obvious aspect, of course, is that the two sexes grow up with bodies displaying clearly different genital anatomy. This is the basis for the controversial theories of castration anxiety and penis envy. Classic psychoanalytic theory built an insupportable theory of female inferiority on the existence of genital differences, but it was quite accurate in directing attention to the early importance of those differences. Children obviously note the presence or absence of a penis, and they draw conclusions about how the difference occurred. Some of their conclusions can be frightening to either sex and can result in concepts of superiority and inferiority. Moulton [81] recently has extensively reviewed the issue of penis envy, with the objective of restoring it to its rational position in psychodynamic thought. It should be mentioned that, granted the child's view that possessing anything (here, the penis) is predictably preferable to not possessing it, the subsequent anxiety over its possible loss may constitute as great a psychological hazard for boys as penis envy does for girls.

Still more far-reaching consequences of basic physiology are those proceeding from the fact that all humans have female mothers. This is an emotionally loaded truism which, to my knowledge, has received only occasional attention for its obvious relevance to male domination and derogation of women [23, 109]. A girl can achieve healthy sexual identity by identifying with her earliest love object, her mother. A boy must separate himself from mother in much different ways, yet there is always the dual emotional tug of the pleasure of infantile dependency and of the Oedipal attraction, which tend to tie him to that first love. In the need for a separate male identity, males must defend themselves against mother, and *mother* and *women* often become unconsciously synonymous. One of the most primitive and inappropriate but ubiquitous defenses mankind has toward those things by which he is tempted yet believes he must resist, is to devalue that object so as to eliminate the temptation. This may be a major but deeply unconscious reason for failure of males to appreciate and reward females for what they are, and for the male propensity to derogate and patronize them.

The natural selection process in the evolution of *Homo sapiens* cannot fail to have exercised an important role in determining some characteristics of masculinity (such as aggressiveness) and femininity (such as maternalism) that have survival value and in erasing from the species some of those that compromise survival. While examination of evolutionary factors is beyond the scope of the present review, attention is called to Gadpaille [23], LaBarre [52], and Zilboorg [109] for more detailed discussion. Sherfey [95] has also drawn broad, through controversial, theoretical speculations from the evolutionary and physiological aspects of male-female dimorphism.

SUMMARY

To recapitulate, certain physiological and behavioral principles in the development of male-female sexual dimorphism have been evolved from the research discussed:

1. The role of the hypothalamus is specific and determinative in the mediation and regulation of male or female sexual physiology and behavior.
2. There are quite limited critical periods for effecting or modifying physiological and psychosexual development.
3. It is nature's basic predilection to produce a female unless something (androgen) is added during the critical period.
4. There are distinctly different male and female brain structures, organized during critical periods in fetal life by the presence or absence of androgens, for producing and releasing male or female physiological function and masculine or feminine sexual behavior.

5. Learning is of increasing importance to sexual behavior as the phylogenetic scale is ascended. A related phenomenon is the greater significance of peer-group juvenile sex play as compared with mothering in the achievement of effective adult sexual function.
6. The gender of assignment and rearing generally transcends other determinants of sexuality in humans.
7. Criteria are emerging that differentiate significant aspects of masculine and feminine attitudes and behavior and that appear to have some valid independence from cultural influences.
8. The male is more vulnerable than the female in almost every way, with the exceptions of physical prowess and the stresses attendant on female cyclic hormone release. There is greater difficulty in achieving maleness and masculinity, including the problems of separation from the mother, coupled with an increased vulnerability of males to disruption of sexual function and to physical and psychosexual disorders.
9. The cyclic hormones of the female and their effects on the central nervous system constitute an aspect of female physiology that poses a unique extra task in the smooth emotional functioning of human females.
10. There is a positive correlation between abnormally increased fetal androgen and high IQ.

Some important considerations for psychodynamics may be derived from these principles. The overriding importance of rearing — the child's early experiences with its parents — is certainly unchallenged and is even validated. The evidence from the outcome of gender misassignment of human pseudohermaphrodites is definitive. However, parental influence is not the sole determinant; it operates in conjunction with genetic-hormonal-constitutional factors that may, under as yet undefined conditions, potentially influence the ease or difficulty with which normal psychosexual differentiation and development take place. These various factors may contribute differentially to orderly or disordered masculine-feminine differentiation, depending upon the relative strengths of their effects and on the correlation of their effects with the various critical periods of influence on psychosexuality.

The existence of male and female — indeed, masculine and feminine — brain structures seems increasingly well established. The various disorders interfering with normal hormonal organizing effects upon hypothalamic and possibly other neural structures have been demonstrated to produce postnatal effects on sexually differentiating behavior that persist into adulthood. That the influence comes during fetal life is attested to by the fact that the same effects exist even in those patients diagnosed and treated from birth and reared without sexual confusion. That the influences are not completely negated by culturally determined attitudes is indicated by the finding that persons with fetally disordered neural organization exhibit evidences of cross-sex attitudes and behavior even when reared unambiguously under the influence of the cultural expectations and stereotypes appropriate to his or her sex.

To elaborate further on this point, it seems likely that there are definable differences in masculine and feminine behavior, attitudes and preferences that are traceable to the simple biological fact of being male or female (assuming biologically normal development) and that all such differences are not purely cultural artifacts. Such differences concern energy level and expenditure, maternalism, aggressiveness, patterns of erotic arousal and other patterns of behavior preference, body image, and social self-presentation. There is no doubt that these are fragile distinctions, easily distorted or even reversed under adverse rearing and environmental conditions; but they demonstrably exist under undisturbed conditions. It is surely more than coincidental that in the research of Kaye et al. on female homosexuals [47], conducted in an entirely different frame of reference, they found virtually the same behavioral and attitudinal characteristics in prehomosexual girls as those found in fetally masculinized girl. Indeed, much of the identical research reported here has significant implications with respect to the etiology and psychodynamics of homosexuality, which is the focus of the original article from which this chapter was adapted [22].

Both parallel with, and as a consequence of, the different male and female brains are massive biological differences between the sexes, almost all of which operate to the detriment of the male. Not only are males physiologically weaker in terms of disease susceptibility and survival despite their greater size and muscular strength, but also their reproductive function and psychosexual development are much more easily tipped off-balance than are those of females. Males can develop only if there is the proper amount of androgen at the proper critical period of fetal life and if their somata are capable of responding to the androgen.

Learning (and, hence, mislearning) plays a definitive role in males' sexual function and behavior, whereas women can function (albeit without optimal participation) despite total ignorance of sexual behavior. Male sexual stamina is but a fraction of the female's. The male's capacity to perform sexually under adverse psychological or environmental conditions is grossly limited. While psychogenic infertility in females is well documented [21] and inhibitions of pleasurable participation in sexual intercourse are common, the number of pregnancies occurring during rape and unconsciousness and despite massive sexual anxieties is testimony that the woman's procreative function, at least, is far less fragile than is the man's. The greater incidence of homosexuality — indeed, of all paraphilias — among men than among women, and the existence of paraphilias peculiar to men, though there are none peculiar to women, is a cogent argument for male vulnerability to psychosexual mislearning and disorder.

The relationship of androgen to IQ is a curious one. There is no statistically significant sex difference in IQ in the overall normal population, but the association of high IQ with abnormally high level of fetal androgens is clear. There are, however, sex-specific differences in subtest scores among normals. Women score higher in verbal subtests, whereas men score higher in mathematical and space-form perception subtests. Those distinctions may have had survival value in the evolution of *Homo sapiens,* but it is difficult to comprehend the significance for normals of a finding that is as yet demonstrable only in pathological conditions.

All this produces substantial contributions to the understanding of the etiology and psychodynamics of masculine-feminine differences:

1. There are, indeed, innate biological differences between males and females that help determine their mental, emotional, and behavioral characteristics and contribute to predictable expressions of femininity and masculinity. The growing understanding of the normal sequence leading to biologically appropriate sexually dimorphic identification and behavior, makes an ever more lucid case for the naturalness of such behavioral distinctions in the absence of one or another kind of interference.

2. Despite the differentiating roles played by genetic code and the neural organizing functions of fetal hormones, the etiological effect of early childrearing is reaffirmed as the major influence determining sexual identity and the adaptation or maladaptation to innate sex roles.

3. The subtlety of fetal hormonal effects and the particular vulnerability of masculine psychosexual differentiation and of maleness in general suggest that one should not insist upon finding a history of radical disturbances in the child-parent relationship of every person with confused sex-role identities in order to credit the critical importance of early rearing experiences. The analyst — indeed, all students of human sexuality — must recognize how subtle the conflict may be, how very little conflict it may require to disturb psychosexual development (especially in the male), and must be alert, both therapeutically and prophylactically, to the almost subclinical quality of the pathogenic influences that may produce conflicted sexual identities. It is clinically naive to depend on the conscious memory of such persons to "prove" or "disprove" the role of early interactions with parental figures in the etiology of their maladaptation.

4. One must at least consider the possibility that undetectable embryonic disorders may produce conditions that make it easier for an individual to develop cross-sex attitudes and behavior (or, conversely, may make it more difficult for an individual to develop sex-appropriate attitudes and behavior).

5. Biological research offers some new support for the psychoanalytic theory of bisexuality, through the evidence that the embryonic bisexual potential is not solely anatomical but may become functional as well under various conditions of disordered development. At the same time, the evidence exposes a significant deficiency in the psychoanalytic theory of psychosexual development in that the theory does not embody the concept of continuing psychosexual differentiation [66].

6. The central importance of maternal (or, generally, parental) influence must be reconsidered, and greater significance must be accorded to peer relationships in childhood, particularly childhood sex play. It cannot be denied, of course, that the opportunity for childhood sex play and children's attitudes toward their own sexuality depend heavily on mother and father and on the cultural attitudes that filter down through the parents. This has important implications in regard to childrearing, sex education, and child therapy.

7. The worldwide expression of male domination over the "weaker" female and "male chauvinism" may be only partially related to hormone-determined superior male strength and aggressiveness [24] and the female need for protection and sustenance due to childbearing and nurturance. These facts may only have made male domination possible, and the

true origins may be subtler, but shared, unconscious determinants. Male domination may partly be a defense against the all-powerful mother, a need to repudiate universal dependency wishes and Oedipal strivings. And it may express a denial of the omnipresent evidence that the man is more fragile and vulnerable, both physically and psychosexually, than the woman. Such a differential in psychosexual stability may help explain the fact that studies of group sex and wife-swapping [4, 84] have found not only that women participate more readily and with less apparent conflict but also that when such behavior is condoned, they enter much more freely and frequently into homosexual activities, with little apparent damage either to their heterosexual identities or function.

8. Accumulating knowledge about the biological origins of masculine-feminine differences carries the obligation that the knowledge be used to try to eliminate irrational inequities. But change is appropriate only in some, not all, expressions and consequences of these differences. Clearly none of the innate differences operate in the aggregate to the detriment of women in comparison with men. They cannot be used as weapons against women.

But one cannot repudiate the whole gamut of innate masculine-feminine traits without a different kind of potential danger to the species. To enforce shifts in sexual identity and characteristics that run contrary to those that both biology and evolution have bred into the species risks disintegration of the individual, disorientation of task performance, and maladaptive influences on children. And regardless of destructive potential in some instances, innate characteristics cannot be "learned out" of the species. Lamarkian inheritance of acquired characteristics is a wishful fantasy. Short of eugenics and genetic engineering, the evolution of a new set of masculine-feminine attributes will require countless generations. Realities, including sex-linked qualities, must be recognized, not denied, before they can be dealt with.

And men will have to learn means other than devaluing women to achieve and maintain a separate masculine identity. Male mothering does not seem, in this author's opinion, to be the remedy; the potential hazards to healthy sex identity are ominous. Maternalism is instinctual to females, not only in this species but in mammals generally. Children need exposure to the mutual complementarity of the uniquely masculine and feminine qualities of both parents, both sexes.

Masculinity and femininity are not created in a vacuum by capricious environmental and cultural influences. Constructive changes are unlikely if innate differences are denied. The interaction of the sexes can be usefully understood only if one accepts the inevitabilities inherent in the fact that the two sexes, from conception to death, grow up in different bodies.

REFERENCES

1. Baker, H. J., and Stoller, R. J. Can a biological force contribute to gender identity? *American Journal of Psychiatry* 124:75, 1968.
2. Bakwin, H. The sex factor in infant mortality. *Human Biology* 1:90, 1929.
3. Barraclough, C., and Gorski, R. Studies on mating behavior in the androgen-sterilized female rat in relation to the hypothalamic regulation of sexual behavior. *Journal of Endocrinology* 25:175, 1962.
4. Bartell, G. Group sex among the mid-Americans. *Journal of Sex Research* 6(2):113, 1970.
5. Beach, F. Sexual behavior in mammals. *Physiological Reviews* 27:240, 1947.
6. Childs, B. Genetic origin of some sex differences among human beings. *Pediatrics* 35:798, 1965.
7. Ciocco, A. Sex differences in morbidity and mortality. *Quarterly Review of Biology* 15:59, 1940.
8. Dalton, K. Schoolgirls' behavior and menstruation. *British Medical Journal* 2:1647, 1960.
9. Dalton, K. Menstruation and crime. *British Medical Journal* 2:1752, 1961.
10. Dalton, K. *The Premenstrual Syndrome.* Springfield, Ill.: Thomas, 1964.
11. Dalton, K. Ante-natal progesterone and intelligence. *British Journal of Psychiatry* 114:1377, 1968.
12. Dalton, K. Menstruation and examinations. *Lancet* 2:1386, 1968.
13. Diamond, M. A critical evaluation of the ontogeny of human sexual behavior. *The Quarterly Review of Biology* 40(2):147, 1965.
14. Drellich, M., and Waxenberg, S. Erotic and Affectional Components of Female Sexuality. In J. Masserman (Ed.), *Sexuality of Women.* Science and Psychoanalysis, Vol. X. New York: Grune & Stratton, 1966.
15. Ehrhardt, A., Epstein, R., and Money, J. Fetal androgens and female gender identity in the early-treated adrenogenital syndrome. *Johns Hopkins Medical Journal* 122:160, 1968.
16. Ehrhardt, A., Evers, K., and Money, J. Influence of androgen and some aspects of sexually dimorphic behavior in women with the late-treated adrenogenital syndrome. *Johns Hopkins Medical Journal* 123:115, 1968.
17. Ehrhardt, A., Greenberg, N., and Money, J. Female gender identity and absence of fetal gonadal hormones: Turner's syndrome. *Johns Hopkins Medical Journal* 126:237, 1970.

18. Ehrhardt, A., and Money, J. Progestin-induced hermaphroditism: I.Q. and psychosexual identity in a study of ten girls. *Journal of Sex Research* 3(1):83, 1967.

19. Everett, J., Sawyer, C., and Markee, J. A neurogenic timing factor in control of the ovulatory discharge of luteinizing hormone in the cyclic rat. *Endocrinology* 44:234, 1949.

20. Fisher, A. Chemical and Electrical Stimulation of the Brain in the Male Rat. In R. Gorski and R. Whalen (Eds.), *The Brain and Gonadal Function*. Brain and Behavior, Vol. 3. Berkeley: University of California Press, 1966. P. 117.

21. Gadpaille, W. Amenorrhea and Infertility in the Hysterical Character. In *Collected Award Papers*. Port Chester, N.Y.: Gralnick Foundation, 1966. P. 131.

22. Gadpaille, W. Research into the physiology of maleness and femaleness. *Archives of General Psychiatry* 26:193, 1972.

23. Gadpaille, W. *The Cycles of Sex*. New York: Scribners, 1975.

24. Goldberg, S. *The Inevitability of Patriarchy*. New York: William Morrow, 1973.

25. Goy, R. Experimental control of psychosexuality. *Philosophical Transactions of the Royal Society of London; B: Biological Sciences* 259:149, 1970.

26. Grant, E., and Pryse-Davies, J. Effect of oral contraceptives on depressive mood changes and on endometrial monoamine oxidase and phosphatase. *British Medical Journal* 3:777, 1968.

27. Hamburg, D. Effects of progesterone on behavior. *Research Publications of the Association for Research in Nervous and Mental Disease* 43:251, 1966.

28. Hamburg, D., and Lunde, D. Sex Hormones in the Development of Sex Differences in Human Behavior. In E. MacCoby (Ed.), *The Development of Sex Differences*. Stanford, Calif.: Stanford University Press, 1966. P. 18.

29. Hamburg, D., et al. Studies of Distress in the Menstrual Cycle and the Postpartum Period. In R. Michael (Ed.), *Endocrinology and Human Behavior*. London: Oxford University Press, 1968. Pp. 94-116.

30. Hamilton, J., Walter, R., Daniel, R., and Mestler, G. Competition for mating between ordinary and supermale Japanese medaka fish. *Animal Behavior* 17:168, 1969.

31. Hampson, J. G. Hermaphroditic genital appearance, rearing and eroticism in hyperadrenocorticism. *Bulletin of the Johns Hopkins Hospital* 96:265, 1955.

32. Hampson, J. L., and Hampson, J. G. The Ontogenesis of Sexual Behavior in Man. In W. Young (Ed.), *Sex and Internal Secretions*. Baltimore: Williams & Wilkins, 1961. P. 1401.

33. Harlow, H., and Harlow, M. The heterosexual affectional system in monkeys. *American Psychologist* 17:1, 1962.

34. Harlow, H., and Harlow, M. Social deprivation in monkeys. *Scientific American* 207:136, 1962.

35. Harlow, H., and Harlow, M. The Effect of Rearing Conditions on Behavior. In J. Money (Ed.), *Sex Research: New Developments*. New York: Holt, Rinehart, Winston, 1965. P. 161.

36. Harris, G. The Development of Neuroendocrinology. In J. French (Ed.), *Frontiers in Brain Research*. New York: Columbia University Press, 1962. P. 191.

37. Harris, G. Abstracts of proceedings of the Singapore conference. *Journal of Reproductivity and Fertility* 5:299, 1963.

38. Harris, G. Sex hormones, brain development and brain function. *Endocrinology* 75:627, 1964.

39. Harris, G., and Levine, S. Sexual differentiation of brain and its experimental control. *Journal of Physiology* 163:42, 1962.

40. Hart, B. Neonatal castration: Influence on neural organization of sexual reflexes in male rats. *Science* 160:1135, 1968.

41. Janowsky, D., and Davis, J. Ovarian hormones, monoamines, and mental illness. *Scientific Proceedings in Summary Form*, Vol. 69. 123rd American Psychiatric Association Meeting, San Francisco, 1970.

42. Janowsky, D., et al. The menstrual cycle. *Archives of General Psychiatry* 17:459, 1967.

43. Janowsky, D., et al. Monoamines and ovarian hormone-linked sexual and emotional changes: A review. *Archives of Sexual Behavior* 1:205, 1971.

44. Jones, H., and Scott, W. *Hermaphroditism, Genital Anomalies and Related Endocrine Disorders* (2d ed.). Baltimore: Williams & Wilkins, 1971. P. 76.

45. Jones, H., and Scott, W. *Hermaphroditism, Genital Anomalies and Related Endocrine Disorders* (2d ed.). Baltimore: Williams & Wilkins, 1971. P. 197.

46. Jost, A. Problems of fetal endocrinology: The gonadal and hypophyseal hormones. *Recent Progress in Hormone Research* 8:379, 1953.

47. Kaye, H., et al. Homosexuality in women. *Archives of General Psychiatry* 17:629, 1967.

48. Kinsey, A., Pomeroy, W., and Martin, D. *Sexual Behavior in the Human Male*. Philadelphia: Saunders, 1948. Pp. 446-509, 642-689.

49. Kinsey, A., Pomeroy, W., and Martin, D. *Sexual Behavior in the Human Male*. Philadelphia: Saunders, 1948. P. 610.

50. Kinsey, A., Pomeroy, W., Martin, D., and Gebhard, P. *Sexual Behavior in the Human Female*. Philadelphia: Saunders, 1953. P. 642.

51. Kollar, E., Beckwith, W., and Edgerton, R. Sexual behavior of the ARL Colony chimpanzees. *Journal of Nervous and Mental Diseases* 147(5):444, 1968.

52. LaBarre, W. *The Human Animal*. Chicago: The University of Chicago Press, 1954.

53. Lewis, V., Ehrhardt, A., and Money, J. Genital operation in girls with the adrenogenital syndrome: Subsequent psychologic development. *Obstetrics and Gynecology* 36(1):11, 1970.

54. Lisk, R. Hormonal Implants in the Central Nervous System and Behavioral Receptivity in the Female Rat. In R. Gorski and R. Whalen (Eds.), *The Brain and Gonadal Function*. Brain and Behavior, Vol. 3. Berkeley: University of California Press, 1966. P. 98.

55. Lisk, R., and Suydam, A. Sexual behavior patterns in the prepubertally castrate rat. *Anatomical Record* 157:181, 1967.
56. MacLean, P. New Findings Relevant to the Evolution of Psychosexual Functions of the Brain. In J. Money (Ed.), *Sex Research: New Developments.* New York: Holt, Rinehart, Winston, 1965. P. 197.
57. MacLean, P. Studies on the Cerebral Representation of Certain Basic Sexual Functions. In R. Gorski and R. Whalen (Eds.), *The Brain and Gonadal Function.* Brain and Behavior, Vol. 3. Berkeley: University of California Press, 1966. P. 35.
58. Masica, D., Money, J., Ehrhardt, A., and Lewis, V. I.Q., Fetal sex hormones and cognitive patterns: Studies in the testicular feminizing syndrome of androgen insensitivity. *Johns Hopkins Medical Journal* 124:34, 1969.
59. Masters, W., and Johnson, V. *Human Sexual Response.* Boston: Little, Brown, 1966.
60. Michael, R. Action of Hormones on the Cat Brain. In R. Gorski and R. Whalen (Eds.), *The Brain and Gonadal Function.* Brain and Behavior, Vol. 3. Berkeley: University of California Press, 1966. P. 82.
61. Money, J. Hermaphroditism, gender and precocity in hyperadrenocorticism: Psychologic findings. *Bulletin of the Johns Hopkins Hospital* 96:253, 1955.
62. Money, J. Components of eroticism in man: I. The hormones in relation to sexual morphology and sexual desire. *Journal of Nervous and Mental Diseases* 132:239, 1961.
63. Money, J. Cytogenetics and psychosexual incongruities, with a note on space-form blindness. *American Journal of Psychiatry* 119:820, 1963.
64. Money, J. Developmental Differentiation of Femininity and Masculinity Compared. In S. Farber and R. Wilson (Eds.), *Man and Civilization: The Potential of Woman.* New York: McGraw-Hill, 1963.
65. Money, J. Influence of hormones on sexual behavior. *Annual Review of Medicine* 16:67, 1965.
66. Money, J. Progress of knowledge and revision of the theory of infantile sexuality. *International Journal of Psychiatry* 4:50, 1967.
67. Money, J. Influence of hormones on psychosexual differentiation. *Medical Aspects of Human Sexuality* 2(11):32, 1968.
68. Money, J. Behavior genetics: Principles, methods and examples from XO, XXY and XYY syndromes. *Seminars in Psychiatry* 2(1):11, 1970.
69. Money, J. Use of an androgen-depleting hormone in the treatment of male sex offenders. *Journal of Sex Research* 6(3):165, 1970.
70. Money, J. Clinical aspects of prenatal steroidal action on sexually dimorphic behavior. Unpublished.
71. Money, J. Sexually dimorphic behavior, fetal hormones and human hermaphroditic syndromes. Unpublished.
72. Money, J., and Alexander, D. Psychosexual development and absence of homosexuality in males with precocious puberty. *Journal of Nervous and Mental Diseases* 148:111, 1969.

73. Money, J., and Ehrhardt, A. Prenatal Hormonal Exposure: Possible Effects on Behavior in Man. In R. Michael (Ed.), *Endocrinology and Human Behavior.* London: Oxford University Press, 1968. P. 32.

74. Money, J., Ehrhardt, A., and Masica, D. Fetal feminization induced by androgen insensitivity in the testicular feminizing syndrome: Effect on Marriage and Maternalism. *Johns Hopkins Medical Journal* 123:105, 1968.

75. Money, J., Hampson, J., and Hampson, J. L. Sexual incongruities and psychopathology: The evidence of human hermaphroditism. *Bulletin of the Johns Hopkins Hospital* 98:43, 1956.

76. Money, J., Hampson, J., and Hampson, J. L. Imprinting and the establishment of gender role. *A.M.A. Archives of Neurology and Psychiatry* 77:333, 1957.

77. Money, J., and Lewis, V. I.Q., genetics and accelerated growth: Adrenogenital syndrome. *Bulletin of the Johns Hopkins Hospital* 118:365, 1966.

78. Money, J., and Meridith, T. Elevated verbal I.Q. and idiopathic precocious sexual maturation. *Pediatric Research* 1:59, 1967.

79. Money, J., and Mittenthal, S. Lack of personality pathology in Turner's Syndrome: Relation to cytogenetics, hormones and physique. *Behavior Genetics* 1:43, 1970.

80. Money, J., and Pollitt, E. Cytogenetic and psychosexual ambiguity. *Archives of General Psychiatry* 11:589, 1964.

81. Moulton, R. A survey and re-evaluation of penis envy. *Contemporary Psychoanalysis* 7:84, 1970.

82. Neumann, F., and Elger, W. Proof of the Activity of Androgenic Agents on the Differentiation of the External Genitalia, the Mammary Gland and the Hypothalamic-Pituitary System of Rats. In A. Vermeulen and D. Exley (Eds.), *Androgens in Normal and Pathological Conditions.* Excerpta Medica International Congress Series No. 101. New York: Excerpta Medical Foundation, 1965.

83. Neumann, F., and Elger, W. Permanent changes in gonadal function and sexual behavior as a result of early feminization of male rats by treatment with an antiandrogenic steroid. *Endokrinologie* 50:209, 1966.

84. O'Neill, G. C., and O'Neill, N. Patterns in group sexual activity. *Journal of Sex Research* 6(2):101, 1970.

85. Pfaff, D. Cerebral Implantation and Autoradiographic Studies of Sex Hormones. In J. Money (Ed.), *Sex Research: New Developments.* New York: Holt, Rinehart, Winston, 1965. P. 219.

86. Phoenix, C., Goy, R., Gerall, A., and Young, W. Organizing action of prenatally administered testosterone propionate on the tissues mediating mating behavior in the female guinea pig. *Endocrinology* 65:369, 1959.

87. Rogers, C., and Davenport, R. Effects of restricted rearing on sexual behavior of chimpanzees. *Developmental Psychology* 1(3):200, 1969.

88. Rossi, A. Maternalism, Sexuality and the New Feminism. In J. Zubin and J. Money (Eds.), *Contemporary Sexual Behavior: Critical Issues in the 1970's.* Baltimore: Johns Hopkins University Press, 1973. P. 145.

89. Sawyer, C. Reproductive Behavior. In J. Field, H. Magoun, and V. Hall (Eds.),

Handbook of Physiology: Neurophysiology II. Washington, D.C.: American
Physiological Society, 1960. P. 1225.

90. Sawyer, C., and Robison, B. Separate hypothalamic areas controlling pituitary
gonadotropin function and mating behavior in female cats and rabbits. Journal
of Clinical Endocrinology 16:914, 1956.

91. Schneider, R., Costiloe, J., Howard, R., and Wolf, S. Olfactory perception
thresholds in hypogonadal women: Changes accompanying administration of
androgen and estrogen. Journal of Clinical Endocrinology and Metabolism
18:379, 1958.

92. Segal, S., and Johnson, D. Inductive influence of steroid hormones on the neural
system: Ovulation controlling mechanisms. Archives d'Anatomie Microscopique
et de Morphologie Experimentale 48:261, 1959.

93. Shaffer, J. Masculinity-Femininity and Other Personality Traits in Gonadal
Aplasia (Turner's Syndrome). In H. Beigel (Ed.), Advances in Sex Research.
New York: Harper & Row, 1963. P. 219.

94. Shainess, N. Psychiatric evaluation of premenstrual tension. New York State
Journal of Medicine 62:3573, 1962.

95. Sherfey, M. The evolution and nature of female sexuality in relation to psychoanalytic theory. Journal of the American Psychoanalytic Association 14:28,
1966.

96. Sigusch, V., Schmidt, G., Reinfeld, A., and Wiedemann-Sutor, I. Psychosexual
stimulation: Sex differences. Journal of Sex Research 6(1):10, 1970.

97. Sobel, E. (in discussion of L. I. Gardner). Biochemical Events at Adolescence.
In L. Meiks and M. Green (Eds.), Pediatric Clinics of North America: Symposium
on Adolescence. Philadelphia: Saunders, 1960. P. 24.

98. Stoller, R. Sex and Gender. New York: Science House, 1968. P. 13.

99. Stoller, R. Sex and Gender. New York: Science House, 1968. P. 65.

100. Szontagh, F., Jakobovits, A., and Mehes, C. Primary embryonal ratio in normal
pregnancies determined by sex chromatin. Nature 192:476, 1961.

101. Tiger, L. Male dominance? Yes. A sexist plot? No. New York Times Magazine, Oct. 25, 1970, p. 35.

102. Tricomi, V., Serr, D., and Solish, G. The ratio of male to female embryos as
determined by sex chromatin. American Journal of Obstetrics and Gynecology
79:504, 1960.

103. Washburn, T., Medearis, D., Jr., and Childs, B. Sex differences in susceptibility
to infections. Pediatrics 35:57, 1965.

104. Whalen, R. Differentiation of the Neural Mechanisms Which Control Gonadotropin Secretion and Sexual Behavior. In M. Diamond (Ed.), Perspectives in
Reproduction and Sexual Behavior. Bloomington: Indiana University Press,
1968. P. 305.

105. Wilkins, L., Jones, H., Jr., Holman, G., and Stempfel, R., Jr. Masculinization of
the female fetus associated with administration of oral and intramuscular
progestins during gestation: Non-adrenal female pseudohermaphroditism.

Journal of Clinical Endocrinology and Metabolism 18:559, 1958.
106. Wilkins, L., Lewis, R., Klein, R., and Rosenberg, E. The suppression of androgen secretion by cortisone in a case of congenital adrenal hyperplasia. *Bulletin of the Johns Hopkins Hospital* 86:249, 1950.
107. Yamamoto, T. Hormonic factors affecting gonadal differentiation in fish. *General and Comparative Endocrinology* 1(Suppl.):311, 1962.
108. Young, W., Goy, R., and Phoenix, C. Hormones and Sexual Behavior. In J. Money (Ed.), *Sex Research: New Developments.* New York: Holt, Rinehart, Winston, 1965. P. 176.
109. Zilboorg, G. Masculine and feminine. *Psychiatry* 7:257, 1944.
110. Zuger, B. Gender role determination. *Psychosomatic Medicine* 32:449, 1970.

8

The Stimulus-Value-Role Theory of Marital Choice

Bernard I. Murstein

The choice of a marital partner is one of the most difficult decisions that a person makes in his lifetime. Few individuals have approached the eve of their wedding without some shred of doubt as to whether they were making the right decision. The ever-mounting divorce rate testifies that, for the majority, this doubt must be interpreted as evidence of realistic misgivings rather than of neurotic indecision.

There are several reasons why, heretofore, indecision has been a constant feature of marital choice. First, individuals are asked to predict future behavior in marriage on the basis of rather limited courting behavior that bears little resemblance to the daily realities of marriage. What will it be like to eat the spouse's cooking day after day? Will the spouse be able to keep a cool head when the baby refuses to drink the formula and cries to the point where husband and wife feel they are going berserk? Will the spouse be of comfort the day the boss fires the individual for alleged indifference on the job? Will the ardent sexual desire, so flattering before marriage, prove to be only conquest-directed sex, which extinguishes quickly when it is available on a daily basis? Will the spouse then, out of the need for variety, choose another as the object of the sex drive? In addition, it is extremely difficult to determine which of an individual's personal characteristics will change over time and which will not.

In the broad sense, the decisions to be made by a nubile person are (1) to marry or not to marry and (2) if the decision is to marry, whom to marry. Each of these decisions will be treated in some detail in the following pages. The various theories of marital choice will be discussed, with emphasis on the author's stimulus-value-role theory.

TO MARRY OR NOT TO MARRY?

Since the onset of history, the vast majority of men and women have married. In recent decades, however, more men and women have married than ever before. Well over 90 percent of adult men and women are married or will marry before they die. The increase in the marriage rate since the nineteenth century in the United States has come about for several reasons: heterosexual contacts are more available because of more balanced sex ratios in the different geographical areas than the ratios that existed in pioneer times. Also, affluence and economic well-being are more widespread, so that it is uncommon today for someone to delay marriage because he is not in an established financial position — a reason that often delayed or prevented marriage in the nineteenth century. Further, increasingly, organizations serve as explicit or implicit marriage markets. There are currently singles weekends, singles apartments and singles cruises that explicitly bring the unmarried together, with at least the suggestion that marriage may be in the offing. The college or university is now recognized by parents and students alike as the best marriage market in the nation, where individuals of homogeneous age, education, and often socioeconomic status, are thrown together for four years or more.

There can be little doubt that our society is oriented toward marriage and the family. It gives favorable tax rates, more status, better-paying jobs, and quicker promotions to the married. It does this because their needs are perceived as greater, and because people have indirectly been taught to believe that "family" people are somehow better than single ones.

It is not difficult to trace the antecedents of this belief. Among the Puritans, for example, it was understood that all Christian men and women

ought to marry. It was the approved means of procreating and raising
children, it permitted lawful sexual cohabitation, and it provided both
citizens for defending the colonies against Indians and labor for the farms
and trades. Not to be overlooked was the fact that colonial marriage
offered companionship and permitted the secular and religious training of
children to a much greater degree than is carried out within the family
today.

Such was the importance of the family in the community that confirmed bachelor men were looked upon as only one degree removed from
lepers. They paid a singles tax yearly for their obstinacy and were sometimes required, if they chose to live in town, to stay in special bachelors'
quarters. When moving to another town, they often had to present themselves to the town officials with a letter from officials in the previous town
attesting to their good character [30].

For women such pressures were unnecessary, for to be single was
punishment enough. Professions for unmarried women were quite scarce,
and economic self-sufficiency was virtually impossible. Single women
either lived with their parents, occupying a low status, or moved to the
homes of other relatives, where they were assigned menial domestic
chores to pay for their upkeep.

The situation is quite different today. The world is in no need of additional population. Children are no longer an economic asset but a financial burden, and much of their education and schooling has become the
province of schools and peers. Sex is available for many people without
resort to either marriage or prostitution; and as more and more women
enter the labor market, fewer and fewer women must marry to provide
economic security for themselves.

Why then do people marry? They chiefly marry for love, companionship, status, sex, and children. We shall analyze love and companionship
in further detail shortly. Marriage, we have already noted, brings certain
status privileges that singleness does not. But are we not contradicting
ourselves in stating that people marry for sex when we state that sex can
readily be had outside of marriage? Not really, if we note that people
marry for *marital* sex, which for many is rather distinct from unmarried
sex. Marital sex differs not only in that it is less apt to be encumbered
by guilt, but also in that it is much more convenient than premarital sex,
in which a lesser commitment connotes more of an exchange approach to

the relationship. The unmarried man, for example, may take the woman
to dinner and a show, and she may grant him sexual favors. Marriage,
however, often signifies a commitment and, in a sense, frees the participants
somewhat from a barter relationship.

Children are desired, of course, even in an overpopulated world because
of the personal and emotional satisfaction. Also, from the point of view
of economics, a sharp reduction in population would result in undercon-
sumption of goods and a depression. Accordingly, a limitation of two
children per family would eventually result in a slight decrease in population because not everyone will marry and not every married couple will
be fecund.

To understand the current importance of love and companionship in
marital choice, we shall briefly adumbrate the evolvement of the modern
theories of marital choice in the United States.

WHOM TO MARRY?

Current Theories of Marital Choice

Nineteenth-century theories of marital choice have been described elsewhere [29, 30]. The focus here is on theories that are still current. Most
of the theories vary in the extent to which the determining variables are
believed to be idiosyncratic to, or within the choice of, the individual, as
opposed to their being more impersonally and culturally determined.

The first of these theories, which most psychoanalysts have held for
some time, is that marital choice is largely unconscious. Kubie [20], for
example, believes that the process of marital choice is not amenable to
scientific study. Jung [12] believed that the search for a mate was guided
by unconscious archetypes. In Jung's own words, "You see that girl, or at
least a good imitation of your type, and instantly you get the seizure; you
are caught. And afterward you may discover that it was a hell of a mistake" [12].

Freud [13] saw two types of marital choice. In his view, the human
being originally possesses two types of sexual object choices. One is patterned after himself and the other after the woman who tended him, usually
his mother. Love for a substitute mother is called *anaclitic* (dependency),
and the love that takes itself as the object is called *narcissistic*. For reasons
not explained, men are more apt to be the anaclitic type, whereas women

are the narcissistic type. This is not a hard and fast rule, however, because there are examples of female anaclitics and male narcissists. Within each of these types, there are several paths to object choice. A person may love [13]:

1. According to the narcissistic type:
   a. what he is himself (i.e., himself)
   b. what he once was
   c. what he would like to be
   d. someone who was once part of himself
2. According to the anaclitic (attachment) type:
   a. the woman who feeds him
   b. the man who protects him

Psychoanalysts have done little or no research on verifying these or other psychoanalytic concepts, instead focusing retrospectively on a narrow range of middle- and upper-class couples who were already married and experiencing personal and marital maladjustment. The little effort that has been expended in testing psychoanalytic beliefs regarding marital choice has been largely undertaken by sociologists, who have focused on the Oedipal and Electra choice patterns. The efforts [18, 22, 42] have not confirmed psychoanalytic theory.

At the other end of the continuum from the theory of unconscious choice lies the concept of marital choice as a conscious decision. The individual is said to possess an image of an ideal spouse and to seek a real person who approaches this ideal as closely as possible. The ideal might be highly idiosyncratic or largely determined by societal or subgroup norms.

The most quoted study in this respect is that by Anselm Strauss [37]. His sample consisted of 373 college-level white Chicagoans who were either engaged or recently married and who filled out a questionnaire about their ideal and actual partners. Supplementary information came from interview data of 50 additional, similar subjects.

Strauss found that eight-tenths of his subjects reported that they had held an ideal of a spouse, and only one in seven thought their ideals were unconscious. About half reported that they compared their actual partner and ideal when deciding on a choice. Some 59 percent had found their physical ideal and 74 percent their personality ideal.

The influence of an ideal-spouse image has been rejected by Udry [41] in a study of 90 engaged college students. However, serious conceptual and methodological flaws (which space does not permit discussing further) vitiate the force of his conclusions. Even so, objection can be raised to Strauss's findings. Can one rely on the testimony that the image guided choice *before* the spouse was selected, or was it rather that a vague unrealized image was clarified by simply taking on the qualities of the flesh-and-blood partners? The influence of the ideal on marital choice, therefore, awaits future research.

Sociology of Marital Choice

By far the greatest amount of research on marital choice has been done by sociologists. A divergence of opinion has arisen, however, concerning the influence of sociological factors on marital choice. There is a common core of agreement on the initial importance of such variables as age, socioeconomic status, propinquity, race, previous marital status, and educational level, all of which reinforce homogamous selection. It is also apparent that these variables are not independent of each other but tend to interact. Thus, propinquity may, in part, result from the fact that individuals with similar cultural backgrounds tend to live close to each other [10].

A divergence of opinion arises in regard to whether these cultural variables tend to serve as a screen for excluding candidates, or whether they actually are instrumental in the specific choice made. For sociologists like Kernodle [17], Reiss [34], and Coombs [8], the cultural and social variables are not only important initially; they take precedence over individual and psychological variables, which are held to be only derivatives of the sociological conditions. Little weight is given to biological or genetic determinants or even idiosyncratic environmental influences.

An extreme case is that of Reiss [34], who seems to discount completely the importance of individual need patterns when he says, "From our point of view, the love object could have been a number of people with similar sociocultural characteristics. Chance factors led to it being this particular person. Thus, even here an 'individualistic' explanation is not needed."

However, all sociologists do not omit psychological factors from their theories of marital choice; this is clearly evident in the *value* theory of Coombs [8]. He acknowledges the presence of individual differences in the socialization process. He states, " . . . each person forms a somewhat unique system of values. Thus we may speak of both 'personal' and 'cultural' values."

In a study of matching on the basis of values, Coombs [9] finds empirical support for his theory that value similarity is a positive factor for individuals who date each other. He found that people with similar values are more likely to want to continue the relationship than are those with dissimilar values.

The other position in regard to the role of sociological variables has been strongly championed by Robert F. Winch [43]. Winch acknowledges the initial importance of the aforementioned sociological variables that reenforce homogamous marital choice but denies that they are the major determinants of marital choice. Rather, he maintains that they define a field of eligibles from which the choice is made on the basis of unfulfilled personality needs. Winch describes two types of personality needs [43]:

Type I: The same need is gratified in both A and B but at very different levels of intensity. A negative interspousal correlation is hypothesized.

Type II: Different needs are gratified in A and B. The interspousal correlation may be hypothesized either to be positive or negative, contingent upon the pair of needs involved.

Winch's theory is, thus, essentially a two-stage one; sociological factors determining the field of eligibles and personality needs determining the specific person chosen. His primary focus has been on the second stage, or personality stage. To test his theory, he studied 25 married couples. One member of each couple was an undergraduate student at Northwestern University. The subjects were tested by means of a number of psychological tests, interviews, and case histories. The research was based on a series of personality needs adapted from Henry Murray's book *Explorations in Personality*. The interviewers rated the subjects on these needs according to their performance during "need-interviews comparing the couple's complementarity to chance expectations." The results generally supported the theory.

Winch's findings, however, have found little support among other researchers. He has been attacked by fellow sociologists [5, 17] as a dabbler in areas where no self-respecting sociologist should dabble — in psychology and psychoanalysis. He has also, in their eyes, slighted the importance of sociological variables in determining marital choice by his positing of a successive-stage relationship between sociological and psychological variables rather than an interactional one, in which the sociological variables serve as the determining factors and the psychological variables as the derivative factors.

Much of this criticism is petty and seems to imply that the search for knowledge must be made along prescribed lines within disciplines. But more serious criticism has come as a result of the empirical attempts of other researchers to verify Winch's findings.

Rossow [35] found the theory vastly oversimplified and Tharp [39] criticized the methodology. The list of failures to replicate Winch's findings is rather large. Only a sample need be mentioned: Schellenberg and Bee [36]; Murstein [23, 24]; Heiss and Gordon [14].

Winch has made a spirited attack on the research findings contrary to his theory [44]. He has, nonetheless, admitted that some of the criticisms are valid and has not hesitated to modify his theory. He now favors an approach combining complementary needs with the satisfaction of role norms [1]. Where complementary need satisfaction is in accordance with the role norms for husbands and wives, the pairing of the man and woman should be highly stable. Where complementary needs and role norms are in conflict (e.g., in the case of a passive husband and a domineering wife) greater difficulty should ensue.

Other research efforts have avoided the question of order of importance of sociological and psychological determinants but have taken it for granted that both operate in some unspecified interaction. These efforts might better be termed *approaches* rather than *theories* since none of them is sufficiently detailed nor rigorously enough defined to be capable of testing. Nonetheless, they do present other factors for consideration in understanding marital choice.

The importance of similarity in other than cultural background variables has been emphasized by Burgess and Locke [6]. Reviewing the literature on marital choice, they found six factors to be influential: (1) propinquity, (2) group membership, (3) disapproval of marriage outside the ingroup, (4) concept of the ideal mate, (5) psychological similarity of prospective partner to one's parents, and (6) homogamy, or the tendency to marry another like the self. Their review of the literature suggests that the homogamy principle finds support in all of the aforementioned areas, but the authors did not put forth a clear-cut theory accounting for these findings.

Another factor that is becoming increasingly the center of concern in interpersonal relationships is the relationship of the overall attractiveness of the individual to his ability to attract others. Boalt [4] has incorporated this into his *summation* theory, which he describes as follows:

> . . . in a sample of newly contracted marriages, husband and wife will be more or less evenly matched or each other's equals . . . every point on which one . . . is superior will tend to be associated with other points on which he is inferior, and vice versa. In other words, despite certain differences, husband and wife will prove to be very much on a par if all the circumstances are taken into consideration.

Boalt provides no data to test this assumption but does suggest a method of measurement for future research.

Recently, Cattell and Nesselroade [7] suggested a variation of the egality or exchange approach described above. Their *completion* hypothesis states:

> . . . every person tends to seek in a partner much the same set of desirables — good looks, intelligence, emotional stability, etc. — but more so to the extent that he or she lacks them. . . . [Thus] a marriage becomes viable because, as a team, it has the necessary qualities for adjustment and survival as a small group unit even though the members do not have them singly.

However, the authors could present only a rather weak test of this hypothesis in their data and did not find it confirmed.

A significant advance in the problem of relating cultural and psychological variables occurred with the work of Kerckhoff and Davis [16] and their presentation of a *filter* theory. Their data, derived from college couples, suggest that in the first stage of a relationship two people choose each other on the basis of similar values and that those who fail to agree on values break off the relationship. If these short-term relationships are analyzed for psychological compability, at this early stage, by comparing the expectations of one partner with the role that the other desires to play, no degree of compatibility beyond chance is found. If, however, couples who have been going together for a considerable amount of time (longer than 18 months) are studied, the common values held by the couple prove to be no longer selective, but the *psychological-compatibility* principle has taken over. Presumably, at this point, those with different values have broken off, and the couples have had enough time to test their mutual expectations for a spouse and their partner's ability to fulfill them.

For nearly a decade this provocative study was unchallenged and un-replicated. Recently, however, a replication undertaken by Levinger, Senn, and Jorgensen [21] has disturbed the "tidiness" of the Kerckhoff and Davis findings. Using essentially the same measuring instruments and two large samples from the Universities of Colorado and Massachusetts, the authors failed to confirm any of the earlier findings. Their explanation is essentially twofold. Relationships among college youth have accelerated in development and the Farber Index of Values and the Firo-B questionnaire, used earlier to measure value consensus and role compatibility, respectively, are now seen as less appropriate. Also, the authors question whether a relationship leading to marriage, which is essentially a pairing commitment, can be successfully predicted from the responses to individual-oriented measures.

In sum, whether pessimism or optimism is the correct reaction to earlier research depends on the point of view. The fact that no viable theory has yet emerged may be a cause for pessimism. However, the increasing quality of research and the realization, apparent in recent research, that earlier theories have been oversimplified and are badly in need of verification, is a cause for optimism. It is hoped that current research may profit from the willingness of earlier researchers to plod ahead with little earlier data or adequate measuring instruments to guide them.

STIMULUS-VALUE-ROLE THEORY

My own theory, the *stimulus-value-role* (SVR) theory, is an attempt to build on the pioneering efforts of earlier researchers.

The two principles that form the scaffold of the theory are: (1) marital choice involves a series of sequential stages (at least three), which are labeled *stimulus, value,* and *role,* and (2) at any given point of the relationship, its viability can be determined as a function of the equality of exchange subjectively experienced by its participants.

Sequential Stages

Stimulus In an "open field," where interaction is not forced, one person may be drawn to another because of his perception of the other's physical, social, mental, or reputational attributes. Because attraction is based largely on noninteractional cues, this stage is based on *stimulus* values. The stimulus stage is of crucial importance in an open-field situation, for, if the other person fails to provoke sufficient attraction, further contact is not sought. Although the "prospect" in question might be a highly desirable person in other ways than initial attraction, the other person, because he forgoes opportunities for further contact, never finds this out; consequently, physically unattractive individuals or persons whose stimulus value may be low for a particular individual (e.g., those of other races and religions) are unlikely to be seriously considered as marital candidates by a high-stimulus-value person.

Value Stage If mutual stimulus attraction exists between a man and woman, they either initiate or increase their interaction so that they enter the second, or *value comparison,* stage. This stage is so named because the individuals assess their value compatibility mainly through verbal interaction.

The couple may compare their attitudes toward life, politics, religion, sex, and the role of men and women in society and marriage. The fact that the couple is interacting at this stage also permits more continuous and closer scrutiny of physical appearance, as well as of such other important factors as temperament, world view, and ability to relate to others.

It is possible that closer appraisal of physical qualities and temperament will lead to a changed opinion regarding the desirability of the partner, and this may result in an attempt to terminate the interaction as soon as gracefully possible. But if contact has been made on the basis of strong stimulus attraction, it is more likely that the couple will remain in the second stage and continue to assess value compatibility.

Should the couple find that they hold similar values in important areas, they are apt to develop much stronger positive feelings for each other than they experienced in the stimulus stage. One reason for this is that when a person meets another with similar values, he gains support for the conclusion that his own values are correct; his views are given social validation. Further, many values are intensely personal and are so linked to the self-concept that rejection of these values is experienced as rejection of the self, and acceptance of them implies validation of the self. Provided that person has a reasonably positive self-image, he tends to be attracted to those persons he perceives as validating it. Also, perceived similarity of values may lead to the assumption that the one likes the other, and there is empirical evidence that people like those who they think like them [2].

Last, persons who have similar values are likely to engage in similar activities and thus reward each other by validating each other's commitment to the activity. Moreover, because these activities are similar, they are apt to have similar reward value in the world at large, which further draws the couple together, since they share equal status in their milieu. In sum, the holding of similar values should be a major factor in drawing two individuals together.

Role Stage It is possible that the couple may decide to marry on the basis of stimulus attraction and verbalized value similarity. However, for most persons, these are necessary, but not sufficient, conditions for marriage. It is also important that the couple be able to function in compatible roles. *Role* means "the behavior that is characteristic and expected of the occupant of a defined position in a group" [11]. A role is thus a norm for a particular relationship and for particular situations. The role of husband, for example, may be perceived by the wife as embodying tenderness and acceptance of her. This role, however, does not necessarily clash with another role of the husband, that of ability to aggressively maintain the economic security of the family. There are, in short, a multiplicity of roles for the different kinds of situations that one encounters.

In the premarital phase, however, the partner's ability to function in the desired role is not as readily observable as is his verbalized expression of views on religion, economics, politics, and on how men should treat women. Knowing, for example, how much emotional support the partner will give when, for example, the other fails a history examination indicates an advanced stage of intimacy. Thus the role stage is last in the time sequence leading to marital choice.

Exchange Principle

Although romantics may believe that love overrides all material considerations, the second principle of the SVR theory holds that love depends on equality of exchange. The exchange principle as applied to social behavior evolved from pioneering efforts by Thibaut and Kelley [40] and Homans [15].

Essentially, these approaches maintain that each person tries to make social interaction as profitable as possible, *profit* being defined as the rewards a person gains from the interaction minus the costs he must pay. *Rewards* are defined as the pleasures, benefits, and gratifications that an individual gains from a relationship. *Costs* are factors that inhibit or deter the performance of more preferred behaviors. A young man living in the Bronx, for example, might like a young lady from Brooklyn whom he has met at a resort. Back in the city, however, he may doubt that the rewards he might gain from the relationship would be worth the costs in time and fatigue of two-hour subway rides to Brooklyn.

Closely allied to rewards and costs are assets and liabilities. *Assets* are the commodities (behaviors or qualities) that the individual possesses that are capable of rewarding others and, in return, causing others to reciprocate by rewarding the individual. *Liabilities* are behaviors or qualities associated with an individual that are costly to others and thus, by reciprocity, costly to the self.

A man who has the liability of being physically unattractive, for example, might desire a woman who has the asset of beauty. If his nonphysical qualities are no more rewarding than hers, she gains less than he does from the relationship and, thus, his suit is likely to be rejected. Rejection is a cost to him, because it may lower his self-esteem and increase his fear of failure in future encounters; hence, he may decide to avoid attempting to court women he perceives as being much better looking than he is unless he has other compensatory assets, such as wealth or prestige.

Contrariwise, he is likely to feel highly confident of success with a woman less attractive than he is since he risks little chance of rejection (low cost). However, since the reward value of such a conquest is low, the profitability of such a move is also low. As a consequence, a socially experienced person is likely to express a maximum degree of effort and also obtain the greatest reward at the least cost when he directs his efforts at someone of approximately equal physical attraction, assuming all other variables are equal.

During the first moments of interpersonal contact, the person may attempt to supplement his visual impression of the other with information regarding the other's role in society, professional aspirations, and background. Thus, persons who are physically attracted to each other are likely to be evaluated by one another on the basis of the total amalgam of stimulus characteristics, even though, for a given trait, gross disparities may exist. Men, for example, tend to give more weight to physical attractiveness in a partner more than women do, whereas women give greater weight to the professional aspirations of the partner. Accordingly, although physical attraction may play a leading role, it is hypothesized that the weighted pool of stimulus attractions that each possesses for the other will be approximately equal if courtship is to progress.

Research Findings with the SVR Theory

One of the most important assertions of the SVR theory is that both the need complementarity and homogamy theories are inadequate in accounting for marital choice because the individual seeking a marriage partner is concerned with neither similarity nor complementarity of needs. Rather, he seeks a partner who represents a fusion of his ideal self and ideal spouse, although, as we shall see shortly, he may be prepared to lower his aspirations somewhat if he perceives himself as not possessing high marital assets in his own right.

In general, however, when one is about to marry, he does tend to idealize his partner and to see him as close to his ideal-self and ideal-spouse concepts. This being the case, the tendency of an individual to marry someone he perceives as being similar or different depends largely on how closely his self-concept is to that trinity of desiderata, his ideal spouse, his ideal self, and his perceived partner (Fig. 1).

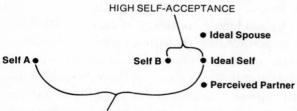

Figure 1 *A*, whose self-concept and ideal-self concept are far apart (low self-acceptance), will see his partner as unlike him, whereas *B*, whose self and ideal self are close together (high self-acceptance), will see his partner as similar to himself. (From *Love, Sex, and Marriage Through the Ages* by Bernard I. Murstein, p. 392. Copyright © 1974 by Springer Publishing Company, Inc., New York. Used with permission of the publisher.)

This figure shows that individual B, who is highly self-accepting, is thus likely to perceive himself as very similar to his partner. Individual A, who is not highly self-accepting (i.e., there is a greater distance between his self-concept and his ideal-self concept), tends to view himself as relatively dissimilar to his partner. In my research [26, 27, 29] this model has been strongly validated. The model also tends to explain the contradictory nature of earlier studies, which sometimes supported the "opposites attract" theory and sometimes the homogamy theory. The model suggests that a person who is dissatisfied with himself will have complementary perceptions of his partner, whereas a highly self-accepting person will perceive his partner as similar to himself.

Another aspect of SVR theory is that men occupy a higher status than women in contemporary American society [30]; consequently, the confirmation of the man's self- and ideal-self concepts by his partner should be more important to progress in courtship than is confirmation of the woman's concepts. Further, when the man has personality difficulties (a neurosis, for example), the effect should be more inimical to the probability of marriage than neurosis in the woman. Both these hypotheses have been confirmed for college couples [26]. Concerning neurosis, the man's degree of neurosis affected the courtship progress of the couple significantly, but the woman's mental health showed no significant association with courtship progress [25].

In accordance with the exchange-theory aspect of SVR theory, it has been shown that a greater-than-chance similarity of physical attractiveness, self-acceptance, values, and neurosis, to name just a few variables, exists among persons in advanced courtship [26]. A fuller treatment of SVR theory, including its applicability to married couples and to friendship, will be found in the symposium *Theories of Attraction and Love* [29]. A discussion of the applicability of SVR theory to interracial marriage has appeared elsewhere [31].

Finally, a complete discussion of the theory, research methodology, tests utilized, and results will appear in the forthcoming book *Who Will Marry Whom? Theory and Research in Marital Choice* [32].

Implications of the SVR Theory

The SVR theory, particularly in its emphasis on exchange, or barter, seems to discount entirely the importance of love in courtship. The omission is intentional. The word *love* seemingly adds little to our understanding of a relationship. Does *love* refer to feeling? Many people who believe they love their spouses do not show it in their behavior.

Is love then behavior? Many people behave in loving fashion toward their spouses but wistfully state that they are not really in love with them. They refer to love as a state of excitement that they find lacking in their relationship. Another person believes he is in love because he has certain cardiorespiratory symptoms in the presence of his beloved. Time, however, can diminish these symptoms dramatically. Still another declares that he loves a person he barely knows — she is the true embodiment of all his ideals. But it is the image he adores, not the girl, whom he scarcely knows.

Let me summarize. An enduring affectionate relationship (love?) generally occurs most readily between equals in status, because they are most capable of satisfying each other's needs equally. Furthermore, to love someone, as I conceive of love, means that a person fulfills his own important needs in the relationship as well as those of the partner (usually needs related to identity, competence, and self-esteem).

To be even relatively sure that the partner satisfies the individual's important needs takes time. Most persons do not reveal all their needs during the early stages of courtship. Only when they feel comfortable and accepted do they gradually reveal themselves; hence love based on realistic appraisal will appear, at the earliest, rather late in courtship and in most cases not until after marriage.

Most people do not wait long enough before marrying to ascertain that they love and are loved. They use either of two alternatives: They note that some needs are readily met (e.g., intellectual, sexual, and empathy needs) and predict or hope that other needs that have not yet been met (or perhaps even recognized) will be fulfilled later.

A second group of people, more immature or need driven, may find one important need met (e.g., the need for beauty) and go on to make sweeping generalizations, imagining the beloved to be perfect in all respects. They project all their fantasies onto the partners, and in the early days of courtship, the data are sufficiently ambiguous that harsh reality does not correct the exaggerations. Some of these people unconsciously fear the disappointment that reality might bring and, therefore, rush into marriage on the basis of inadequate data.

The SVR theory points out just what aspects people react to at first and what factors influence them later. Persons who marry before reasonably negotiating the third (role) stage, for example, have less probability of achieving a durable love relationship and marital success than those who have negotiated it; however, those who have at least moved through the second (value comparison) stage have a higher probability of success than those who marry on the basis of only the first (stimulus) stage of satisfaction (e.g., physical attractiveness). It should be understood, nevertheless, that even those who marry on the bases of high stimulus, value compatibility, and role compatibility are not automatically assured of success but possess only a better chance of marital success than those having less fully developed relationships. Marital success cannot be guaranteed because, to name only two reasons, (1) some needs are not yet conscious (if they ever are to become so) at the time of marriage and (2) people and needs change with time because of changes in the environment and in interpersonal relationships and because of aging.

The SVR theory also suggests a much more conscious, bargaining, approach to marriage than the usual marriage-for-love stereotype. In my opinion, "love" without reference to the beloved's status and qualities occurs about as spontaneously as did the fainting spells of the early cinema heroines. For most people, love's dart is allowed to strike only when the other's marital assets are as good as or better than one's own.

There is indeed no greater testimony to the validity of the exchange portion of SVR theory than the marriage of those at the bottom of the marriage totem pole. When a fat, unattractive girl of mediocre intelligence working at a menial occupation marries a fat, unattractive man also working at a menial job, they may both profess that they are utterly charmed by the other. Yet it is probable that had they been accepted by an attractive, slim professional, they would have found the fat person less desirable, all other things being equal. The limited marital assets of some people force them to marry others with equally limited assets; consequently, it would be more correct to say that such people settle for, rather than choose, each other, although this fact may be denied by rationalization and idealization.

SVR theory also suggests how one of the great interpersonal tragedies of our current society might be avoided. Our society abounds in open-field social situations in which people do not have to interact with others socially unless they want to. There are dance halls and bars where singles go and interact with those who please the eye. This may be an adventurous experience for those who are physically attractive; it is not for the unattractive. Men, however, occupy a higher status in society than do women; as a result, ugliness works a greater hardship on a woman, for a homely man can bargain his superior status for looks, whereas a homely woman cannot.

Physical attractiveness and many of the other variables in the stimulus stage are crucial in an open field in determining who will interact with whom. They do not determine who will be happy with whom. In fact, there are, doubtless, a great number of cases where a man and woman would manifest considerable value-stage and role-stage compatibility if they ever met and had the opportunity to develop a relationship. Yet if one of the two is considerably less physically attractive than the other, the chances are that they will never meet in an open-field situation.

I could argue that society should abandon the cult of beauty to assure many of its citizens greater happiness. No doubt this belief is as true as is the one that wars are detrimental to the progress of mankind. Yet, for the present, overreaction to good looks is a part of reality, just as war is. Let me therefore focus on what is feasible rather than what ought to be.

It seems to me that, in the loneliness of increasingly urbanized society, much more could be done to create congenial closed-field situations in which individuals could learn a great deal about each other without immediate focus on marriage. These closed-field situations would enable the participants to get to know the other members of the group fairly well and would facilitate the discovery of value comparison and role fulfillment, which count more toward marital success than does physical attraction.

There already are a number of good closed-field situations. The small college seminar is ideal for enabling people to interact and learn about each other in a nonstatus situation. Some specialized clubs, such as Parents without Partners, serve the same purpose. These groups have legitimate nonmarital purposes, but it is no secret that they can serve as marital markets for those who are "shopping." Indeed, the first thing that an interested single person should do when moving to a new city is to join a special-interest club that contains a large number of eligible marriage partners. Such a move is particularly wise if the person is physically unattractive. Physically attractive persons, especially women, do not need closed-field situations as much, for the world will find them, bringing as such people do, great rewards in status to those who associate with them.

Although the SVR theory is more detailed and extensive than earlier theories, it by no means may be regarded as more than a rough design for further extension and development. Currently, its chief shortcoming lies in the fact that it makes it appear that each person is completely free to choose whomever he wants whenever he wants. In actuality, parents and peers influence the course of the relationship in subtle and not-so-subtle ways. Family and societal networks can be conveyor belts in moving a couple of whom they approve along the route to marriage by treating them as if they were already a couple.[1] As time passes, therefore, it becomes increasingly difficult to get off this conveyor belt until the final destination, marriage, is achieved.

Another factor worthy of research in regard to SVR theory is measuring the strength of the desire to marry. Presumably, a person who has little desire to marry may be quite content to be the lover but not the spouse of even the most compatible mate. Another person who is eager to marry, may seize the opportunity to marry another of only modest compatibility. Indeed, the person who rejects the opportunity of marrying the highly compatible mate at age 25 may marry someone far less compatible at age 30. Thus, it is clear that desire to marry acts as a suppressor variable that dampens the degree of compatibility necessary for matrimony.

Just what makes a person ready to marry at one stage rather than at another stage is not clear. Some people will not marry until their professional training is completed, whereas others find this factor no impediment. As people age, they may find that a fear of isolation and loneliness in middle age pushes them into matrimony more than do the traits of the partner. Yet others, still in their early twenties, seem to be able to determine when a compatible partner comes along and marry quickly.

Closely allied to the decision to marry may be the critical incident that either moves the couple swiftly into marriage or weakens or breaks the relationship. One example of a critical incident is a job transfer of one member of the couple (usually the man) to a distant city. If the partner goes too, a commitment to marriage has usually been made.

The SVR theory is, in sum, replete with assertions and predictions. (In the book *Who Will Marry Whom?*, 39 tested hypotheses are presented.) A

[1]Many of these emendations stem from several helpful discussions with Robert G. Ryder.

theory that can be tested often has a short and sweet life — at least in its original form. The principal reason for this is that many theories are incorrect, either in whole or in part. But even if a theory is essentially correct, it can never be general enough nor detailed enough to account for all possible personality types, environmental conditions, and changing motivations. A useful theory, therefore, is tested and modified by many researchers much more quickly than is an exotic, untestable theory. If the SVR theory is modified or altered radically as a result of testing, it might be gloriously metamorphosed or even destroyed. But, as the aged grandpa in *The Happy Time* said when his sons told him that his nightly forays with the Widow La Touche would stop his teeth from aching *permanently,* "The one who knows of a better way to die, will he step forward?" [38]

REFERENCES

1. Bermann, E., Compatibility and stability in the dyad. Unpublished, 1966.
2. Berscheid, E., and Walster, E. *Interpersonal Attraction.* Reading, Mass.: Addison-Wesley, 1969.
3. Blood, R., Jr., and Wolfe, D. *Husbands and Wives.* New York: Free Press, 1965.
4. Boalt, G. *Family and Marriage.* New York: McKay, 1965. P. 28.
5. Bowman, C. Uncomplimentary remarks on complementary needs. *American Sociological Review* 20:466, 1955.
6. Burgess, E., and Locke, H. *The Family.* New York: American, 1960.
7. Cattell, R., and Nesselroade, J. Likeness and completeness theories examined by sixteen personality factor measures on stable and unstable married couples. *Journal of Personality and Social Psychology* 7:351, 1967.
8. Coombs, R. A value theory of mate-selection. *Family Life Coordinator* 10:51, 1961.
9. Coombs, R. Value consensus and partner satisfaction among dating couples. *Journal of Marriage and the Family* 28:165, 1966.
10. Eckland, B. Theories of mate-selection. *Eugenics Quarterly* 15:71, 1968
11. English, H., and English, A. *A Comprehensive Dictionary of Psychological and Psychoanalytical Terms.* New York: McKay, 1958.
12. Evans, R. *Conversations with Carl Jung.* Princeton: Van Nostrand Reinhold, 1964.
13. Freud, S. On narcissism (1914). In *The Standard Edition of the Complete Psychological Works of Sigmund Freud,* transl. and ed. by J. Strachey with others. London: Hogarth and Institute of Psycho-Analysis, 1957. Vol. 14, p. 90.
14. Heiss, J., and Gordon, M. Need patterns and the mutual satisfaction of dating and engaged couples. *Journal of Marriage and the Family* 26:337, 1964.

15. Homans, G. *Social Behavior: Its Elementary Forms.* New York: Harcourt, 1961.
16. Kerckhoff, A., and Davis, K. Value consensus and need complementarity in mate selection. *American Sociological Review* 27:295, 1962.
17. Kernodle, W. Some implications of the homogamy-complementary needs theories of mate selection for sociological research. *Social Forces* 38:145, 1956.
18. Kirkpatrick, C. A statistical investigation of the psychoanalytic theory of mate selection. *Journal of Abnormal and Social Psychology* 32:427, 1937.
19. Knupfer, G., Clark, W., and Room, R. The mental health of the unmarried. *American Journal of Psychiatry* 122:841, 1966.
20. Kubie, L. Psychoanalysis and Marriage: Practical and Theoretical Issues. In V. Eisenstein (Ed.), *Neurotic Interaction in Marriage.* New York: Basic Books, 1956.
21. Levinger, G., Senn, D., and Jorgensen, B. Progress toward permanence in courtship: A test of the Kerckhoff-Davis hypothesis. *Sociometry* 33:427, 1970.
22. Mangus, A. Relationships between young women's conceptions of intimate male associates and of their ideal husbands. *Journal of Social Psychiatry* 7:403, 1936.
23. Murstein, B. The complementary need hypothesis in newlyweds and middle-aged married couples. *Journal of Abnormal and Social Psychology* 63:194, 1961.
24. Murstein, B. Empirical tests of role complementary needs, and homogamy theories of marital choice. *Journal of Marriage and the Family* 29:689, 1967.
25. Murstein, B. The relationship of mental health to marital choice and courtship progress. *Journal of Marriage and the Family* 29:447, 1967.
26. Murstein, B. Stimulus-value-role: A theory of marital choice. *Journal of Marriage and the Family* 32:465, 1970.
27. Murstein, B. Self ideal-self discrepancy and the choice of marital partner. *Journal of Consulting and Clinical Psychology* 37:47, 1971.
28. Murstein, B. What makes people sexually appealing? *Sexual Behavior* 1:75, 1971.
29. Murstein, B. A Theory of Marital Choice and its Applicability to Marriage Adjustment. In B. Murstein (Ed.), *Theories of Attraction and Love.* New York: Springer, 1971.
30. Murstein, B. *Love, Sex, and Marriage Through the Ages.* New York: Springer, 1974.
31. Murstein, B. A Theory of Marital Choice Applied to Interracial Marriage. In L. Abt and I. Stuart (Eds.), *Interracial Marriage.* New York: Grossman, 1973.
32. Murstein, B. *Who Will Marry Whom? Theory and Research in Marital Choice.* New York: Springer, 1976.
33. Murstein, B., and Glaudin, V. The use of the MMPI in the determination of marital maladjustment. *Journal of Marriage and the Family* 30:651, 1968.
34. Reiss, I. Toward a sociology of the heterosexual love relationship. *Marriage and Family Living* 22:139, 1960.
35. Rossow, I. Issues in the concept of need complementarity. *Sociometry* 20:216, 1957.
36. Schellenberg, J., and Bee, L. A re-examination of the theory of complementary needs in mate selection. *Marriage and Family Living* 22:227, 1960.

37. Strauss, A. The ideal and the chosen mate. *American Journal of Sociology* 52:204, 1946.
38. Taylor, S. *The Happy Time.* New York: Dramatists Play Service, 1950.
39. Tharp, R. Psychological patterning in marriage. *Psychological Bulletin* 60:99, 1963.
40. Thibaut, J., and Kelley, H. *The Social Psychology of Groups.* New York: Wiley, 1959.
41. Udry, J. The influence of the ideal mate image on mate selection and mate perception. *Journal of Marriage and the Family* 27:477, 1965.
42. Winch, R. Further data and observation on the Oedipus hypothesis: The consequence of an inadequate hypothesis. *American Sociological Review* 16:784, 1951.
43. Winch, R. *Mate-Selection.* New York: Harper & Row, 1958.
44. Winch, R. Another look at the theory of complementary needs in mate selection. *Journal of Marriage and the Family* 29:756, 1967.

9
Death of A Spouse*

David Maddison
Beverley Raphael

When death disrupts a marital relationship, the possible adverse consequences
are of such frequency and magnitude as to justify our regarding the death of
a spouse as an extremely important public health and social problem.
Moreover, we believe that there is excellent evidence, much of which is
set out in this chapter, for regarding this particular life crisis as a crucial
area for both preventive psychiatry and preventive medicine in general.

This is especially true when one views the death of a spouse in the framework of contemporary *crisis theory*. Although implied by earlier workers
(for example, Eliot [24]), Gerald Caplan [11] in particular emphasized the
operational value of considering the terminal illness and death of a spouse
as a life-crisis situation for the survivor. All the basic assumptions of
crisis theory may be applied, and indeed tested, in this context. There is
probably general agreement that a crisis is a time-limited intrapsychic
state, arising as a consequence of some hazardous life event, in which the
individual's habitual coping techniques are relatively ineffective. Specifically, the bereaved spouse is, to a greater or lesser extent, beset by feelings

*This work has been supported at various stages by the Foundations' Fund for Research in
Psychiatry, the Grant Foundation, Inc., the National Health and Medical Council of Australia, the
New South Wales Institute of Psychiatry and the University of Sydney.

187

of confusion, perplexity, and anxiety, with or without accompanying somatic symptoms. Anger, shame, and guilt may also be prominent in varying combinations during this crisis state. The bereaved spouse may urgently need to develop new modes of coping in order to resolve a painful feeling of uncertainty. An additional and crucially relevant assumption of the model is that the bereaved spouse is maximally susceptible to influence during this time. Such influence may be of vital importance in determining whether he emerges from the bereavement with an improved coping capacity or whether he is thereafter handicapped by inappropriate or ineffective defensive styles that decrease his ability to adjust, either immediately or in the future.

The person in crisis is likely to seek support from members of his family and persons in his social network, and their influence is likely to be more pronounced than usual because of his lowered defenses. This conceptualization takes into account not only the psychodynamic makeup of the bereaved but also the quality of his social network and the nature of his interactions with others of importance to him. An understanding of conjugal bereavement in these terms provides a coherent theoretical framework for offering the surviving partner a form of supportive intervention that will maximize his effectiveness in working through the problems of loss and adapting to his new state.

Because of the differing mortality rates for the two sexes in Western society, most of the empirical data concerning conjugal bereavement have been derived from studies of widows. Although there *are* reasons for believing that the mourning process should not differ too much whether one is talking about a bereaved husband or about a bereaved wife, obviously the role strains and identity changes for a widower are substantially different from those imposed on a widow (an observation for which there is little documentary evidence). But in this chapter we will be referring in particular to the consequences of conjugal bereavement for widows — and the assumption cannot always be made that the findings are applicable to a population of widowers, particularly when we are considering the social consequences of bereavement.

THE CONSEQUENCES OF CONJUGAL BEREAVEMENT

Broadly speaking, three types of outcome can follow any crisis. First, there may be improved adaptation — physically, psychologically, or socially. The frequency of this sort of response following conjugal bereavement is difficult to ascertain, but it seems most unlikely that it is very high. Lopata [44] mentions that some of her widowed subjects who perceived a change in their identities saw this as positive, with the development of previously unutilized aspects of their personality. Isolated cases have been described in which bereavement was followed by a remission of psychiatric illness, notably depression [29], schizophrenia [15], and psychosomatic illness [74]. These quite exceptional examples might appeal to those who, like the cynic John Gay, consider that "the comfortable estate of widowhood is the only hope that keeps up a wife's spirits."

Second, there may be a return to the precrisis equilibrium, although even this will probably be associated with some alteration in identity, especially for the woman whose adult identity was substantially built up through continuous interactions with her husband.

Our major preoccupation must be, however, with the third possible outcome, that of "malresolution" of the bereavement crisis by widow or widower. This malresolution may occur in many and varied forms, and, unfortunately, there is abundant evidence that bad outcomes are both frequent and severe.

Death

Folklore, fiction, and contemporary newspapers provide much anecdotal evidence for the frequency of death during the period of shock or mourning following bereavement, and this observation has been well presented by Engel [26]. Parkes [61] showed that widowers over the age of 55 had a 40 percent higher mortality in the six months following conjugal bereavement than married men of the same age. A "broken heart" — heart disease — was the major cause of these deaths, although there was also a real increase in deaths due to other diseases. Of the total number of widowers, 5 percent had died during the first six months, nearly half of these from the same disease as the wives. Kraus and Lilienfeld [36] found that the higher mortality was particularly marked in widowers aged 25-34 and that it tended to decrease with age, though still staying consistently above the death rate for control groups of married men of all ages. In those under 35 years of age, there was up to 10 times the expected death rate for several leading causes of death, principally cardiovascular disease; and in the age group 20-24 there was nine times the expected rate of suicidal deaths. McMahon and Pugh [50] confirm the high suicide rate among the conjugally bereaved, both male and female, and consider this to be a true bereavement effect.

Ekblom [23], studying conjugally bereaved males and females over the age of 75, demonstrated that the mortality rate among the survivors during the first 12 months was 15 percent higher than predicted, and during the first month was double the expectation. Cox and Ford [16] have also described an increased mortality, their death rates for widows being especially high during the second half of the first year. Rees and Lutkins [66] demonstrated that in a semirural area of Wales, the death rate for bereaved relatives during the first year after the loved one's death was seven times that of the nonbereaved controls; when the bereavement was that of a spouse, the death rate among the survivors was 10 times higher than that of the controls. The physical situation in which the loved one's death occurred affected the mortality of the bereaved even further, ranging from double the rate if the death occurred in the hospital to a fivefold increase if it occurred on the highway. While it is possible that other factors could contribute to this increased death rate among the survivors (for example, a mutual selection of poor-risk mates, or a shared unfavorable environment), most studies that consider these possibilities suggest that it is the bereavement itself that is the prime or only causal factor.

Morbidity

There is substantial evidence for the occurrence of increased morbidity following conjugal bereavement, whatever measures are used for the assessment of subsequent health deterioration.

Self-Assessment Reports of health impairment range from 43 percent of subjects at a mean period of two years and two months following the bereavement [54] to 27 percent at the end of the first year [58].

Use of Medical Services Parkes [56] examined the rates at which a group of London widows consulted general practitioners before and after their bereavement. Whereas in the six months prior to the bereavement there was an average of 2.2 consultations per patient, the number rose to 3.6, 2.6, and 3.0 per patient in the three six-month periods following the bereavement. The rate was higher in all age groups, but those under 65 years old showed a particularly marked increase in the rate of consultation for depression and other psychological symptoms, whereas those over 65 showed a particularly marked increase in the rate of consultation for somatic symptoms.

Symptomatology Our own controlled study of the health of 375 widows in Boston and Sydney [51] showed the frequency and extent of deterioration in physical and mental health as judged by a health questionnaire administered 13 months after the bereavement, and it also indicated the frequency of certain symptoms. Marked health deterioration was judged by independent examiners to be present when a score of 16 or more was obtained on this questionnaire. Scores of four or less seemed to represent no significant health deterioration.

Table 2 Health Deterioration in Bereaved and Nonbereaved Women in Sydney, Australia, and in Boston, Mass.

	Number of Subjects	Degree of Deterioration (percent)		
		Marked	Moderate	None
Boston widows	132	21.2	35.6	43.2
Sydney widows	243	32.1	36.2	31.7
Total widows	375	28.0	36.3	35.7
Boston controls	98	7.2	31.6	61.2
Sydney controls	101	2.0	28.7	69.3
Total controls	199	4.5	30.2	65.3

Table 2 shows that 21 percent of Boston widows and 32 percent of Sydney widows were judged to have had a marked deterioration in health during the year following the spouse's death, the prevalence of health deterioration being significantly higher (p $<$ .001) than the health deterioration reported by a matched sample of nonbereaved middle-aged women. Disturbances in sleep, appetite, and weight were prominent when compared with the prevalence of these symptoms in a nonbereaved matched control group, as were headaches and various psychosomatic symptoms affecting every bodily system. The studies of Marris [54], Hobson [34], and Parkes [58] all confirm the frequent occurrence of such symptoms in a bereaved population.

Psychosomatic Illness Psychosomatic illnesses, in particular, ulcerative colitis [43], asthma [48], leukemia [31], and hyperthyroidism [41], are reported to have been precipitated by bereavement. The relevant studies were uncontrolled, however, and some include losses other than those due to death. Schmale [68], in his study of 14 women who had experienced the "psychic trauma" of the death of a spouse, found that 8 developed somatic illness. Our own study [51] fails to show any increase in the frequency or severity of major psychosomatic diseases, such as asthma and migraine.

Psychiatric Illness Approximately two out of every five of our subjects had major difficulty with "nervousness" and insomnia during the year following bereavement, and one in every eight subjects feared total "nervous breakdown" during this period. Other phobic and anxiety symptoms were also common. One widow in eight had consulted a physician for depression, though only 1.3 percent of our total sample had required hospitalization for this reason. Parkes [55] has demonstrated, in a study of patients admitted to a psychiatric hospital, that the number of patients whose illness followed the death of a spouse was six times greater than expected. In his study of bereaved psychiatric patients, Parkes considered that 28 percent were suffering from neurotic or reactive depression, a finding not dissimilar from that of Singh [70], who noted reactive depression in 40 percent of bereaved Indian psychiatric patients. Lindemann [42] described agitated depression as one type of distorted grief reaction, but offered no comment on its frequency.

Indeed, virtually every type of psychiatric illness has been claimed to occur following bereavement. Hypochondriasis, phobias about death and major illness, obsessions, manic illness, and schizophrenia-like conditions have all been described, though the last seems to be distinctly rare. Endogenous depression of the anergic type is also rare, although Anderson [4] described 4 percent in his sample. Alcoholism may develop or, if previously established, relapse or worsen. The Boston widows in our sample, but not the Sydney widows, reported an increased consumption of alcohol in the year after the husband's death when compared with nonbereaved controls. Conversely, the Sydney widows, but not the Boston widows, showed a substantial increase in the consumption of sedatives and tranquilizing drugs. This parallels the finding of Parkes [56] that widows under the age of 65 had a sevenfold increase in the consumption of sedatives in the first six months following the bereavement, the increase being maintained at a slightly lower level throughout the next year (see Table 3).

The important concept of anniversary illness, introduced by Hilgard [33], has more recently been elaborated by Pollock [63]. There is strong evidence that psychiatric illness may appear, or may recur or worsen, around the time of the wedding anniversary and the anniversary of the death itself and other dates that were of special significance in the marriage.

Social "Morbidity"

Most widows complain to some extent of social isolation and loneliness. Many find that some previously gratifying relationships are no longer available or that the gratification previously gained in these contacts has markedly diminished; this is particularly true for relationships with married couples in which the widows had previously been involved together with their spouses. Parkes [58], in his uncontrolled study of London widows, found that they were frequently isolated, spending much time alone at home and only rarely making more social contacts than previously; this finding has been paralleled in our own work. There is some evidence that widowers are likely to be even more isolated and depressed than are widows [72].

Lopata [44, 45, 46] has provided a great deal of valuable information from her extensive sociological study of 301 widows in metropolitan Chicago, investigating in particular their integration into society. She analyzed the ways older women handled the disengagement from society brought about by the husband's death, and the problems in social relationships that ensued. The more multidimensional the involvement of her husband in a woman's life, the more disorganized became the widow's social relationships after his death, changes occurring either in the types of social role and relationship with which she is involved or in her level of

Table 3 Prevalence of Certain Symptoms and Complaints in Bereaved and Non-bereaved Women in Sydney, Australia, and Boston, Massachusetts

Symptom or Complaint	Percent Total Widows (no.=375)	Percent Total Controls (no.=199)	p[a]	Percent Boston Widows (no. = 132)	Percent Sydney Widows (no.=221)	p[a]
General nervousness	41.3	16.1	0.001	40.9	41.2	n.s.
Depression	22.7	5.5	0.001	17.4	25.3	n.s.
requiring medical treatment	12.8	1.0	0.001	9.1	14.0	n.s.
requiring hospitalization	1.3	0	0.05	0.7	1.8	n.s.
Fear of "nervous breakdown"	13.1	2.0	0.001	12.1	14.5	n.s.
Insomnia	40.8	12.6	0.001	35.6	44.8	n.s.
Migraine	4.8	3.0	n.s.	1.5	6.3	0.02
Headache	17.6	9.0	0.01	14.4	19.5	n.s.
Blurred vision	13.7	7.5	0.02	12.1	15.8	n.s.
Indigestion	9.9	4.5	0.01	10.6	9.5	n.s.
Difficulty in swallowing	4.8	1.5	0.02	6.1	4.5	n.s.
Excessive appetite	5.4	0.5	0.001	3.0	5.9	n.s.
Anorexia	13.1	1.0	0.001	9.8	16.3	n.s.
Weight gain	8.5	9.0	n.s.	10.6	6.3	n.s.
Weight loss	13.6	2.0	0.001	9.1	16.7	0.05
Menorrhagia	3.4	0.5	0.05	3.0	2.7	n.s.
Chest pain	10.1	4.5	0.01	4.5	14.0	0.01
Dyspnea	12.0	4.5	0.001	8.3	14.0	n.s.
Asthma	2.4	1.5	n.s.	2.3	2.3	n.s.
Drug intake − increase	37.3	11.1	0.001	20.5	48.0	0.001
marked increase	5.9	0.5	0.001	2.3	8.1	0.01
Alcohol intake − increase	6.7	2.0	0.001	9.1	3.2	0.05
Smoking − marked increase	11.7	1.5	0.001	14.4	9.0	n.s.
Frequent infections	2.1	0	0.01	3.0	1.8	n.s.
General aching	8.4	4.0	0.001	6.8	9.5	n.s.
Reduced work capacity	46.7	26.1	0.001	43.2	50.2	n.s.

[a]Probabilities calculated by chi-square analysis with 1 degree of freedom. *Note:* n.s. = chi-square value < 0.05 level of significance.

194

engagement with them. It is clear that urbanization, industrialization, and the increased complexity of society, because they produce a constant shifting of people and their roles, make it increasingly difficult for the widow to return to her past social network. The alternative, i.e., entering into new social roles, is also difficult, because older widows in particular lack the ability to replace past relationships with new ones that possess an equally satisfying intimacy. Society does little to facilitate the reengagement of those whose life pattern has been disrupted or who, for other reasons, are unable to find satisfying involvements, basing its neglect on the rationalization that those people who are socially isolated have become so of their own free choice.

Lopata found a sizable number of widows who were relatively isolated or living at a minimal level of contact with a few nearby children, siblings, and friends. She considers that the major reason for their isolation is that they have "not been socialized to analyze logically the resources of their environment, to choose desired social roles, to prepare themselves for entrance into interaction scenes, to be willing to be tested by secondary criteria, and generally to rebuild their lives." Blau [7] also noted that older New York widows felt that widowhood had an adverse effect on their friendships, experiencing a loss of contact with some friends and a change in the quality of their relationship with others. Widows who do have confidants, however, may, despite living alone, have a higher morale and life satisfaction than married women without such emotionally supportive relationships [47].

There is also considerable evidence that widows constitute a minority group facing discrimination, poverty, and exclusion from full participation in society. They are seen as handicapped in that they lack a mate, much of the discrimination against them being based on the fact that they are visibly different in any situation requiring a male escort. Their loneliness is often exploited, and they may be dealt with unfairly in business affairs. They also tend to be avoided because their grief and their loneliness are threatening to others, who are made anxious by such emotions. They are passive females, lacking a defined function in a male-dominated, function-oriented culture. The average age at which women are widowed in the United States, according to Lopata, is 56; and such women tend to be regarded as old in a youth-centered society.

In the United States, widows may also be members of other minority groups — racial or ethnic ones — and as such have an additional reason for feeling threatened by their community. They form a disproportionately large segment of the poor, poverty restricting their lives and proving particularly difficult for those who had had a higher standard of living. Probably 50 percent of widows experience a considerable drop in financial status following widowhood, and their level of poverty is frequently extreme, particularly for the nonwhite and the elderly living alone. Aitken-Swan [1] showed that at least 29 percent of younger widows in Australia (especially "civilian" widows, as distinct from servicemen's widows), had incomes at a poverty level. Those most affected were those who did not own their own homes and who had three or more dependent children. Besides their problems of loneliness and rejection, their income was so low that they could not provide proper food for their children, and they had great difficulty in earning additional money.

Widows, then, tend all too frequently to be downwardly mobile in a society that idealizes upward mobility. Most widows wish to help themselves. They appreciate opportunities that may be presented for reentry into society, having no wish to rely on the passive acceptance of charity. Conditions in Australia have improved to some extent following Aitken-Swan's survey, with the provision of additional allowances and support and the availability of subsidized retraining programs. There still remains, however, in any culture, an enormous problem for the older widow, who is frequently poorly educated in an increasingly educated world; and for this group in particular major economic and social difficulties remain.

Family Relationships

Family relationships are also likely to be altered following bereavement. The problems inherent in living alone, difficult though these may be, may well be replaced by an entirely different set of problems if the widow moves in with one of her married children. This situation often reactivates conflicts that both mother and child had regarded as worked through and "closed" many years before. In our studies of the social network of the widow in the first few months after bereavement, we have been struck by the frequency with which her conflicts are heightened by invitations from one or more of her children to live with them. She resents any feeling that she is being unduly pressured, doubts (often with good reason) the sincerity of the invitation, and senses clearly some of the important conflicts that are likely to arise when she moves into a three-generation household in which her role is likely to be poorly defined. If her married children suggest that she go to each family in turn, for a limited period, she has even more reason to suspect that they are probably motivated by a sense of duty, rather than by any genuine desire to offer her a new and more rewarding life. There are times, of course, when financial considerations make it urgent that she accept such an offer from a member of her family. Yet it is probably true that this usually constitutes an additional crisis (as defined on p. 217) if the offer comes immediately following the bereavement, and it may create problems.

If such a domestic realignment is made, the complex emotions involved are sometimes handled by the widow with gross denial; she purports to believe that all is running smoothly in her new home, yet may consult a physician within a short space of time and complain of numerous psychogenic symptoms. Only then does it become evident, as confirmed by her daughter and son-in-law, for example, that the three-generation family arrangement is working poorly, with much rivalry manifested in many of the family relationships, perhaps most particularly between the widow and her daughter. Anecdotal evidence from psychiatric practice makes it clear that this type of contrived family setting often has serious deleterious effects on members of the second and third generations, quite apart from the unhappiness that it can bring the widow herself. It is hardly surprising that widows who are able to support themselves in their own home, both financially and emotionally, state that they have greater peace, quite, and independence. Perhaps the ideal situation is one of "intimacy at a distance," with the widow living near, but not actually in, her child's house and with appropriate contact and support readily available. Dubourg and Mandelbrote's [22] findings on mentally-ill widows support this proposition.

Sometimes the widow's social interactions are reduced to what has been called a society of widows. While the widow may see this as representing a great drop in her social status, we have some evidence from our own work to suggest that there is a particular comfort for many widows in the empathy they feel can come only from someone who has worked through, or who is currently working through, an identical loss. We have been told repeatedly of interactions that seemed to be evidence of that special understanding only another widow could provide. Undoubtedly for this reason, the widow-to-widow program developed by Silverman

[69] has been able to assist many widows who have few social contacts. Organizations of war widows and civilian widows perform a similar function; most are geared, largely if not entirely, to assistance with material problems and the provision of agreeable recreational outlets for the widow in a group of her peers. Within these limits they seem to perform a useful function, but it is extremely difficult to agree with the suggestion of Cumming and Henry [20] that such groups offer a degree of gratification sufficient to incite the envy of the married.

As already described, the widow is likely to undergo a considerable change in her identity, especially when a great deal of her identity was derived from her interactions with her husband and his ties with the outside world. Though many of Lopata's widows refused to admit that they had changed in this dimension, many gave contradictory evidence. For lower-class, poorly educated women, whose husbands had not been so important to the wives' identity formation, it is more likely that there will be no change. The women who reported marked change were likely to have been socially active and integrated, to have had a higher education, and to have had husbands of higher occupational status. Some of these changes had indeed been in a positive direction; their grieving completed, these women might in fact feel more competent, more independent, and freer, busying themselves and developing aspects of their identities that had previously been undernourished because of their dependence on their husbands.

Work Adjustment

Most of the subjects in our samples asserted that, if possible, they wanted to work. Of the 21 widows described by Parkes [58], 14 were working 13 months after their husbands' deaths, half of these having taken a job for the first time. The other half returned to work on an average of 12 days after the death. Our own study of the health of widows, however, showed that 47 percent reported a diminished work capacity during the first year after the husband's death. The comparable figure for non-bereaved middle-aged women is only 26 percent — a statistically significant difference.

Sexual Adjustment

There is a striking lack of empirical data concerning the sexual adjustment

of the widow, suggesting that this problem is perceived as particularly
threatening not only by the widows and members of their immediate
social network but also by "objective" scientific investigators. Many
widows report that early and inappropriate sexual advances have been
made toward them, sometimes even by close friends of the deceased
husbands. Others feel that they are shunned for fear of the sexual demands that they may make, perhaps most particularly toward the husbands
of their friends. In working with voluntary organizations that provide
guidance in practical matters for the widow, and most particularly for her
children, we have been struck by the high level of sexual anxiety shown
by some of the male volunteers, indicated by elaborate anecdotes derived
from what are largely, if not wholly, fantasy perceptions of the widow as
sexually insatiable. It does appear likely that the younger widow, still in
the phase of intense sexual involvement with her husband, will experience
a substantial sexual deprivation and our clinical work with some of these
younger recently bereaved widows provides evidence of the difficulty
which at least some of them have adjusting to the absence of sexual gratification. Promiscuity certainly is one (uncommon) type of maladaptive
response, particularly during the period of transition from old object
relationship to new. Sexual involvement becomes less intense from the
middle years onward, so that sexual need probably plays a lessened role
in the adjustment problems of the older widow [72].

Remarriage

Chances of remarriage are higher for widowers than for widows, because
there are more available women than men. A study of remarriage in the
elderly [49] demonstrated that widowers tended to remarry in about
three years and widows in about seven years; over half had known the
new spouse for a long time, often for most of their lives. Of these new
marriages, 75 percent were rated as successful. Success was more likely
if the first marriage had been a good one, if the remarriage was motivated
by needs for love and companionship rather than by material factors, if
the wife was somewhat younger, if the children approved, and if relationships with both families were good. Marris [54] found that, during the
years they were studied, 17 percent of his widows in the 20- to 24-year-
old age group remarried, compared with 1 percent of those aged 50 to 59.
   In our own studies, we were surprised to find how frequently the

subject of remarriage had been brought before the widow by relatives or friends, sometimes within a few days or weeks of the husband's death. The widow's response was almost always strongly unfavorable, even though she often conceded that she felt that her friend or relative was acting with good intentions. We were left with the distinct impression that, whatever else one might say to a widow during the height of crisis, a discussion, or even a hint, of some future romantic liaison is always distasteful.

GRIEF AND MOURNING: AN ANALYSIS

Normal Grief and Mourning

Following Bowlby [8], we use the term *grief* to refer to that peculiar amalgam of anxiety, anger, and despair following the experience of what is feared to be an irretrievable loss. *Mourning* is used to describe the whole complex sequence of psychological processes and their overt manifestations, beginning with angry efforts at recovery and appeals for help, proceeding through apathy and disorganization of behavior, and ending when some more or less stable organization is beginning to develop.

Extended and detailed descriptions of acute grief have been given by Lindemann [42] and Parkes [58], from which it is evident that the following features are characteristic:

1. An initial period of shock, numbness, disbelief, and denial, lasting from one to seven days, often punctuated by outbursts of tearfulness and restlessness, sometimes with extremely disturbed behavior.

2. Lindemann believes that the bereaved suffers, almost universally, a syndrome characterized by "sensations of somatic distress, occurring in waves, lasting 20 minutes to an hour at a time; a feeling of tightness in the throat; choking, with shortness of breath; need for sighing and an empty feeling in the abdomen; lack of muscular power; and an intense subjective distress described as tension or mental pain."

3. The individual's mental state is generally altered, with feelings of unreality and a sense of increased emotional distance from others. There are pangs of intense pining for the dead person; these are related to unconscious impulses to search for him. There may be a misperception of the deceased's presence, with the experience of something akin to an auditory or visual hallucination, sensations which sometimes lead the recently bereaved person to fear that he is going insane [65].

4. Crying seems to be a universal accompaniment of normal grieving, being particularly marked during the first month and then gradually decreasing.

5. Irritability, bitterness, and anger are characteristic features. These feelings are often surprising and disturbing to the bereaved, and may again be interpreted by the bereaved as an indication of approaching insanity. Anger experienced toward the dead person himself (which is far from rare) tends to be seen as totally alien to the mores of our culture and is thus likely to create additional distress.

6. Lindemann considers it a normal aspect of the grieving process for the survivor to go over and over the events of the death, looking for evidence that his own failure has in some way contributed to it. Parkes did not, however, find guilt to be a major problem in normal widows, though when present it did tend to correlate with initial anger.

7. Activity levels may fluctuate greatly throughout the day, with incessant talking, restlessness, and aimlessness being frequent. The grief-stricken person may be unable to initiate and maintain organized patterns of activity, and may thus become dependent on others to stimulate him to appropriate action. Each fragment of an everyday task seems to require a major effort.

8. Other features of normal grief may be anorexia, insomnia, vivid dreams, and occasional episodes of panic.

We owe to Freud [28] the original and still provocative description of mourning in psychodynamic terms. Freud [28] noted that mourning, if properly conducted, left little energy for other purposes or interests and, is one of his best-known passages, emphasized that "reality testing has shown that the loved object no longer exists, and it proceeds to demand that all libido shall be withdrawn from its attachment to that object. This demand arouses considerable opposition. . . ." In a passage that is exceptionally important for those who work with the conjugally bereaved, he notes that "each single one of the memories and expectations in which the libido is bound to the object is brought up and hypercathected, and detachment of the libido is accomplished in respect of it. . . . when the work of mourning is completed the ego becomes free and uninhibited again."

Bowlby's [8] exposition of the processes of mourning has much heuristic value. He considers that the early phase of yearning and protest is marked by crying and anger because it is akin to the infant's instinctual cry for the mother, triggered by separation experiences. These behaviors function adaptively in an attempt to accomplish reunion and to prevent recurrence of the loss. Of cardinal importance for those who work with bereaved people is Bowlby's assertion, amply documented from our own experience, that the expression of angry strivings to recover the lost object represents a sign of health, enabling the object in due time to be relinquished.

In the phase of behavioral disorganization, both the fact and the permanence of the loss are accepted, resulting in despair. Painful though this period may be, there is general agreement among all those who have worked with bereavement that this phase of mourning must be tolerated. Only if old patterns of interaction with objects are broken down is it possible to develop new ones, related to new objects. Each time the individual is bereaved he must accept the destruction of part of his personality before he can organize himself afresh toward a new object; this is a necessary part of being alive, but one which human beings are reluctant to face.

In the phase of reorganization of behavior, the mourning person again takes an interest in the external world and does indeed find fresh objects to replace the lost one. He now experiences a renewal of the capacity to make and to maintain love relationships.

Pathological Grief and Mourning

Bowlby [9] has described four main variants of pathological mourning in adults, all of them familiar to those who work with bereaved people.

1. Persistent unconscious yearning for the lost object is predominant in one of these forms, although it may well be present but deeply repressed in all forms of pathological mourning. The person remains oriented toward the lost object and continues to live as though the dead spouse were present or retrievable — the person lives in the past. He or she remains preoccupied with the lost object in thought and action, not only organizing his or her life as if it were still recoverable but also continuing to weep for it and to display ill-temper and dissatisfaction with friends and oneself. There may ensue a steady deterioration in social relationships, leading to a progressive isolation. Frank anxiety and depressive syndromes may occur.

2. Reproach is a normal feature of mourning. Reproach is related to attempts to recover the lost object and is directed overtly toward the deceased, toward the bereaved person herself, or toward third parties, such as physicians and others who are seen as connected with the loss. But reproach may become pathological in intensity, toward whatever target it is directed, or its direction may be altered in pathogenic ways; for example, reproach may be directed entirely away from the self toward third parties, producing a paranoid clinical picture, or entirely away from the object and toward the self, producing a depressive picture. The angry, reproachful feelings toward the original object thus become unconscious and persistent. In healthy mourning, loving memories of the lost person are strong enough to hold these angry reproaches in check, permitting their limited expression and thus enabling the bereaved to master the loss.

Parkes [57] has demonstrated that excessive guilt is strongly associated with pathological mourning. It can arise in several ways. We have found that the circumstances of the death are not infrequently such as to lead the survivor to the conviction that he or she played some significant part, even though perhaps small, in the death itself — for example, in situations in which the wife sees herself as having persuaded her husband, "against his better judgment," to have some major surgical procedure that, as it turned out, caused or hastened his death. In other instances, perhaps realistically, perhaps not, extreme guilt is generated in the survivor because of the belief that he or she neglected certain aspects of her husband's care that might have been crucial in determining the outcome. Another important clinical problem arises when the death of one partner supervenes in a highly pathological, intensely ambivalent marriage: strong possessive tendencies and a great deal of anger previously had been directed toward the lost person, and the survivor is required to live with the guilt that springs from knowing that, consciously or unconsciously, she often wished the lost person dead.

The circumstances of the death itself may have been such as to maximize angry feelings toward the dead person. There are abundant examples in our own files: when the death has been due to suicide; when, more subtly, the survivor considers that the death was induced or hastened by the deceased's failure to comply with appropriate medical instructions, or even to seek medical advice; or when the deceased persisted with seriously self-destructive habits, such as heavy smoking although suffering from emphysema. Lindemann [42] and Parkes [57] both noted that pathological grieving could be recognized by the presence of hostility — fury — directed toward specific persons. In circumstances of this type reproaches might initially have been aimed, more or less appropriately, at the lost person, but it would seem more common for them to be diverted elsewhere, and severe guilt would, of course, be experienced if they are turned back against the self. In our own study of social network factors during the bereavement crisis (see p. 210), we found a highly significant tendency for those widows who experienced a bad outcome to have perceived their environment as blocking their expression of such affects as guilt and anger. On the contrary, those women who resolved the crisis satisfactorily did not feel that they had encountered such blocking, and, in fact, appeared to have had a permissively supportive network that enabled these affects to be ventilated.

3. A bereaved person sometimes limits the expression of his own grief and concentrates instead on succoring some other individual who has also been bereaved or who is seen as deprived in some other major way. The bereaved person projects onto the vicarious figure his own affects of grief and helplessness, plus his yearning for the lost object and his anger at the desertion. Children or sick persons, perceived as helpless and in need of help, are often selected for this purpose. Although this proxy response may be a component of normal mourning, the situation is pathological when this style of coping is predominant.

In many instances the younger widow expresses various aspects of her grief through her children, thereby minimizing her own distress. She focuses on one child's dependent needs, thus partially escaping a confrontation with her own dependence; she foresees serious sexual difficulties for another child, thus minimizing her own feelings of sexual need; with yet another child she emphasizes his sense of loss and emptiness. If such children are able to be directly observed, it is not uncommon to find abundant evidence of projective identification, the child being found in fact to be coping reasonably well, in striking contrast to his mother's pathological but unrecognized reaction.

4. In a fourth type of pathological mourning, the reality of the loss is denied so that instinctual response systems are not evoked to deal with it. A secret belief may be maintained that the object will return, even though

publicly the loss is accepted. A relationship may be continued in fantasy with the lost person, and because of uncorrected reference to reality the picture of the lost object becomes grossly distorted by idealization. The belief is kept secret because to discuss it would run the risk of disillusionment, so that the lost one would indeed have to be given up; therefore intimate relationships that might tempt the survivor to share her precious memories and hopes are fraught with risk and are therefore avoided. Another way in which disorganization may be avoided is by the mechanism of ego-splitting, enabling the subject to contain completely self-contradictory beliefs about the reality of the loss. Grieving may be postponed for several years [21], later becoming activated in response to some precipitating factor, such as another bereavement or an anniversary. This type of pathological mourning is rarely identified in research studies of bereaved people. One might guess that a person falling into this group might be one of those people who are unwilling to participate in any discussion of their bereavement, for to do so would risk shattering their particular defense systems. Anecdotal evidence from clinical experience also suggests that this denial mechanism may exist in at least some of those bereaved people who make an extraordinarily hasty (and often disastrous) remarriage.

Identification

One of the most contentious topics in the psychology of grief and mourning is the part played by identification. Lindemann [42] described one type of pathological grief reaction as characterized by acquisition of the symptoms of the deceased's last illness, and Parkes [57] has found this to be relatively prominent in his study of bereaved psychiatric patients. Freud [28] had nevertheless seen identification as occurring, at least to some extent, in normal mourning; and a critical part of psychoanalytic theory rests on the assumption that personality growth is substantially dependent on the introjection of important aspects of objects that are lost or in danger of being lost, the ego of the developing child thereafter being modified to conform with the introject. Identification can then be said to have occurred. In terms of bereavement, such an introjection serves the purpose of preserving in memory the relationship with the dead person.

Krupp [37] has significantly helped our understanding of this problem by proposing four possible forms of identification of the bereaved person with the deceased:

1. Constructive identification with vital and satisfying aspects of the object and the relationship, comparable with the identifications that follow separation from parents in the Oedipal stage, during adolescence, and in young adulthood.

2. Personality identification, in which the mourner adopts the mannerisms, traits, and characteristics of the loved one. These identifications may be transient and variable, their presence at any point having a dynamically determined purpose.

3. Symptomatic identification with the deceased person's last illness. This mechanism is strongly associated with pathological mourning, resulting in what amounts to conversion symptoms, simultaneously representing the unconscious gain of bringing the lost one back as well as punishment in accordance with the talion principle. In our own study such identifications were most frequently seen in women who showed evidence of previous masculine identification problems. One of Krupp's patients, a man, fluctuated between this type of identification when he felt guilty because he wanted the deceased dead and a personality identification when he wanted the deceased alive.

4. Depressive identification, some degree of which is an inevitable accompaniment of mourning, but which is of limited extent in healthy grief. In pathological forms of mourning it is excessive and persistent; by treating himself as the hated object, the survivor can maintain the fantasy that he has not lost it.

Grief and Mourning in the Elderly

There is adequate evidence to show that the older person views death quite differently from the younger person; its inevitability for both himself and his spouse confronts him much more forcefully. This realization is due to a number of factors: the prevalence of illness and physical impairment, the loss of many of his family and friends, diminished psychosocial support from his environment, disengagement from his social network [20], the process of his life review [10], and the knowledge that his time is running out.

There is also considerable evidence, however, that the nature of the tie between two elderly spouses is probably quite different from that existing between younger ones. In the very old, if both spouses are feeble, and both do what they can [12], often they are so intimate as to be symbiotic in a simple sense — if one dies, the other cannot survive. Sexual factors are of greatly lessened significance in the relationship. Emotional ties and mutual warmth may, however, be greater than in the middle years, when, as Troll [72] points out, many marriages are rated as unsatisfactory, only to be considered improved later.

From the limited evidence available, mourning in the elderly would appear to be qualitatively different. Inhibition of overt grief appears to be frequent, being replaced by somatic reactions. Stern, Williams, and Prados [71] found little overt grief or guilt was manifested at this time of life, but rather an idealization of the deceased, often to a bizarre degree, with irrational hostility toward living persons in the environment, especially those of the same sex as the deceased. Accentuation of preexisting somatic symptoms or the onset of new somatic illness frequently occurred. Gramlich [30] also found grief to be chronic, inhibited, and prolonged in the elderly, the emotional reactions being suppressed and the most common manifestation being somatic pain and distress. Incorporation of the lost one's physical symptoms was not infrequent. Parkes's study [56] of the health records of London widows also demonstrated that those over 65 showed an increased consultation rate for somatic symptoms, while those under 65 had increased consultation rates for psychological symptoms.

Is Grief a Disease?

Under the provocative title *Is Grief a Disease?* Engel [25] offered many cogent arguments for the view that it was valuable to regard grief as a disease syndrome, bringing forth a good deal of evidence of the type already mentioned in this chapter. Much earlier, Freud [28] had stated: "Although grief involves grave departures from the normal attitude to life, it never occurs to us to regard it as a morbid condition and to hand the mourner over to medical treatment." It is certainly useful, on the one hand, to be reminded that the seemingly ubiquitous human experience of grief may have disastrous consequences. On the other hand, there would seem to be considerable danger, at least for primary care-givers, in defining in terms of a medical model a segment of human experience that is both inevitable and necessary and (as so heavily emphasized by Bowlby) growth-promoting, in a fundamental sense. Clayton et al. [14], in a prospective study of 40 bereaved relatives, 19 of whom were bereaved spouses, considered that the profile of symptoms derived from their subjects warranted the definition of bereavement in terms of a model of a mild reactive depression. This, too, would seem to have unfortunate implications for the management of conjugal bereavement.

SOCIAL-NETWORK FACTORS IN BEREAVEMENT

The survivor of a marital dyad that has been involved in mutually supportive relationships with family and community, through a strong and empathic social network, will certainly have very different problems of adjustment compared with the survivor of an isolated and alienated pair, living an anomic existence, whether or not there have been children. It was pointed out many years ago that human behavior is always a function of two sets of variables, those involving the person and those involving the situation in which that person is functioning; and Blackman and Goldstein [6] have recently enunciated, using their own empirical data, that one crucial aspect of the environment is an interaction with close, face-to-face members of the community, with "the exchange of emotional support and services." They have advanced the concept of a "credit network," by means of which a person may receive emotional support and temporary services when in a state of crisis; his position in the credit network (and perhaps people keep informal, barely conscious, track of this) may determine the amount of support available. Their observations suggest that individuals who have fewer available supports manifest more psychological symptoms, and Cumming [18], in an otherwise extremely pessimistic paper, believes that there is evidence to suggest that "anyone bound to a small group of common goals and shared values, in which there is a certain minimum specialization of roles, may be provided with one element of protection against mental illness, no matter what kinds of stresses he must endure." This is echoed by Blackman and Goldstein [6]: "Failure to be involved in such a network of credits . . . increases the probability that disability will result from a given amount of stress because no support will be available."

Our original retrospective study [53] of conjugal bereavement investigated the interpersonal transactions that were considered by the widow to have occurred during the crisis, and it related these to the subject's ultimate outcome as measured by general assessment of her health 13 months after her husband's death. The research instrument was a semi-structured interview schedule designed to tap the widow's perception of her environment during crisis; more precisely, it aimed to render a detailed accounting of the interactions that took place between the widow and the members of her social network and, most important, to determine whether she saw these as helpful or unhelpful. It was part of our intention to assess, as precisely as possible, those forms of interpersonal exchange that the widow considered would have been helpful during the crisis period but which the environment failed to supply, these being referred to as "needs."

From our total sample of 375 subjects, we interviewed in this way 39 "bad-outcome" and 42 "good-outcome" widows, selected so that the two groups would be matched as closely as possible on the social and personal variables for which data were available. Attempts to assess the importance of specific persons produced little that was statistically significant, the one exception to this being that there was a significant tendency for good-outcome subjects in our Sydney sample to have perceived the doctor in attendance at the time of the husband's death as helpful and for bad-outcome subjects to have seen him as unhelpful ($p < .05$). It was also noted that, though the majority of the husbands of good-outcome subjects had not died in the hospital, when they had done so, widows had seen the hospital staff as helpful. This was in contrast to the finding that, of the bad-outcome subjects interviewed in Sydney, 12 husbands out of 19 had died in the hospital, and five of the 12 widows had perceived the hospital staff as unhelpful.

More important findings related to the widow's perception of the helpfulness of particular interpersonal transactions rather than of particular people. It is important to note that the great majority of widows, both those who resolved their crisis without subsequent health impairment and those whose health deteriorated in the year after the husband's death, experienced many helpful interactions with their environment. The difference between bad-outcome and good-outcome groups was determined by the greater number of nonhelpful interchanges reported by the former subjects, the bad-outcome women perceiving their social environment as overtly or covertly hostile, nonsupportive, and failing to meet their needs. In the Boston study the presence of "unmet needs" was clearly of the greatest importance in differentiating the two groups; in the Sydney replication this aspect was less prominent, though the subjects still tended to see the environment as opposing their task of mourning [52].

More specifically, widows who subsequently proceeded to a bad outcome could be shown to have preceived some quite specific interpersonal problems during the bereavement crisis. They expressed the feeling that a person or persons in the environment had overtly or covertly opposed their free expression of emotions, particularly those of grief and anger. There was recurrent mention by subjects in this group of the belief that other people seemed to be shocked by the widow's feelings, telling her to control herself and pull herself together, and that, on the other hand, attempts seemed to have been made to minimize her grief by a process of generalization, pointing out to her the sufferings of other widows or telling her just how much grief was appropriate for a widow to feel. In other instances, the bad-outcome widow considered that important people in her environment were themselves upset to an extent she believed inappropriate or even competitive, or were being incongruously cheerful, or claimed to share her grief and understand exactly how she was feeling, which the subject thought was patently untrue.

Another important finding was that the bad-outcome widow considered that persons in her environment were actively attempting to focus her attention on the present and the future, these exchanges being seen as actively unhelpful. Many such widows, during the first three months following the death, had an overtly hostile response to the type of conversation that tried to arouse their interest in new activities, the development of new friendships, or the resumption of old hobbies and occupations. Another area of interaction with the environment was represented by a series of interchanges that we could group together under the heading "review of the past"; whereas some bad-outcome subjects considered that they needed assistance in this area, i.e., that they lacked an empathic person with whom they could discuss their past life and, in particular, their relationship with their husbands, other bad-outcome widows had found some interchanges in this category unhelpful. Two important such interchanges had a religious orientation, and from this area of our study we developed the conviction that unsolicited discussions on religious topics during the bereavement crisis were only occasionally perceived as helpful. Subjects who already had a religious belief tended to regard such interventions as gratuitous and unnecessary, while subjects without any profound religious conviction found such attempts at comfort meaningless and often extremely irritating.

It must be emphasized that it is the subject's *perception* of her environment that has been the variable under study throughout this work. Clearly there is a very real possibility that the widow's own longstanding modes of interpersonal relationship may in some instances have contributed, perhaps markedly, to the nonsupportiveness she perceived around her; her own behavior, perhaps lifelong, perhaps manifested most intensely during the terminal stages of her husband's life, may have driven away from her, or induced hostility in, those people who might have been supportive figures in the social network. It is also possible that at least some of the unhelpfulness and hostility perceived in the environment is caused by projection of her own unrecognized hostile feelings. On balance, however, the evidence from our studies strongly suggests that, while massive projection may be important in some individual instances, "objective" insensitivity, overt or covert hostility, a failure of empathy, and a relative or complete ignorance of the emotional needs of the widow played a much more significant part. There seems to be abundant evidence that many people in the environment of the widow, including some members of the so-called helping professions, had actively behaved in ways that, however much these persons may have believed themselves to be helping, had been in active opposition to those psychological processes required for the satisfactory resolution of object loss.

Several of the widow's social relationships appeared to be of particular importance during the bereavement crisis. Mother-daughter kinship ties are suggested by several workers to be those most heavily and profitably utilized in times of stress, as described by Halbertsma [32] in a working-class district, where such ties offer mutual assistance in times of illness or death. In our study, there was a tendency for the middle generation to interact with mothers or daughters or both. Often their own mothers, however, perhaps themselves widowed, were perceived as reacting non-supportively during the bereavement crisis. When the relationship between the widow and her mother was a mutually gratifying one, the mother's support seemed to have been invaluable, but when the mother was reported as being unhelpful at this time, or as failing to meet the widow's needs, this seemed to pose a particular problem. The mothers who had themselves been widowed at a relatively early age often claimed to have all the answers to the problems of bereavement — answers which were, however, quite unacceptable to their daughters.

The importance of the female in kinship ties makes many other sources of support potentially available for the bereaved woman. These female-linked kinship networks are evidenced by the facts that the place of residence is commonly closer to that of the wife's parents, there is a greater proportion of interaction with the wife's relatives, and mutual aid is provided more frequently along the female line. Sisters and nieces (sisters' daughters) may well provide considerable support, but the mother-daughter tie, the widow's turning to her adult or adolescent daughter, tends to be of the greatest value.

Mother-daughter ties tend to be stronger than those between mother and son from the time the children reach adulthood, just as sister-sister ties tend to be stronger than those between sister and brother or between brothers. In the mother-son relationship, the son may offer instrumental support, but there is little reciprocation of services such as characterizes the relationship between mother and adult daughter, enjoyment of each other's company and assistance between mothers and sons tending to decrease following widowhood.

The problem is very different for the widow, usually substantially younger, whose children are themselves dependent and sorely in need of support following the bereavement. The younger widow lacks the supportive ties that her older counterpart is likely to have with adult children, and the altered patterns of family interaction following the husband's death may create serious role strains for her. She is not only required to fill both maternal and paternal roles, but she is also expected to be both comforter and bereaved. Her own needs during the crisis may substantially affect her relationships with her children and her involvement with them, and when she cannot respond emotionally to her children's needs they suffer a double deprivation. Although the younger widow tends frequently to say that she is grateful for the presence of her dependent children because they are considered by her to provide some partial distraction from her own problems and to give meaning to her continued existence, mothers all too frequently feel that they must hide their grief in their children's presence, and their own mourning thus becomes inhibited [40]. Frequently there is indeed a mutual inhibition of grief, rationalized as a protective mechanism to prevent the other members of the family from being upset. The magnitude of the child's own disturbance is not always easy to assess without direct evaluation, and the widow may be threatened or enraged when the outward manifestations of mourning in the child or adolescent seem inadequate to her, particularly when such inhibited grief in the young is followed by delinquent or quasi-delinquent behavior [13] that has a clear relationship to the bereavement. The relative or complete lack of response in the very young child, who has failed to grasp the significance and permanence of his father's death, may also prove a burden to the grieving mother. As described previously, projective identification may distort the widow's perception of her children's real needs and qualities and thus impair her ability to relate to them; one of our subjects, for example, seemed to be expressing mainly her own feelings of withdrawal and isolation when she described her son as being remote from everybody since his father's death.

The bereaved person's altered relationships with the children may place the latter in new roles that may subsequently prove threatening to all parties. Older but still adolescent children may be thrust prematurely into adult roles to ease the parent's own anxieties; e.g., a son may be expected to take over as the man of the family. One of our subjects symbolized this by giving her son, a week after her husband's death, his father's clothes to wear. A younger son may be taken into his mother's bed in an attempt to gratify her primitive needs for bodily warmth and comfort, and the Oedipal conflicts reactivated and inflamed in such a situation may lead to excessively close cross-generational and cross-sexual ties, with a serious warping of the child's later psychosexual development.

Some widows may be threatened by their own feelings of childlike dependence and may flee from these into exaggerated independence. The need to fill both maternal and paternal roles may be beyond the capacity of the immature and dependent woman, as well as extremely threatening to her if her own sexual identification rests on insecure foundations; her response may be to adopt one role or the other to an extent so exaggerated that it clearly indicates the degree of overcompensation involved. Any of these mechanisms and responses may operate to distort the subsequent family adjustment, making it increasingly pathogenic for all its members.

Members of the husband's family seem unlikely to offer much support to the widow beyond the time of the funeral. Marris [54] cites only two widows (out of a total of 72) who reported that members of the husband's family visited them more often, on their own initiative, after his death. He suggests that this may be a strongly class-linked phenomenon; in the East End of London, the area of his study, a man tends to marry into his wife's family, sharing her company with her mother with as good grace as he can, and visiting his own family largely on his own or with his children. Our own studies, both in Boston and Sydney, have abundantly confirmed the extent to which the two family groups may drift apart after the death, particularly when there has been animosity beforehand. Quarrels may develop over the disposition of the husband's possessions, there may be disagreements about funeral arrangements, and, in particular, the widow may consider that there has been a failure to keep promises concerning attention to the children, coupled with the withholding of financial support that she believed could have been given without hardship. The studies showed that in some instances the widow considered that her husband's family made distressing inferences that she had failed to take adequate care of him or had not really appreciated his good qualities. Members of the husband's family, and, in particular, the husband's mother, were also listed among those who had distressed or angered the widow by suggesting that her loss was less substantial than that suffered by one or more members of the husband's family. Sad to relate, there are indeed some mothers who say to a grieving widow, "You have lost a husband, but I have lost a son."

In a different population again, Lopata [45] found a similar lack of support emanating from the husband's family. Only one in four of her sample of Chicago widows reported any visiting by these relatives after the funeral; indeed, 64 percent stated that the in-laws did not even help with the funeral arrangements.

SOCIOCULTURAL FACTORS

The influence of socioeconomic status in determining the outcome of the bereavement crisis is uncertain. (Poverty as a consequence of bereavement was discussed earlier in this chapter.) There is no positive correlation between poverty and bad outcome as determined by health criteria; and our own studies have not revealed any relationship between the widow's social class and the success of her coping techniques. Certainly we have found that the younger, lower-class widow with many dependent children and few material resources may present a picture of extreme deprivation, and Parkes [60] did find a lower socioeconomic status to be one factor predictive of bad outcome in his young widows and widowers. It also follows from Lopata's work that, while middle-class widows may experience a greater life disorganization than lower-class widows, because they were more affectively and more variously involved with their husbands, they also appear to have more facility for reentry into society.

Cultural factors also influence the response to death. Most societies have evolved culturally sanctioned rituals in order to deal with death and the regaining of social equilibrium as quickly as possible. Probably the most important consideration is the extent to which a culture provides for the open expression of grief and other emotions and defines a clear role for the bereaved person. It may well be that the rites of passage sanctioned by the culture influence the pathogenicity of the cultural response to bereavement.

Western cultures, of course, provide relatively little formal ritual or structured societal support for the widow, who is left without a clearly defined role to play, either during the bereavement crisis itself or in the following period of reorganization of her life. Except in certain cultures or subcultures that have more formal mourning requirements, such as special clothes to wear, a defined period for grieving, and religious ritual, expectations of the widow are variable and uncertain. She may hear, for example, of widows who are openly enjoying the attentions of other men within a few months, but she has little but her own feelings to guide her in determining whether or not this is acceptable behavior. It might also be suspected, though there are no empirical observations on this, that the grieving problems of widowers may be greatly magnified in an Anglo-Saxon society, where the cultural expectation remains that men should not make too much display of their grief.

Our own work in the United States and Australia has found a significantly greater health deterioration in Australian widows, compared with their North American counterparts. There is no easy explanation for this, but in view of the fact that the Boston subjects were predominantly Roman Catholic, with many women of Irish and Italian descent, there is certainly the possibility that the widows' supportive networks, and indeed the attitudes of the subcultures toward grief and mourning, differ significantly in the two areas in such a way as to favor the American subject. One obvious difference is the much greater degree of ritualization that surrounds death in these segments of contemporary American society, with a much higher frequency of embalming and public "viewing" of the body, together with more precisely defined customs through which family and friends formally share in the mourning process. One particular challenge for future research is presented by the need to determine, in a variety of cultures, whether the widely differing practices concerned with the expression of grief, and the different prescription of roles for the bereaved, do in fact have any correlation with the ultimate outcome of conjugal bereavement. Yamamoto et al. [75], for example, in their study of Japanese widows, suggest that the specific cultural beliefs of ancestor worship, whereby the deceased becomes an ancestor in daily communication with the widow at the family altar, influence the expression of mourning, because the lost object is not fully lost.

STUDIES IN PREVENTIVE INTERVENTION

Despite the considerable gaps in knowledge that still exist, it can be argued that sufficient data have already been accumulated concerning the consequences of conjugal bereavement to justify a variety of attempts at preventive intervention [11], ultimately designed to deliver to bereaved people a form of care-giving that will maximize their chances of resolving the crisis without pathological consequences. There is a need to improve the quality of the help available to people in crisis from the so-called caretaking agents, particularly physicians and clergymen.

Also important is the strengthening of the individual's social network in these detribalized times in ways that will lock the bereaved person more securely into a situation in which spontaneous help of a nonprofessional kind will be more readily forthcoming. Organizations for widows and widowers have an important role to play in this regard. Silverman [69] has developed a supportive network that mobilizes the experience and the capacity for service of other widows.

The effectiveness of these group approaches [35] is difficult to assess. Evaluation of such programs to date is frequently based on the judgment that all help given is beneficial, which smacks of omnipotent autocracy rather than of scientific methodology [64]. Moreover, there would appear to be the very real risk that such broadly based approaches may interfere with the adaptive devices of those who would otherwise benefit from the crisis experience. Attention must therefore be given also to individual approaches to preventive intervention, though these, too, tend to be poorly conceptualized. The literature is full of references to the use of reassurance, positive transference, direct advice, and environmental manipulation, without any justification of why these should be used, apart from the gratifications they provide the intervener.

In the study of preventive intervention, it is of critical importance to be able to predict, with a reasonable degree of accuracy, which bereaved persons are at substantial risk of unfavorable outcome. In making such a prediction, the evidence gathered from our earlier studies of conjugal bereavement has permitted the formulation of criteria which, when applied in certain combinations to an unselected group of widows by independent raters of proven reliability, furnish a group of subjects of whom 80 percent would, without intervention, proceed to a bad outcome. These criteria are as follows:

1. Perceived unhelpfulness of the environment, as determined by a defined frequency of "unhelpful" and "needed" responses in that section of the evaluation interview that deals with the widow's perception of the supportiveness of her environmental network.

2. The presence of additional concurrent crisis situations, wherein the individual, despite perhaps seemingly adequate coping resources, faces such overwhelming problems that the task of adjustment is likely to be beyond his capacities — and those of most people. Examples of such situations are the death of another important family member during or just prior to the conjugal bereavement itself, the discovery of illegitimate pregnancy in a teenage daughter, and the diagnosis of serious illness in oneself or in another family member.

3. The mode of death may have been such as to maximize anger, guilt or self-reproach (see p. 218). One example involved a widow who was enraged because her husband had chosen to make a small repair to the roof of their home at the exact time they were due to go out on a social visit. Immediately after she shouted at him to hurry, he lost his footing

and died in the resultant fall onto the concrete below.

4. A preexisting pathological marital relationship, characterized by extreme dependence or ambivalence in the relationship between the survivor and the deceased.

Many of these criteria, it will be noted, fit the earlier descriptions in the literature of those factors likely to be associated with pathological grief reactions. Similar factors were found by Parkes [60] to relate to poor outcome in his prospective study of Boston widows and widowers, although he also included low socioeconomic status as an additional predictor.

Now well in progress are studies of the effect of crisis intervention in such a high-risk group, intervention being carried out only during the crisis period itself, arbitrarily defined as the first three months following the bereavement. Intervention, carried out by an experienced psychiatrist, involves selective support of the various aspects of ego functioning shown to be impaired during the widow's interaction with her social network [64]. The widow is actively encouraged to express her sadness, anger, and guilt; highly individualized attention is paid to those aspects of her defensive style that interfere with this expression of affect or with her acceptance of the actuality of the loss. She is also encouraged to go over thoughts and memories of her husband in her review of the relationship. Any concurrent crisis situation is assessed and dealt with, as are feelings about the preexisting marital relationship and the special circumstances of the death.

The health of these subjects has been compared, 13 months after the bereavement, to the health of a control group of widows, assessed as being at similar risk of bad outcome but randomly allocated to a nonintervention group. In this way the effectiveness of this type of intervention has been established.

Further consideration might well be given to those factors that influence our raters to use "mode of death" as a predictive criterion. The social setting in which the death of a spouse occurs is, of course, variable and plays a part in many instances. Krupp and Kligfeld [38] referred to the perceived "timeliness" or "untimeliness" of the death. A death at the end of a full and satisfying life together, when major life goals have been attained and the process of disengagement from society has begun, presents to both the dying person and the survivor very different problems of adjustment compared with a premature death in the early years of marriage, when life and family goals still lie ahead, and involvement between the partners is intense. Moreover, sudden death presents a very different coping problem from the gradual and painful adaptation required in a prolonged terminal illness. We have found, contrary to a good deal of the folklore about bereavement, that those women whose husbands die instantly or with minimal warning are no more likely to develop health deterioration than are those who have substantial foreknowledge of the death [53]. The evidence does indeed suggest that a protracted period of dying presents its own problems, in that it may maximize preexisting ambivalence and lead to pronounced feelings of guilt and inadequacy in the nursing person, soon to be the bereaved. When such a death has involved deformity and mutilation, additional intrapsychic problems are involved for the wife, as well as the physical strain of heavy nursing or repeated hospital visiting and the torment resulting from close contact with her husband's pain and suffering. Repeated and unpleasant changes of dressing, injections, the home-nursing procedures required to deal with incontinence, or the anguish of dealing with a spouse whose mental state has so changed that he is no longer recognizable as the person who was once dearly loved, all may lead the spouse to long for the death and to feel considerable guilt in doing so. One of our subjects, for example, was mourning a husband who had had a parotid-gland tumor that had required 32 operations over a period of 25 years. Several years before his death, his tongue had been amputated, he emitted an extremely bad odor, and his face was grossly disfigured.

On the other hand, when the period of fatal disease has extended beyond a few months, anticipatory mourning may well have taken place so that grief for the death itself may be attenuated.

THE MANAGEMENT OF CONJUGAL BEREAVEMENT

Management of the dying patient and his family begins with the knowledge that one partner in a marriage is suffering from a fatal illness. There have been several valuable contributions in recent years toward the understanding of this problem, for example, those of Kübler-Ross [39], Cramond [17], and Roose [67]. Often there is initial denial of the seriousness of the illness by one or both partners, which may be a necessary phase of their coping. It has been shown, for example, that 19 percent of a group of terminally ill people told quite specifically and directly the nature and prognoses of their illnesses later insisted that they had no knowledge of what was wrong with them [2]. Such denial is maintained because the knowledge of impending death is too overwhelming to be immediately comprehended, and harsh confrontation of this denial will be of no avail or, worse, seriously destructive. General support for both partners is essential during this stage, and communications showing the beginning of a more honest recognition of the nature of the illness may start to appear, often in disguised form. The patient's queries concerning the future and his tentative discussion of anticipated everyday events may represent ways of approaching the question of whether he does indeed have a future.

Both the dying partner and the survivor may go through stages resembling the phases of mourning in their attempts to adapt to the fact that this is a terminal condition. The denial and disbelief of the initial phase of shock and numbness may give way to angry protest, but later some degree of calm acceptance may appear. All too frequently, however, and sometimes with medical sanction and even at the physician's insistence, a ludicrous charade is required to be played out, in which both partners in the marriage are aware that the illness is a fatal one, yet each is prevented from any sort of realistic discussion about the issues involved because of the false belief that the other partner does not know and must be kept in ignorance. Sometimes, even in the presence of full awareness, there is a necessary isolation of affect, with the feelings of anxiety, hopelessness, and anger cut off from consciousness in order to enable the accomplishment of such necessary tasks as the preparation of property settlements by the dying spouse or the nursing care by the healthy partner. There may be fluctuating levels of hope throughout this period, interspersed with episodes of angry protest, bargaining with God, and depression as anticipated losses are mourned. Both the dying spouse and his partner may experience anticipatory grieving, feeling acute pain as they share the memories of shared past experiences and relinquish, one by one, their anticipated hopes and goals, as well as the love relationship itself. Aldrich [3] emphasizes that this form of anguish may be even more intense for the well-integrated person who has had a full and rich life and, in a very real sense, much more to lose.

Throughout this phase the dying person requires a relationship marked by consistent, empathic support, in which he can feel free to express his sadness and anger, his guilt concerning past failures, and his fears of the future. His helplessness in the face of increasing dependency, weakness, and physical impairment, his fears concerning loss of control and his anguish at any mutilation or specific impairment that might be involved in the process of dying, all these can be subjects for a series of discussions that will help him toward a more comfortable and less bitter terminal phase.

The surviving spouse also requires a supportive relationship in which she can ventilate her own fear, guilt, and anger, and wherein some of her dependent needs can be met. Dependency conflicts may be greatly mobilized, both because of the threatened loss of dependent gratification and because of identification with the helplessness of the dying person. A good deal of anger may be stimulated by the knowledge of impending loss, the present and anticipated frustration of needs, and the problems of caring for a dying person. Hostility may be even more of a problem if the illness is interpreted by her, realistically or not, as in part self-induced, or if the husband's terminal illness is seen by a disappointed or ambitious wife as representing the end of all her hopes.

Serious guilt may follow such aggressive feelings, particularly in relationships in which ambivalence has been intense. Symptoms of depression seem particularly likely to appear if the surviving partner feels that she has made some sort of contribution to his illness or to the rapidity with which the patient died.

Sexual conflicts may also be aroused. Identification with the patient may highlight previous sexual inadequacies or make them conscious, particularly if the terminal illness has involved surgery of a type likely to activate castration anxiety or if it arises from carcinoma of the breast or from disease of any other organ with a sexual connotation. Diseases that are mutilating and disfiguring are also important in this connection. Sublimation or other defenses may need to be mobilized to deal with the survivor's sexual drives when they are no longer gratified by the terminally ill person. When sexual activity is extended outside the marital relationship, guilt is likely to be extreme, as such sexual behavior often has a markedly hostile basis.

In summary, awareness of these potential areas of conflict in the dying person and his spouse should enable the care-giver to offer a valuable psychotherapeutic relationship, alleviating distress, promoting an adaptation that is as meaningful as possible, and working through any anticipatory grieving. Further communication between the two may be encouraged, and the destructive conspiracy of silence that so often impairs a relationship, denying both partners a valuable emotional closeness in this last phase of their marriage, can be avoided.

Management of the Bereaved Spouse

Lindemann suggested in 1944 that 8 to 10 interviews with the bereaved would assist the work of mourning and resolve the state of acute grief, but there has, in fact, been little scientific investigation of the management of the recently bereaved. Most expositions have concentrated on the care of patients with clearly pathological forms of grieving, such as the reports of Barnacle [5], Fleming and Altschul [27], Paul and Grosser [62], and Volkan and Showalter [73].

There is considerable clinical evidence for the proposition that if grief is suppressed or inhibited it will later seek full expression in some pathological form. Our own studies have demonstrated that those widows who do poorly are significantly different from those who achieve a satisfactory outcome following bereavement in that they perceive their environment as suppressing their grief. It follows, then, as indicated in our studies on preventive intervention, that bereaved individuals should be helped, when necessary, with their task of mourning. This would seem to be particularly necessary for those in whom it can be established (by the use of certain defined criteria) that there is a high probability of crisis malresolution. During the initial stage of disbelief, denial should not be confronted harshly. A supportive and empathic presence should suffice, with a possible taking over of everyday tasks beyond the bereaved's capacity. It is important for care-givers to be accessible for further discussion should the bereaved person seem to desire it. When the true work of mourning begins, there should be active encouragement of the expression of sadness, anger, and guilt, coupled with support in reviewing the lost relationship, discussing its various positive and negative aspects as it is gradually relinquished — bit by bit.

It is appropriate, for example, to provide an opportunity for the bereaved person to express her hostility and to discuss its sources, such as the desertion and deprivation she perceives in the death and the anger that may be aroused in her by certain behaviors within her social network. When guilt seems to be an important affect, this, too, should be able to be expressed, and, when necessary, its sources discussed and explored. In some instances the bereavement will have revived conflicts associated with earlier object losses, including earlier bereavement, and these may need to be examined if they are considered to be important factors in hindering current expression of affect. Defense mechanisms that impair the recognition or expression of emotion may also require interpretation, such as when prolonged denial operates to inhibit sadness or anger, displacement disguises the true object of these affects, or projective identification results in only a surrogate grief.

Conflicts that come to the fore because of the deprivation resulting from the death, such as those associated with unsatisfied dependent or sexual needs, may also require to be worked through, although cultural taboos in Western society seem to make the area of sexual frustration the most difficult one to handle. Altered family relationships may also require some type of supportive intervention. An important part of the management of the bereaved spouse may involve work with her children, directly or indirectly, in order to assist their own grieving reactions, work with the family unit as a whole, or even work with other significant network members.

Such support will be most beneficial if available during the bereavement crisis itself. It must be offered in such a form that, while gratifying some of the intense dependence needs of the bereaved, does not produce in her a sense of helpless inadequacy. At the termination of the intervention period, when the supportive relationship is coming to an end, it is important also to deal with the transference mourning and loss that may be expressed, in disguised form, during the last few contacts. Interpretation of this behavior and the associated affects may well be of critical importance in aiding the task of mourning.

There is little evidence to suggest that pharmacotherapy is an appropriate method for the management of grief. Examination of our own data shows that those who did badly used significantly more psychotropic medications than those who did well. Although not necessarily suggesting that these two findings were causally related, we can at least conclude that such preparations do little to help. In those circumstances in which a true depressive illness has supervened, antidepressant medication may, of course, be a valid and effective form of treatment, as indeed may electrotherapy. This brings us, however, into a quite different area — the management of the pathological sequelae of bereavement, a task that is still a serious challenge to the clinical psychiatrist.

REFERENCES

1. Aitken-Swan, J. *Widows in Australia: A Survey of Economic and Social Conditions of Widows with Dependent Children.* Sydney: Council of Social Services of New South Wales, 1962.
2. Aitken-Swan, J., and Easson, E. Reactions of cancer patients on being told their diagnosis. *British Medical Journal* 1:779, 1959.
3. Aldrich, C. The dying patient's grief. *Journal of the American Medical Association* 184:329, 1963.
4. Anderson, C. Aspects of pathological grief and mourning. *International Journal of Psychoanalysis* 30:48, 1949.
5. Barnacle, C. Grief reactions and their treatment. *Diseases of the Nervous System* 10:173, 1949.
6. Blackman, S., and Goldstein, K. Some aspects of a theory of community mental health. *Community Mental Health Journal* 4:85, 1968.
7. Blau, Z. Structural constraints on friendship in old age. *American Sociological Review* 26:429, 1961.
8. Bowlby, J. Processes of mourning. *International Journal of Psychoanalysis* 42:317, 1961.
9. Bowlby, J. Pathological mourning and childhood mourning. *Journal of the American Psychoanalytical Association* 11:1, 1963.
10. Butler, R. Research and clinical observations on the psychologic reactions to the physical changes of aging. *Mayo Clinics Proceedings* 42:596, 1967.
11. Caplan, G. *Principles of Preventive Psychiatry.* New York: Basic Books, 1964.
12. Clark, M., and Anderson, B. *Culture and Aging.* Springfield, Ill.: Thomas, 1967.
13. Clarke, J. The precipitation of juvenile delinquency. *Journal of Mental Sciences* 107:1033, 1961.
14. Clayton, P., Desmarais, L., and Winokur, G. A systematic study of normal bereavement. *American Journal of Psychiatry* 125:168, 1968.
15. Cohen, M., and Lipton, L. Spontaneous remission of schizophrenic psychosis following maternal death. *Psychiatric Quarterly* 24:716, 1950.
16. Cox, P., and Ford, J. Mortality of widows shortly after widowhood. *Lancet* 1:163, 1964.
17. Cramond, W. Psychotherapy of the dying patient. *British Medical Journal* 3:389, 1970.
18. Cumming, E. Unsolved problems of prevention. *Canada's Mental Health*, Suppl. 56, 1968.

19. Cumming, E. The Multigenerational Family and the Crisis of Widowhood. In W. Donahue et al. (Eds.), *Living in the Multigenerational Family*. Ann Arbor, Mich.: Institute of Gerontology, 1969.

20. Cumming, E., and Henry, W. *Growing Old*. New York: Basic Books, 1961.

21. Deutsch, H. Absence of grief. *Psychoanalytical Quarterly* 6:12, 1937.

22. Dubourg, G., and Mandelbrote, B. Mentally ill widows. *International Journal of Social Psychiatry* 12:63, 1966.

23. Ekblom, B. Significance of socio-psychological factors with regard to risk of death among elderly persons. *Acta Psychiatrica Scandinavica* 39:627, 1963.

24. Eliot, T. The adjustive behaviour of bereaved families: A new field for research. *Social Forces* 8:543, 1930.

25. Engel, G. Is grief a disease? *Psychosomatic Medicine* 23:18, 1961.

26. Engel, G. A life-setting conducive to illness — the giving-up given-up complex. *Bulletin of the Menninger Clinic* 32:355, 1968.

27. Fleming, J., and Altschul, S. Activation of mourning and growth by psychoanalysis. *International Journal of Psychoanalysis* 44:419, 1963.

28. Freud, S. Mourning and melancholia (1917). In *The Standard Edition of the Complete Psychological Works of Sigmund Freud*, transl. and ed. by J. Strachey with others. London: Hogarth and Institute of Psycho-Analysis, 1957. Vol. 14, pp. 237-258.

29. Friedman, J., and Zaris, D. Paradoxical response to death of a spouse. *Diseases of the Nervous System* 25:480, 1964.

30. Gramlich, E. Recognition and management of grief in elderly patients. *Geriatrics* 23:87, 1968.

31. Greene, W., and Miller, G. Psychological factors in reticuloendothelial disease. *Psychosomatic Medicine* 20:124, 1958.

32. Halbertsma, H. Working-class systems of mutual assistance in case of childbirth, illness and death. *Social Science and Medicine* 3:321, 1968.

33. Hilgard, J. Anniversaries in mental illness. *Psychiatry* 22:113, 1959.

34. Hobson, D. Widows of Blackton. *New Society* 24:13, 1964.

35. Jacobsen, G., Strickler, M., and Morley, W. Generic and individual approaches to crisis intervention. *American Journal of Public Health* 58:338, 1968.

36. Kraus, A., and Lilienfeld, A. Some epidemiological aspects of the high mortality rate in the young widowed group. *Journal of Chronic Disease* 10:207, 1959.

37. Krupp, G. Identification as a defense against anxiety in coping with loss. *International Journal of Psychoanalysis* 45:303, 1965.

38. Krupp, G., and Kligfeld, B. The bereavement reaction — a cross-cultural evaluation. *Journal of Religious Health* 1:222, 1962.

39. Kübler-Ross, E. *On Death and Dying*. London: Tavistock, 1970.

40. Langer M. *Learning to Live As a Widow*. New York: Messner, 1957.

41. Lidz, R. Emotional factors in hyperthyroidism. *Psychosomatic Medicine* 11:2, 1949.

42. Lindemann, E. Symptomatology and management of acute grief. *American Journal of Psychiatry* 101:141, 1944.

43. Lindemann, E. Modifications in the Course of Ulcerative Colitis in Relationship to Changes in Life Situations and Reaction Patterns. In H. Wolf (Ed.), *Life Stress and Bodily Disease*. Baltimore: Williams & Wilkins, 1960.

44. Lopata, H. Identity in marriage and widowhood. Unpublished, 1971.

45. Lopata, H. The social involvement of American widows. *American Behavioral Science* 14:41, 1971.

46. Lopata, H. Widows as a minority group. *Gerontologist* 2:67, 1971.

47. Lowenthal, M., and Haven, C. Interactions and adaptation: Intimacy as a clinical variable. *American Sociological Review* 33:20, 1968.

48. McDermott, N., and Cobb, S. A psychiatric survey of 50 cases of bronchial asthma. *Psychosomatic Medicine* 1:201, 1939.

49. McKain, W. *Retirement Marriages*. Agricultural Experiment Station Monograph no. 3, Storrs: University of Connecticut, 1969.

50. McMahon, B., and Pugh, F. Suicide in the widowed. *American Journal of Epidemiology* 81:23, 1964.

51. Maddison, D., and Viola, A. The health of widows in the year following bereavement. *Journal of Psychosomatic Research* 12:297, 1968.

52. Maddison, D., Viola, A., and Walker, W. Further studies in conjugal bereavement. *Australian and New Zealand Journal of Psychiatry* 3:63, 1969.

53. Maddison, D., and Walker, W. Factors affecting the outcome of conjugal bereavement. *British Journal of Psychiatry* 113:1057, 1967.

54. Marris, P. *Widows and Their Families*. London: Routledge & Kegan Paul, 1958.

55. Parkes, C. Recent bereavement as a cause of mental illness. *British Journal of Psychiatry* 110:198, 1964.

56. Parkes, C. Effects of bereavement on physical and mental health — a study of the medical records of widows. *British Medical Journal* 2:274, 1964.

57. Parkes, C. Bereavement and mental illness. *British Journal of Medical Psychology* 38:1, 1965.

58. Parkes, C. The first year of bereavement. *Psychiatry* 33:444, 1970.

59. Parkes, C. Psychosomatic aspects of bereavement. In O. Hill (Ed.), *Modern Trends in Psychosomatic Medicine*. London: Butterworth, 1970.

60. Parkes, C. Determination of outcome following bereavement. *Proceedings of the Royal Society of Medicine* 64:279, 1971.

61. Parkes, C., Benjamin, B., and Fitzgerald, R. Broken hearts: A statistical study of increased mortality among widowers. *British Medical Journal* 1:740, 1969.

62. Paul, N., and Grosser, G. Operational mourning and its role in conjoint family therapy. *Community Mental Health Journal* 1:339, 1965.

63. Pollock, G. Anniversary reactions, trauma and mourning. *Psychoanalytical Quarterly* 39:347, 1970.

64. Raphael, B. Crisis intervention: Theoretical and methodological considerations. *Australian and New Zealand Journal of Psychiatry* 5:183, 1971.

65. Rees, W. Hallucinations of widowhood. *British Medical Journal* 4:37, 1971.

66. Rees, W., and Lutkins, S. Mortality of bereavement. *British Medical Journal* 4:13, 1967.

67. Roose, L. The dying patient. *International Journal of Psychoanalysis* 50:385, 1969.
68. Schmale, A. Psychic trauma during bereavement. *International Psychiatry Clinics* 8(1):147, 1971.
69. Silverman, P. The widow-to-widow program: An experiment in preventive intervention. *Mental Hygiene* 53:333, 1969.
70. Singh, R. A controlled study of bereavement and grief reactions at the Patna Medical College Hospital, Patna, India. Unpublished, 1967.
71. Stern, K., Williams, G., and Prados, M. Grief reactions in later life. *American Journal of Psychiatry* 198:289, 1951.
72. Troll, L. The family of later life: A decade review. *Journal of Marriage and the Family* 33:263, 1971.
73. Volkan, V., and Showalter, C. Known object loss, disturbance of reality testing and re-grief work as a method of brief psychotherapy. *Psychiatric Quarterly* 42:358, 1968.
74. Wear, L. Disorders of communion — some observations on interpersonal tensions in general practice. *Lancet* 1:103, 1963.
75. Yamamoto, J., Okonogi, K., Iwasaki, T., and Yoshimura, S. Mourning in Japan. *American Journal of Psychiatry* 125:1660, 1969.

10

Theories and Research on Marriage: A Review and Some New Directions

George W. Goethals
Robert S. Steele
Gwen J. Broude

This chapter presents a review of the pertinent psychological literature on marriage, with the major focus on the theory of research on marital adjustment and marital psychopathology. Briefly outlined are, first, views on the "ideal marriage," in this chapter also called *ideal symbiotic relationship*. A further review of the literature focuses on four approaches to the analysis of marital dyads: the sociocultural, the motivational, the phenomenological, and the psychodynamic. Finally, a summary is provided, along with an attempt at a synthesis. We hope this chapter will provide the reader with an awareness of the vast literature on marriage.

VIEWS ON THE "IDEAL MARRIAGE"

Marriage in Western culture since 1900 can be seen as a relationship between two people, ideally developing out of a romantic attachment of each to the other; the goal of the relationship is a mutual increase in each partner's happiness [126]. Happiness is often impossible to achieve, however, because marital expectations of both partners are often too great and are bound to be frustrated. Freud [55] criticized "civilized" marriage because it was held out to young people "as a refuge for the sexual instinct,"

229

whereas in many cases it actually involved a renunciation of libidinal satisfaction for both partners, with the frustration from this renunciation often leading to neurosis. Despite Freud's disaffection for marriage as the ultimate cure for "what ails you," we still find in psychoanalytic writers like Erikson [45] an idealization of marriage, in some form, as the natural home for the expression of genital love and adult creativity. Erikson [45] says:

. . . Genital activity may help two individuals to use one another as anchors against regression; but mutual genital love faces toward the future and the community. It works toward a division of labor in that life task which only two of the opposite sex can fulfill together: the synthesis of production, procreation, and re-creation in the primary social unit of some family system. (pp. 71–72)

Erikson further speaks about the genital relationship's allowing each partner to be "maturely different," with immature patterns of relationship being absorbed within mutual genitality so that "differences between the sexes become a full polarization within a joint life-style" Hence, Erikson envisions a relationship in which each partner is fully differentiated as an individual, both being true to their sex and yet both working together as a unit, presumably the marital dyad, to satisfy self and other and to fulfill their responsibilities as mature members of society.

Although he makes no specification that the marital dyad is the most natural place to evolve an ideal two-person relationship, Fairbairn [47] does specify the parameters of such a relationship under his conception of mature dependence. For Fairbairn, mature dependence

. . . is characterized by a capacity on the part of a differentiated individual for co-operative relationships with differentiated objects. So far as the *appropriate biological object* is concerned, the relationship is, of course, genital; but it is a relationship involving evenly-matched giving and taking between two differentiated individuals who are mutually dependent, and between whom there is no disparity of dependence. (p. 145)

Fairbairn goes on to point out that this is, of course, only a conceptually ideal state and is never completely realized, for no one's libidinal development is so good that he could achieve such a state of nonlibidinally demanding object-relatedness. Both Erikson and Fairbairn seem to be stressing the idea that in the ideal two-person relationship each partner is accepted by the other as an individual with his own needs and wishes and that within the dyad there is an attempt by each mature individual to fulfill both his own and the other's needs, without resorting to pregenital modes (Erikson) or transitional or infantile modes (Fairbairn) of interpersonal interaction.

Symbiosis

It is important at this point in the review to offer a theoretical position that may amplify the present positions offered by the psychoanalytic material reviewed so far. In the opinion of the authors, most attempts to define love from the point of view of psychoanalytic theory have been largely unsuccessful. The reason for this is interesting and intriguing, particularly in light of the fact that psychoanalytic theory prides itself in dealing with this most powerful of emotional states. The primary confusion seems to arise from the assumption in most psychoanalytic thinking that when one has reached a certain stage of genital development, an emotional state, love, is an automatic corollary. Even the most cursory reading of the anthropological literature or an examination of non-middle-class standards suggests that sexual gratification per se is by no means related to or a predictor of an emotional relationship. Many cultures and subcultures see sexual gratification in a highly matter-of-fact way and attach little if any emotional significance to adult sexual relationships. While tenderness and affection can be expressed toward children and while there can indeed be extremely strong ties of family loyalty, the emotional overtones so characteristic of modern Western romantic attachment are entirely absent.

To shed some light on this subject, some considerations of the antecedent conditions for powerful "pair-bonding" require a digression. Thus, in this section we will consider two different but closely related theoretical issues. We propose to deal with *symbiosis* in human life; while symbiosis is obviously related to what is presently known as *attachment theory,* its differences from it will become evident in the discussion.

Theoretical Background and Considerations

Probably the most important matter to examine is how and in what way the ideas to be discussed are the same as, or different from, the work of John Bowlby [27]. This is particularly true since any discussion of symbiosis in a psychological sense is related to psychological dimensions of *attachment*. The similarities are disposed of relatively easily. In the appendix to his book, Bowlby discusses the contribution that psychoanalytic theory, in particular, has made to the study of attachment; or more specifically, the attachment that exists between mother and child. He demonstrates that the child's attachment to its mother is a critical experience not only for human beings but also for other species. If the experience of attachment does not provide, to use Winnicott's phrase, "good-enough mothering" [183], the development of the personality in general and of the affective system in particular will be disturbed. Our discussion differs from Bowlby's in placing quite different emphasis on similar materials.

Bowlby discusses the work of Freud, Fairbairn, Balint, and other object-relations theorists with respect to how their conclusions can be utilized to describe attachment; however, he does not bring into account the more general issue of object relationships per se, nor does he specify how object relationships per se are related to attachment. Furthermore, while Bowlby does discuss the fact that if early attachments are not satisfactory, later attachments may be difficult or precarious, he does not discuss specifically how and in what way early attachments or lack of them affects the emotional and affective tones of later object relationships. In other words, Bowlby, by the definition of his work, is primarily concerned with attachment and its importance in human life; and because of this focus, he pays little systematic attention to the interaction between early and late object relationships that have, among other aspects, the quality of attachments.

Symbiosis may be described as follows: it consists of a powerful emotional attachment of a positive kind between one object and another. It is characterized as and called *symbiosis* rather than *attachment* because in symbiosis each party provides for the other something that the other does not have. Symbiosis might then be seen as a kind of attachment that, as a prime prerequisite, involves complementation of what exists in one object by what exists in another.[1] Thus, symbiosis can never be seen as an isolated phenomenon. By definition it is not only interpersonal but interpsychic.

---

[1] This definition is at variance with the customary biological definition of symbiosis as a state of life where each of two parts is a necessary condition for survival of the other.

The world and psyche of one person demand complementation by another for the establishment of a symbiotic field. It follows, of course, that any interference with such a complementary interpersonal interface will be vigorously resisted, and, if interrupted, extremely serious revisions of affect or personality, or both, are inescapable.

Freud presented a number of ideas that are central to any theory that deals with symbiosis: probably the most important idea is contained in a paragraph from Lecture XX, "The Sexual Life of Human Beings" [61]. In speaking of the nursing relationship, Freud states:

Sucking for nourishment becomes the point of departure from which the whole sexual life develops, the unattainable prototype of every later sexual satisfaction, to which, in times of need, phantasy often enough reverts. The desire to suck includes within it the desire for the mother's breast, which is therefore the first object of sexual desire; I cannot convey to you any adequate idea of the importance of this first object in determining every later object adopted, of the profound influence it exerts, through transformation and substitution upon the most distant fields of mental life. (p. 275)

Freud, in this brief paragraph, is dealing with the essence of certain ideas critical for understanding his view of personality development. First, Freud states that the whole of sexual life develops from the nursing relationship. Second, he suggests that the nursing relationship is probably the prototype of every later satisfaction and that regression to this stage in times of need is a human characteristic. There is also the implication that this first relationship is probably the most satisfactory a human being ever has. Third, Freud makes specific his conviction that the desire to suck includes the desire for the mother's breast itself. Finally, and most important in this context, is Freud's insistence that this first object determines every later object adopted through transformation and substitution. Thus, to Freud, the nursing relationship is a matter not only of attachment but also of object relationship; modifications, transformations, and substitutions of this *first* object relationship will affect all other object relationships.

Freud is not dealing in metaphorical terms in this discussion. He is dealing specifically with the genesis of sexual object relationships; and the existence of sexual satisfaction is as concrete in infancy as in later life. In Lecture XX [61] he states:

Interpretation finds most to do in regard to the sexual activities of the infant, as you will perceive; and no doubt you will find reason for objections. This interpretation is formed on the basis of analytic investigation, working backwards from a given symptom. The infant's first sexual excitations appear in connection with the other human functions important for life. Its chief interest, as you know, is concerned with taking nourishment; as it sinks asleep at the breast, utterly satisfied, it bears a look of perfect content which will come back again later in life after the experience of sexual orgasm. (p. 274)

It has thus been established that human beings have their first object relations very early in life, and when they find them pleasurable, this pleasure is not only a precursor of but also an analogue to later genital sexual satisfaction. Freud has thus established the primacy of the object tie between parent and child. Further, he has suggested that this object tie is sexual in nature and will affect, in a variety of ways, all subsequent object relationships.

Many ideas in the work of Freud bear summarizing. The first of these is Freud's emphasis on a period of time in human life when object relationships are formed. The relationships formed early in life will affect the pattern of all subsequent relationships. Second, Freud sees in the biological dependency of man the genesis of object relationships, and in the psychology of man, the need for a redefinition that significantly involves object loss during the Oedipal crisis. Object loss not only creates a new internalized domain of the personality but in addition brings with it an overtone of depression. Furthermore, Freud sees very important differences in the Oedipal situation as it is experienced by men and women.

The limitations in Freud's discussions of object choice and object loss are not content ones. Freud's theory is limited in that he does not make specific the relationship between the early experience with love and what will occur later as the person attempts to form new attachments with a different technique at his disposal. We know very generally from Freud, then, that there is *some* relationship between parental attachments and what will happen later in life; we know that these early attachments will predispose one toward certain patterns of genital sexuality; but we do not know the precise and systematic relationship between early and late experiences. Thus, there is the need to elaborate on Freud's basic data.

Anticipating Object Loss

Anna Freud has suggested in two important theoretical reviews [52, 53] that the central task of adolescence is the reorganization of the defenses. Faced with extremely powerful new libidinal drives, the adolescent defends himself against turning back and regressing to older objects and at the same time defends himself against commitment to new objects. The fear of and defense against new objects may be quite intense because at this time not only are old object ties attractive, but also repressed memories of object loss in earlier years are revived. One knows he should not go back, but he is afraid to go forward.

In a series of papers begun in 1940, Fairbairn [46, 47] has added an even more complex consideration. Critical for our discussion is Fairbairn's insistence that the libido is always object directed rather than simply directed toward the release of tension, as Freud asserts.

Fairbairn suggests that, because of the especially precarious nature of original object ties as a consequence of what mothering is — and is not — in modern society, a generalized suspicion, even rejection, of object relationships later in life is inevitable in certain instances. Fairbairn makes the point that we are all essentially split and all have a certain amount of distrust in our capacity to love and give, because our attempts to love have not been consistently reciprocated, nor has the object always been there to love us when we required it. What Fairbairn does is carry Anna Freud's thinking one step further: not only does one defend against object ties, but one feels incapable of loving, and, when a love object approaches, drives it away out of anticipation of disappointment. Thus, whereas Sigmund Freud sees adult relationships shaped as a consequence of the experience of both attachment and loss in early life, Fairbairn sees later experience as impeded by the anticipation, not the consequence, of an unsatisfactory experience.

Balint makes valuable suggestions as to what specific aspects of adult relationships may interfere with successful object relationships in later life. In his essay *Eros and Aphrodite* [10], Balint discriminates between what he calls *fore-pleasure* (essentially physical arousal) and what he calls *end-pleasure,* namely, the experience of full orgasm. It will be remembered that Freud viewed the sleeping, satiated infant as the precursor of the adult after orgasm (see page 234). Balint sees this relaxation after end-pleasure as the capacity to permit complete and profound regression. To have the capacity through orgasm with a trusted partner to return to a state of complete helplessness is to reexperience as an adult the helplessness that characterized primary love. It is not profane in this context to suggest that what Balint was really restating is the old Biblical concept that unless one becomes like a little child, one cannot enter the kingdom of heaven. The central point that must be kept foremost is that adult sexuality and its expression, paradoxically, require the capacity of the individual to tolerate regression. Balint is explicit on this [10].

This [fore-pleasure, i.e., pregenital satisfaction] could also be described as a short recapitulation of one's own sexual development before every sexual act. . . . Thus harmonious genital love requires a constant testing of reality in order that the two partners may be able to discover, and to satisfy, as much as possible of each other's needs and wishes in the fore-pleasure. . . This work causes considerable strain on the mental apparatus, and only a healthy ego is able to bear it. Still, it cannot be relaxed, till just before the orgasm. Then, however, the happy confidence emerges that every-thing in the world is now all right, all individual needs are satisfied, all individual needs sunk, only one — identical — wish has remained in which the whole universe submerges, and both subject and partner become one in the "mystical union."

But one should never forget that this supreme happiness is to a very large extent an illusion, based on a regression to an infantile stage of reality testing. This is the most primitive stage of object-relationship, called by Ferenczi the passive object-love. Healthy people are elastic enough to experience this far-going regression without fear, and with complete confidence that they will be able to emerge from it again. (p. 116)

The essence of Balint's thinking, then, that is germane to our discussion is that the experience of the genital relationship, by definition, assumes the capacity to regress.

SELECTED REVIEW OF THE PSYCHOLOGICAL LITERATURE ON MARRIAGE

The ideal dyad and the perfect symbiosis are but postulates — models of perfection rarely achieved in nature; the reasons for imperfection are manifold and analyses of the imperfections vary greatly. We proceed to an extensive review of the psychological literature on marriage, our purpose being to elucidate the major analytic dimension of four different approaches to the analysis of marital dyads: (1) the sociocultural, (2) the motivational, (3) the phenomenological, and (4) the psycho-dynamic.

The Sociocultural Approach

We alluded earlier to Freud's criticism of marriage. In a highly mobile, atomistic society, his comments are probably even more pertinent.

Each partner must play many roles in a marriage, and in a society that is in a state of flux and in which people from widely divergent backgrounds often marry each other, there is usually a great deal of conflict between the role expectation of each mate for himself and for the other [39, 126]. This conflict becomes manifest in marital discord. Spiegal [150] presents the sociocultural view of marital problems precisely.

... the sources of tension [in a marriage] can be related to differences and incompatibilities in cultural value orientations and, as a corollary, in definitions of social role expectations [by the partners]. (p. 2)

The studies of cultural value orientations and role expectations can, to a great extent, be analyzed in terms of Parsons and Bales's idea [133, 134] that in a group there are two major axes on which roles are differentiated — the power axis and the instrumental-expressive axis. Dealing first with the instrumental-expressive axis, Langborne and Secord [103], in a study of unmarried college students, showed that women wanted their future spouses to be achieving, to have high moral qualities, and to be succorant, whereas males wanted their future wives to be orderly, good social mixers, nurturant, sensuous, sensitive, and good managers of domestic affairs. Hill [86] and McGinness [122] in similar studies found comparable results. Gorer [73] found that lower-class and working-class males in Britain valued very highly both maternal and housekeeping skills in a spouse. It seems then that a model role differentiation for husbands and wives did exist, and that the differentiation was along the lines of Parsons's instrumental-expressive axis [161], the husband being ideally involved in " 'instrumentally' establishing the desired relations to external goal-objects" and the wife involved in the expressive role of "the maintenance of integrative relations between the members" of the family and internal maintenance of the system. Studies by Corsini [33], Luckey [116, 117], and Taylor [157], all on mates' perceptions of themselves and their spouses, have shown that the accurate perception by the wife of the husband's self-image is vital to marital happiness; and Burgess and Locke [31] and Uhr [166] have shown that for a marriage to be happy, the husband's personality has to remain consistent, while the wife's has to change to adapt to her mate. These studies support the idea that marital discord is avoided if the wife carries out the expressive function (adapting to the husband for the maintenance of the system and being capable of correctly perceiving what he feels he is, so that she can adapt to him) and thereby conforms to modal role expectations. Corsini [33] also shows "for a marriage to be rated as happy, the husband [has] to be a stereotyped conforming individual," he has to conform to the modal role of instrumentality. Studies on role conflict by Ort [132] and Jacobsen [91] showed that happiness or adjustment in marriage "is a function of playing the role expected for the self, and the mate's playing the role expected for the mate." Hurwitz [87] has developed the Index of Strain, which measures "the difference between the rank order of role performance and role expectation" for married couples. He has found that the happiness of husbands in marriage is significantly related to a lack of discrepancy between role performance and role expectations for both themselves and their wives, while for wives there is no correlation of their happiness with their own or their husbands' Index of Strain. Some support is also given to the idea that wives change more (they meet more of their husbands' expectations) than do husbands (they meet fewer of their wives' expectations) and that the husband's satisfaction of having his role expectations met, and not the wife's, is the important factor in marital harmony. In Parsons's terms, the wife's skill in the expressive role of maintaining "integrative relations" in terms of fulfilling her husband's expectations of what a wife should be is vital to the husband's satisfaction in marriage. A general statement that sums up these studies and that ties in well to the statement by Spiegel is provided by Tharp [161]:

. . . marital satisfaction is a function of the satisfaction of needs and/or expectations specific to [modally defined] husband and wife roles. (p. 115)

Dealing with the power axis of role differentiation in marriage, Bales and Slater [7] say that the allocation of power "often presents a problem of integration of the system" once differentiation into instrumental and expressive roles has occurred. Power is usually allocated along the lines of function, with the husband in the instrumental role having a "vested interest in change, usually for the sake of some improved adjustment vis-à-vis the environment" and the wife in the expressive role having a "vested interest in maintaining the internal state of affairs of the system in [a] steady state." Blood and Wolfe [22] present the following hypothesis about allocation of power in marriage:

The sources of power in . . . marriage must be sought in the comparative resources which the husband and wife bring to the marriage . . . A resource may be defined as anything that one partner may make available to the other, helping the latter satisfy his needs or attain his goals. The balance of power will be on the side of that partner who contributes the greater resources to the marriage. (p. 12)

In their study of 731 urban and suburban housewives in Detroit, and 178 farm wives in rural Michigan, Blood and Wolfe [22] present a great deal of data to support this hypothesis. First, they found that the allocation of power to either the husband or wife basically divided along the lines of instrumental and expressive role functioning, which supports the Bales and Slater idea — the husband makes decisions about his work and the car, and the wife makes decisions about a family doctor and food. Four areas, however, depended on joint decisions or were allocated, depending on other variables — insurance, vacations, type of living quarters, and the wife's working. Blood and Wolfe found that, depending on the resource differentials of husband and wife, the one with the greater resources tended to make more decisions or take a larger part in the decision-making in these four areas, and thereby gained the greater decision-making power in the marriage. Some of the resource areas investigated were social status, occupation, income, job status, education, and organizational membership. In any one of these areas, the higher the husband ranked in relation to other husbands, the greater number of decisions he made in the marriage. Also, as the differential between husband and wife (in any one of these areas) increased in favor of the husband, his power over decisions also increased. However, the lower the husband was in relationship to other husbands on any of these variables and the less the differential between husband and wife, or the greater the wife's resources in these areas, the more decisions she tended to make in regard to vacations, insurance, and so on. In view of these findings, Blood and Wolfe state that "the patriarchal family is dead" and that allocation of power is based on the comparative resources of each mate in the marriage:

No longer is the husband able to exercise power just because he is the "man of the house." Rather, he must prove his right to power, or win by virtue of his own skills and accomplishments in competition with his wife. (p. 29)

Findings by Snow [149] among 112 young married couples add some additional evidence to Blood and Wolfe's study. On an adjective checklist,

Snow asked each mate to check adjectives that described his perception of his role performance, his perception of the spouse's role performance, his role expectation, and his perceptions of his spouse's role expectations. Snow found that wives expected the husband's role to be more dominant and saw their husbands as more dominant. While husbands expected the husband's role to be more dominant than the wife's, they saw their wives as equal in dominance to themselves. Both the husbands and wives seemed to feel that a priori male dominance is part of the husband's role; while wives had this expectation fulfilled (they saw their husbands as more dominant), the husbands did not find that their performance met expectations (they found their wives equally dominant). Snow views this discrepancy as a potential area of conflict in the marriage, and when we examine Veroff and Feld's work [169], we will see that men are indeed in conflict about proving their "right to power" in the marriage.

So far we have dealt with marital sociopsychopathology in terms of a sociocultural view that has allowed us to differentiate marital health from pathology largely on the basis of marital satisfaction versus dissatisfaction, satisfaction being a function of whether or not the modal role expectations of the spouses were met in the marriage in terms of instrumental and expressive roles and in terms of the allocation of power by "resource differentials." This approach allows us a glimpse of the interactive process of marriage, but to get closer to those specific elements that produce marital discord, it is necessary to examine the motivational literature on marriage.

The Motivational Approach

In regard to motivational studies on marital interaction, we are still dealing with studies that decide health or pathology on the criteria of marital satisfaction and happiness versus marital dissatisfaction and unhappiness, but our level of analysis is defined in terms of individual needs that, within the interaction of marriage, either facilitate or hinder an individual's marital adjustment. We will see that much of what has been said about motivational factors in marital discord falls neatly along the analytic dimensions that we have talked about in the sociocultural approach. There are three major motivational studies that we will consider: Winch's [181] study on need complementarity; Katz, Glucksberg, and Krauss's [94] study on need interrelationship using the Edwards Personal Preference Schedule (EPPS), and Veroff and Feld's [169] study using the Thematic Apperception Test (TAT) and looking at needs as they are related to marital adjustment.

Few hypotheses have caused as much controversy in the field of marital studies as Winch's hypothesis of need complementarity. Tharp [161] summarized the theory concisely:

Briefly stated, the theory holds that though homogamy of social characteristics [similar social backgrounds, interests, education, and so on] establishes a "field of eligibles," mate selection within this field is determined by a specific kind of *heterogamy of motives* — complementarity. This complementarity may be of two kinds: (a) that in which partners differ in degree of the same need, or (b) differ in kind of need. That mate is selected who offers the greatest probability of providing maximum need satisfaction, as the partners act according to their complementary patterns of motives. (p. 104)

Winch [181] tested this hypothesis on a sample of 25 married undergraduates. He used 12 of Murray's needs, classified into 44 subvariables by whether they were operative in or outside the marriage and whether they were overtly or covertly expressed. Winch used case histories, interviews, TATs, and case conferences to assess the needs of each member of a couple. The results of the TAT need analysis were opposite to those predicted, the case history analysis of needs was inconclusive, and only the interview need analysis and the case conference need analysis confirmed the hypotheses of interspousal need complementarity. On this Winch [180] concludes that:

. . . the bulk of the evidence, therefore, supports the hypothesis that mates tend to select each other on the basis of complementary needs. (p. 554)

We will not report Winch's findings here because their validity is questionable. Several attempts at replication [26, 94, 140] have obtained opposite results. Tharp [161] feels that "the complementary-need hypothesis is not tenable," and we think Tharp's conclusion is sound.

Katz, Glucksberg, and Krauss [94], in an attempt specifically to test the complementary patterning of interspousal needs as predicted by Winch for 21 need-pairings, administered a modified EPPS to 56 volunteer married couples. They found "five relationships contradictory to the complementarity hypothesis, and none supportive of it." This study also dealt with the relationship of need satisfaction in marriage to one's own and one's spouse's needs, and because of this we will explore the study in depth. Besides administering the EPPS, the investigators also provided the subjects with descriptions of the needs being assessed on the EPPS and asked them, to the extent they had any of these needs, whether the spouse satisfied, thwarted, or did not affect the need in any way. The subjects were also asked to predict how the spouse would reply on these questions. For each subject, self-ratings on satisfaction scores were added together and a total need satisfaction score was obtained. Then the 20 highest scores and the 20 lowest scores for both males and females were taken to form the high-satisfaction and low-satisfaction groups. The correlation of husband and wife total satisfaction scores was .55. In regard to interspousal similarity of needs for women [94]:

. . . three notable relationships were found between total satisfaction and resemblance of own [the wife's] and spouse's EPPS scores. High Satisfaction wives as compared with Low Satisfaction wives, showed a trend toward less similarity to their husbands on Aggression (p < .10). On Nurturance and Succorance . . . High Satisfaction wives were significantly more similar to their husbands than were Low Satisfaction wives. (p. 206)

For men, similarity of needs with their wives was less for high-satisfaction men than for low-satisfaction men on achievement (p < .02), succorance (p < .05), and dominance (p < .10). For high-satisfaction men, their succorance was significantly related to their wives' nurturance (p < .05).

For the individual EPPS scores, total satisfaction of needs in the marriage for wives was related significantly positively with the wives' nurturance and succorance, and with their husbands' EPPS scores on nurturance (p < .10) and achievement   (p < .02). There were two trends toward negative relationship between wives' total satisfaction and their husbands' EPPS scores on abasement and autonomy.

The husbands' total satisfaction scores were negatively related to their own EPPS scores on affiliation (p < .10) and dominance (p < .10).

Total satisfaction of husbands showed four significant relationships with EPPS scores of their wives. Two were positive: Succorance (p < .05) and Nurturance (p < .02). Two were negative as was a trend, Autonomy (p < .05), Dominance (p < .05), and Aggression (p < .10). (p. 207)

Because the findings by Katz et al. overlap with those of Veroff and Feld, we will hold off further discussion of the Katz et al. findings until we have outlined Veroff and Feld's study [169]. Veroff and Feld, participating in a national survey, scored TAT protocols of 513 women and 461 men, all of whom were married but not to each other, for n (need) Affiliation, n Achievement, and n Power using scoring systems in Atkinson [5], with some of their own modifications. They also obtained data on marital satisfaction versus marital unhappiness (dissatisfaction) by using a questionnaire. Veroff and Feld reported on the relationship of motives in marriage to husband and wife satisfaction for several age and educational groupings. To make analysis of these findings easier, we have summarized them in Table 4. The findings of Katz et al. [94] for individual motives of each spouse as related to his or her own satisfaction and his or her mate's satisfaction, are also reported in Table 4. In a discussion of these two sets of data and their interrelationships, we also want to show how a transition from motivational data to the Parsons and Bales [134] conceptions of role dimensions in marriage can be made, hopefully demonstrating that the data from both areas supplement each other and that the motive-by-role interaction plays a vital part in marital satisfaction or dissatisfaction.

Nurturance and Succorance   Murray [130] says:

The n Succorance is the tendency to cry, plead, or ask for nourishment, love, protection, or aid; whereas n Nurturance is the tendency to satisfy such needs in a succorant O [other]. Thus, the two needs are complements. (p. 181)

In the Katz et al. [94] study, the satisfaction of both the husband and the wife was related to the wife's being high on nurturance and succorance. Also, they found the complementary relationship between the husband's succorance and the wife's nurturance to be significantly related to marital satisfaction for husbands. These relationships can probably best be explained if we consider potential need satisfactions in marriage and the expectation that the wife will play the expressive role. The level of interpersonal need fulfillment would be greatest if the need to nurture and the need to receive nurturance, i.e., succorance, were approximately equal in each of the partners; this way neither partner would suffer tension from oversatiation or deprivation, which could lead to conflict [109]. Hence, the relationship between husband's succorance and wife's nurturance makes excellent sense, for if the husband is high on succorance and the wife is high on nurturance, both will be satisfied; and if both persons are low, they both will remain satisfied. However, with one low (presumably

Table 4 The Relationship of Motives in Marriage to Husband and Wife Satisfaction with Marriage. (Motive listed is equivalent to motive's being high.)

	Wife		Husband	
	Own	Husband	Own	Wife
Satisfaction	Nurturance [94] Succorance [94] Affiliation [H, O, T] Achievement [H, Y, T] Power [C, Y, M, T]	Nurturance [94] Achievement [94]	Achievement [C, Y, O]	Succorance [94] Nurturance [94]
Dissatisfaction or unhappiness [169]		Autonomy [94] Abasement [94]	Affiliation [94] Dominance [94] Affiliation [H, Y, C, M] Achievement [H, Y, M] Power [H, O, C, O, T]	Autonomy [94] Dominance [94] Aggression [94]

NOTE: H = high school group [169]; C = college group [169]; Y = young group [169]; M = middle-aged group [169]; O = old group [169]; T = all ages [169].

SOURCE: Modified from Katz, Glucksberg, and Krauss [94] and Veroff and Feld [169].

244

the wife low on nurturance, because the wife's being high on nurturance is related to satisfaction for both husbands and wives), and the other (presumably, the husband) high (on succorance), the husband would not obtain gratification and the wife would feel constant pressure to give gratification. The conflict would most likely result in dissatisfaction.

The finding that on nurturance and succorance needs, satisfied wives tend to be more like their husbands than unsatisfied wives, offers some support to the Burgess and Locke [31] and Uhr [166] ideas that the wife's adaptation is vital to marital happiness. In other words, if the wife provides the emotional give (nurturance) and take (succorance) that the husband requires, then the marriage will be satisfactory (in terms of need gratification) for both husband and wife. The importance of succorance and nurturance in the wife coincides well with Parsons's concept that the wife assumes the expressive role, for succorance and nurturance are both concerned with the management of emotional matters in the marriage.

Affiliation The wife's own high affiliation is positively related to marital satisfaction for high school-educated women in Veroff and Feld's study, while for husbands, high affiliation is related to dissatisfaction or unhappiness in both the Katz et al. study and in the Veroff and Feld study for young high school-educated men and for middle-aged college-educated men. What do these results mean?

Veroff and Feld [169] suggest that entrance into marriage is associated with high n Affiliation (divorced people who remarry have higher n Affiliation than ones who do not remarry), but that fulfillment of the affiliative need in marriage is different for husbands and wives. Because of the fact that among the high school-educated group of women high n Affiliation is significantly related to happiness for the older women only, Veroff and Feld [169] suggest that as marriages become desexualized for women, the possibility of affiliative satisfaction in a companionate marriage is enhanced.

The lack of affiliative satisfaction for men is reflected in both the Katz et al. study and the Veroff and Feld study. Veroff and Feld [169] explain their findings by the fact that men with high n Affiliation are more likely to be engaged in social activities with friends than are men with low n Affiliation. "This result suggests that men with high affiliation motivation who feel distressed in marriage may be reacting to the interference with affiliative behavior with friends that marriage can cause."

Achievement Veroff and Feld found that for college-educated males, n Achievement was positively related to marital satisfaction, and Katz et al.

found that for wives, their husbands' achievement as measured on the
EPPS was positively related to the wives' marital satisfaction. This seems
to demonstrate that the fulfillment of role expectations for one's self and
for one's spouse is positively related to marital satisfaction, the husband's
high n Achievement leading him to successful instrumentality in the world,
and the wife deriving satisfaction from having her expectations met by
her husband's playing the instrumental role.

An integration of the Katz et al. findings with the Veroff and Feld
findings on need achievement in the high school-educated sample will,
we think, provide an additional idea of how roles and interspousal need
interactions affect each other in terms of marital satisfaction. Veroff and
Feld found that for young high school-educated men, n Achievement was
positively related to marital dissatisfaction (problems) and for young high
school-educated women, n Achievement was positively related to marital
satisfaction (negatively related to problems). Katz et al. [94] found that
satisfied husbands had wives who were dissimilar to them on achievement,
whereas dissatisfied husbands had wives who were like them on achievement.

Perhaps young high school-educated males who have high n Achievement are not sure that their educations will allow them to fulfill their
various career choices [94]. Furthermore, if their wives are also high in
n Achievement, the husbands might feel conflict over their assumed right to
take the instrumental role in the family. Young high school-educated
wives who are high in n Achievement, on the other hand, have achievement
possibilities open to them both at home and in a career and may be able
to satisfy their n Achievement in either place. (For young high school-
educated women, both career n Achievement and home n Achievement
are negatively related to marital problems [94]).

Autonomy   The findings of Katz et al. [94] — that the high autonomy
of the spouse was associated with lack of satisfaction in the marriage for
both husbands and wives — is not surprising, considering the high degree of
interdependence that characterizes American marriage [109]. It is interesting that the autonomy of one spouse causes dissatisfaction for the
other spouse. This dissatisfaction could arise from three possible sources.
The husband's dissatisfaction when the wife is autonomous is probably due
in part to the contravention of the husband's role expectations for the wife.
She is supposed to be the integrative, expressive partner, and her autonomy
needs probably do not facilitate her playing the expressive role. Second,

autonomy in one spouse violates the culturally defined expectation of great interdependence that the other spouse might hold. Finally, the other's autonomy might pose a threat to the marriage, for example, the autonomous one might break out of the marriage and leave the other.

Power, Dominance, and Aggression   If one recalls Blood and Wolfe's [22] findings and statements concerning male power in the family and Snow's finding [149] that males were in conflict over their position of dominance in the marriage, Veroff and Feld's [169] findings about *n* Power and marital satisfaction make complete sense. Veroff and Feld [169] state that:

. . . college-educated husbands with high power motivation reported problems with their marriage . . . . These men also reported that marriage was restrictive. In contrast, college-educated women who were power motivated . . . felt less restricted by their marriages and reported fewer marriage problems and more marital happiness than those with low power motivation. The college-educated women seem to be more able to assert themselves in their marital relationship (perhaps this is because there is a small differential between their own and their husbands' educational resources) and obtain satisfaction from this assertive role. This power assertion by women seems most possible with the more egalitarian norm for the husband-wife relationship that exists in this social group. [Blood and Wolfe would argue that the egalitarian norm of power pertains to all groups; however Veroff and Feld did not find conflict over power in either the grade school or high school samples.] This norm, however, appears to create difficulties for the college-educated man who has high power motivation; egalitarian marriage threatens his position of power, opens up the possibility of his weakness. (pp. 118–119)

The finding of Katz et al. [94], that for husbands their own dominance and their wives' dominance and aggression cause dissatisfaction, probably reflects the male's difficulty in reconciling or establishing a balance between his own power and that of his wife. Wives who exercise too much power in terms of dominance or aggression have husbands who are dissatisfied, and yet the husband who is too dominant is not satisfied in marriage either. Zybon's [187] finding that wives low in dominance had more stable marriages also fits with these data. As Bales and Slater [7] state, "Power . . . allocation between specialists often presents a problem of integration of the system, once specialization occurs." The areas of power and dominance-submission are ones that are vital to the four approaches to marital studies that we are considering; in all these approaches power and dominance-submission play a crucial role in determining marital adjustment. As we have seen, the allocation of power in the marriage through "differential resources" as it interacts with the power motive can either facilitate (for college women) or disrupt (for college males) marital happiness. This is an excellent example of the interaction of a motive (*n* Power), role expectation (who will lead), and role differentiation (who, in fact, leads) in determining marital satisfaction.

In the phenomenological and psychodynamic approaches, we will also see that the axis of power differentiation is important in the determination of marital pathology.

The Phenomenological Approach

The orientation of research in the phenomenological and psychodynamic approaches is quite different from that of either the sociocultural or motivational approaches. Both the phenomenological and psychodynamic approaches gather their data from intensive work with pathological families, and instead of differentiation along the lines of satisfaction and dissatisfaction, there is a differentiation among the types of pathological processes in marriage.

The phenomenological approach relies on observational work with families and a description in terms of what is observed in the family process to explain family pathology. The work of Bateson, Jackson, Haley, and Weakland [16], with their communications approach, and Laing and Esterson's [101] work with families of schizophrenics provide the general orientation of this approach. Haley [79], in explaining the theoretical view of family process that is common to this approach, says that a family is an "error-activated" system, in which any deviation of a family member that upsets the homeostasis in the family automatically triggers processes that work to reinstate equilibrium. "Such a system contains within itself self-corrective processes which permit it to continue to function in 'habitual ways.'" Jackson [88] views such "habitual ways," or stereotyped, compulsive, infantile means of family interaction, as a sign that certain healthy (i.e., flexible) mechanisms have broken down and the family has become locked into a system where, Spiegal [150] says:

Phenomena take place unwittingly, not only because of the unconscious dynamics within each person but also because of the operations of the systems of relations in which the members of the family are involved. (p. 2)

The communications approach does not talk about these "unconscious dynamics," but Dicks [39] does so in great detail, and we will discuss his work later. Haley [79], however, does talk about "the operations of the systems of relations" in the family network. He says:

The range of behavior of family members is set largely by the other family members. . . . Two sorts of governing processes occur in the family: the family members behave in an error-activated way if one member exceeds a certain established limit [role expectations], but individual family members also attempt to be the ones who set or establish that limit. It is at this second level the control problem enters the picture in the disturbed family. . . . At this second level, the problem is this: who is going to tell whom what to do and so govern the limits of behavior. (p. 134)

Jackson [88] states the power dimensions of the control problem as follows: ". . . all persons implicitly or explicitly are constantly attempting to define the nature of their relationships." (p. 126). In mature (healthy) relationships, he says, each partner in the marriage "defines areas in which he determines the nature of the relationship," and there is mutual agreement by both mates on these definitions of activity and control differentiation. The definitions of areas of control depend on cultural factors (modal roles) and special skills (allocative resource power), and in a healthy relationship there is agreement on the definitions that will be used in defining areas of control. In other words, in healthy relationships there are role expectations in common and individual motive disposition that allow the mates to agree on how the marriage will operate.

In contrast to the mature relationship, Jackson [88] says:

In a pathologic relationship, we see rather than areas of control a constant sabotaging or refusing of the other's attempts to define the relationship [problems in power differentiation]. (p. 127)

Jackson [88] sees that a pathological relationship may be indicated when instead of agreements on issues of control being worked out, there is a one-way trend in control definitions; that is, one of the mates "increasingly appears to define the nature of the relationship."

Spiegal [150] elaborates 11 methods by which a member of a marital unit may attempt to control a mate or define his or her area of control

over a mate and thereby achieve homeostasis. Five of these methods are
"manipulative ego attempts by persuasions or some other means (coaxing,
evaluating, masking, postponing) to get the other to comply with his expectations." One method, role reversal, can either be manipulative or lead to an
agreed-on mutual modification of control. The other five methods "are based
on mutual insight rather than manipulation. They lead to a novel solution
of the role conflict underlying the disequilibrium." These methods are
joking, referral to a third party, exploring, compromising, and consolidating.
Of course, any attempt by one mate to use a tactic to establish equilibrium
can be countered or "sabotaged" by the other mate [88]:

The communication methods used to refuse, negate, or sabotage the other's attempt
to define the nature of the relationship may range from a simple, direct "no" to
complex multilevel messages in which covert denial is further obscured by itself being
denied. This is the essense of the "double bind" situation. (p. 127)

Jackson [88] provides the first categorization and description of the
different types of pathological family interaction that we will discuss.

Since relationship messages are constantly being exchanged, it is likely (within certain
limits) that a family can be characterized by maneuvers used. The extent to which
relationship messages are implicit (e.g., symptoms of various kinds), explicit, commands,
helpless or "one-down" ploys, will vary from family to family. It is possible to classify
families or relationships into four types on the basis of the transactions used to define
the nature of the relationship. These four categories are: stable satisfactory, unstable
satisfactory, stable unsatisfactory, and unstable unsatisfactory. (pp. 129–130)

A stable satisfactory relationship is one in which it is possible for either
partner to explicitly discuss the relationship and comment on the effects
that the other's behavior is having on him or her. In this type of relationship
disequilibrium does occur, but equilibrium is reestablished through open,
explicit communication, not masked, double-bind communications. This
is the ideal, or mature, relationship [88].

The unstable satisfactory marriage differs from the stable satisfactory
marriage only in that the periods of instability last longer and agreement
about a new point of equilibrium is harder to arrive at in the unstable
satisfactory marriage. Often stable satisfactory relationships become unstable unsatisfactory when profound changes in the relationship, resulting
from internal or external causes, must be adjusted to (for example, the

death of a parent, the birth or marriage of a child, the absence of a partner)
and when the mechanisms of adjustment are not adequate to the problem.
These relationships, however, are basically strong, and short-term intervention by a therapist is usually quite effective [88].

An unstable unsatisfactory relationship is one where no explicit or implicit agreement
is reached upon the question of who is in control of the relationship or areas within it.
It is characterized by the need to redefine the relationship the moment it becomes
defined so that stable periods are brief, and unstable periods are long. The discussion
that takes place between the parties is apt to be not at a relationship level, but at a
level of details. Each party tends to take behavior of the other party as a challenge at a
relationship level without this ever being discussed. Maneuvers to control the relationship are made with simultaneous denials that these are maneuvers [masking, double
binds]. Often psychosomatic or hysterical symptoms are used as ways of defining
the relationship since they are messages which can be denied as messages. (p. 132)

There is usually competition over dependency in these relationships,
neither one allowing the other to be either dependent or independent.
Jackson feels that "many of the serious psychosomatic disorders and possibly
psychoses of rather acute onset come from this group." The network
constellation of these families makes therapeutic care for any member
almost impossible without the whole family's being treated, because the
error-activated system of control automatically responds to any one member's
change, and coerces him back into old patterns of relating.

The stable unsatisfactory relationship is an insidious form of the unstable unsatisfactory relationship. For in the unstable unsatisfactory
relationship, it is obvious that the whole family network is in turmoil
and that the problems of one family member are, in part, an outgrowth
of the nature of family interaction. The stable unsatisfactory family,
however, is calm and united — the patient is the only one who is crazy.
There is a united front in these families, for they have "agreed never to
make an issue of who is in charge of the relationship or areas within it"
[88]. There is almost no give and take or change in these families; they
are marked by inflexibility and compulsiveness. Family members do things
because of an outside structural definition (religious codes, "my parents
did it this way," and so on) that has been adopted to control family interaction. This fact provides these families with a particularly impersonal
quality. There is usually an isolation from outside contact so that no dis-
rupting elements will challenge the system. In fact, these families usually
refuse to cooperate in family therapy.

The reason for the pathology-producing interaction in unstable unsatisfactory marriages is not really explained by either Haley [78] or Jackson [88]. They describe the phenomenon and the nature of the masked and double-bind communications that maintain the systems, but they provide no etiology of the structure of the relationship.

An explanation of these phenomena takes us in two directions, and the approach of Jackson and Haley is a transition point between two other approaches. Spiegal [150] takes a sociocultural viewpoint in explaining the discordant working of these relationships. He says that in "the incompatibilities in cultural value orientations" and "social role expectations" the members of a marital dyad cannot reach agreement over who does what. This disagreement between role expectations and role performance causes strain, tension, and anxiety that lead to various and, Jackson would say, usually unsuccessful ways of trying to reach a point of agreement. The other explanation of these phenomena takes us into the psychodynamic considerations of marital conflict.

The Psychodynamic Approach

The infantile ideas about the nature of marriage, which are not often retained by the conscious memory, have great significance for the symptoms of later neurotic illnesses. ([56]; p. 57)

Dicks [39] has produced the best explanation yet of the dynamic etiology of marital psychopathology. Dicks's explanation of the etiology of the unsatisfactory unstable relationship described by Jackson provides the cornerstone of his theory. Dicks feels that the masked, or double-bind, communications that maintain such marital systems arise from a "collusive process" built on "mutually projective identifications" that bind the partners in a union "around which some sort of joint ego boundary" is drawn. The double-bind communications are used by each partner to protect himself, the other, and the dyad from his own unconscious objects (internal and projected onto the other), which, if not disguised, masked, or denied from awareness, would destroy the ego, the other, and the dyad. The members in an unsatisfactory unstable relationship talk only about details and not about the relationship, because communication about the relationship would mean an examination of the motives and character that each has attributed to the other. This examination would be too dangerous because it would unmask material that the central ego has been

keeping from awareness since infancy, when the first objects were split
off as being too threatening. The essence of the double-bind communication
is that, if it is questioned by the other, it can be denied as a communication so that in the communication both members of the dyad are protected.

We have jumped headlong into Dicks's system in attempting to explain
the etiology of the double bind and to show how the transition point between a sociocultural view and a psychodynamic view lies in the work of
phenomenological family studies. We shall now discuss Dicks's approach
to marital psychopathology, and bring in around his work the other pertinent studies.

Dicks sees as pathological or disturbed any marriage that uses childish,
regressive defense mechanisms that foster communications that help
maintain an unconscious collusive dyadic system. He views such a marriage
relationship itself as neurotic and, within this relationship, the marital
partners as disturbed. He is not talking about marriages in which one or
the other partner has a diagnosed psychopathological ailment; in fact, in
only a few of his patients was this the case [39].

Dicks [37] says:

A marital relationship (like any other) is the resultant of the interaction of forces
inherent in two personalities with a long history, fashioned out of participation in
past object relationships, needs and pressures, from the cradle onwards, in the complex
fields of their individual and social pasts. (p. 183)

Dicks sees that in a mature healthy union there must be "a mutual affirmation of the other's identity as a lovable person" [39]. Each partner must
accept the other as a whole object; indeed what makes a union mature,
among other things, is the gratification of "childlike, unashamed dependence"
in the other "by caressing words and actions, both immediate and in the
sense of continual 'thoughtfulness' and cherishing in daily relations" [39].
When one denies the dependent, needy part of himself or of the other
through fear, hate, or rigidity, or belittles it as "sloppy" or "babyish"
then there is a denial of the fact that oneself or the other is a real person
with manifold needs that require satisfaction [39]. In disturbed marriages,
one or both partners have persistent need demands that have never been
satisfied by the parental figures; because these demands have not been
satisfied, the object-need relationship became so frustrating and hate-
arousing to the child that the potential for that relationship (the libido

cathexis to the object) is split off from the central ego and repressed. The split-off parts of the ego lie dormant until a new situation of intimacy, like marriage, occurs, at which time these needy parts become reactivated. With the reactivation of previously split-off repressed elements, the ego must carry out renewed defensive processes to keep these infantile, hating, and exciting demands from awareness, because the demands call up also the fears and frustration that attended them in childhood. If the relationship is a mature, healthy one, the ego need not do this, for in the relationship there will be an acceptance of the "libidinal child," and each partner will obtain from the other gratification of heretofore ungratified needs. However, if there is not an acceptance of the other's "libidinal child," then both partners' egos must carry out defensive processes to deny that needy aspect in themselves [38]. At the heart of the defensive processes lie collusion, idealization, and projection.

To trace how the defensive processes work within a marriage, we must go back to that point at which a marital partner is chosen. Dicks [38] says:

I visualize the obscure process of mate selection . . . as largely based on unconscious signals or cues by which the partners recognize in more-or-less central ego-sytonic person the other's "fitness" for joint working-through or repeating of still unresolved splits or conflicts inside each other's personalities, while at the same time, paradoxically, also sensing a guarantee that with that person they will not be worked-through. Thus they both hope for integration of the lost parts by finding them in the other, and also hope that by collusive "joint resistance" or mutual defence this painful growth can be by-passed. It is these rigid defences which tend increasingly to invade the stage to the distress and impoverishment of the partners' sense of identity and ego strength. (p. 128)

In the same vein, Ackerman [2] says:

In the neurotic marriage . . . the infantile situation is repeated but not resolved, making further maturation difficult or impossible so that the pathologic relationship continues in repetitive, circular movements. (p. 98)

For both marital partners then, defensive processes are directed at keeping the split-off parts of the ego in repression and thereby keeping the self-images safe. For this to happen, each partner must be as the other wishes him to be and must be allowed by the other to remain as he wishes to be. Any real movement in the system calls up defensive processes (it is an error-activated system in Haley's terms [78]) in the partner to maintain the structural defenses of the relationship. Dicks expands on two such defensive processes, collusion and idealization.

Freud [59] defines idealization as "a process that concerns the object; by it that object, without any alternation in its nature is aggrandized and exalted in the mind." Idealization by one or both partners of the other partner works to keep the idealizing partner safe. Dicks [39] says:

By denying the reality of ambivalent hate or anger, and by the variants of projective identification, one or both spouses attribute to the partner those bad feelings they must not own themselves, or else make the partner all good and exalted while themselves taking on all the guilt and badness. Idealization prevents the treatment of the partner as a safe, real person, and thus hinders the continuation of growth into a full mutual commitment because the "other half" of the ambivalence [love or hate] is not offered for reality testing — one is, oneself, acting a false part. (p. 43)

Dicks sees idealization of the marital partner as being at the base of both hysterical defenses (often manifest in impotence or frigidity) and depressive defenses (anxiety withdrawal, guilt), for at the base of these defenses is an attempt to avoid commitment that would call up previously repressed highly ambivalent feeling toward the partner, who is kept safe because he is idealized.

If there are shared, collusive idealizations that the partners hold of each other, a protective structure is formed "within which the semblance of an adult marriage can be lived without seriously disturbing the slumbering inner object worlds of the partners" [39]. This is probably the dynamic relationship that underlies Jackson's stable unsatisfactory marriages. For collusively idealized marriages are marked by great rigidity, neither partner breaking the idealized role image that the other has unconsciously formulated for him and projected onto him. Each plays his role, as prescribed by the other, perfectly. Mittelmann [123] also talks about idealization of the spouse. He says, as does Dicks, that if there is mutual identification, although the relationship becomes restricted, there may be both satisfaction in the marriage and increased self-esteem for both partners.

When idealization of the mate breaks down or mates hold contradictory idealization for self and other (at the sociocultural level, this is an incompatability of role expectations), marital tension and discord usually result. With a breakdown of idealization there is usually regressive behavior on the part of both partners, because each now sees the other as the frustrating nongiving object on the model of the frustrating parent. Dicks [39] describes the process:

The parties treat each other as if the other were the earlier object, the regression occurs in the means used to coerce or persuade the parent image [a projective identification onto the other] with the old, childish resources for revenge or for gaining favor. Forbidding and rejecting qualities are attributed and evoked each by the other. It is as if the "bad object" [the over-exciting or over-rejecting object] is shuttled to and fro in their contest which is indeed the essence of *collusion*. (p. 58)

Mittelmann [123] describes this same kind of process as mutual identification and feels that when the process becomes habitual it "may contain the original reaction to the parent or other infantile experience[s]."

Ackerman [1] talks about an important element of the collusive process when he speaks about the fact that in some pathological marriages each partner "yearns to complete the self through union with the other. The psychic identity of the marital couple [then] derives from this union." The idea that the partner may be chosen, unconsciously, because he is felt to possess aspects that have been lost to the self has been expressed by Jung [93] in his concept of anima and animus unions. Dicks [39] sees unions of this type as the result of the partner having been unconsciously perceived as a symbol of lost, because repressed, aspects of the subject's own personality. In these unions there is the need for unconscious *complementariness*, a kind of division of function by which each partner supplies part of a set of qualities through the collusive mechanism of projective identification, the sum of which creates a complete dyadic unit. This joint personality, or integrate, enables the partner:

. . . to rediscover lost aspects of their primary object relations which they had split-off or repressed, and which they were, in their involvement with the spouse, reexperiencing by projective identification. The sense of belonging [in such dyads] can be understood on the hypothesis that at deeper levels there are perceptions of the partner and consequently attitudes toward him or her *as if* the other were part of oneself [a good definition of projective identification] [39].

The problem with this type of collusive dyad is that one partner may come to persecute the other just as the lost object (usually the libidinal object) has been persecuted by the subject (usually his antilibidinal ego). Perhaps the essence of the tension inherent in all collusive dyadic interactions is that they are carried out on an unconscious level by the mechanism of projective identification and that, because they are unconscious and motivated by split-off infantile needs, they are ambivalent. If the infantile need satisfaction is ever frustrated by the partner, the ambivalence becomes expressed, love turns to hate, and the partner is subjected to the opposite of what he has been getting. This treatment may in turn induce in the partner the previously unexpressed pole of his own ambivalence, and the dyad becomes caught in the regressive expression of infantile emotions. The collusive process however does not stop here, for each partner may, through projective identification, attribute those bad qualities "that made him do it" to the other and try to escape feelings of guilt or remorse over his own rage. Or, if the need to maintain the other as perfect is strong enough, one mate may accept all the guilt in order to maintain the goodness of the idealized spouse. So within the collusive marital dyads, even outbreaks of primitive infantile emotion are subject to management by the collusive mechanism of projective identification. The collusive process offers a dynamic explanation of those marriages in which the mates stay together even though there seems to be only hate and animosity. In commenting on these terribly embattled ("cat-and-dog") marriages Dicks [37] says:

No doubt at times we may attribute such "loyalty" to a sense of duty, especially where there are children, or to habit plus social conformity pressures (such as fear of admitting failure publicly or letting down their own values). At other times one senses that there is a genuine relationship, a *mutual collusion of clinging to the object.* The ambivalent, hostility-soaked relationship represents . . . the highest common denominator of object-love of which the given partners are capable with each other. The particular means of communicating their love needs to each other in heavily disguised and oblique ways . . . often conceal a good deal of real libidinal investment in the relationship. (p. 195)

There have been several investigators who have studied pathologic marital phenomena closely related to Dicks's idea of collusion and the formation of joint ego boundaries that accompany collusive processes. One of the first workers in the field of marital psychopathology, Oberndorf [131], presented a paper on a *folie à deux.* Each partner identified his mate with previously lost objects. The husband identified his wife with his lost mother and the wife her husband with her lost father, and because the identifications were complementary, the projective systems supported each other and the pathological symptoms manifested by each before marriage became mutually shared by both in marriage. In *folie à deux*, the anxiety and guilt can become so great, as one partner evaluates the other's fears in terms of his own inner conflicts and then reacts against the other for causing his own inner turmoil, that the partners become forced closer together in attempts somehow to assuage their guilt and combat their helplessness. A joint fantasy often forms and the overt symptoms of fear and anger are projected outside the marital dyad to the rest of the world, thereby setting up a mutual paranoid phantasy within the dyad [123, 131].

Dicks expressed the idea that in the mate-selecting phase the collusive process was already starting; and findings by Slater and Woodside [148] on postwar marriages of lower-class normal and neurotic males support this. Slater and Woodside found that neurotic men tended significantly more often to pick mates who were neurotically predisposed than did normal men.

The work of Kohl [98] gives additional support to the idea that the collusive process establishes joint ego-boundaries and becomes an error-activated system. Kohl investigated the reactions of 39 marital partners to the psychological improvement of their spouses, who were mental patients. He found that in all 39 cases the first observable signs of psychopathology in the nonpatient spouse came when the patient was showing symptomatic improvement or obvious progress. The complementary patterning in these units was clearly expressed by the fact that 21 marital partners reacted with depression and acute anxiety at the patients' signs of recovery. Kohl [98] says that this is because:

The previously passive and submissive partners appeared to be reluctant to relinquish their dominant roles gained for the first time through the patients' illnesses. On the other hand, the aggressive partners appeared to be unwilling to relinquish their long established dominant roles at a time when their over-dependent spouses displayed the first signs of healthy aggression and expression of resentment. (p. 1038)

These marital systems were obviously error-activated; one partner's improvement leads to an automatic implicit communication (a symptom) by the other partner that is an attempt at restoring the old balance. It is also of interest that dominance-submission problems were at the center of the mates' adjustment difficulties, another indication of the significance of power differentiation in marital pathology.

In this study, Kohl made another interesting finding — it was often the healthier partner who first sought treatment (Oberndorf [131] observed the same) and there seemed to be no "awareness of the pathologic nature of their marital adjustment" [131] by either partner. In fact, at the time of the patient's admission, both partners denied marital conflict, and emphasized the ideal nature of their marriage. They also expressed fears that psychotherapy would destroy their marriage. They were in collusion to save the dyad, to them the healthy product of their collusive fantasy systems.

The work of Kohl takes us into the area of dominance-submission, which Dicks [39] calls the second axis around which marital conflict revolves. The first axis, as we have seen, revolves around the fact that the partner somehow does not play that fantasized unconscious role that is assigned him by the repressed infantile needs of the spouse. In other words, there is some conflict, not at the sociocultural ego level but at the unconscious level, over the fantasy role expectations for the mate and the actual or at times fantasized role performance of the mate. The conflict, because it is over unconscious unfulfilled needs, is disguised by the collusive dyadic setup and emerges only as symptoms — sulks, headaches, frigidity, impotence, and so on. Conflicts over role performance and overdominance or passivity are almost always intertwined, and we will have to consider dominance-submission conflicts in the context of both unconscious and sociocultural role expectations for self and other in the dyad. Dicks [37] makes two subdivisions of dominance-passivity (submission) conflicts:

> The subdivisions are in terms of whether dominance is exerted by repressing (or suppressing, denying) passivity, or passivity is emphasized as a defense against aggression. In neither case is the attitude successful because of the underlying ambivalence, and because of the complexity of the partner's role expectations. (p. 192)

Those who use dominance as a defense include husbands who insist that they must be the head of the household; they are afraid to be tender and have a deep fear of being swallowed or destroyed by their wives if they do display tenderness, which for them equals weakness. This type of dominance usually works if the wife has the need to play "the long-suffering or placidly acquiescent maternal role" [37], although the wife usually becomes hurt or sees through her husband's behavior, because it does not often meet her needs or fulfill her role expectations of him. In women, the dominant role

is assumed as a primary marital relationship position either to conquer the
sadistic father image that is projected onto the husband or to deny the
passivity of the maternal role — or as a secondary position in reaction to
dominance displayed by the husband.

When both partners fear aggression or destructive action, they usually
produce, through projective identification, idealizations of each other and
the relationship. As we have seen, this mutual submissive-passive defense
leads to a stagnant marriage, one in which all feeling becomes taboo.
Husbands with a strong fear of aggression in themselves usually become
terrified of their wives' reactive dominance to their own submissive behavior. They usually meet any dominant behavior in their wives with
apathy and withdrawal into activities outside the home. "This passive
resistance makes matters worse and is . . . interpreted by the wives as
withdrawal of love" [37], which in turn leads to even more shrewish behavior (secondary dominance).

Passivity, when used as a defense by wives, must usually call on the aid
of hysterical or phobic mechanisms "which contain both the appeal to
be succored by the husband and the power-through-weakness motive by
which he is forced to become a slave" [37]. The hysterical and phobic
mechanism undoubtedly must be used by passive women, because it is
consistent with the female role and the implicit symptomatic message is
used to make sure that the spouse knows that his wife is not happy being
the "little woman."

Probably the greatest tragedy of the dominance-submission conflict is
that children become an integral part of it; and every investigator in the
field stresses the notion that children raised in unhappy homes (Terman,
[158], and many others) tend significantly to have unhappy marriages.

Mittelmann [124] views the dominance-passivity (submission) conflicts
as so central to marital discord that he classifies marital relationships in
terms of the reciprocal patterns of dominance and passivity around which
the dyad revolves. He describes his five categories as follows:

1. One of the partners is dominant and aggressive; the other, submissive, passive, and
   masochistic.
2. One of the partners is emotionally detached; the other craves affection.
3. There is continuous rivalry between the partners for aggressive dominance.
4. One of the partners is helpless, craving dependency from an omnipotent mate; the
   mate is endlessly supportive.

5. One of the mates alternates between periods of dependency and of self-assertion; the other between periods of helpfulness and of unsatisfied need for affection. (p. 98)

Slater and Woodside [148] in turn found that most of the neurotic men in their study had conflicts over unsatisfied dependency needs and either adopted a submissive strategy to gain gratification or denied their needs through aggressive dominance.

Synthesis

Before we present a synthesis of the major ideas that contribute to the concept of symbiosis in marriage, we would like to summarize briefly the analytic dimensions and points of transition among the four approaches reviewed. We started with the sociocultural approach using the idea of Parsons and Bales [134] that there are two axes along which functions are differentiated in any group, the power axis and the instrumental-expressive axis. We have found in every area of investigation that these axes provide the two major dimensions along which marital problems are analyzed. At any level of analysis, sociocultural, motivational, phenomenological, or psychodynamic, we have found that if role expectations, conscious or unconscious, are not met, some type of marital discord will result. Last, we have found that the allocation of power, the problem of control and of dominance-passivity among marital partners, is another area that can cause turmoil in a marriage.

SYMBIOSIS AND MARRIAGE

We have attempted in the three preceding sections of this chapter to raise a number of issues, both directly and by implication, relating to research in the area of marriage psychology. But before the ideas covered in this chapter are synthesized, certain trends should be noted.

First, both the social sciences and psychoanalysis, have, in our opinion, made important errors of omission. In regard to the social sciences, two major deficiencies can be noted. The first of these is essentially definitional. It is hard to determine whether any given study, regardless of its orientation, is studying marriage, the family, or both. A second grave deficiency is that certain methodological constraints, sometimes self-consciously adopted for "scientific rigor," have tended to produce a body of literature that takes us not much farther than common sense. As Jerome Bruner once aptly remarked, there has been a tendency in most studies to sacrifice relevance for elegance. This is not to demean or to dismiss the literature that we have reviewed in such detail. It is rather to suggest that continuing to do research within such a narrow compass will probably not add much knowledge in the next decade. Thus there is the need to think about new methods, new indices that can be used to study marriage *qua* marriage.

The major limitation in psychoanalytic thinking has already been mentioned — the tendency to equate genital maturation with a capacity for love. This may not have been the intent of many writers, but nevertheless it seems to us a major limitation. Another limitation is that psychoanalytic theory has paid little attention (until the work of Bowlby [27]) to the problem and meaning of attachment and dependency. The child at the breast may indeed be going through a psychosexual event or stage, but he is also developing two other powerful motives, those of attachment and dependency.

Until the work of Cuber and Harroff [34] and of Dicks [37, 38, 39] intensity and typology were relatively uninvestigated. Further investigations, such as Mittelmann's [124] and Spiegal's [150], concerned themselves largely with neurotic patterning in marriage. While the earlier work of Jackson [88] discussed family and marriage patterning in terms of a continuum from stable to extremely unstable marriages and families, Jackson's subsequent work was largely on pathological marital dyads.

Both the Dicks and the Cuber and Harroff studies, although taking different points of view, attempted to deal with a typology of marriages (and the plural is important); and their work, taken together, suggests that the complementation implied in Terman's [158] concept of the "united front" can come about in a variety of ways and may, too, involve a number of different levels. Cuber and Harroff, for example, see marriages as ranging from *conflict-habituated* marriages at one extreme to *vital* and *total* marriages at the other. Thus, Cuber and Harroff suggest not only different typologies but also different intensities of relationship.

Dicks, trained both in social anthropology and in psychiatry, suggests further that within any given typology there are levels of depth and interaction. For example, he says [39]:

We can, in theory and in practice, discern *three major levels of sub-systems*, which are internally related to each other, but can vary independently, and have changing importance in maintaining the cohesion of the dyad over different phases.

(a) The *first* and most "public" sub-system is that of sociocultural values and norms. Although in our society selection for marriage has tended towards the valuation of autonomous commitment of the partners to each other on the principle of expected satisfaction of mutual needs, there remain the traditional norms of selection on the basis (as well as the opportunities) of social homogeneity or "homogamy". . . . Though of decreasing importance in a mobile society, homogamy at a social level is a factor for initial cohesion in a certain proportion of marriages.

(b) The *second* sub-system is that of the "central egos," which operates at the level of the personal norms, conscious judgments and expectations also derived from the developmental background of object-relations and social learning preceding the marriage. At this level the sub-culture element can be enriched or diluted by individual variances (even in a socially homogamous partnership) of such factors as: conscious differentiation from parent-generation models; habits and tastes, deeper rebellion, counter-cathexes, and counter-identifications vis-à-vis parental figures and values. At this point the "heterogamy" of free choice becomes possible, and with it potential conflict in one or both partners between sub-culture pressures (now operating intra-personally) and the individual's contrary norms and role expectations.

It is within this second sub-system of interaction that the on-going pulls and pushes of demands of the partners on each other for role performance are continually testing the consistency or inconsistencies of the consciously-held ego-attitudes in actual behavior.

It is here that such qualities of character as flexibility and tolerance of ambivalence of self's and partner's conations and attitudes are the essential equipment for meeting the other partner's manifestations of individual identity and divergent maturation.

The second sub-system, insofar as it works well, would correspond to Fairbairn's "mature dependence" characterized by a capacity on the part of differentiated individuals for co-operative relationships with differentiated objects.

(c) The *third* sub-system. This is the area which I called "the unconscious forces" flowing between the partners, forming bonds of a "positive" and "negative" kind, often referred to as "transactions." It is topologically the field in which we locate the drives towards satisfaction of object-relational needs which have undergone exclusion from awareness in the course of transition from primary towards more differentiated object-seeking. According to the intensity of conflict during this development, the pathways of dynamic flow from self to object are more or less open along that developmental line, or are deflected into segregated channels or blind alleys at various phases along the line. These are the "repressed" or "split-off" internal ego-object relations, as envisaged by object relations theory. Their dynamic presence influences the integrity or potential contradictoriness of the central ego's perception of its own object needs and the directness with which it can perform its psycho-social roles in seeking the object and maintaining gratifying relation with it. I hold that it is the "mix" of the more or less unconscious interaction of object-relations in this third sub-system which governs the longer-term quality of marriages. (pp. 129–131)

Contrast these ideas with a statement made by Cuber and Harroff [34]:

The typology concerns relationships not personalities. A clearly vital person may be living in a passive-congenial or devitalized relationship and expressing his vitality in some other aspect of his life — career being an important preoccupation for many. Or, possibly either or both of the spouses may have a vital relationship — sometimes extending over many years — with someone of the opposite sex outside of the marriage.

Nor are the five types to be interpreted as *degrees* of marital happiness or adjustment. Persons in all five are currently adjusted and most say that they are content, if not happy. Rather, the five types represent *different kinds of adjustment* and *different conceptions of marriage.* This is an important concept which must be emphasized if one is to understand the personal meanings which these people attach to the conditions of their marital experience.

Neither are the five types necessarily stages in a cycle of initial bliss and later disillusionment. Many pairings started in the passive-congenial stage; in fact, quite often people intentionally enter into a marriage for the acknowledged purpose of living this kind of relationship. To many the simple amenities of the "habit cage" are not disillusionments or even disappointments, but rather are sensible life expectations which provide an altogether comfortable and rational way of having a "home base" for their lives. And many of the conflict-habituated told of courtship histories essentially like their marriage. (pp. 60–61)

It would be well to summarize the ideas of Cuber and Harroff and of Dicks. Cuber and Harroff have made an extremely important observation insisting that their study, from a sociological point of view, concerns itself with relationships and not personalities. Second, Dicks, starting from what he calls the "public sub-system of marriage," goes beyond that in his second and third subsystems not only to include a consideration of marriage (as has Cuber) but also to provide a theoretical framework for considering personalities within marriage as well. Moreover, in the theoretical structure that Dicks proposes, it is possible to begin to consider systematically the effective dimensions of a marriage as well as its structural attributes.

This chapter provides the reader with a theoretical framework in which the intensity dimensions of a continuing marriage relationship can at least be considered systematically. We are suggesting that, particularly in cultures such as our own, where nuclear families are the norm if not always the reality, the meaning of marriage in terms of mutual dependency becomes paramount. Furthermore, the implicit problem of fear of loss that can be found in adults outside a nuclear setting must be considered. In our estimation these matters have not been treated systematically, and it is time that they should be. What we have called *symbiosis theory* is thus an attempt to redefine certain aspects of genitality so that psychical involvement in a love relationship may be made more visible.

REFERENCES

1. Ackerman, N. W. *The Psychodynamics of Family Life.* New York: Basic Books, 1958.
2. Ackerman, N. W. The Psychoanalytic Approach to the Family. In J. H. Masserman (Ed.), *Individual and Familial Dynamics.* New York: Grune & Stratton, 1959.
3. Ainsworth, M. D. The Effects of Maternal Deprivation: A Review of Findings and Controversy in the Context of Research Strategy. In J. Bowlby et al. (Eds.), *Deprivation of Maternal Care.* New York: Schocken Books, 1966.
4. Allport, G. *Becoming.* New Haven, Conn.: Yale University Press, 1955.
5. Atkinson, J. W. (Ed.). *Motives in Fantasy, Action and Society.* New York: Van Nostrand Reinhold, 1958.
6. Bales, R. F. *Personality and Interpersonal Behavior.* New York: Holt, Rinehart, Winston, 1970.
7. Bales, R. F., and Slater, P. E. Role Differentiation in Small Groups. In T. Parsons and R. F. Bales (Eds.), *Family, Socialization and Interaction Process.* New York: Free Press, 1955.
8. Balint, E. How will this marriage work? *Comprehensive Psychiatry* 7(5):1, 1966.
9. Balint, M. Early Developmental States of the Ego. Primary Object-Love. In *Primary Love and Psycho-Analytic Technique.* New York: Liveright, 1965.
10. Balint, M. Eros and Aphrodite. In *Primary Love and Psycho-Analytic Technique.* New York: Liveright, 1965.
11. Balint, M. *The Basic Fault: Therapeutic Aspects of Regression.* London: Tavistock, 1968.
12. Bannister, K., and Pincus, L. *Shared Fantasy in Marital Problems.* Welwyn, Hertfordshire: Codicote Press, 1965.
13. Barry, H., III, Bacon, M. K., and Child, I. L. Definitions, Ratings and Bibliographic Sources for Child-Training Practices of 110 Cultures. In C. S. Ford (Ed.), *Cross-Cultural Approaches.* New Haven, Conn.: Human Relations Area Files Press, 1967.
14. Barry, H., III, and Paxson, L. M. Infancy and early childhood: Cross-cultural codes 2. *Ethnology* 10(10):466, 1971.
15. Barry, W. Marriage research and conflict. *Psychological Bulletin* 73(1):41, 1970.
16. Bateson, G., Jackson, D., Haley, J., and Weakland, J. Toward a communication theory of schizophrenia. *Behavioral Science* 1:251, 1956.
17. Bell, N., and Vogel, E. (Eds.). *A Modern Introduction to the Family.* Beverly Hills: Glencoe Free Press, 1960.
18. Bernard, J. Infidelity: Some Moral and Social Issues. In J. H. Masserman (Ed.), *The Dynamics of Work and Marriage.* New York: Grune & Stratton, 1970.
19. Bettelheim, B. *The Empty Fortress.* New York: Free Press, 1967.
20. Binswanger, L. *Being-in-the-World.* New York: Basic Books, 1963.
21. Blaine, G., and McArthur, C. *Emotional Problems of the Student.* New York: Appleton-Century-Crofts, 1961.

22. Blood, R. O., and Wolfe, D. M. *Husbands and Wives: The Dynamics of Married Living.* New York: Free Press, 1960.
23. Blos, P. *On Adolescence.* New York: Free Press, 1962.
24. Bossard, J., and Ball, E. *Family Situations.* Philadelphia: University of Pennsylvania Press, 1943.
25. Boszormenyi-Nagy, and Framo, J. (Eds.). *Intensive Family Therapy.* New York: Harper & Row, 1965.
26. Bowerman, C., and Day, B. A test of the theory of complementary needs as applied to couples during courtship. *American Sociological Review* 21:602, 1956.
27. Bowlby, J. *Attachment and Loss. Attachment,* Vol. I. London: Tavistock, 1968.
28. Brady, J. P., and Levitt, E. E. The scalability of sexual experiences. *The Psychological Record* 15:275, 1965.
29. Brecher, E. M. *The Sex Researchers.* Boston: Little, Brown, 1969.
30. Broude, G. J. *Norms of Pre-Marital Sexual Behavior: A Cross-cultural Study.* Los Angeles: University of California Press, 1975.
31. Burgess, E. W., and Locke, H. J. *The Family: From Institution to Companionship.* New York: American Book, 1945.
32. Bychowski, G. Schizophrenic Patterns. In V. W. Eisenstein (Ed.), *Neurotic Interaction in Marriage.* New York: Basic Books, 1956.
33. Corsini, R. S. Understanding and similarity in marriage. *Journal of Abnormal Psychology.* 52:327, 1956.
34. Cuber, J. F., and Harroff, P. B. *Sex and the Significant Americans: A Study of Sexual Behavior among the Affluent.* Baltimore: Penguin, 1965.
35. Dicks, H. V. Personality traits and national socialist ideology. *Human Relations* 3(2):111, 1950.
36. Dicks, H. V. Observations on contemporary Russian behavior. *Human Relations* 5(2):111, 1952.
37. Dicks, H. V. Experiences with marital tensions in the psychological clinic. *British Journal of Medical Psychology* 26(3,4):181, 1953.
38. Dicks, H. V. Object-relations and marital studies. *British Journal of Medical Psychology* 34:125, 1963.
39. Dicks, H. V. *Marital Tensions.* New York: Basic Books, 1967.
40. Dominion, J. *Marital Breakdown.* London: Penguin, 1968.
41. Ehrmann, W. *Premarital Dating Behavior.* New York: Holt, Rinehart, Winston, 1959.
42. Eisenstein, V. W. (Ed.). *Neurotic Interaction in Marriage.* London: Tavistock, 1956.
43. Eisenstein, V. W. Sexual Problems in Marriage. In V. W. Eisenstein (Ed.), *Neurotic Interaction in Marriage.* London: Tavistock, 1956.
44. Erikson, E. *Childhood and Society.* New York: Norton, 1950.
45. Erikson, E. *Identity, Youth and Crisis.* New York: Norton, 1968.

46. Fairbairn, W. R. D. *Psychoanalytic Studies of the Personality*. London: Tavistock, 1952.
47. Fairbairn, W. R. D. *An Object Relations Theory of Personality*. New York: Basic Books, 1954.
48. Farnsworth, D. *Mental Health in the College and University*. Cambridge, Mass.: Harvard University Press, 1957.
49. Fenichel, O. *The Psychoanalytic Theory of Neurosis*. New York: Norton, 1945.
50. Fisher, S., and Mendell, D. The communication of neurotic patterns over two and three generations. *Psychiatry* 19(1):41, 1956.
51. Fox, R. The Alcoholic Spouse. In V. W. Eisenstein (Ed.), *Neurotic Interaction in Marriage*. London: Tavistock, 1956.
52. Freud, A. *The Ego and Mechanisms of Defense*. New York: International Universities Press, 1946.
53. Freud, A. Adolescence. *Psychoanalytic Study of the Child*, Vol. 13. New York: International Universities Press, 1958.
54. Freud, S. The transformations of puberty: three essays on the theory of sexuality (1905). In *The Standard Edition of the Complete Psychological Works of Sigmund Freud*, transl. and ed. by J. Strachey with others. London: Hogarth and Institute of Psycho-Analysis, 1953. Vol. 7, pp. 207–243.
55. Freud, S. Civilized sexual morality and modern nervousness (1908a). In *Standard Edition*, 1953. Vol. 9, pp. 177–205.
56. Freud, S. On the sexual theories of children (1908b). In *Standard Edition*, 1953. Vol. 9, pp. 205–227.
57. Freud, S. The most prevalent form of degradation in erotic life (1912). In *Standard Edition*, 1953. Vol. 11, pp. 177–195.
58. Freud, S. Psychoanalytic notes upon an autobiographical account of a case of paranoia (1911). In *Standard Edition*, 1958. Vol. 12, pp. 3–80.
59. Freud, S. On narcissism: An introduction (1914). In *Standard Edition*, 1957. Vol. 14, pp. 67–73.
60. Freud, S. Mourning and melancholia (1917). In *Standard Edition*, 1957. Vol. 14, pp. 237–243.
61. Freud, S. Introductory Lectures on psycho-analysis: Lecture XX. The sexual life of human beings (1916). In *Standard Edition*, 1963. Vol. 16, pp. 303–320.
62. Freud, S. Introductory lectures on psycho-analysis (1916–1917). In *Standard Edition*, 1963. Vol. 16.
63. Freud, S. New Introductory Lectures on psycho-analysis (1933). In *Standard Edition*, 1964. Vol. 22.
64. Freud, S. New Introductory Lectures on psycho-analysis: Lecture XXXI. The anatomy of the mental personality (1933). In *Standard Editon*, 1964. Vol. 22, pp. 57–81.
65. Friedman, L. J. *Virgin Wives: A Study of Unconsummated Marriages*. London: Tavistock, 1962.

66. Futterman, S. Personality trends in wives of alcoholics. *Journal of Psychiatric Social Work* 23:37, 1953.

67. Goethals, G. W. Factors Affecting Permissive and Nonpermissive Rules Regarding Premarital Sex. In J. M. Henslin (Ed.), *Sociology of Sex: A Book of Readings.* New York: Appleton-Century-Crofts, 1971.

68. Goethals, G. W. Review of D. S. Marshall and R. C. Suggs (Eds.), Human sexual behavior: Variations in the ethnographic spectrum. *American Journal of Sociology* 77(4):806, 1972.

69. Goethals, G. W. Symbiosis and the life cycle. *British Journal of Medical Psychology* 46:91, 1973.

70. Goethals, G. W., and Klos, D. S. *Experiencing Youth: First-Person Accounts.* Boston: Little, Brown, 1970.

71. Goethals, G. W., and Whiting, J. W. M. Research methods: The cross-cultural method. *Review of Educational Research*, Dec., 1957. P. 441.

72. Goodrich, D., et al. Patterns of newlywed marriage. *Journal of Marriage and the Family* 30:383, 1968.

73. Gorer, G. *Exploring English Character.* London: Cresset, 1955.

74. Guntrip, H. *Schizoid Phenomena, Object-Relations and the Self.* New York: International Universities Press, 1958.

75. Guntrip, H. *Personality Structure and Human Interaction.* London: Hogarth, 1961.

76. Haire, N. (Ed.). *Sexual Reform Congress.* London: Kegan Paul, 1930.

77. Haley, J. The family of the schizophrenic. *Journal of Nervous and Mental Disease* 129:357, 1959.

78. Haley, J. Marriage therapy. *Archives of General Psychiatry* 8:213, 1963.

79. Haley, J. Whither Family Therapy? In J. Haley, *The Power Tactics of Jesus Christ.* New York: Avon, 1969.

80. Handel, G. Psychological study of whole families. *Psychological Bulletin* 63:19, 1965.

81. Harlow, H. F. The nature of love. *American Psychology* 13:673, 1958.

82. Harlow, H. F. The Development of Affectional Patterns in Infant Monkeys. In B. M. Foxx (Ed.), *Determinants of Infant Behavior,* Vol. 1. New York: Wiley, 1961.

83. Harlow, H. F., and Harlow, M. K. The Affectional Systems. In A. M. Schrier, H. F. Harlow and F. Stollnitz (Eds.), *Behavior of Nonhuman Primates,* Vol. 2. New York: Academic, 1962.

84. Harlow, H. F., and Zimmerman, R. R. Affectional responses in the infant monkey. *Science* 130:421, 1959.

85. Heider, F. *The Psychology of Interpersonal Relations.* New York: Wiley, 1958.

86. Hill, R. Campus values in mate selection. *Journal of Home Economics* 37:554, 1945.

87. Hurwitz, N.   The index of strain as a measure of marital satisfaction. *Social Science Research* 44:106, 1959.

88. Jackson, D. D.   Family Interaction, Family Homeostasis, and Some Implications for Conjoint Family Psychotherapy. In J. H. Masserman (Ed.), *Individual and Familial Dynamics.* New York: Grune & Stratton, 1959.

89. Jackson, D. D. (Ed.).   *The Etiology of Schizophrenia.* New York: Basic Books, 1960.

90. Jackson, D. D. (Ed.).   *Communication, Family and Marriage.* Palo Alto: Science and Behavior Books, 1968.

91. Jacobsen, A. H.   Conflict of attitudes toward the roles of husband and wife in marriage. *American Sociological Review* 17:146, 1952.

92. Jacobsen, E.   Manic-Depressive Partners. In V. W. Eisenstein (Ed.), *Neurotic Interaction in Marriage.* New York: Basic Books, 1956.

93. Jung, C. G.   Marriage as a psychological relationship (1926). In *Collected Works* 17:187, 1931.

94. Katz, I., Glucksberg, S. and Krauss, R.   Need satisfaction and Edwards PPS scores in married couples. *Journal of Consulting Psychology* 24:203, 1960.

95. Kelly, E.   Marital compatibility as related to personality traits of husbands and wives as rated by self and spouse. *Journal of Social Psychology* 13:193, 1941.

96. Kinsey, A. C., Pomeroy, W. B., and Martin, C. E.   *Sexual Behavior in the Human Male.* Philadelphia: Saunders, 1948.

97. Kinsey, A. C., Pomeroy, W. B., and Martin, C. E.   *Sexual Behavior in the Human Female.* Philadelphia: Saunders, 1953.

98. Kohl, R. N.   Pathological reaction of marital partners to improvement of patients. *American Journal of Psychiatry* 118:1036, 1962.

99. Laing, R. D.   *The Self and Others.* New York: Pantheon, 1961.

100. Laing, R. D.   *The Divided Self.* London: Penguin, 1965.

101. Laing, R. D., and Esterson, A.   *Sanity, Madness and the Family.* London: Penguin, 1964.

102. Laing, R. D., Phillipson, H., and Lee, A.   *Interpersonal Perception.* London: Tavistock, 1966.

103. Langborne, M. C., and Secord, P.   Variations in marital needs with age, sex, marital status, and regional location. *Journal of Social Psychology* 41:19, 1955.

104. Leary, T.   *The Interpersonal Diagnosis of Personality.* New York: Ronald, 1957.

105. Lederer, W., and Jackson, D.   *The Mirages of Marriage.* New York: Norton, 1968.

106. Levinger, G.   Task and social behavior in marriage. *Sociometry* 27:433, 1964.

107. Levinger, G.   Marital cohesiveness and dissolution: An integrative review. *Journal of Marriage and the Family* 27:19, 1965.

108. Levinger, G.   Systematic distortion in spouses' reports of preferred and actual sexual behavior. *Sociometry* 29(3):291, 1966.

109. Lewin, K.   The Background of Conflict in Marriage. In M. Jung (Ed.), *Modern Marriage.* New York: Appleton-Century-Crofts, 1940.
110. Lewin, K.   *Field Theory in Social Science.* New York: Harper & Row, 1951.
111. Lidz, T.   *The Family and Human Adaptation.* New York: International Universities Press, 1963.
112. Lidz, T., et al.   The intrafamilial environment of the schizophrenic. II. Marital schism and marital skew. *American Journal of Psychiatry* 114:241, 1957.
113. Lifton, R.   Protean Man. *Partisan Review*, Winter, 1968.
114. Locke, E.   *Prediction and Adjustment in Marriage.* New York: Holt, Rinehart, Winston, 1951.
115. Loehlin, J. C.   *Computer Models of Personality.* New York: Random House, 1968.
116. Luckey, E. B.   Marital satisfaction and congruent self-spouse concepts. *Social Forces* 39:154, 1960.
117. Luckey, E. B.   Perceptual congruence of self and family concepts as related to marital interaction. *Sociometry* 24:234, 1961.
118. Maccoby, E.   *The Development of Sex Differences.* Stanford, Calif.: Stanford University Press, 1966.
119. Maslow, A.   *Motivation and Personality.* New York: Harper & Row, 1954.
120. May, R. (Ed.).   *Existence.* New York: Simon & Schuster, 1958.
121. May, R.   *Existential Psychology.* New York: Random House, 1961.
122. McGinnes, R.   Campus values in mate-selection: A repeat study. *Social Forces* 36:568, 1958.
123. Mittelmann, B.   The concurrent analysis of married couples. *Psychoanalytic Quarterly* 17:182, 1948.
124. Mittelmann, B.   Analysis of Reciprocal Neurotic Patterns in Family Relationships. In V. W. Eisenstein (Ed.), *Neurotic Interaction in Marriage.* New York: Basic Books, 1956.
125. Modell, A.   *Object Love and Reality.* New York: International Universities Press, 1968.
126. Montagu, M. F. A.   Marriage: A Cultural Perspective. In V. W. Eisenstein (Ed.), *Neurotic Interaction in Marriage.* New York: Basic Books, 1956.
127. Murdock, G. P.   *Social Structure.* New York: Macmillan 1949.
128. Murdock, G. P.   Cultural Correlates of the Regulation of Premarital Sex Behavior. In R. A. Manners (Ed.), *Process and Patterns in Culture.* Chicago: Aldine, 1964.
129. Murdock, G. P. et al.   Outline of Cultural Materials (4th ed.). New Haven, Conn.: Human Relations Area Files Press, 1965.
130. Murray, H.   *Explorations in Personality.* New York: Oxford University Press, 1938.
131. Oberndorf, C. P.   Folie à deux. *International Journal of Psychoanalysis* 15:14, 1934.

132. Ort, R. S.   A study of role-conflicts as related to happiness in marriage. *Journal of Abnormal Psychology* 45:691, 1950.
133. Parsons, T.   Family Structure and Socialization of the Child. In T. Parsons and R. F. Bales (Eds.), *Family, Socialization and Interaction Process.* New York: Free Press, 1955.
134. Parsons, T., and Bales, R. F.   *Family, Socialization and Interaction Process.* New York: Free Press, 1955.
135. Phillipson, L.   *An Object Relations Test.* London: Tavistock, 1955.
136. Pincus, L. (Ed.).   *Marriage: Studies in Emotional Conflict and Growth.* London: Methuen, 1960.
137. Price, G. M.   A study of the wives of 20 alcoholics. *Quarterly Journal of Studies on Alcohol* 5:620, 1945.
138. Reider, N.   Problems in the Prediction of Marital Adjustment. In V. W. Eisenstein (Ed.), *Neurotic Interaction in Marriage.* New York: Basic Books, 1956.
139. Rogers, C.   *On Becoming a Person.* Boston: Houghton-Mifflin, 1961.
140. Rosenblatt, P. C.   A cross-cultural study of child-rearing and romantic love. *Journal of Personality and Social Psychology* 4:336, 1966.
141. Rosenblatt, P. C.   Marital residence and the functions of romantic love. *Ethnology* 6:471, 1967.
142. Rosenblatt, P. C., Fugita, S. S., and McDowell, K. V.   Wealth transfer and restrictions on sexual relations during betrothal. *Ethnology* 8:319, 1969.
143. Sapirstein, M. R., and Soloff, A. D.   *Paradoxes of Every Day Life.* New York: Random House, 1955.
144. Schellenger, J. A., and Bee, L. S.   A re-examination of the theory of complementary needs in mate-selection. *Marriage and Family Living* 22:227, 1960.
145. Searles, H.   The effort to drive the other person crazy. *British Journal of Medical Psychology* 32:1, 1959.
146. Shapiro, D.   *Neurotic Styles.* New York: Basic Books, 1965.
147. Shirley, R. W., and Romney, A. K.   Love magic and socialization anxiety: A cross-cultural study. *American Anthropologist* 64:1028, 1962.
148. Slater, E., and Woodside, M.   *Patterns of Marriage.* London: Cassell, 1951.
149. Snow, L.   Role Relationships and Marital Integration. Ph.D. dissertation, Ohio State University, 1966.
150. Spiegal, J.   The resolution of role conflict within the family. *Psychiatry* 20:1, 1957.
151. Stein, M. H.   The marriage bond. *Psychoanalytic Quarterly* 25:238, 1957.
152. Stekel, W.   *Marriage at the Crossroads.* New York: Godwin, 1931.
153. Stephens, W. N.   *The Oedipus Complex: Cross-Cultural Evidence.* Beverly Hills: Glencoe Free Press, 1962.
154. Sullivan, H. S.   *Clinical Studies in Psychiatry.* New York: Norton, 1950.
155. Sullivan, H. S.   *Interpersonal Theory of Psychiatry.* New York: Norton, 1953.
156. Suttie, I.   *Origins of Love and Hate.* London: Kegan Paul, 1935.

157. Taylor, A. B.   Role perception, empathy amd marital adjustment. *Sociology and Social Research* 52:22, 1967.
158. Terman, L. M., et al.   *Psychological Factors in Marital Happiness.* New York: McGraw-Hill, 1938.
159. Tervel, G.   Considerations for a diagnosis in marital psychotherapy. *British Journal of Medical Psychology* 39:231, 1966.
160. Textor, R. B.   *A Cross-Cultural Summary.* New Haven, Conn.: Human Relations Area Files Press, 1967.
161. Tharp, R. G.   Psychological Patterning in Marriage. Ph.D. dissertation, University of Michigan, 1957.
162. Thorne, F. C.   The sex inventory. *Journal of Clinical Psychology* 22(4):367, 1966.
163. Tomkins, S.   *Thematic Apperception Test.* New York: Grune & Stratton, 1947.
164. Trivers, R. L.   The evolution of reciprocal altruism. *The Quarterly Review of Biology* 46(4):35, 1971.
165. Trivers, R. L.   Parental Investment and Sexual Selection. In B. Campbell (Ed.), *Sexual Selection and the Descent of Man,* 1871–1971.   Chicago: Aldine, 1972.
166. Uhr, L. M.   Personality Changes during Marriage. Ph.D. dissertation, University of Michigan, 1957.
167. Van de Velde, T. H.   *Fertility and Sterility in Marriage.* New York: Covici, Friede, 1929.
168. Van de Velde, T. H.   *Sex Hostility in Marriage: Its Origins, Prevention and Treatment.* New York: Covici, Friede, 1931.
169. Veroff, J., and Feld, S.   *Motives in Marriage, Parenthood and Work.* New York: Van Nostrand Reinhold, 1970.
170. Weinstock, A. R.   Family environment and development of defense and coping mechanisms. *Journal of Personality and Social Psychology* 5(1):67, 1967.
171. Whelan T.   Wives of alcoholics: Four types observed in a family service agency. *Quarterly Journal of Studies on Alcohol* 14:632, 1953.
172. White, R.   Competence and the Psychosexual Stages of Development. In M. R. Jones (Ed.), *Nebraska Symposium on Motivation.* Lincoln: University of Nebraska Press, 1960.
173. White, R.   Ego and reality in psychoanalytic theory. *Psychological Issues* 3(3):1, 1963.
174. White, R.   *The Study of Lives.* New York: Atherton, 1963.
175. White, R.   *Lives in Progress.* New York: Holt, Rinehart, Winston, 1966.
176. Whiting, J. W. M.   Sorcery, Sin and the Superego: A Cross-Cultural Study of Some Mechanisms of Social Control. In C. S. Ford (Ed.), *Cross-Cultural Approaches: Readings in Comparative Research.* New Haven, Conn.: Human Relations Area Files Press, 1967.
177. Whiting, J. W. M.   Methods and Problems in Cross-Cultural Research. In G. Lindzey and E. Aronson (Eds.), *The Handbook of Social Psychology* (2d ed.), Vol. 2. Reading, Mass.: Addison-Wesley, 1968.

178. Whiting, J. W. M.   Causes and Consequences of the Amount of Body Contact Between Mother and Infant.   Paper presented at the American Anthropological Association Meeting, New York, Nov. 18, 1971.
179. Whiting, J. W. M., and Child, I. L.   *Child Training and Personality: A Cross-Cultural Study.*   New Haven, Conn.: Yale University Press, 1953.
180. Winch, R. F.   The theory of complementary needs in mate selection: Final results on the test of general hypotheses.   *American Sociological Review* 20:552, 1955.
181. Winch, R. F.   *Mate Selection: A Study of Complementary Needs.*   New York: Harper & Row, 1958.
182. Winch, R., and Coodman, L.   *Selected Studies in Marriage and the Family.*   New York: Holt, Rinehart, Winston, 1968.
183. Winnicott, D. W.   *The Maturational Processes and the Facilitating Environment.*   New York: International Universities Press, 1965.
184. Worchel, P., and Byrnne, D. (Eds.).   *Personality Change.*   New York: Wiley, 1964.
185. Wynne, L., et al.   Pseudo-mutuality in the family relations of schizophrenics.   *Psychiatry* 21:204, 1958.
186. Young, L. B.   *Population in Perspective.*   New York: Oxford University Press, 1968.
187. Zybon, G.   Role Consensus, Need Complementarity, and Continuance of Marriage.   Ph.D. dissertation, Case Western Reserve University, 1965.

11

The Dimensions of Power Distribution in the Family

Constantina Safilios-Rothschild

Every aspect of marriage and family life is influenced and determined by the exercise of some kind of power. All the ground rules of married life are expressions of power. Yet one of the main reasons why family power has been poorly studied and understood is the fact that it is a variable that pervades all family interactions.

What is family power? Family power is a multidimensional concept expressed by the degree to which one or more members of a family control the important behavioral acts taking place in the family. A powerful family member can effectively determine the nature of the family structure and dynamics so as to best fit his or her wishes, preferences, and needs.

Furthermore, family power, like all other types of power, is unevenly distributed, even when ideology and prevailing societal norms prescribe the equal distribution of power, at least between spouses. Even a couple determined to abide by a strictly egalitarian ideology and to divide power equally between themselves would find their task almost impossible. For one thing, it is difficult to delineate clearly and accurately all the family power units that must be equally divided, and for another, stereotyped beliefs about sex-appropriate behavior present serious obstacles to family power equality. These beliefs, adhered to at least to some degree by even

275

the most liberated men and women, restrict most aspects of power to men and relegate other aspects, often secondary in importance, to women. This distribution of family power on the basis of sex stereotypes is by no means an egalitarian one, because, according to these stereotypes, women are inferior beings with biological, physiological, and intellectual limitations that necessarily place them in a secondary position. Because of these stereotypes about women, social structure barriers exist that make important occupational, educational, and psychological options closed to women [18]. Thus, in most societies women are barred from high-prestige and high-income occupations, and — what constitutes an even more basic restriction of options — married women, and especially mothers, are not supposed to work.

Thus, women's economic dependence on their husbands, their lack of contact with the work world, their being tied down to the house, and their being viewed as having more time than their husbands, because they do not work, restricts to a considerable extent the kinds of decisions women can claim as belonging to their domain. As a class, women have not had the chance to acquire the resources, skills, and expertise that would allow them a share in most important types of family power [5]. Because of their restricted territorial domain (the house), women can (and are given the right to) decide about decoration of the house, food-shopping, meals, managing the house, and a number of issues relating to children. These "feminine" decisions have a definite common characteristic: all of them are time consuming and repetitive. Since women have had much time on their hands because of their obligatory abstinence from work, they have been delegated the implementation of some important decisions, such as those pertaining to children's socialization, and the implementation of some less important decisions, such as food-buying, meal-planning, and so on. Husbands, on the contrary, who have had a wide territorial domain (spreading to work, politics, civic associations, other cities or countries through travel, a wide network of acquaintances, and so on), have made the decisions that involve finance (buying a car, a house, major household items, insurance, and so on), as well as work-related and other major decisions that determine the family life-style. The decisions related to the husband's job have all-pervading consequences on family life-style since they determine where the family will live, the salary level and, hence, the standard of living and the social, educational, and recreational options, the amount of time the husband will spend away from home, the people with whom they will associate with socially, and so on. Wives may decide when to invite friends for dinner but the friends that the couple see are most often the husband's colleagues.

Decisions such as those pertaining to relations with in-laws that have been claimed as the woman's domain by wives as respondents cannot be considered as constituting feminine decisions until enough husbands have been interviewed and their answers substantially agree with those of their wives. Up to now, however, we have mostly the one-sided story given by the wives.

There seem to be three crucial factors, beyond the personality type of the particular spouse involved, that make for an unequal power distribution in the family: (1) the diffuse and all-pervasive nature of power, (2) the prevailing stereotyped beliefs about sex-appropriate behavior, and (3) the inhibiting social-structure barriers facing women, which account for their difficulty in assuming and exerting power.

When, in addition to these factors, personality factors enter into the picture, the added complication may lend further to unbalance the existing inequality; or, on the contrary, it may tend to correct the inequality and restore a more balanced distribution of power between the spouses. A particular wife may be able to convince her husband that she can handle the family financial affairs more competently and she may therefore be entrusted with the major responsibility for economic decisions. Or a husband may think, and convince his wife, that she has bad taste and take over the decision-making (but not the actual work of implementing the decision) concerning decoration of the house, clothes-buying, and so on.

Another question can also be raised. Since, because of the existing sex-differentiated roles and social patterns, women are usually economically dependent upon men and do not share the financial responsibility for the family, can there be, or would it be fair to expect, an equal distribution of power? Regardless of whether or not an equal power distribution between the spouses would be just or realistic when the husband alone bears the financial responsibility and the wife alone the housekeeping and child-care responsibilities, all the available research evidence from couples married for more than five years indicates that, under conditions of unequal sexual differentiation of family responsibilities, an equal power distribution is neither feasible nor desired by either spouse, especially by wives [18].

Wives in this case may be anxious to preserve the unequal but sex-appropriate power distribution and division of labor because they might fear that, by letting their husbands share tasks and decisions labeled "feminine," they would lose rather than gain power. As long as these wives do not wish to, are not allowed to, and are not equipped to work on equal terms with their husband to share the financial responsibility for the family and to function freely and without any discrimination in society, they are not able to share the major types of family power, which remain in their husbands' hands. And since the men are not willingly going to share power with their wives, sharing with them the feminine tasks and decisions would not bring about a corresponding sharing of the masculine tasks and decisions. Thus, unless wives can protect the little power they have because they are women and, therefore, housekeepers and mothers, they might end up having even less power [6].

A TYPOLOGY OF POWER

Since family power is multidimensional, a comprehensive typology of family power would include different types and different levels of power, so that one-to-one comparison is seldom possible between one type and another type of power or between one level and another level of power. However, a tentative typology of power can be made.

Legitimate Power, or Authority

This power is entrusted to one spouse by the prevailing cultural or social norms that designate him or her as the *ex officio* possessor of that power. In the United States and most other societies, it is the husband who still has the legitimate family power or authority, both by law and by the fact that he alone most often has access to financial and other resources necessary for the sustenance and welfare of the family. The wife has no authority to make any decision, especially from the legal point of view, since the law holds the husband responsible for practically all family matters [4, 9]. In North America and several other Western societies, the authority of the husband is not challenged or weakened by other male family members, as is sometimes the case in the larger-than-nuclear family systems of other societies. In this country, there are seldom fathers (his or his wife's), older or younger brothers, or adult, married sons living with him (or when they do live together they are not vested with such authority) that can in any way diminish his authority. Despite lip service given to egalitarianism by some middle-class people, husbands are still expected to be, and are rewarded for being, dominant and are ridiculed for yielding power to their wives.

Decision-Making Power

This type of power may be subdivided into major decision-making power and everyday decision-making power. The former type of power affects and determines the family's life-style and the very fact that there will be a family, while the latter type of power determines the range of variation within the established family framework. For example, the decision concerning how the food money will be spent usually has a much lesser impact on family life than the decisions concerning how much money can be spent on food and how all the available money should be used. The research indicates that the distribution of minor and major decisions is not random nor according to who is the better qualified of the spouses. It seems, on the contrary, that husbands consistently make the major decisions and wives the minor decisions (with the exception of childrearing decisions), as perceived by both husbands and wives (although, or course, there are differences between their perceived decision-making). Thus, wives decide on the time-consuming, repetitive, and relatively unimportant matters that American husbands do not wish to bother with, preferring to spend their time and energy on work, politics, friends, and leisure.[1] Furthermore, in the case of some of the important feminine decisions, such as the rearing of children, the husband may make some of the crucial rule-setting decisions while letting his wife implement them and make the routine decisions [15].

Influence Power

Influence power refers to the degree to which formal or informal, overt or covert pressure of some kind is successfully exerted by one spouse on the other, so that his or her point of view about a pending decision prevails despite the initial opposition of the other spouse [17].

[1] From the author's unpublished data on family dynamics among black and white middle- and lower-class couples collected in Detroit in 1960–1970.

This type of power has been always thought to be the most significant available to women, who, devoid of legitimate authority, can work only behind the scenes. Thus, it has been widely argued that women have always had much more family power than most survey studies showed and they themselves were willing to admit. According to this argument, wives manage to covertly exert power under the condition that they do not allow this fact to come out in the open in front of their husbands or third parties. This pattern of behavior attributed to wives indicates that they have no option in regard to power — officially they cannot appear to be powerful. They must seem weak and powerless because they do not have the right to challenge their husband's legitimate power openly even when, in fact, they do have power.

How do these observations and assumptions hold in the light of the research on influence power? An interview study carried out in Detroit, in which 178 husbands and wives were interviewed separately, showed that influence power is exerted by both men and women, but in accordance with prevailing sex stereotypes. That is, men tend to rely much more than women on direct verbal techniques, that is, discussion and persuasion, or one-sided persuasion, while women rely much more on indirect, sometimes nonverbal, techniques, such as "sweet talk," and affection, anger, crying, pouting, and the silent treatment. Furthermore, the more a spouse perceives himself or herself as having a considerable say in the family decision-making, the more he or she tends to rely on verbal rather than nonverbal influence techniques. This is particularly true for wives, who, when they perceive themselves as powerful, or when they work, or when they have a college education, and so on (and can therefore claim resource power), tend to primarily rely on verbal techniques [16].

The trends in these research findings seem to be clear and consistent. There are probably two different types of influence power, each obtainable by entirely different means. One type, verbal influence power, is obtained by means of persuasive verbal techniques and can take place only when the influencer and the one influenced enjoy nearly equal power. Two equals (equals is not used here in its absolute sense) openly try to convince each other, or one tries to persuade the other.

The second type, nonverbal influence power, is obtained by means of emotional and sexual techniques and seems to be the only type of influence that can be used when the influencer is far apart from the one influenced in terms of possession of power. Thus, the spouse who is devoid of

legitimate power and of resource power (and other types of power discussed in this chapter) — usually the wife — often cannot discuss matters
with nor persuade her husband because he vetoes her plans or he regards
her arguments as illogical, silly, and unfounded. Or she does not even
dare present her arguments because he becomes violent or threatens her.
Thus, the wife has access only to the typical feminine weapons of the weak,
such as crying, sulking, "buttering the husband up" by preparing favorite
foods, and being sweet and affectionate to him hoping that he will be more
responsive to her wishes.[2]

Resource Power

Resource power is the power with which a spouse is vested because he or
she is offering to the other spouse scarce, desirable, or absolutely necessary
resources [2]. Thus, for example, the husband of a not particularly
attractive wife who has four young children and has no salable skills, who
provides her with a comfortable and high-status life (perhaps the chance to
attend courses at a university), will tend to have a considerable resource
power over his wife. Of course, his wife may have high affective and expert
or dominance power, or both, so that in fact she is as powerful as or more
powerful than her husband. But in most marriages in which there are
several (usually three) young children and the wife does not work, the
power scene is stacked against the resourceless wife unless she has unusual
interpersonal and manipulative skills, or an extraordinarily attractive appearance, or a domineering personality.[3] Her resources as housewife and
mother, despite the fact that they represent absolutely necessary services
for the family unit, tend to be rated secondary activities and woman's
work; they are viewed as unskilled, low-prestige jobs that have always been
unpaid [1, 5]. When, on the contrary, a woman works — and in an occupation that is not significantly below that of her husband in terms of income and
prestige — she is able to exert considerable resource power and to share with
her husband's major decisions [17]. Similarly, educational or political

[2]It is interesting to note that even when husbands perceive that they have less decision-making
power than their wives do (a rare situation) they do not resort to nonverbal techniques but instead
they defy their wives' power by going ahead and doing what they themselves wish. They thus
exert defiance power, which is possible for them only because husbands have both legitimate and
resource power.
[3]There are, of course, some indications that the prevailing sex-appropriate socialization practices
tend to give women better manipulative and interpersonal skills than they give men. Thus, women
have a "fighting chance" for power through the use of "underground" influence techniques.

resources of the wife give her backing to demand and obtain resource power in competition with her husband.

Expert Power

Expert power is the power a spouse claims and is granted on the basis of his expertise, special knowledge, skills, and experience in particular areas. For example, a wife with training and experience in accounting or book-keeping may be granted expert power in major financial management and investment decisions, although this is the husband's area of legitimate power. Or a husband who is a child psychologist may be granted considerable expert power in decisions concerning the socialization and the care of the children although his wife has legitimate power or authority in this area.

Affective Power

Affective power is the power that is given to a spouse by the spouse who is the more affectively involved. In other words, the spouse who is more in love with the other or who has the greater weakness for the other tends to yield considerable affective power to the less affectively involved spouse. Love can thus be dysfunctional for the spouse who cannot live without the other, who needs many expressions of love from the other spouse, who cannot tolerate or permit himself or herself to displease the spouse in any way. Thus, the spouse more in love can be more easily manipulated by the other spouse by the controlling, withdrawing, and bestowing of affection, tenderness, warmth, and sex.

The spouse more in love, on the contrary, exerts less affective power in manipulating the same affective and sexual rewards, first, because he or she can withdraw the rewards only with great difficulty, and second, because the spouse who is less in love can much better tolerate the temporary withdrawal or curtailing of affection and sex [17]. However, when it is the wife who is the spouse less in love, she may not always be in a position to use the love-sex ploy effectively because she is a woman and therefore certain options are closed to her. If she does not work and is therefore financially and psychologically dependent upon her husband, she may be psychologically unable to tolerate emotional and sexual distance or hesitant to risk displeasing her husband. Furthermore, her husband usually controls a considerable amount of expert and resource power (in addition to authority), and he can punish her withdrawal of sex by, for example, restricting the amount of money she may spend on clothes. Depending therefore on the dynamics of a particular marriage and the values placed on love, sex, and financial resources, a wife less in love than her husband is more or less effective in obtaining power through the withdrawal of love or sex, or both [18].

Finally, a wife's chances to get power through withdrawal of love and sex are further diminished by the fact that after some years of marriage wives are seldom in the less-in-love position. Regardless of who was more in love at the onset of the marriage, in most cases the husband, because of a much wider network of relationships and of opportunities to develop his personality, has a much greater probability of eventually being less in love with his wife than she is with him [3]. The husband may have other meaningful relationships with more attractive women, or he may simply have become gradually dissatisfied with his spouse because she has not developed along with him, or he may feel that his wife can be easily exchanged for another spouse, probably one more desirable than she [8].

Dominance Power

Dominance power is the power that a domineering spouse usurps, or claims, or forces the other spouse to yield by such techniques as physical coercion, violence, and threats of violence [7, 10, 12]. Dominance power is not based on any particular resource, skill, or expertise that the claimant has, but simply on his or her sheer bossiness.

While dominance power is theoretically possible for wives, it is, in fact, often out of their reach. Because they are born female, women are socialized to be unaggressive, submissive, and opinionless. A girl who does exhibit aggressive or domineering behavior is usually punished or ridiculed for inappropriate and unfeminine conduct. Thus, many women learn to suppress their tendencies and needs for power and dominance and to submit to domination as a sign of femininity and of love.

Men, on the contrary, are encouraged to become dominant, aggressive, and to impose their opinion. They are rewarded and admired when they behave in these ways, and they are expected to continue this behavior pattern throughout life. For this reason, boys are taught from an early stage in their socialization how to dominate in interpersonal relations, how to impose their opinion, and how to be boss — training that women lack, even when, through some "mistake" in their socialization, they are women who *do* have their own opinions and who *do* wish to dominate. Such women are caught in a dilemma, having to choose between power and femininity, two extremes that society wants them to believe are incompatible.

Furthermore, men are usually much stronger physically than women. But even when a stronger woman marries a physically weaker male, it is not acceptable that she beat, or threaten to beat, her husband. A man's beating or threatening to beat his wife may not be considered desirable or be encouraged, but it is often tolerated, unless the beating reaches extremes and the wife complains to the police. There is research evidence that wife-slapping and wife-beating occur much more often in all social strata than is usually admitted or reported. The lack of reporting may be more frequent the higher the social class [5]. Thus, husbands have a double advantage over their wives in their ability to exercise dominance power.

Tension-Management Power

Tension-management power is the power that one spouse may have because of a talent in managing existing tensions and disagreements so that the marriage can go on even when the basic conflicts cannot be entirely resolved. The spouse who can function thus as an arbitrator can also in the process of tension management find ways to gain for himself or herself a considerable amount of power by turning the tensions to his or her own benefit. Since there are different levels and ways in which any particular argument or conflict can be settled, or managed, the spouse who is skillful in this area can find the most advantageous way and level and thus come to possess considerable power.

Moral Power

Moral power[4] refers to the power a spouse may claim by having recourse to a legitimate and respectable set of norms that indicate the "fairness," "justice," or "rightness" of his or her claim for power. A husband, for example, may have recourse to traditional norms prevailing in his parents' and grandparents' families, or to legal norms that support his claim to un-questionable power over his wife. Or a wife may be able to demand and

---

[4]This type of power was suggested to the author by Henry Grunebaum in his comments on an earlier draft of this chapter.

obtain more equitable distribution of power by having recourse to the cherished egalitarian ideology, or in the case of a more liberated husband, to the norms and attitudes emanating from the Women's Liberation Movement. A spouse may, of course, claim power on the basis of some moral ground only to the extent that the other spouse also believes in the validity of the particular moral ground. Thus, wives may not believe that tradition nor what their husbands' parents did justifies their husbands' claim to power. And some husbands may believe that most women are biologically and intellectually inferior to men, and cannot, therefore, see how women can justifiably claim an equal amount of power.

LEVELS OF POWER

Most types of power can be exercised at different levels, some of which will be described here.

The Orchestration, or Rule-Setting, Level

At this level decisions are made about who should be allowed to win an argument, who should be vested with what type of power and how much of it, and what the division of labor will be [13, 15, 17]. At this level the rules regarding the power distribution in a particular family are set. The spouse who has considerable power at the orchestration level is the one who sets the pace for the entire family and is the more powerful of the two, even when he or she relegates decision-making power in different areas to the other spouse, who becomes the implementor.

The Implementation Level

At this level, particular decisions are made about particular issues, or one spouse wins over the other in a particular argument or disagreement. A spouse having more power than the other at the implementation level may have less overall power if the other spouse is more powerful at the orchestration level. After all, the implementor cannot easily nor without sanctions go beyond the limits set by the orchestrator, who has determined the range of freedom and power that the implementor may enjoy.

Women very often are cast in the role of implementor by their husbands, who determine for them the limits within which they may act. This gives wives an illusion of power since they may sometimes confuse their implementing with active involvement in family power and decision-making.

On the basis of other criteria, four levels of involvement in family power and decision-making can be distinguished:

The Decision-Making Level

This is the level at which a particular decision is made and verbalized by one spouse and apparently accepted by the other. However, the fact that a particular decision has been made does not necessarily guarantee that it will be carried out in exactly the way in which it has been formulated — or that it will be carried out at all. Whether it will be enacted as decided, or modified and to what extent, or enacted at all depends on the degree of opposition from a disagreeing spouse or other family member, the degree of power the disagreeing person has and the extent to which he or she can influence the enactment. In some cases, the power "orchestrator" in a family may decide that the other spouse or family member should make a particular decision (and thus derive considerable gratification from this victory) only to be later defeated because the decision either is not enacted or is enacted in a very modified version.

The Enactment Level

At the enactment level, a decision is carried out after a particular matter has been decided on. The enactment of a decision is sometimes simple, but it usually requires the cooperation of other family members. Sometimes the person who has made the decision is the person who also enacts it. In the cases, however, in which the decision-maker happens to be a generally powerful person (especially at the orchestration level) and the enactment of the decision is time- and energy-consuming, he or she may relegate the enactment to another family member. The way in which the decision is enacted and the extent to which it may be modified or its direction reversed, as well as the probability of its being enacted at all, depend on the enacting spouse's feelings about the decision, the powerful spouse's support of the decision, the potential sanctions that he or she could impose in case of deviations from the original formulation, and the power balance between the spouses. The less powerful the enacting spouse or family member, the greater the probability that the decision will be enacted according to the wishes of the powerful spouse. The more powerful the enacting spouse or other family member, the greater the chance that he or she can circumvent the decision by obstructing its enactment.

Finally, on the basis of yet another set of criteria, family power may take place at the following two levels:

The Overt Level

At the overt level, different types of power, but especially decision-making power, are openly expressed, verbalized, and publicly recognized.

The Covert Level

At the covert level, different types of exercised power are not openly admitted. Most power is exercised at the covert level, since the other spouse and family members are thus not openly challenged and tend to rebel against the power figure less often and less effectively. Also, the fact that power can be and is exercised at the covert level permits the spouse or other family member who does not have legitimate power to exercise it if the spouse who *has* authority does not like to be challenged openly. In such cases the one spouse (especially if he or she has power at the orchestration level) may consistently allow the other spouse to have power at the overt level, while reserving for himself or herself power at the covert level, as well as at such other levels as the orchestration and the enactment ones.

Family power exercised at the covert level should not be confused with influence power. Only one type of influence power — nonverbal influence power — is exerted at the covert level. Other types of power (resource, affective, tension-management power) may be exercised at the covert level by powerful but diplomatic family members. In this way the powerful husband (or occasionally, the powerful wife) can enjoy all the power he wants while at the same time maintaining smooth interpersonal relations in the family and high marital satisfaction with his dominated spouse, who will tend not to feel oppressed.

The Assessment of Family Power

It is very difficult to assess a person's standing in the family power structure precisely. Because family power is multidimensional, it is difficult for any family member to know exactly how much power he has and can exercise. The different types of family power at different levels and areas are not cumulative, and they do not carry the same weight. Furthermore, it is often difficult to assess who has more power in a particular issue because of the time lag and other factors that usually exist between decision-making and enactment and also because different family members may be exercising power in different ways and on different levels. In addition, the power structure in a family is by no means rigid and permanent. It tends, on the contrary, to be fluid and to change during the various stages of family life, and from one event to another [2, 11, 14]. Such an event may be the employment of the wife in a job with a good salary (or the wife's leaving such a job), the addition of an adult to the family, such as a parent, the chronic illness or disability of a spouse, an economic depression or a high unemployment rate, or an event bringing about both attitudinal and social-structure changes, such as the Women's Liberation Movement. Other events may be the infidelity of one spouse, the awareness of one's own or the other spouse's attractiveness to others, or a spouse's success or fame. Such fluidity makes the accurate assessment of the power structure at a given point even more difficult, since it necessitates a detailed analysis of the influence exercised by all the significant factors.

Besides the difficulties inherent in family power assessment, perceptual distortions can further complicate the situation. Since the exercise of power is an area of great importance for each spouse or family member, there can be a number of conflicting motivations resulting from opposite ideologies, normative constraints, and personality needs. Some men and women want to think that they have the upper hand in their families because that image of themselves is crucial to their self-concepts. Others, especially women who think of themselves as sweet, feminine, and accommodating, need to perceive themselves as having little power in the family and as being facilitators. Some working women who see themselves as liberated may want to believe that they have considerable power in the family, and this belief may strongly color their perception of the on-going power processes.

Because the perception of the family power structure is greatly influenced by the spouse's needs, motivations, self-concept, and ideologies, as well as by the nature of the marital relationship and the degree of satisfaction with it, the power assessment of one spouse often differs significantly from that of the other. Since this assessment is inherently quite difficult, each spouse tends to focus on the power processes that are consistent with his or her preferred power distribution model. But since it is the perceived reality that affects and determines people's behavior, it is the perceived power structure rather than any objectively determined one that is valid for each spouse [15].

The Role of Family Therapists Regarding Power

Family therapists and counselors have to deal with each spouse's subjective assessment of the family power structure as a valid datum, and they often have to deal with two discrepant assessments without being able to determine what is the real power structure. A couple's discrepant assessment of family power structure must not necessarily be taken as a symptom of a pathological marital relationship. It may well represent an appropriate adjustment of spouses with very different needs, motivations, and ideologies — an adjustment that enables them in some cases to be consistent with their self-concepts without creating continuous, unresolved power conflicts. For example, a spouse who believes that marriage ought to be egalitarian and that his or her marriage *is* egalitarian may be able to cope with the existing unequal power distribution by means of a perceptual emphasis on those power aspects that present a more egalitarian picture. The other spouse, however, may be able to tolerate the existing unequal power distribution either because of a lesser commitment to egalitarian ideals or because he or she is favored (or at least perceives himself to be favored) by the existing power inequality. Thus, an apparent perceptual discrepancy, far from indicating dissatisfaction or strain, may often indicate a solid and viable modus vivendi.

However, a spouse may be dissatisfied with the family power structure that he or she perceives. It may be possible to help such a person by making him or her aware of the different types and levels of family power, especially the ones in which he or she is exercising more (or less) power than he or she thinks. But such an awareness-raising can be effective only if it is accompanied by an open discussion of the spouse's needs, motivations, and ideologies that may conflict and result in a dysfunctional perception of family power structure. Many women may wish, on the one hand, to have considerable power over their family, while they may like, on the other hand, to be subordinate, feminine women in the traditional sense. Such women are caught on the horns of a power dilemma. A few of them may manage to obtain considerable power, not only nonverbal influence but also affective power, expertise power, or major decision-making power, either because they possess resources equal to or higher than those of their husbands or because their husbands do not wish to carry the family responsibilities and safeguard only their privacy and personal rights. These women may perceive that the power distribution is egalitarian, or they may perceive themselves as more powerful than their husbands and, thus, partly satisfy their needs, partly because they simultaneously feel unhappy about their unfeminine behavior. Research studies have shown that these women report a low degree of marital satisfaction and tend to transfer their anxiety about their unfeminine behavior to their husbands, whom they accuse of being weak and ineffectual [2]. Since relationships in which the woman holds the higher position are not institutionalized in any society, both men and women feel quite uncomfortable and dissatisfied when they find themselves in one. Stereotypes still strongly prescribe that men must be stronger, smarter, and have more expertise and resources in order for both the husband and the wife to be happy. And this prescription precludes the liberation of men and women and their possible enjoyment of unequal marital relationships in which the wives have more resources, greater expertise, skills, income, or prestige than their husbands do.

The therapists have an especially important role today, when both long-established and young couples, as well as young people and adults about to marry, have to be helped find comfortable relationships in a difficult transitional period. Those already married for several years may often need help in renegotiating the original marital contract and in redefining the original ground rules. In many instances, wives, motivated by their changing status and roles, may need advice and support as they initiate the resocialization of their husbands (and of their children) for new marital and familial relationships and interactions. Since it is to be expected that women will increasingly acquire more resources, skills, and expertise and that society will increasingly open to them a greater number of options, wives will start to compete with their husbands for equal family power and will sometimes gain it. Husbands will have to be helped to cope with this potentially threatening change by arriving at a redefinition of *masculinity* that makes being understanding and supportive of their wives, having less power than their wives, or earning less than their wives perfectly compatible with maleness. Husbands may have to become able to accept occasionally, or perhaps even permanently, both the lower position in an unequal marital relationship and an unequal family power structure without feeling diminished, humiliated, or less of a man. Similarly, women must be helped to redefine *femininity* so that they can still consider themselves sexually attractive and feminine even if they are powerful, famous, earn high incomes, and make important decisions. Only through such redefinitions of *masculinity* and *femininity,* free from sex stereotypes and behavioral clichés, can husbands and wives find a model of power distribution that will best correspond to each spouse's needs and talents and that each will feel comfortable with. This does not imply that the power struggle within the family will be diminished in any way, but rather that it will be not between men and women as categories but between individuals with a particular set of abilities and talents, free of sex-related handicaps.

REFERENCES

1. Benson, M.   The political economy of women's liberation. *Monthly Review,* September, 1969.
2. Blood, R., Jr., and Wolfe, D.   *Husbands and Wives.* New York: Free Press, 1960.
3. Cuber, Jr., and Harroff, P.   *The Significant Americans.* New York: Appleton-Century-Crofts, 1965.
4. Gallen, R.   *Wives' Legal Rights.* New York: Dell, 1967.
5. Gillespie, D.   Who has the power? The marital struggle. *Journal of Marriage and the Family* 33:445, 1971.
6. Goode, W.   *World Revolution and Family Patterns.* New York: Free Press, 1963.
7. Hallenbeck, P.   An analysis of power dynamics in marriage. *Journal of Marriage and the Family* 28:200, 1966.
8. Heer, D.   The measurement and bases of family power: An overview. *Marriage and Family Living* 25:133, 1963.
9. Kanowitz, L.   *Women and the Law, the Unfinished Revolution.* Albuquerque: University of New Mexico Press, 1969.
10. Komarovsky, M.   *Blue Collar Marriage.* New York: Vintage Books, 1967.
11. Michel, A.   Comparative data concerning the interaction in French and American families. *Journal of Marriage and the Family* 29:337, 1967.
12. O'Connor, L.   Male dominance, the nitty-gritty of oppression. *It Ain't Me, Babe* 1(8):9, 1970.
13. Ryder, R.   Dimensions of early marriage. *Family Process* 9:51, 1970.
14. Safilios-Rothschild, C.   A comparison of power structure and marital satisfaction in urban Greek and French families. *Journal of Marriage and the Family* 29:345, 1967.

15. Safilios-Rothschild, C.   Family sociology or wives' family sociology? A cross-cultural examination of decision making. *Journal of Marriage and the Family* 31:290, 1969.
16. Safilios-Rothschild, C.   Patterns of familial power and influence. *Sociological Focus* 2:71, 1969.
17. Safilios-Rothschild, C.   The study of family power structure: A review 1960–1969. *Journal of Marriage and the Family* 32:539, 1970.
18. Safilios-Rothschild, C. (Ed.).   *Toward a Sociology of Women.* Lexington, Mass.: Xerox College Publishing, 1972.
19. Safilios-Rothschild, C.   Family Power and Love Within the Context of Exchange Theory. In D. H. Olson and R. E. Cromwell (Eds.), *Power in Families.* San Francisco: Allen Jossy-Bass. In press.

12

The Implications of Projective Identification for Marital Interaction*

John Zinner

Of the many variables that influence the marital interactional system, the focus of this chapter is on those operating at an unconscious intrapsychic level. Less accessible to observation than are sociocultural values and conscious expectations, these unconscious forces are nevertheless as potent as they are obscure. They exert a significant influence on marital object choice [1] and continue to affect the moment-to-moment quality of the relationship. Moreover, the unconscious fantasies that determine marital interaction extend to include perceptions of, and behavior toward, children, and hence have important consequences for their psychological development. More specifically delimiting our topic, we shall here draw on our psychoanalytic understanding of the individual to examine the interpersonal consequences of the defense mechanism of projective identification.

DEFINITION OF PROJECTIVE IDENTIFICATION

Projective identification is an activity of the ego that modifies perception of the object and, in reciprocal fashion, alters the image of the self. These

*This study was performed while the author was Staff Psychiatrist, Adult Psychiatry Branch, National Institute of Mental Health, Bethesda, Md.

conjoined changes in perception influence and may, in fact, govern behavior of the self toward the object. Thus, projective identification provides an important conceptual bridge between an individual and an interpersonal psychology, since our awareness of the mechanism permits us to understand specific interactions *among* persons in terms of specific dynamic conflicts occurring *within* individuals.

Jaffe [5] has provided a careful review of the evolution of the concept of projective identification, including recognition of the clinical phenomenon before its naming in 1946 by Melanie Klein. At that time, Klein defined projective identification as "a combination of splitting off parts of the self and projecting them on to another person" [6], later adding "the feeling of identification with other people because one has attributed qualities or attributes of one's own to them" [7]. Klein saw this as a defensive mode evolving from an early infantile developmental stage that is characterized by splitting of the ego and objects as a defense against anxiety. In this connection it is important to recall Anna Freud's [3] earlier elaboration on Edward Bibring's concept of "altruistic surrender" in terms of projection and identification. Here the self finds in others a "proxy in the outside world to serve as a repository" for the self's own wishes. Anna Freud views this defensive mode as providing vicarious gratification of the projected impulse. Implicit in her formulation is the willingness, unconscious or not, of the recipient of the projections to collude in providing vicarious gratification on behalf of the other. In the absence of this collusive process the defense fails, or the projection is "lost," an extrapolation of the view of Malin and Grotstein [9] made from a somewhat different perspective:

What is projected would be lost like a satellite rocketed out of the gravitational pull of the earth. . . . A projection, of itself, seems meaningless unless this individual can retain some contact with what is projected. That contact is a type of internalization, or, loosely, an identification.

Relationship Between Subject and Object

The meaning of the word *identification* used in this context has generated considerable discussion [5]. In general, the term *projection* alone has not been considered sufficient to describe the entire defensive operation. As noted above [9], the individual who is projecting must "retain some contact with what is projected" or the "projection of itself is meaningless." In our conceptualization, *identification* (as in "projective identification") refers to the relationship between a subject and his projected part as he experiences it within the object. The subject's behavior in this relationship is directed by two principles. The first is that the subject interacts with, or relates to, that projected part of himself in the object as he would interact with the self-part were it internalized. Freud [4] has given us an example in characterizing the "falsification of judgment" which accompanies the idealization of loved objects:

The tendency which falsifies judgment in this respect is that of idealization but now it is easier for us to find our bearings. We see that the object is being treated in the same way as our own ego, so that when we are in love a considerable amount of narcissistic libido overflows onto the object. It is even obvious, in many forms of love choice, that the object serves as a substitute for some unattained ego ideal of our own ego, and which we should now like to procure in this roundabout way as a means of satisfying our narcissism.

The second principle governing behavior of the projecting subject toward the recipient object is that efforts must be made to involve the latter as a collusive partner in conforming with the way in which he is perceived. From an existential point of view, Laing [8] notes:

We are denoting something other than the psychoanalytic term "projection." The other person does not wish merely to have the other as a hook on which to lay his projections. He strives to find in the other, or to induce the other to become, the very embodiment of that other, whose cooperation is required as "complement" of the particular identity he feels. . . impelled to sustain.

In summary, the characteristics of a relationship in which projective identification plays a determining role are: (1) the subject perceives the object as if the object contained elements of the subject's personality, (2) the subject can evoke behaviors or feelings in the object that conform with the subject's perceptions, (3) the subject can experience vicariously the activity and feelings of the object, and (4) participants in close relationships are often in collusion with one another to sustain mutual projections, i.e., to support one another's defensive operations and to provide experiences through which the other can participate vicariously.

For projective identification to function effectively as a defense, the true nature of the relationship between the self and its projected part must remain unconscious, although the individual may feel an ill-defined bond or kinship with the recipient of his projections. The disinheriting of the projected part is not so complete that the subject loses his capacity to experience vicariously a wide range of the object's feelings, including those which the subject has himself evoked. These vicarious experiences contain features associated not only with gratification but with punishment and deprivation as well.

PROJECTIVE IDENTIFICATION WITHIN A MARRIAGE

The projection of disavowed elements of the self onto the spouse has the effect of charging a marital relationship with conflict that has been transposed from an intrapsychic sphere to an interpersonal one. One woman whose "cat-and-dog" marriage was undergoing conjoint treatment stated, "I feel better when my husband hates me than when I hate myself." While it is certainly true that projective identification has lessened the anxiety occasioned by her own self-recrimination, such a defense wreaks havoc on the marriage because it requires, to be effective, a continuing state of conflict within the dyad. This conflict need not be overt but may be implicit in the form of polarized perceptions that marital partners have of one another. These polarizations preempt the possibility of sharing feelings and of collaborative behavior. Hence a wife might experience herself as emotionally labile and her husband as cold and logical. Similar polarities within the marriage are strong-weak, frigid-lusty, helpless-effective, rageful-even tempered, depressed-cheerful.

CASE 1   Mrs. A. possessed strong phallic assertive strivings, although their expression was inhibited by guilt and a fantasized fear of their destructiveness. On the other hand, Mr. A.'s own active aggressiveness was in conflict with passive longing. The defensive economy of each mate was served by projection of the wife's aggressiveness onto the husband and by reciprocal projection onto her of his view of himself as helpless. Mr. A. could thereby experience the fulfillment of his own passive wishes through his wife while she likewise obtained covert vicarious satisfaction through his competitive success at work and, more intimately, his phallic potent orientation in sexual relations. Such a polarization of the helpless wife and effective husband can be quite stable and self-perpetuating and finds considerable reinforcement in contemporary society. This apparently robust system could be easily destabilized, however by Mrs. A.'s assuming the initiative during intercourse. At this point, her husband would become anxious and lose his erection, since her behavior would undermine his defensive view of her as the passive one.

For similar reasons it is a familiar experience in the individual treatment of married persons to learn of the reawakening of intrapsychic conflict in the untreated spouse as the mate in psychotherapy begins to internalize previously projected conflict.

The operation of projective identification within marriage, however, is more than a matter of externalization of disavowed traits. We find that the contents of the projected material contain highly conflicted elements of the spouse's object relationships with his or her own family of origin. Although it is commonplace to think of a husband selecting a mate who is "just like the girl who married dear old Dad," we are referring to the unconscious striving to reenact conflicted parent-child relations through such an object choice. Highly fluid role attributions occur in which a husband, for example, may parentify his spouse, or on the other hand, infantilize her by experiencing the wife as the child he once was. The externalization of aspects of old conflicted nuclear relationships serves not only a defensive need but also a restorative one — a need to bring back to life, in the form of the spouse, the individual's lost infantile objects, both "good" and "bad." Jaffe [5] has similarly commented on this dual function of projective identification.

It follows from what has been said that the operation of projective identification in marital relationships bears close resemblance to the transference that forms in psychoanalytic therapy. Barring an unanalyzed countertransference in the therapist, however, the treatment situation should not be characterized by the collusive interplay of mutual projections that obtain within the marital dyad. Nevertheless, just as we anticipate some degree of transference in treatment, we likewise always find some elements of projective identification operating within the marriage. We may speak of a continuum of projective identification in the relationship. At one end, the most primitive form of the mechanism is at play — self and object representations are fused and perceptions of the object may be so distorted as to be frankly delusional. At the "healthy" end of the continuum, the self may achieve an empathic grasp of the subjective world of the object by the selective use of the self's own prior experience within his own nuclear family. Where a particular relationship lies along this continuum is determined by the quality and developmental level of internalized nuclear object relations, by the capacity of spouses to experience one another as separate, differentiated individuals, and by the intensity of the need for defense. To the extent that a spouse uses projective modes less as a way of externalizing conflict and more as an instrument for approximating shared experience, the marital relationship approaches the healthy end of the continuum.

Effects on the Family

Our recognition of the importance of projective identification derived from our studies of families of disturbed adolescents carried out at the National Institute of Mental Health. We found that within our population of troubled families, parents' images, or "delineations," of their offspring were often distorted and that these distortions served the defensive economy of the parents. These parental defensive delineations of adolescents were projective identifications and led to reenactments of the parents' earlier experience with their own families of origin. Our adolescent subjects tended to identify with their parents' distorted images of them, and this led to significant developmental problems in the formation of adolescent identity. We observed frequently that the use of projective identification by individual family members caused them to appear as if they were psychologically unconflicted, since the elements of conlict were externalized and distributed among the family members through projection [10, 11]. Meanwhile, the family, as a whole, appeared to be the equivalent of a single conflicted psychic entity. We have illustrated this phenomenon in the case of the family of an acting-out adolescent [12]. The adolescent's behavior represented the unconflicted expression of impulse while the parents, disavowing their drives, spoke for the harsh directives of the superego. As a unit, however, the family could be viewed as a complete psychological organism where both drive and prohibition were represented.

Marital Therapy

Our therapeutic methods involve conjoint marital therapy as well as individual and conjoint family sessions. We found that the very processes involving projective identification that were found to operate within the whole family group were active as well within the marital dyad. The seminal work on the implications of projective identification for marital object choice and subsequent marital interaction was performed by Dicks [2] in the Marital Unit of the Tavistock Clinic. Dicks's comprehensive clinical studies of marriage have not yet received the attention they deserve in the United States; they merit being a basic reference for all students in the field. Dicks treated a number of what he called "collusive marriages" in which interaction was, to a large extent, determined by mutual projective identifications. He viewed these dyads as if they were a "joint personality," characterized by "a kind of division of function by which each partner supplies a set of qualities, the sum of which created a complete dyadic unit." Here it can be seen how our observation of the family as a "single psychic entity" converges with Dicks's formulation of the marital "joint personality." The phenomena described above is illustrated by excerpts from the conjoint marital therapy of Mr. and Mrs. C.

CASE 2   The C.'s marriage was beset by overt conflict from its inception 25 years previously. During courtship, warnings by friends that the relationship was doomed only seemed to strengthen the couple's resolve to be married. Each spouse perceived himself and his mate as if they were polar opposites. Mr. C. was seen as exceedingly rational, ruminative, incapable of affectionate intimate ties, contemptuous of emotional display, and indifferent to sex. In contrast, Mrs. C. was viewed as volatile, impulsive, clinging, and erotic. Each of the partners could maintain such single-minded percepts of himself and the other through the projection of conflicting aspects of their personality onto their mate. Hence, Mr. C. feared the destructiveness of his anger and vicariously experienced the volatile temper of his wife while he simultaneously criticized her outbursts. At times, the intensity of his hostility would overwhelm his projective defense, and he would fly into rages. These were experienced as dissociative lapses, as not a part of himself, and he would finally repress the rage.

Faced with the growing independence of and eventual separation from their daughters in late adolescence, both parents struggled to maintain a positive alliance with their children. Mr. and Mrs. C. shared the fantasy that the filial ties could not endure parental ambivalence. Therefore, each competed to be the "all-good" parent while envisioning the mate as the "bad" one, whose relationship with the daughters was one of unmitigated hostility. Their competition is demonstrated in an excerpt from couple's therapy that followed a family session attended for the first time by Cheryl, the eldest daughter, who lives away from home.

CASE 2 (Excerpt 1)

Husband   Well, poor old Cheryl was, of course, somewhat at a disadvantage yesterday, in that she'd never been here before. That was not her only disadvantage, I guess. Those two girls are real antagonists, as you could see. Or I don't know that you could see. Cheryl was very mad afterwards. She said she would leave the family, and I wouldn't be responsible for her finances, and so on.

Wife   And she wouldn't — she didn't talk to me. Arthur told me that she hated me.

Husband   She was very mad because of Barbara's [Mrs. C.'s] outburst about her not cooperating yesterday at home.

Wife   And that he was the only one who she liked.

Husband   No, she didn't say that.

Wife   That's what you told me.

Husband   No, no, she didn't say that.

Wife   No, she didn't say it, you did.

Husband   Well, she was — she said that she hated you.

Wife   Yeah.

Husband   And that she'd been home at Christmas and she'd tried to do something, and you chewed her out. And so she wouldn't take it anymore, and so on. And I said, well, you'd better come on back now. She said she was arranging to stay in Wilmington this summer.

Wife   But she arranged that a long time ago.

Husband   I like Cheryl — I like them all. I think it's just a pity that they're so antagonistic. I was very pleased that you [the therapist] intimated that maybe they both had a battle of inferiorities rather than a battle of, to some extent, the exchange of superiority on one side crushing a weaker force on the other. Because I don't think either one of them are that superior. Cheryl likes to score points on doing the proper thing. And, of course, doing it, as many children do, more outside of the home than in — that kind of thing.

Wife   Well, anyhow, you did tell me last night that it was because I was so bitchy that she was this way.

Husband   Well, I think you do the extremes of violent outbursts, which are rather crushing. And maybe I'm the Caspar Milquetoast in the deal, although I have my outbursts, but not so often, I think.

Wife   So you see where the blame is placed. Ask him.

Husband   Well, I think — I would say just as a matter of fact, and maybe this is a normal thing, I think these kids look upon me as a — well, Joan [the younger daughter] said something about they were getting to know me better. This sort of surprised me.

Wife   Because of this?

Husband   Yes, that's right. She said this. And, they look upon me as someone who can help them with their —

Wife   No, they don't. They just dread asking you anything, because you go on at 30 miles an hour and —

Husband   No, I think they ask me more — they've asked me more in the first — in this year than they have in a long time.

Wife   I remember when Cheryl would ask you something and you'd go on. Finally you'd end by hitting her over the head or slapping her on the cheek. And —

Husband   That was in high school. She used to — they used to annoy me if they came to me and then wouldn't accept anything.

Wife   And then you slapped her. Yeah.

In this excerpt each member of the couple is vying to be the loving, giving parent in contradistinction to the angry, depriving one. The shared ambivalence they might feel toward their children is obscured by their regression to a preambivalent state where the loci of love and hate are split, through projective identification, between the partners in this collusive dyad. Mr. C. blames Cheryl's alienation from the family on his wife's "crushing" "violent" outbursts, while he perceives himself as "someone who can help" his daughter. In defense, Mrs. C. tries to reverse this polarization by reminding her husband of his striking Cheryl in her high-school years when she "would ask you for something." Insofar as he was the "crusher" then, she can experience herself as the "good" mother who retains the positive tie to her daughter.

In Dicks's terminology, the division of function is accomplished by the parceling out within the C.'s dyad of the affects of love and hate. The psychological incompleteness of each partner is manifested by the lack of ambivalence. They do represent a "joint personality" in the sense that the dyadic unit contains the ambivalence that is lacking in each individual.

A crucial aspect of the therapeutic work is to encourage the internalization of conflict within each partner in the marriage. After all, the intrapsychic conflict is only perpetuated by virtue of its externalization, whereas resolution can occur only when the struggle is experienced as residing within the individual. In the case of Mr. C.'s fear of his anger, for example, interpretations are directed with this in mind. During another marital therapy session, Mr. C. accused his wife of "blowing her cool" at a pair of very provocative house guests who happened to be close relatives.

CASE 2 (Excerpt 2)

Therapist   So you feel that anger and love can't reside in you at one time, because one pushes the other out — love pushes out any possibility of anger and anger pushes out love and when the two can't reside in you, well, I think you have to take one of the feelings and put them in Mrs. C. [*Mr. C.:* Yeah.], in this instance, so that Mrs. C. is the angry one and you're the loving one because it's very difficult for you to say, "I'm loving and I'm angry."

Husband   Yeah. (*tearfully*) Yeah, you're cooking with gas. I think, and it may relate to the fact, I mean as far as, in my amateurish use of the term of, of really getting boiling mad where I'm dangerous, as Wendell Willkie said, and this I don't really do because I would — I don't trust myself. I can remember as a kid, my sister and I used to have some royal battles like the — like when I threw the books, and maybe this is the key motif of — of the symphony of my existence, that I have a trigger. Certain things are like that. I mean this might never have happened — you know — well, we'll work on this business.

Mr. C. has tentatively begun to internalize the "boiling mad" aspect of himself previously projected onto his wife. The Caspar Milquetoast self-definition yields to a more authentic one of a man who is deeply concerned about control of his hostility, recalling earlier experiences within his family where his anger led to schisms between himself and his sister.

Having thus illustrated the defensive division of function within the marriage that is effected by projective identification, let us look at some ways in which this same process led to reenactment of earlier relationships within Mrs. C.'s family of origin. We will focus, in this example, on her experience of being devalued or "crushed" in the marriage and, reciprocally, of her own prominent devaluation of her husband. Both Mr. and Mrs. C. have acquired superegos of the harshest variety. Taking advantage of this structural condition, it was painfully common to discharge hostility by generating guilt and self-hatred in the spouse. In order to lighten the burden of their punitive consciences, each perceived its recriminations as emanating from the mate rather than from within themselves. On one occasion, a third and younger of the C.'s offspring began to do poorly at school. Mrs. C. was agonized by this, blaming herself severely for being a "bad mother." In the midst of this torment she turned to her husband during a family session, asking, "Arthur, where have I failed?" Mr. C. willingly enumerated her faults until the therapist intervened. Nevertheless, the husband's criticism relieved her considerably of the anguish that followed from her blame of herself. Now she was able, with great indignation, to fight with her critic, and she was single-minded in her defense of her mothering capabilities.

In the following excerpt from a marital therapy session, Mrs. C. has grasped that her relationship with Arthur recreates her interaction with her mother who "made me feel completely worthless." She does not yet appreciate how she evokes this devaluing behavior in others, but this becomes apparent in her transference attitude toward her therapist.

CASE 2 (Excerpt 3)

Wife   . . . and their feelings. I mean, my parents must have been very unhappy people, too, or they wouldn't have behaved the way they did. And I

	won't ever know why or so forth, but maybe these are kind of basic. . . just feelings rather than any specific incidents. Until I am able to understand them and try to cope with my feelings toward them, I don't think I'm going to be able to cope with my feelings toward Arthur. Does that make sense to you?
Therapist	Well, why don't you elaborate.
Wife	This is just about where I've gotten. And now I'm — and I'm working back. I'm — I hate to take the whole — this amount of time away, we need to discuss things. Okay?
Therapist	Away? Take it away from what?
Wife	From Arthur. You — shall I go on?
Husband	Shall she go on? Or would you rather hear a few words —
Wife	I figured —
Therapist	Well, I'm just — I'm confused about —
Wife	Okay, I'll unconfuse you, I think.
Therapist	I'm confused by your guilt a little bit. In other words, you're in a little bit of a box anytime you start reflecting on your own life and feeling sad about it. Then you start hating yourself because you're pitying yourself.
Wife	Yeah.
Therapist	That's a trap for yourself, because you can't — it's hard to do thinking if you start feeling that you're indulging yourself too much just by thinking.
Wife	Well, I —
Therapist	And then you feel you're taking up too much time in here, as if all of — and that may reflect one of your own earlier feelings that you didn't have rights to feeling bad, didn't have rights to your anger, and —
Wife	And any time, you see, when I was a child I would get so angry that I would say something back to my mother, I was instantly told, "You don't talk that way to your mother." And, consequently, I guess I still feel this. And I don't think this way about your mother or your father or — and so forth. But last night I was thinking, well, goddamn it, my mother was able to make me feel completely worthless, all of my growing up. And maybe what has happened is that I — Arthur was able to bring these same feelings out. And consequently I felt quite comfortable with Arthur. Because these were feelings I had lived with for so many years. No, I, I feel I am gaining the strength to face these feelings for the first time that my mother has felt for me. And I was again, oh, my God! I mean, go back into the past! I do remember when I was a freshman in college and I was rehearsing for a play, and the head of the drama department was directing it, and the play was coming up Sunday. Anyhow, things were very, very tense, and he turned on me at one point and screamed and ranted and raved. And my first reaction was, "Oh, my God, I've done something horrible again." Then I looked at the script and I saw that I was right. And that he was wrong. And I told him so. And I can remember still that glorious feeling: "By God, I didn't take the blame for something I was right about." And, of course, he quickly then said, "Oh, my God, I, I'm sorry," and so forth. So that — it was the very first time in my conscious recollection that I was able to talk back and say, "I'm

	right, you're wrong." In a very concrete situation. Now probably in feelings — I still wasn't able to feel not guilty about something that somebody jumped on me about. Well, anyhow, that brings us up to this feeling that I am wondering if it's a part of me Arthur has supplied over the years, is this need of mine that, that I had grown up with. Now is this a logical kind of reasoning of mine, or am I on the wrong track in my analyzing?
Therapist	It makes sense to me.
Husband	I'm a mother substitute as a crusher? Is that what you're —
Wife	I am saying that I seem to have a need to feel uncomfortable with myself, that I am not a worthy person, et cetera. I've said it once, hell.
Husband	You mean that your — that in order to be comfortable you feel uncomfortable. That was like what someone said about people that are so bored, that they don't know that they're bored, which I've been working on.
Wife	Arthur, don't you hear anything, huh?
Husband	Yes, but —
Wife	Well, what did you hear?
Husband	You're saying that you grew up feeling uncomfortable and crushed down, and, therefore, you got used to it and so now you still have to be that way. And I stand in the locus of your mother, making you feel uncomfortable. I was just saying it's an irony that you only feel comfortable when you're uncomfortable. It seems to be a little illogical.
Therapist	Well, it is a puzzle. I mean, that is, you know, another one of the reasons that it makes a lot of sense to me that what you say is — that I see you right here soliciting criticism.
Wife	From who?
Therapist	For example, by asking me whether you're on the right track in your discoveries of yourself.
Wife	Well, I honestly —
Therapist	"Am I right or wrong?" And that's really soliciting —
Wife	Well, what I'm doing to you is what I . . . my students do to me and what I've done to my teachers. If I'm practicing something in a certain way, I don't want to go through a whole damn week practicing it wrong.
Therapist:	But this isn't the theater. This is about self-discoveries and about yourself. I think you really are soliciting my judgment about you. And it fits in with your saying that perhaps one of the needs that has — that you have asked to be fulfilled and has been fulfilled is that judgments are made about you or criticisms, and then you for some reason have a need to experience this bad feeling about yourself. And if I had said, "No, it sounds like you're on the wrong track," I think you would have felt terrible.
Wife	Then I'd have to go through the whole damn process again and start all over again.

Mrs. C. speaks, in this interaction, of the parallel between her mother's and husband's devaluation of her worth. She attributes her tolerance of Mr. C.'s derogation primarily to habit, that is, " . . . because these were feelings I had lived with for many years." We would go a step further, however, to say that she is actively seeking to reenact through Arthur her experience with her mother. Because she has been successful, she feels "quite comfortable with Arthur." Evidence for her attempts to recruit a collusive partner to relate to her as her mother did is found in her behavior toward the therapist. At an unconscious level, her reflections constitute a performance in his behalf — "Does that make sense to you? . . . Shall I go on?" She associates, in a metaphorical vein, to her conflict with the drama-department chairman and her need to be told whether she is right or wrong. Soon thereafter, she turns to the therapist to ask, "Now is this a logical kind of reasoning of mine, or am I on the wrong track in my analyzing?" At first, the therapist does collude as her mother-judge by responding, "It makes sense to me," but he subsequently extricates himself from the collusion by interpreting her efforts at "soliciting criticism." As much as Mrs. C. wishes to disassociate herself from the familiar interaction ("It was either right or wrong. It wasn't a matter of anything else"), she is nevertheless reluctant to relinquish it ("If I'm practicing something in a certain way, I don't want to go through a whole damn week practicing it wrong").

Almost obscured in this excerpt is a glimpse of the other side of the coin, that is, Mrs. C.'s own inclination to devalue, to derogate: "Arthur, don't you hear anything, huh?" The reenactment of the mother-daughter relationship allows for a fluidity of identifications. Mrs. C., identified with her mother, is quite accomplished in making her husband feel worthless. In this situation, Mr. C. becomes for her the devalued child she once was. The common denominator then is the quality of the relationship between Mrs. C. and her mother. Which member of the marital dyad assumes which role is of secondary consequence as long as the subjective experience, the affective tone, of the earlier relationship is recreated. In the following excerpt, Mrs. C. discusses her concern that she is doing to her husband what her mother has done to her father, and through her identification, the scope of the reenactments is expanded to include now her own marriage as a reliving of her parents' marriage.

CASE 2 (Excerpt 4)

Therapist   What you've said makes me wonder about your own father. You rarely mention your father.

Wife   I feel that my mother was the stronger one there, and I think she did a
          beautiful job of castrating him, and I suspect I have doubts about my
          doing the same thing to Arthur. Maybe the right word isn't *doubt*, but
          I expect I do the same thing to Arthur. Guilt — I feel guilty everytime I
          fight back.

Therapist How do you mean castrated? She cut him down?

Wife   Constantly. He just wasn't any good. He wasn't anything according
          to her.

Therapist Just what?

Wife   Complete failure as far as she was concerned, and I thought that — I
          remember when they came to visit us, must have been about 10 years
          ago. It was the first time I got — saw my mother — as a lady that had
          done a real swell job.

Therapist What did you really see?

Wife   That I don't think — that he was perhaps not as bad as she led him to
          think.

Therapist Well, what's your perception of him?

Wife   Oh, he's very good, very kind. He's never been able to make a lot of
          money. See why I'm comparing? Why I'm doing the same thing to
          Arthur? My mother's always acted and — he had many of the same charac-
          teristics as Arthur — constantly talking and nobody listens. He writes
          beautiful letters, elegant letters, they ought to be published, just like
          Arthur. When you talk to him, it's completely undisciplined thoughts,
          just like Arthur, going on and on and on. And I think my greatest fear
          is that I do to Arthur what my mother did to my father.

This excerpt, in addition to demonstrating Mrs. C.'s identification with
her mother as a severe appraiser of the worth of others, also expresses a
secret admiration for a devalued father: "Oh, he's very good, very kind."
"He writes beautiful letters, elegant letters, they ought to be published."
We see that in being married to Arthur, Mrs. C. is also reliving a relationship
with an overtly denigrated but covertly valued father: "He was perhaps
not as bad as she led him to think." This element of positive attachment
to her father — obscured out of allegiance to mother — provided the leverage
for a substantial revision, during treatment, of her perception of and behavior toward her husband.

Because of schisms between her parents, Mrs. C. had come to feel that
a positive tie to one precluded intimacy with the other. During the transference relationship, the therapist-mother did not abandon Mrs. C. because
of her affection for her husband-father. Mrs. C. came to understand that
she could care for both, and without retaliation.

No attempt has been made here to present a comprehensive picture of the rich unconscious underpinnings of the C.'s marriage. Rather, we have selected excerpts that illustrate our main themes. Mr. C's intrapsychic conflict over his anger (Excerpt 1) is transposed onto the interpersonal field through the mechanism of projective identification. He discharges his hostility through the vicarious experience of his wife's volatility, which he disavows in himself. This disavowal permits him, in fantasy, to sustain a relationship with his daughter that is seemingly free of ambivalence. By virtue of the integration of his severe prohibitions on anger and her unbridled expression of hostility, the couple become, in Dicks's term, a joint personality. Interpretation by the therapist of this process of externalization (Excerpt 2) leads to an internalization, albeit tentative, of Mr. C.'s own conflict and to the elaboration of pertinent genetic material. The marital interactions generated by projective identification represent the reenactment of earlier object relationships in the spouses' families of origin (Excerpts 3 and 4). This process bears a strong resemblance to the formation of the transference, and, in fact, efforts are made to recruit the marital therapist as a collusive participant in this reenactment (Excerpt 3).

Although this chapter is not directed primarily at the treatment process, some comments stimulated by the aforementioned clinical material are appropriate. We hope that we have demonstrated how an appreciation of unconscious forces enriches our understanding of the marital relationship. Beyond that, this understanding illuminates the path for our therapeutic interventions. Intrapsychic conflicts that have been externalized through projective identifications must be reinternalized with the aid of our interpretations, since the process of working through can only be achieved at an intrapsychic level. Interventions that are aimed at modifying the behavior of the spouse who is the recipient of projections so that he or she is no longer a collusive partner have their parallel in individual therapy in the form of the analyzing of the countertransference. The transference in conjoint marital therapy must be closely attended to since the unconscious forces that influence the marital dyad are equally at play in the triad that now includes the therapist. For these reasons we concur with Dicks [2], who emphasized "the importance of grasping the meaning of unconscious communication as the essential part of marital therapy worthy of the name."

REFERENCES

1.   Dicks, H. V.   Object relations theory and marital studies. *British Journal of Medical Psychology* 36:125, 1963.
2.   Dicks, H. V.   *Marital Tensions. Clinical Studies Towards a Psychological Theory of Interaction.* New York: Basic Books, 1967.
3.   Freud, A.   *The Ego and the Mechanism of Defence* (1936). New York: International Universities Press, 1946.
4.   Freud, S.   Group psychology and the analysis of the ego (1921).   In *The Standard Edition of the Complete Psychological Works of Sigmund Freud*, transl. and ed. by J. Strachey with others.   London: Hogarth and Institute of Psycho-Analysis, 1955, Vol. 18, p. 112.
5.   Jaffe, D. S.   The mechanism of projection: Its dual role in object relations. *International Journal of Psycho-analysis* 49:662, 1968.
6.   Klein, M.   Notes on some schizoid mechanisms. *International Journal of Psycho-analysis* 27:99, 1946.
7.   Klein, M.   On Identification. In M. Klein, D. Heimann, and R. E. Money-Kyrle (Eds.), *New Directions in Psychoanalysis.* New York, Basic Books, 1956.
8.   Laing, R. D.   *The Self and Others: Further Studies in Sanity and Madness.* Chicago: Quadrangle, 1962.
9.   Malin, A., and Grotstein, J. D.   Projective identification in the therapeutic process. *International Journal of Psycho-analysis* 47:26, 1966.
10.   Zinner, J., and Shapiro, E. R.   Splitting in families of borderline adolescents. *Seminars in Psychiatry.* In press.
11.   Zinner, J., and Shapiro, R. L.   Projective identification as a mode of perception and behavior in families of adolescents. *International Journal of Psycho-analysis* 52:523, 1972.
12.   Zinner, J., and Shapiro, R. L.   The family as a single psychic entity: Implications for acting-out in adolescence. *International Review of Psychoanalysis* 1(1, 2):179, 1974.

III

Treatment of Marital Problems

The prevention and treatment of marital problems is a relatively new field. As mental health professionals, we are impressed with the large and increasing number of people who are seeking us out for help with their marriages. This interest in understanding and changing a relationship appears to be more a demand from the client than an innovation of the professionals, who have tended to devote their attention to the problems and psychology of the individual. The client hopes and expects that the mental health professional who has been able to help the individual will also be able to help the couple.

There are perhaps three major forces that have converged to bring about the search for a marital therapy system. The first is the historically important trend that marriages are increasingly thought of as an emotional relationship and decreasingly as an economic one. This has been described in greater detail in the first section of the book, particularly by Demos and Abernethy, but it is worth recalling the present-day expectations of couples for mutual support, companionship, help in coping with the psychological problems of life, and sexual satisfaction.

The second force that has been instrumental in couples seeking marital therapy is the women's movement and the changes in our society which led to it and which can be subsumed under this rubric. The woman of today is less inclined than the woman of the past to assume sole or major responsibility for the success or failure of her marriage. Today a married woman is less likely to seek individual psychotherapeutic assistance for a marital problem, but rather she may insist that her husband join her in whatever therapy is undertaken.

The third force in the evolution of marital therapy is the growing belief that disturbed human relationships are at the core of psychological problems — a view pioneered by Freud with his emphasis on the importance of early childhood experiences. Object relations theorists within psychoanalysis have emphasized and expanded this approach. The interpersonal psychiatry of Sullivan is also of great importance in this trend. More recently the study of family relationships and family therapy have further enlightened us as to the complementary nature of human interaction. And finally, the work of Masters and Johnson has made it clear that even sexual problems, such as frigidity and premature ejaculation, which were thought to be problems of individuals and frequently unaffected by individual treatment, can be successfully treated if viewed as problems within a relationship.

Thoughtful therapists have always been haunted by the role that marriage, the most intimate of human relationships, plays in the psychotherapy of individuals. Time and again, what has been accomplished in therapy sessions has been undone in the home. In the era of individual treatment, the only options considered were to advise a separation, to refer the spouse to his or her own therapist, or to terminate the treatment for the sake of the marriage.

Gradually the marriage itself has come under direct scrutiny. This scrutiny has taken both individual and group forms with a common theoretical perspective, namely, that the actual interpersonal experience, the "here and now," is of crucial significance for the resolution of marital problems. Instead of focusing only on the past of each partner, the therapist must choose when and how to focus on the present behaviors of the individual partners in relation to each other, taking into account their capacities for empathy and understanding. An emphasis on impediments to communication is central to treatment, since changing behavior, fostering empathy, and encouraging problem-solving depend on verbal, as well as emotional, sharing.

All human learning can be conceptualized as occurring in three main ways: through insight, through imitation and identification, and through behavioral conditioning (or reinforcement). These three modes of learning or influence are useful and necessary to marital therapy. Perhaps the most attention has been devoted to helping patients achieve insight, since insight is the precursor of a change in attitude and thus a change in behavior. Yet mechanisms such as initiation and identification with the attitudes and person of the therapist are undoubtedly equally important and powerful influences that can be effectively harnessed for use in the therapeutic process. For instance, when the therapist takes seriously the feelings and thoughts of one spouse, within an atmosphere where both feel understood, an opportunity for the other spouse to do likewise exists. These possibilities exist to an even greater extent in the group treatment of couples.

Many therapists have found it useful to alter marital interaction patterns by giving the couple specific instructions about behaviors in which they are to engage — in other words to use conciliatory or reinforcement teachings. The treatment of sexual dysfunctions, as discussed in the chapter by Offit, is a prime example of the influence of carefully thought-out behavioral directives. Some marital therapists view the giving of instructions or tasks as the central role of the therapist and view modified behavior as the major, and sometimes the only, goal of therapy. Other therapists eschew the giving of instructions, believing that it interferes with the attainment of insight, which they believe is a prerequisite for change. Our own perspective is that attempts to influence a couple's behavior through a directive should usually be viewed by both therapist and couple as a form of interpersonal experiment. If the couple attempts the task, they may well learn and gain insight from it, since acting differently, even if unspontaneously, permits one to see things differently. If they do not attempt the task, the reasons why they do not require exploration. The exclusively "directive" therapist runs the danger of leaving his patient changed in a particular aspect of behavior but without the insight to cope with future problems and possibly also of being identified with an authoritarian person. On the other hand the exclusively "insight-oriented" therapist has the problem that a couple may gain insight into their relationship but not know how or be able to change their behavior toward one another; their therapist is then wise but ineffectual, as is the couple. Marriage therapists, we believe, are well advised to strike a middle course by attending carefully to behavior and suggesting changes in a way that both fosters understanding and permits the couple to experience the therapist and the therapy as helping them to explore and experiment with new ways of behaving and relating to one another.

The therapist's attitude toward the couple is an important part of marital therapy. Here we have much to learn from the existential therapists who have emphasized the importance of the therapist's attempt to experience the world as the patient does. Nowhere is this more important than in work with married couples who are living with each other and experiencing the world in part through the other's eyes. Feeling understood is a precious experience; want of it is often what prompts an individual to seek therapy. It is difficult to describe how to achieve empathy, but the therapist will do well to remember its importance and to attempt the task of empathizing with each member of the couple. An emotional relationship experienced firsthand is much more alive, moving, and complex than it may seem when viewed objectively. However, the therapist must not only be involved empathically, but must also maintain his or her objectivity.

In a stimulating article, Loevinger has emphasized the fact that human beings have the paradoxical ability to shift cognitive modes, perhaps so as to avoid change or to change in undesired ways. An example will clarify what is meant. For instance, a husband may suggest to his wife that there is a certain reason that underlies her behavior and hopefully with the insight he is helping her achieve, she can now change. The wife, on the other hand, may perceive this comment as merely the continuation of an argument or as maliciously intended criticism carried out in the guise of promoting insight. The experience thus acts as negative reinforcement. Another example is that of a parent who lectures a misbehaving child or spanks the child in an attempt to impart insight into the causes of an undesirable behavior through negative reinforcement. The parent may find, however, that the child will identify with the parent and learn to lecture or to hit siblings and friends. Similarly, the therapist runs the danger that verbal interpretations of a patient's behavior will be experienced as negative reinforcement, that behavioral directives will be experienced as an opportunity to identify with an authoritarian person, or that his or her caring and gentle style will be experienced as insufficiently reinforcing to bring about change. We are therefore stressing both on theoretical grounds and from practical experience that the therapist will do well to work flexibly with couples using the tools of psychoanalytic exploration, behavioral therapy, and a caring, interested, and hopeful outlook.

In conclusion, we view that it is a matter of great importance that a marital therapist be clear about his or her own values with regard to marriage. They are an important influence on the course of therapy. The therapist's views of the appropriate division of work between the sexes, of divorce and fidelity, and of relationships with extended family and kin are obvious instances. More subtle, but we believe also more important, are feelings about the importance of intimacy, honesty, affection, and the need for, and quality of, sexual relationships. The therapist's own marriage and that of his or her parents will inevitably influence what is felt to be desirable. These are values which also have their impact on the type of therapy chosen and the quality of the therapeutic relationship, but ultimately we believe that the therapist's own attitudes will remain as the most important residual effect of the shared therapeutic hours.

The various chapters in Part III provide the basis for the treatment of married couples with the gamut of problems. In discussing the prevention of marital difficulties, Lieberman in his chapter has done a yeoman's task in an almost unexplored area. Clearly, our efforts in this direction are in their infancy. The other chapters of Part III form a logical sequence, beginning with the need for diagnostic assessment, proceeding to the problems of forging a meaningful therapeutic alliance, and then to the actual work of therapy, both in conjoint and group situations. The integration of the principles of dynamic marital treatment and sex counseling is emphasized in the chapter by Offit. The description and delineation of the various syndromes of marital disharmony is in its beginning stages. In this

delineation the cultural and historical factors that affect the manifestations of mental disharmony cannot be ignored. In his chapter Willi
describes in detail one unique marital constellation. It is an example
of the kind of detailed clinical analysis that we will no doubt see more
of in the future.

Finally Wahle, in her chapter, deals with the importance and challenge
for the therapist in acting as an objective and skilled agent of change while
at the same time bringing to the therapeutic experience the warmth and
humanness of his or her own unique personality.

13

The Prevention of Marital Problems

E. James Lieberman

> Marriage is the only adventure
> open to the cowardly.
> — Voltaire

In the five years from 1968 to 1973, the divorce rate in the United States jumped 50 percent; the number of couples divorcing annually averaged about 750,000, involving some 1.5 million adults [12]. Most divorces also involve children. Couples without children are more readily divorced than are couples with children, but they have fewer marital problems. This is one of many paradoxes to be found in a psychosocial overview of contemporary American marriage.

A high incidence of marital problems is reflected in statistics on homicide: the family is the main site of lethal arguments. Therapists, lawyers, and judges see the full-blown problems too late to repair the damage, much less prevent it. Yet prevention is needed, because treatment resources are inadequate in quantity, if not in efficacy.

Recently much attention has been paid to the prevention of suicide, drug abuse, and crime in the streets — problems that touch fewer people directly than does marital failure. There should be no quarrel about the importance of prevention in all these areas. But the ubiquity of marriage problems and the primacy of the family in child socialization suggest that prevention of marital and family problems is the foundation of preventive

315

psychiatry, since many other personal and social problems stem from the failure of the family.

The role of the clinician in prevention of family breakdown must be broadened. If all divorcing couples sought counseling, there would not be nearly enough mental health professionals to handle them. More counselors are needed, of course, but an increase is not a substitute for primary prevention. Therapists usually treat people in serious difficulty; that is, most people do not consult therapists until the problem is major. An exception occurs when a child is being treated, and the therapist also finds the parents' marriage in need of treatment. Unfortunately, few child specialists are oriented toward marriage counseling. But their concern must extend even farther, beyond the office to the large number of people at risk of having problems, including those now married and those to be married. Clinicians and family-life educators must take notice of each other and of the schools, doctors' offices, courts, banks, and churches — all the places where trouble can be detected early and where critical decisions are made.

A DEMOGRAPHIC PERSPECTIVE

Vital statistics deserve much more attention from socially responsible clinicians than they are now getting. There is a wealth of information about marriage, parenthood, and divorce in the United States with which professional and lay people should be familiar. The following summary of this information is based on the comprehensive study by Carter and Glick [4] and on a subsequent paper by Glick and Norton [12].

Lest the incidence of problems seem overwhelming, it should be noted that since 1940 the rate of increase of the married segment in the United States has been five times the rate of increase of the divorced segment. The divorce rate is up in most of the world, and the trend is such that the gap is closing between countries with a low rate and countries with a high rate. Instead of the 13-fold gap between top and bottom of a generation ago, the gap is now fivefold. But the United States is far ahead in the divorce rate. The number of divorces per 1000 married couples per year is 10.7 in the United States, 6.7 in Austria, and 5.0 in Sweden. On the low side, Canada, France, Norway, the Netherlands, and the United Kingdom have a rate of under 3 per 1000. The United States, along with some other economically developed countries, experienced peak divorce rates from

1945—1952, and these peak rates have now been reached again. The
modal duration of marriage in years before divorce ranges from under
one year to over seven; in the United States it was one to two years
(in 1963), with the most common age for the wife 20 to 24 years old and
for the husband 25 to 29 years old. Divorces tend to be concentrated in
the younger age groups, with the highest rate among teenage spouses (25
per 1000 per year) and an only slightly lower rate in the 20- 24-year-old
group. Other countries have fewer teenage marriages but also far fewer
divorces among couples under 20 years of age (below 4 per 1000). In the
United States, either there is less hesitation to end a poor marriage
promptly, or the high rate of young marriage predisposes to a high percentage of failure [4].

Marriage rates for teenagers increased worldwide in the period 1936
to 1963, with the United States far ahead. Indeed, most other countries
reported higher marriage rates for men over 60 years old than for those
under 20. By 1960, 10 percent of single teenage girls (15 to 19 years old)
married each year in the United States — about twice the rate in other
countries. The trend toward youthful marriage has now ended and is
showing a reversal, with a higher proportion of women remaining single
past the age of 20 [4].

Since most couples have a child in the first three years of marriage, and
most divorces occur within the first 15 years, 60 percent of divorces involve minor children. In this country, for every 100 divorces there are
130 children involved; excluding childless couples, the average number of
children involved per divorce is 2.14. The trend has been toward more
children's being involved — 700,000 in 1967 — reflecting a greater willingness of parents to be divorced than was true in the past. This coincides
with higher educational levels and employment rates for women and
changing mores about marriage and divorce. [4]

The Depression, World War II, and the postwar period affected marriage
rates, so that our recent history lacks a period with a "normal" marriage
pattern for older persons. In the late 1960s, a "marriage squeeze" developed, consisting of a surplus of marriageable girls as compared with
young men. This resulted from the baby boom after 1945, the female
half of which reached the traditional marriage age before the male group.
In such a situation, one might predict (1) more girls having to wait until
the boys are old enough, (2) a narrowing of age difference between

husbands and wives in this group (although there will also be some "raiding" of other age groups for spouses, and even married men might be considered fair game), and (3) a rise in the average woman's age at marriage, a trend that has already been observed. In the last decade, the average age of women at marriage has increased by six months, but other factors affecting marriage age may also be responsible. The advent of more effective contraception, safer and more available abortion, and more liberal attitudes toward premarital sex have reduced certain obvious pressures to marry prematurely. The annual removal of up to 500,000 young men to Vietnam, most of them unmarried and eligible, also had some effect on marriage rates in the period after 1965.

Divorced people remarry at higher rates than single people marry. This may not be surprising, but it deserves some thought. Obviously, most people who end marriages are not condemning the institution of marriage per se since so many marry again. Often there is a third party in the background, offering the prospect of remarriage as an incentive to divorce. As the number of women with a higher education and the number of women in the labor force have increased, the sexes have become more exposed to one another. Marriages are therefore under greater pressure than ever because of the quantity and quality of other possible relationships [4].

Of those people who are divorced before age 25, one-half of the women and one-third of the men remarry within a year. The median duration of marriage before divorce is about seven years; the largest cluster of divorcing couples do so within the first or second year of marriage. The stability of remarriages approximates that of first marriages. Because of increased longevity and the increased divorce rate, most remarriages today follow divorce rather than death of a spouse, a reversal of the former pattern. One-fourth of the people marrying today are remarrying. This leads to a situation in which the total marriage rate is high, the divorce rate is high, and more young women are staying single longer. The apparent paradox is explained by a drop in the rate of first marriages [4].

There are major promarriage developments — among them, an increase in the percentage of married persons and an increase in the percentage of adult life spent married. Between 1940 and 1960, the willingness to enter marriage readily, terminate it, and try again was reflected in increases in percent married and percent divorced, with a decrease in percent single. The percentage of adult life spent married increased between 1940 and

1964, for men from 50 percent to 68 percent, for women from 56 percent to 62 percent [4]. As permissiveness toward divorce increases, one might assume that free choice becomes a larger factor in sustaining those marriages that endure. This is the silver lining in the cloud of marital breakdown.

Although the trend is now away from teenage marriage, the impact of the earlier trend toward it will be felt for some time to come. To illustrate: in 1966, among women age 45—49, 28 percent had married before age 20; among women age 25—29, 49 percent had married before age 20 [4]. It is not surprising, then, that the divorce rate jumped so high in the late 1960s.

There were about 3 million divorced and 2 million separated persons in the 1960 population. The median age at divorce for men was 34 (three-fourths of divorced men were under 45 at the time of divorce); women averaged three years younger. Teenage marriages have the highest rate of dissolution: one-third are over within 20 years, which is about twice the rate for later-marrying couples. Marital breakdown is correlated with dropout status from high school or college, and marital stability generally increases with eduational level, more so among men. Other correlates of marital stability are good employment and income. The burdens of poverty and racism are evident in the higher rates of separation, divorce, widowhood, and single status among non-whites. For example, half of white women are widowed by age 70, but half of nonwhite women are widowed by age 63. Not until age 85 are half of all men widowers [4].

Risk of hospitalization for mental illness varies with marital status, and mental patients who are married have a better statistical chance for recovery. Among psychiatric inpatients, for every 100 who are married, there are 204 widows, and 2250 single males [4]. This striking figure probably reflects a greater societal tolerance for disturbed females rather than a drastically higher illness rate among males. It can also be accounted for by the "mating gradient," which describes the tendency for men to marry down in social status and women to marry up, with a hard core of unmarriageable males at the bottom of the social ladder and females at the top. The single females are better equipped to cope alone than are the single males.

Three-fourths of husbands are older than their wives: the median differential is 2.7 years, down from 3 years (1948—1960 figures), About one-seventh of wives are older than their husbands. The rest are same-age pairs. Men have been marrying at a much earlier age than they used to, in large part because working wives provide an economic base that never existed before. Now there are more marriages among people in their twenties, fewer among people in their teens and thirties. (But nonwhites, it appears, have to postpone marriage longer to get the equivalent job and income of their white counterparts.)

In 1960, husbands over 55 years old were, on the average, 3.6 years older than their wives, whereas husbands under 35 were only 1.9 years older [4]. This narrowed age gap will reduce the incidence and duration of widowhood that results from the shorter life span of men.

When immigration rates were high, there used to be a surplus of males in the United States; foreign-born men tended to marry late, and thus many came to this country without wives to balance off their number. Now there is a balance between the sexes, with a steadily increasing surplus of women in the aging population. There are about 9 million widows, and 2 million widowers [4], evidence of a mental health challenge surpassing even that of divorce, but underplayed in a society that abhors aging.

Homogamy — the tendency of like to marry like — is pervasive in our society. Although laws against interracial marriage were struck down in 1966, the phenomenon is still rare: it occurs in less than 1 percent of all marriages. Mixed-religion pairings, mostly Protestant-Catholic, constitute about 5 percent of marriages. Both types of mixed marriages cause discussion and consternation out of proportion to their failure rate, which is little worse than that of homogamous marriages.

Childbearing has become more of a universal phenomenon in the society, as has marriage. All but 3 or 4 percent of Americans marry now — a higher percentage than in most countries. Americans are sold on marriage and parenthood, although the price appears high in terms of divorce and separation. Among women born between 1900 and 1910, 8 percent were single, 26 percent were childless; among women born between 1930 and 1950, 4 percent were single, 10 percent were childless. The average interval between marriage and birth of the first child is about one and one-half years — too short according to studies of marital adjustment; and these figures do not include premarital conceptions. There has been a decline of average family size from 4 to 2.5 children. Women tend to have a few extra years child-free in their late thirties now, because childbearing is accomplished sooner. The number of couples experiencing the "empty nest" is remarkable. In the twentieth century, an average of nine years (or 25 percent) has been added to married life. The average interval between age at marriage and the death of one spouse, usually the husband, has increased from 35 to 44 years. This fact, plus changes in childbearing patterns, has increased the average empty-nest marital stage from one year to 12 years. The mental health implications are obvious. Eighty percent of couples will survive to see their last child marry; a generation ago only 50 percent did [4]. The phenomenon of divorce after 20 or more years of marriage is increasing, but this phenomenon involves only a tiny fraction of divorces. Like other sensational phenomena, the empty-nest divorce seems to be more frequent that it is: 85 percent of all divorces occur to women under 45. Perhaps 3 percent of married women above that age will be divorced — 97 percent will not [12].

MARITAL ADJUSTMENT AND STABILITY

Little is known about marital adjustment or happiness. Concepts and definitions of success, satisfaction, and adjustment are difficult; subjective reports are relied on in an area where social norms are hard and fast, and researchers are often caught up in value-laden assumptions. Bradburn [3] suggests that happiness and unhappiness are not part of one continuum but coexist, so that some people are low on both and others are high on both. This describes many marriages, which differ as much in the intensity of feeling and involvement as in the direction of feeling.

Research in the 1960s, reviewed by Hicks and Platt [15], confirms some well-established findings: marital happiness correlates with higher socioeconomic status of husband, with homogamy by age, socioeconomic status, and religion, and with affection and esteem for the spouse. The instrumental, traditional male role appears to have a greater importance than was realized by social scientists. Research oriented to the companionship aspects of marriage suggests a positive relationship between affective involvement, communication, accurate empathy, and happiness. A new typology of marriages emerged: happy-stable, unhappy-unstable, and, to the surprise of some, unhappy-stable. This last applies to those who tolerate misery well, or who simply will not view divorce as an option.

No mention was made of a fourth type, happy-unstable, although with higher expectations for happiness, and experimentation with sex, group marriage, and the like, it may well be that some marriages fit this description. When marriages that are judged to be stable by others dissolve, sometimes the others are shocked and may even feel threatened, because they may have considered the broken marriage happier than their own. They may be right. Evidently there are many durable marriages with less happiness than some unstable marriages have [10]. The issue is complicated by the need to conduct research over time or retrospectively so that the whole family life-cycle can be encompassed.

Children have profound effects on the marital dyad. Couples with unplanned children have lower-than-average adjustment scores [6]. And couples who delay parenthood after marriage have lower divorce rates: the longer the interval to first birth, the less likely divorce is [5].

Major studies of marital adjustment and happiness of a generation ago found the vast majority of couples to be content; up to 80 percent were in the higher-status groups [15]. These studies have since been criticized because of the value assumptions that rate marriages that are conflict free and conventional, no matter how dull, dishonest, and undemocratic they may be, as good marriages. Recent studies may seem pessimistic at first glance but it must be considered that the emphasis is on different qualities of life, for example, vitality, creativity, and independence [15]. This is entirely fitting at a time when many people are rethinking the values of marriage and family life, and are no longer satisfied with traditional attitudes. As aspirations go up, marital satisfaction may fluctuate greatly, depending on the persons involved, the time in the family life-cycle, and external circumstances. The prevention of marriage problems in the future depends on much more than finding a key to adjustment. Prevention of problems means facing conflict, growing in a relationship, reevaluating commitment, and cultivating joyful intimacy. Marital health is not merely the absence of divorce.

SOCIETAL NORMS THAT UNDERMINE MARITAL SUCCESS

Our social norms still support marital fidelity and stability, premarital chastity, and postmarital childbearing. These ideals are often unrealized, which is not surprising. What is surprising is the extent to which social institutions fail to support these ideals. There is virtually no social deterrent to early marriage, although it predisposes to divorce. Laws barring marriage of minors are breached at a whim, especially when the girl is pregnant. Divorce proceedings are costly and difficult (though becoming less so), as though attempting to maintain family stability. Easy pathways to marriage are coupled with stringent divorce laws, a model better suited to designing rat traps than happy families. The social system requires people to abide by a decision to marry made when they were immature and when under duress of sexual pressures if not pregnancy.

Who let them into marriage to begin with? The agents of society who encounter prospective nuptial couples are, at most, the marriage-license clerk, the physician or laboratory technician, and the clergyman or justice of the peace. Of these, only some clergymen have the time, interest, or skill to inquire about a couple's relationship and to offer guidance. From the mental health standpoint, few of these agents are qualified to assess and assist at what is a critical time in the life-cycle for two — and ultimately many more — people. We cannot, as a society, be proud of our approach to marriage.

Until recently, most couples in the United States used no method of contraception prior to the birth of the first child [20]. Information and technology have advanced in the last decade so that planning of the first birth is more common, but it still misses the groups that need it most: the poor, the less educated, and the very young. There is no single factor of greater importance in the enhancement of marriage and parenthood, and in the mental health of families in general, than of birth-planning on the basis of informed consent prior to the first pregnancy and each succeeding pregnancy [7, 18, 20, 27].

Since the medical profession controls the channels to the best methods of birth-planning, it has the chief responsibility to raise the topic with couples who present themselves for premarital examination and certification. The offer of birth-control services must be done sensitively (perhaps with the question, "Do you want to have children right away?"), but it must be done. Research has shown that many couples who wish information will wait until the doctor (or nurse) initiates discussion [14].

Of course, the doctor's office is not the place to begin family-planning education. The schools must lead off, and they have the appropriate context in well-established courses on health, family living, home economics,

biology, and so on. The failure to teach young people the elementary
facts about family formation, their own bodies, and the social consequences
of various patterns of behavior is manifest in the high rates of unwanted pregnancy, out-of-wedlock parenthood, venereal disease, and abortion. Direct
evidence concerning the impact of sex education on marital success is
lacking, but the burden of proof, in view of indirect evidence, must be on
those who say it does not help. In the future, sexual ignorance, premature
marriage, and excess fertility will have a higher cost than ever for the individuals concerned and for the community.

There is much more than sex education to be done in the schools in
regard to marriage preparation. Indeed, the need for sex education may
lessen as the mass media become more involved. With the emergence of
the nuclear family of high mobility, children grow up with a limited view
of child development. They are stratified by age from the earliest years
and may have very little contact with children and adults of varying ages
unless they happen to grow up in an age-mixed neighborhood. The school
is responsible for the age stratification, and the school can remedy the
situation by creating more arrangements for age-mixing. There should be
a day-care center in every high school. From sixth grade on, children
should assist in classrooms of younger children. High-school students
should follow young couples through pregnancy and birth experiences
and should become competent in infant care. Senior citizens should be
involved with children of all ages to balance the experience of the community and as evidence of the life cycle and the interdependence of people
of all ages.

Nothing short of this can be considered adequate preparation for family
life in the world of the future, when tradition will have less hold — and
less to offer [23].

In the United States, marriage counseling is an underdeveloped profession. While most of the mental health disciplines are engaged in it,
and marital as well as family therapy is now recognized as part of the
treatment spectrum, marriage and family counseling lack the status given
the other therapies [1]. In Great Britain and other Commonwealth
countries, a system of marriage counseling by selected trained and super-
vised lay people has emerged since World War II. Although the counseling
has not been rigorously evaluated (neither has psychotherapy here), it is
generally regarded as a successful program. Each year some 18,000 couples

are counseled in Great Britain alone by people who spend at least three hours a week counseling. Their work is probably monitored better than comparable work by professionals — a significant benefit to the client [31].

There has been debate and some experiments with mandatory counseling before divorce is granted. If there were enough trained people (including trained laymen), the idea would be worth implementing; but as suggested above, the problems associated with too-early marriage and too-early childbearing are not likely to be solved by talk after the fact.

Conversely, any reasonable approach to increasing the average age of marriage and of childbearing (the median age for women having their first child is 22) is sure to increase both the quality and durability of marriage. This is not to say that all teenage marriages are unsuccessful. Nonetheless, it is scientifically reasonable and simply humane to have marriages contracted in so far as possible by people with informed consent, not under duress and not with unrealistic expectations. The steps outlined above for schools would be helpful. Of course, if more young people delay marriage, approximating the pattern in some other countries, we can expect a corresponding increase in premarital sexual experience. The increasing availability of birth control should forestall any rise in premarital pregnancy, and, as will be shown, responsible premarital sex must be recognized as an option for young people today.

PRIMARY PREVENTION AND PREPARATION FOR MARRIAGE

Marriage counseling, court reconciliation services, and arbitration services are beyond the scope of this chapter, although they might be subsumed under the public health terms *secondary and tertiary prevention.* Such services uncover important data on the sources and course of marital problems, and those who provide these important services also need to be aware of primary prevention, which is the focus here.

Several psychiatrists have written on the theme of primary prevention in relation to marriage. Greene [13], whose approach is clinical, has developed a "well-marriage" unit, and suggests annual visits by the couple for the first three years of marriage, followed by a visit once every five years. His marital checkup employs psychological tests, an emphasis on improved marital communication, and a framework of developmental stages in marriage. The well-marriage unit approach, in operation since

1964, also deals with early-stage problems, and any therapist may refer or bring a couple for consultation. Saul [26] presents a casebook on marriage problems and their prevention. Kirsten Auken [2], the late Danish psychiatrist, emphasized housing and other material considerations, as well as emotional maturity, as prime factors in marriage problems. A British psychiatrist, Dominian [8], emphasizes sociological variables in primary prevention: increased age at marriage, no premarital pregnancy, and a successful engagement period of nine months or more. He favors marriage preparation courses and family-planning.

Premarital counseling is fine in principle but weak in practice. The number of trained professionals is too small to cope with the number of marriages — more than one million annually. The only hope is that counseling principles be utilized by the gatekeepers to the institution of marriage: clergymen and physicians [25]. School counselors would be a potential resource for group premarital counseling, an approach that has psychological as well as logistic advantages for adolescents [11]. At least one department store has introduced premarital counseling as part of its bridal services; and perhaps the mass media will fulfill more of its great potential for realistic communication about sex, marriage, childrearing, and family life.

All high-school, college, and church-related teaching on marriage and the family may be considered primary prevention. Evaluation of such efforts is difficult because (1) not all students are exposed to them, (2) varied materials and methods are used, and (3) frank exploration of student attitudes and practices has not been the rule. Large numbers of young people in the past avoided such courses if possible, while others sought them out for easy marks rather than for marriage preparation. Such courses today, at least at the college level, are attracting more interest, probably reflecting a trend toward behavioral science generally, greater frankness with issues, and more worthwhile material in the marriage preparation field, from consumerism to childcare, sex, contraception, and abortion. One publication, which serves as an index to 30 of the most commonly used college texts [17] provides a good overview of the field. The textbooks of the 1960s have a generally conservative thrust and are pale by comparison with the statements of Judge Ben Lindsey [21], Bertrand Russell [24], and Havelock Ellis [9]. However, texts of the 1970s are much bolder [29, 32].

Premarital sex is naturally of interest to young people who take these courses, a fact recognized by textbook authors, who devote considerable space and energy to the matter. The texts of the 1960s, like their predecessors, tend to uphold the virtues of premarital chastity but acknowledge widespread departure from that standard, and most recognize that premarital sex experience does not necessarily lead to unhappy marriage. Although none of the authorities treat sex as an end in itself, some, placing social convention or personal prejudice ahead of objective evidence and analysis, give the impression that premarital chastity is an end in itself. It is necessary, now that the threat of pregnancy can be met, to provide other reasons for chastity, or else abandon the effort. The failure of many marriage textbooks to deal adequately with contraception is shocking, to say the least, and may be a sign of the author's (and publisher's) reluctance to give up the old deterrents to premarital sex.

Instead of polarizing premarital chastity and premarital intercourse as right and wrong, one might better try to establish right and wrong reasons for chastity and for sex — before and after marriage. Chastity has little meaning unless it is by choice, and young people must be equipped to make informed choices about whether and when to engage in sexual intercourse.

Marriage textbooks offer advice on many matters, but their treatment of the more philosophical issues, including those pertinent to adjustment and mental health, seems too general to be helpful. Maturity, sensitivity, unselfishness, and so on, are important in good human relations, but they come across as platitudes unless good case examples are given. As Russell [24] pointed out, romance depends in part on the unattainability of its object. Marital problems begin to be felt after romance has faded. Marriage based on love is better than arranged marriage, if freedom of choice is a value, but informed consent is hardly possible at a very young age, when the power and beauty of adolescent romance overshadows the reality of commitment to lifelong companionship.

To keep the romance in a marital relationship, sex must not be taken for granted after the wedding any more than premarital chastity was taken for granted in the generations past, when sex was a wife's duty and a husband's prerogative. Recent changes in attitudes include the emergence of extreme responses that proclaim the death of the family, the futility of lifelong marriage, and the right to extramarital sexual freedom. These are provocative attitude changes that must be handled with a combination of firmness and humility by the therapist, since they are value-laden and not easily subject to scientific proof. Too often, marriage experts are indistinguishable from spokesmen for traditional value positions; this includes physicians, who are de facto experts and gatekeepers for the institution of marriage in states that require premarital certification of health.

It can be argued that young people are ill-equipped to make mature decisions about premarital sex, and society can help some of them avoid disaster by telling them no. But if so, how can society allow young people to marry at all? Why not say no to marriage before age 21? The obvious reason is that social mores dictates early marriage rather than premarital intercourse. But equally obvious is the fact that, for the prevention of marital problems and the building of a stable nuclear family, safe premarital intercourse is better than premature marriage. This is not a condemnation of chastity, but of a system that tacitly builds the primary institution of society — the family — on a foundation of legalized sex for young people. Perhaps one should marvel at the number of marriages that are durable and happy, considering the manner in which so many are contracted.

CONCLUSIONS

In view of the large number and many kinds of marital problems and the difficulty of arriving at criteria of readiness for marriage and of providing reliable guides to behavior, clinicians and others concerned with prevention should make use of objective statistical material for policy-making, program-planning, teaching, and advising. Statistics, too, are imperfect and subject to various interpretations. But they provide a framework within which there is room for testing hypotheses, such as the ones listed below, and using clinical judgment with each individual case. The following hypotheses are concerned with prevention of marital and mental health problems.

1. Too many Americans marry. Of those eligible, 95 percent go to the altar. It is statistically and socially deviant to be mature and never married, yet the high rate of marriage failure suggests that more than 5 percent are unsuited for marriage. Perhaps 80 to 85 percent would be a more realistic percentage if marital breakdown is to be prevented.

2. Americans marry too young. The United States leads the Western

world in marriages before age 20 and in divorces. Early marriage is the single best predictor of marital failure. Delaying marriage would undoubtedly result in a higher percentage of nonmarriage, which is consistent with the paragraph above. Persons unsuited for marriage may not have a chance to evaluate options in adolescence, when sexual and other pressures to marry are intense and when the tendency to conform is also very strong.

3. The transition to parenthood comes too early. Many young marriages result from accidental pregnancy. Many other marriages are constricted, if not ruined, by the birth of a child within the first year or two. If parenthood were truly a matter of informed consent, the average age of parents at the birth of the first child would increase, as would the interval between marriage and parenthood. Couples would have fewer children altogether, with more attention to greater spacing between children, probably about 3 years [19, 33], and a higher percentage would forego parenthood altogether, also a desirable outcome not only personally for those unsuited but communally in view of population pressures and the tragically high number of institutionalized children. Good parenting is, of course, the essential long-range investment in the prevention of future family problems.

4. Women should marry level or downward in age. The present system guarantees a tragic number of widows in years ahead, because women live longer and marry men who are somewhat older. In adolescence girls are perhaps more mature than their male peers, most of whom do not marry until their twenties. Women, too, should postpone marriage and that should be easier to do as sex discrimination in education and employment is reduced, and the double standard regarding premarital sex is abandoned.

5. Laws should be revised to make marrying somewhat more difficult and the process of divorce more humane. Incentives should be given for marriage education as they are for driver education. The present system allows, or entices, young people to commit matrimonial folly, which can then be undone only with great suffering. Making divorce difficult punishes, but does not prevent, matrimonial mistakes. Probably if divorce laws were fairer, marital conflict would be handled more maturely [16]. Couples often rely on the marriage contract as a ball and chain that keeps them from options that are essential to dignity and sanity. Tax laws should be reversed so that they favor the unmarried and nonparents. There is no longer a need to give incentives to marriage and parenthood — if there ever was.

These recommendations will seem utopian to some, diabolical to others. A reduction in the proportion of married people and a delay in the timing of marriage and parenthood presuppose an increase in protected (contraceptive) premarital and nonmarital sexual intercourse. Those who consider this inconsistent with family stability should consider first the present deplorable state of affairs. Available evidence suggests that accidental pregnancy, not premarital sex, is the major threat to marital adjustment.

Those who agree with the recommendations but find them unrealistic should be aware of the need for a program of enlightened education. This means, among other things, a more realistic and diverse treatment of love, sex, marriage, and parenthood in the mass media. Films, magazines, and books are moving ahead in these matters; television and newspapers lag behind but show some improvement. Norman Paul's television film *"Trouble in the Family"* and his radio series *"A Chance to Grow"* are fine examples of what can be done. The mass media reflect, as well as determine, prevalent attitudes, and their power to inform and influence public opinion is immense. The responsibility of the media is commensurately great, as is that of experts on mental health, marriage, and family life; both should take a more active role in the development of sound public opinion. Legislation may be out of the question or ill advised, but much information and discussion are needed to overcome the inertia of tradition and conformity in matters that undermine modern family life.

To conclude, it is not fair to blame the family for the psychosocial ills of our times; the family has not been given a fair trial. It is encouraging to see concern for family and marital health gaining attention and higher status among professional and lay leaders [28, 30] at a time when other preventive medicine and health maintenance concepts are being advanced.

REFERENCES

1. Abse, D. W., Nash, E. M., and London, L. *Marital and Sexual Counseling in Medical Practice.* New York: Harper & Row, 1974.
2. Ard, B. N., Jr., and Ard, C. C. *Handbook of Marriage Counseling.* Palo Alto, Calif.: Science and Behavior Books, 1969.
3. Auken, K. Time of marriage, mate selection and task accomplishment in newly formed Copenhagen families. *Acta Sociologica* 8:128, 1964. Reprinted in Howells, J. G. *Theory and Practice of Family Psychiatry.* New York: Brunner/Mazel, 1971.

4. Bradburn, N. M., and Caplovitz, D. *Reports on Happiness.* Chicago: Aldine, 1965.
5. Carter, H., and Glick, P. C. *Marriage and Divorce: A Social and Economic Study.* Cambridge, Mass.: Harvard University Press, 1970.
6. Christensen, H. T. Timing of first pregnancy as a factor in divorce: A cross-cultural analysis. *Eugenics Quarterly* 10:119, 1963.
7. Christensen, H. T., and Philbrick, R. E. Family size as a factor in the marital adjustments of college couples. *American Sociological Review* 17:306, 1952.
8. David, Henry P. Mental health and family planning. *Family Planning Perspectives* 3:2, 1971.
9. Dominian, J. *Marital Breakdown.* Baltimore: Penguin, 1968.
10. Ellis, H. *Marriage Today and Tomorrow.* San Francisco: Westgate Press, 1929.
11. Farson, R. Why good marriages fail. *McCalls,* Oct. 1971, p. 110.
12. Gangsei, L. B. *Manual for Group Premarital Counseling.* New York: Association Press, 1971.
13. Glick, P. C., and Norton, A. J. Perspectives on the recent upturn in divorce and remarriage. *Demography* 10:301, 1973.
14. Greene, B. L. *A Clinical Approach to Marital Problems.* Springfield, Ill.: Thomas, 1970.
15. Herndon, C. N., and Nash, E. M. Premarriage and marriage counseling. *Journal of the American Medical Association* 180:395, 1962.
16. Hicks, M. W., and Platt, M. Marital happiness and stability: A review of the research in the sixties. *Journal of Marriage and the Family* 32:553, 1970.
17. Kargman, M. W. The revolution in divorce law. *Family Coordinator* 22:245, 1973.
18. Kirkendall, L. A., and Adams, W. J. *The Students' Guide to Marriage and Family Life Literature: An Aid to Individualized Study* (5th ed.). Dubuque, Iowa: William C. Brown, 1971.
19. Lieberman, E. J. Preventive psychiatry and family planning. *Journal of Marriage and the Family* 26:471, 1964.
20. Lieberman, E. J. Reserving a womb: A case for the small family. *American Journal of Public Health* 60:87, 1970.
21. Lieberman, E. J. Informed Consent for Parenthood. *In Abortion and the Unwanted Child.* New York: Springer, 1971.
22. Lindsey, B. B., and Evans, W. *The Companionate Marriage.* New York: Boni & Liveright, 1927.
23. Rossi, A. S. Family development in a changing world. *American Journal of Psychiatry* 128:1057, 1972.
24. Russell, B. *Marriage and Morals.* New York: Liveright, 1929.
25. Rutledge, A. L. *Pre-Marital Counseling.* Cambridge, Mass.: Schenkman, 1966.
26. Saul, L. J. *Fidelity and Infidelity.* New York: Lippincott, 1967.
27. Schwartz, R. A. The role of family planning in the primary prevention of mental illness. *American Journal of Psychiatry* 125:1711, 1969.

28. Silverman, H. L. (Ed.).   *Marital Therapy.*   Springfield, Ill.: Thomas, 1972.
29. Skolnick, A. S., and Skolnick, J. H.   *Family in Transition.*   Boston: Little, Brown, 1971.
30. Vincent, C.   *Sexual and Marital Health.*   New York: McGraw Hill, 1973
31. Wallis, J. H.   *Marriage Guidance.*   London: Routledge & Kegan Paul, 1968.
32. Wiseman, J. P.   *People As Partners.*   San Francisco: Canfield Press, 1971.
33. Wray, J. D.   Population Pressure on Families: Family Size and Child Spacing. *In Rapid Population Growth: Consequences and Policy Implications.*   Baltimore: Johns Hopkins Press, 1971.

14

Diagnosis and Treatment-Planning for Couples*

Henry Grunebaum
Jacob Christ
Norman A. Neiberg

Couples with troubled marriages are increasingly seeking assistance from
mental health professionals. The literature is replete with reports docu-
menting clinical experiences, often successful, with one or another form
of marital treatment. However, little has been offered in the way of guidelines to assist the diagnostician in prescribing the appropriate treatment
for any given couple, except for a single paper by Greene [5]. Traditional
descriptive or dynamic psychiatric diagnosis of individual members of a
couple offers little aid in treatment-planning.

This chapter discusses the diagnostic indications for the various types
of marital therapy, and is thus primarily patient focused. However, certain
features of the various types of therapy will be described to clarify why
a given technique is most appropriate for a particular type of patient. Our
endeavor in this chapter is a preliminary effort at classification. It will,
we hope, arouse controversy; and, indeed, we have sought to be both
explicit and definite rather than tentative and guarded in order to provoke
reactive disagreements. We believe that the field is ripe for efforts that
go beyond descriptions of technique to heuristic attempts at prescription.

*Reprinted with modifications from *International Journal of Group Psychotherapy* 19(2):185,
1969.

This chapter is a revision and extension of an article we wrote in 1968.
In the intervening years, certain social changes have influenced the treatment of couples. First, it is our experience that an increasing number of
couples seek treatment together and that, increasingly, students in the
mental health professions are interested in learning how to treat couples
and families. Second, the importance of interpersonal relationships and
the need to consider seriously their forms and values are highlighted by
the appearance of various alternative group life-styles, such as communes,
group marriages, and swinging. Finally, we have the impression that the
influence of the women's movement has led to a reevaluation of the
marital relationship by many couples and to changes or problems for
some, if not most, couples. Certainly, married people are giving more
thoughtful consideration to whether they should seek treatment on an
individual or on a "couples" basis.

Although this chapter is primarily about assessment and treatment-
planning for married couples, there is no reason to believe that it does
not apply to unmarried couples. Our clinical experience suggests that
unmarried couples are likely to seek assistance when their relationships
are under stress. This typically occurs when one partner wants to formalize
and stablize the bond by marriage, when one partner wants to terminate
the relationship, or when a geographic move is being considered by a
member of the couple. Perhaps even more than in married couples, careful
evaluation of the commitment of each member to the relationship is
necessary. Frequently, the couple needs assistance in effecting a mutually
agreed-on separation.

It may be asked, why not treat every married client as though his or
her symptoms resulted from difficulties in marital interaction (from
"system" problems)? However, it has been widely believed by many mental
health professionals that the only definitive treatment is individual treatment and that problems are always intrapsychic in etiology. Rational
discussion of an intrapsychic-individual approach versus a relational-
marital approach is made difficult because of the following emotionally
charged factors that influence treatment-planning for married couples.

First, as members of a culture in which the individual is valued, it may
be more difficult for patients to seek assistance for shared problems and
for therapists to offer it. Certainly, medical training and much of psychology, which both focus on the individual as the locus of disease, do not

incline therapists to view a marriage as a dynamic system, but rather as two separate people each with his own symptoms. Mental health professionals may dabble in social systems theory, but psychoanalysis, behavior therapy, drug, and other organic treatments are individualistic in orientation. Freud himself was very much aware of the problems posed by the patient's family ("In psychoanalytic treatment, the intervention of the relatives is a positive danger and, a danger one does not know how to meet . . . the patient's closest relatives sometimes betray less interest in his recovering than in his remaining as he is" [4]), and he chose to deal with a patient only if "he was *sui juris* not dependent on anyone else in the essential relations of his life" [4]. It may be suspected that we are all influenced to some degree by these features of our culture and professions.

Second, the admissions procedure of psychiatric institutions often militates against a married person receiving treatment for his or her marriage. A study of the Massachusetts Mental Health Center Walk-In Clinic by Bloch et al. [1] found that 25 percent of all new patients came accompanied by a friend or relative. Approximately 40 percent of these, or 10 percent of the total admissions, were married patients accompanied by a spouse; the spouse was frequently involved in the diagnostic evaluation. A review of the charts and a small-scale interview study of these cases showed that, when the patient was accompanied by his or her spouse, the problem was usually a marital one. Of course, it should be noted that many married patients come to the clinic alone. The individualistic and medical orientation of the clinic may be judged from the fact that, until recently, when a couple came to the clinic secretary (the first staff person encountered), she inquired which one was the patient and asked that person to fill out a form. The staffing patterns of institutions also influence whether couples and families are seen together or individually. In the Walk-In Clinic it is common for the patient and his or her relatives to be seen (when relatives *are* seen) by a single responsible psychiatrist. This has resulted in the family's being evaluated as a whole more often than when a social worker is available to see relatives, as is the case in the inpatient services of the same hospital.

Thus, the structure of the treatment team, with its division of responsibilities and with professional identity involved in doing one's share of the work, may militate against or in favor of couples' being seen together.

In addition to staffing patterns and ingrained bureaucratic procedures, "third-party" payment arrangements are increasingly a major influence on the treatment of couples, since these arrangements often require that there be one designated patient even if a couple is treated conjointly. This is clearly a problem when an interactional view of symptoms is taken.

Finally, daytime clinic hours make it difficult for husbands, particularly working-class men, to come for treatment.

It may be noted in passing that at present there are vehement advocates of seeing all married couples together, just as there are those who believe that family treatment is the Ariadne's thread out of the maze of psychopathology. The evidence necessary to support these assertions is lacking; nonetheless those who believe that new treatments should be tried while they seem to work will undoubtedly use them. Some of those advocates go so far as to insist on involving the couples' extended families in therapy regardless of where these relatives live; and they often use guilt as a motivating force.

Although the impact of an individual's social field is great and the need of families and couples to find scapegoats is also powerful, the individual is entitled to exercise control over his own destiny and may justly seek, and deserves to receive, help on an individual basis.

Finally, it may be noted that a careful review shows that the literature on marriage therapy offers little guidance to the clinician in deciding whether to treat a married person as a member of a couple or as an individual.

In our experience, when a couple comes together to the therapist with the presenting complaint of marital difficulty, a series of joint interviews is initially more desirable than separate, followed by conjoint, interviews. But this approach is not always possible; and when the therapist must see one of the partners first, this, in itself, is a sign of the couple's difficulties in trust and communication. In most cases, adherence to the conjoint interview avoids the pitfall of the therapist's learning a "forbidden secret" from one partner and then, in later joint interviews, becoming a conspirator in the secret, which, most frequently, centers on sexual matters.

CASE 1 Mrs. W. came alone to the first interview, although when she called she had been encouraged to bring her husband. She said, "My problem is, I cannot get pregnant, and my husband's problem is, he is impotent." The facts that her father knew the therapist and that she had revealed at the initial interview that her husband secretly masturbated were major issues in their later joint sessions. Her husband was understandably angry about the one fact and embarrassed about the other.

Even when the precaution of the conjoint interview is taken, it is common for each member of the couple to feel that it is really the other one who is in greater need of assistance. (For a more detailed discussion of the motivational constellation of couples seeking marital therapy, see Chapter 15.)

Greene [5], in a pioneering paper, has discussed the diagnostic implications of therapist factors, practical considerations and treatment prescription after previous failures, as well as the importance of certain dynamic issues. He found that suspicious, jealous, and paranoid people may feel more comfortable initially in conjoint therapy and that people with a "secret," such as inappropriate acting out, may prefer to be seen separately. He also pointed out that immaturity or intense feelings of sibling rivalry, such as may exist if one of the spouses is a twin, may preclude sharing a therapist. These are obvious important considerations in the choice of therapy, especially at the beginning of treatment, but we believe that these dynamic issues must be worked with so that the treatment may be selected for fundamental reasons. That is to say, a couple should have the opportunity to change by learning to share, to trust each other, and to modulate their rivalry.

TREATMENT-PLANNING

During the diagnostic period, three parameters must be assessed and a decision made with regard to each to determine the best course of therapy. The first of these parameters involves the question of whether the couple's difficulties are indeed marital and the extent of their commitment and ability to work on them (Fig. 2). The second parameter involves an evaluation of the extent to which the experienced problem is within the marriage. The third parameter involves the extent to which the problems are acute and ego-alien rather than chronic and ego-syntonic to both partners.

The methods of treatment to be considered are:

1. *Individual psychotherapy for each partner by two therapists.* The therapists may or may not confer regularly with each other. (When they

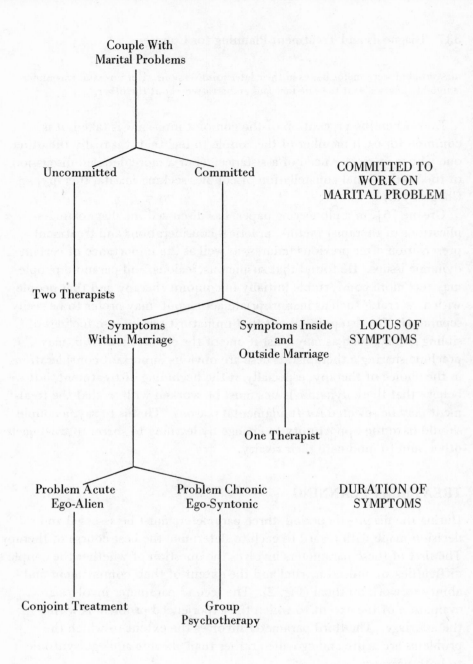

Couple With
Marital Problems

Uncommitted   Committed   COMMITTED TO
WORK ON
MARITAL PROBLEM

Two Therapists

Symptoms   Symptoms Inside   LOCUS OF
Within Marriage   and   SYMPTOMS
Outside Marriage

One Therapist

Problem Acute   Problem Chronic   DURATION OF
Ego-Alien   Ego-Syntonic   SYMPTOMS

Conjoint Treatment   Group
Psychotherapy

Figure 2 Three parameters to be assessed for diagnosis and treatment-planning of marital problems.

do so, and attempt to reconstruct and understand the important events in the life of the couple, they are employing a form of therapy termed *stereoscopic* by Martin and Bird [12].) On the other hand, the therapists often choose to conduct their work entirely separately, as is the case in classical psychoanalysis of two married persons.

2. *Individual psychotherapy for each partner by a single therapist, with or without occasional conjoint meetings.* This treatment was first described by Oberndorf [14] and by Mittelman [13], who discussed their experiences with concurrent psychoanalysis of married couples.

3. *Conjoint treatment with a single therapist or with two therapists.* This form of treatment was probably first described by Watson [16]. Haley [7] is also a proponent of this particular treatment modality.

4. *Couples group psychotherapy.* Group treatment of couples is described by Flint and MacLennan [3], Leichter [10], and Papanek [15].

If marital problems are not a significant issue, or if the couple is uncommitted or unable to work on them but has identifiable personal difficulties, then individual treatment for one or both partners separately is indicated. If, on the other hand, both members are committed to the marriage, are able to communicate with each other, and if marital problems are significant but there are also serious problems outside the marriage, then concurrent individual therapy with the same therapist is indicated. If the couple have symptoms that are experienced almost entirely within the marriage, they should be treated together. Whether they should be seen conjointly or in group psychotherapy depends on the extent to which the problems are acute and ego-alien. (*Ego-alien* refers to the ability of each member of the couple to experience conflict about his or her role in the marriage and to recognize that he or she contributes to the difficulties.) If the discomfort experienced in the marriage is both acute and ego-alien, conjoint treatment is indicated. If the problems are chronic and ego-syntonic, that is, if the problem marriage is a way of life, psychotherapy in a couples group is suggested.

The therapist must be aware that the assessment of the issues confronting the couple is an ongoing task and that, as the issues change, the therapy should correspondingly change. With increasing experience, we have become more flexible in our approach, often seeing a couple both conjointly and for individual sessions. If the therapist and the couple agree on the direction the treatment should take, usually a plan can be developed that can evolve appropriately as the issues change.

PARAMETER 1: TO WHAT EXTENT ARE THE PROBLEMS MARITAL? WHAT IS THE EXTENT OF THE COMMITMENT TO WORKING ON THEM?

We have noted two groups of people who apply or are referred as a couple for marital therapy but who do not have difficulties that are primarily marital. One group is composed of couples in which each member appears to be immature, dependent, and helpless and the marital disorder seems to be more of an expression of their mutual developmental difficulties rather than a marital issue per se. Recently married couples — students, for example — often fall within this category. Both partners may be still deeply and neurotically involved with their primary families, may be financially dependent on them, and may be simply legalizing an adolescent romance. They are not ready for marriage, and usually they have no children. Quite often the future of the marriage is uncertain since it appears to offer so little mutual satisfaction. One may say that these people are married in name only and primarily have individual developmental difficulties requiring individual therapy.

CASE 2   Mr. and Mrs. B., both in their early twenties, had been married for two years. Both were engaged in graduate studies when Mrs. B. consulted the clinic and requested marital therapy for their many problems with each other. Their past histories gave a clue to what was to be done. Mr. B. was the oldest of four sons of an ambitious mother. He had performed well until adolescence, when his mother divorced his father, putting responsibility for the younger children on him. He reacted to this situation by developing stomach symptoms. He recovered his good performance when he left home. After marriage and the birth of a child, his ability to do academic work deteriorated. Mrs. B. had a "bumbling" mother and a strong and competitive father. After her marriage she improved an already good performance to the point when she was equally at ease academically and as a parent, outshining her husband in all respects. The marriage problems seemed to arise from the husband's faltering in his studies, which he blamed on his wife and her demands. The formulation was that these young people were vying with each other for their independent, active, adult roles as if there was just a certain amount of success available to them and as, if one succeeded the other had to fail. In individual psychotherapy, they were able to relate the present problems to the primary relationships with their parents. After a few months their marriage had improved, and each had matured somewhat.

second did well. Falling out of love can be irreversible if it is caused by a change in one's entire life-style or at times reversible if certain intercurrent stresses can be lifted and neurotic interpersonal dynamics altered, particularly if much goodwill exists between the spouses. In any case, couples in which one partner states he or she does not love the other require on-going evaluation, and sometimes trial therapy is necessary to determine their commitment to the marriage and to evaluating their contributions to the difficulties.

If lack of commitment to the marriage is suggested by the couple's questioning whether the marriage will continue, or if one partner has more or less consciously decided that the marriage will not continue, any form of couple treatment, such as conjoint or concurrent therapy, will probably not succeed. Sometimes, however, a couple may agree that they wish to discuss with a therapist whether they should separate and how to cope with the problems that their children and they will face if they do separate. It is vital in situations in which communication between partners is already seriously impaired that each spouse decide explicitly to work with the other partner, or, at least, in the other partner's presence, in resolving the difficulties. Such a minimal commitment is often difficult to attain; and, in these instances, an individual maturation-oriented approach may offer the best chance.

The clinician treating couples must be prepared for the fact that a significant number will end up deciding on a divorce. The percentage will depend largely on the nature of his practice, but it will probably range between 20 and 40 percent. Thus, counseling for divorce will inevitably be part of his work. The feelings and values of the therapist will inevitably influence his view of the relative importance of individual fulfillment as it both conflicts with and fosters loyalty and relatedness. He should bear this in mind as he attempts to assist couples to find the most appropriate course for them.

It has been stated that, if the problems are not primarily marital or the couple is not committed to working on them, both partners should be treated separately by different therapists. This may be considered the traditional method; it had been widely practiced by psychoanalysts and other psychotherapists. The negative side of such an approach is that marital problems have often been treated as resistances, and therapists have been generally inclined to limit themselves to resolving the patient's own contributions to the marital difficulties by tracing these back through the transference to their origins and to an infantile neurosis. The positive side is that the therapist is able to adhere to the therapeutic contract with the patient and to protect the patient's therapy or analysis from interference by relatives by avoiding contact with them as much as possible. In this way, it is believed, the patient has the best opportunity to develop himself and to resolve his or her neurosis.

Detractors of separate therapists for married partners have often claimed that psychoanalysis or intensive therapy with one spouse leads to divorce. Although no data are available, the relative isolation of a marital partner from his spouse during therapy would seem to merit careful study. A considerable number of couples who consulted one of us, privately stated that they wished to be treated by the same therapist since too many of their friends who had been treated by different therapists were subsequently divorced. The methods described in this chapter are innovative; their goals are to diminish the isolating effect of therapy on marriage and to deal with the ongoing and present problems of the spouses.

Mann and Lundell [11] have discussed in detail the problems encountered in the separate treatment of couples by two therapists. Their experience suggests the antitherapeutic influence of the following factors: (1) hierarchical problems that can occur when therapists differ in status and prestige; (2) differences in therapeutic viewpoint; (3) transference-countertransference problems, often involving negative feelings toward the opposite partner or his therapist or both; (4) differences in skill; (5) differences in assessment of improvement, for example, when one therapist regards a given behavior, such as increased self-assertion, as more mature, without regard to its effect on the marriage; (6) "advocacy phenomena," i.e., in discussion with the other therapist, sides are taken; and (7) practical, as well as emotional, impediments to communication between the therapists. The experience and conclusions of Mann and Lundell are much like our own: separate treatment by two therapists has its dangers and difficulties, and, if the focus of treatment is the marriage, all other things being equal, the treatment should be carried out by a single therapist.

Some important considerations in the choice of therapy are the abilities, needs, and experience of the therapist. The therapist who must deal with immature and seriously troubled people in a setting in which he sees first one and then the other spouse, or sees them together, may be overwhelmed

and decide, "The two of them are too much for me." Indeed, a therapist
may be wise, depending on his inclinations, not to become involved in
the treatment of two spouses whose conflicts are so intense or who have
so little ability for self-observation that the therapist feels overburdened.
It may be useful for inexperienced or unmarried therapists to use a stereoscopic approach (see p. 508) as a way of learning to deal with a couple.
It is vital that the therapists be able to communicate with one another,
but the focus must be on the development of a genuine dialogue between
the two spouses.

In summary, separate individual psychotherapy of married couples is
indicated when (1) the marriage does not appear to be the primary problem
and either immaturity or severe psychopathology is present in one partner;
(2) the couple appears uncommitted to the marriage or to working out
their marital difficulties; or (3) the therapist is inexperienced or is inclined
toward this form of treatment.

PARAMETER 2: TO WHAT EXTENT ARE THE PROBLEMS EXPERIENCED AS WITHIN THE MARRIAGE?

Thus far, we have discussed those patients for whom marital problems
appear almost irrelevant or who have little or no commitment to working
on their marriage. Between this group and another group of individuals
at the other end of the continuum, who see their problems as being solely
within the marriage, there is a large group of couples who experience
difficulties both within and outside the marriage. For this group, we
believe, concurrent psychotherapy by a single therapist is most useful.
This treatment technique has been discussed by Grinker [6], who focuses
on some of the advantages and problems. He notes that distortions are
diminished, reality-testing is fostered, affect may be increased, and acting
out diminished in concurrent therapy by a single therapist. On the negative
side, the transference may be overly intense, involving Oedipal and rival-
rous feelings.

Concurrent psychotherapy is individual psychotherapy of two people
who have a close relationship. It is like traditional psychotherapy in that
it works best with patients with clear-cut neurotic problems — people
who can develop and resolve the transference and make use of clarification
and insight. Patients with character problems who do not develop a

workable transference neurosis and those who neurotically blame others for their problems will have difficulty in either individual or concurrent psychotherapy.

The advantage of concurrent psychotherapy when the couple complain of problems both within and outside their marriage is that it places the therapist in a much more satisfactory position for assessing the real situation of each partner. Since any difficulties between the partners are described by each, the therapist, hearing both sides, is less likely to misjudge the situation. For this reason, concurrent psychotherapy is less divisive of marriages than is treatment by two therapists. When both partners are treated, over-identification with either of them is minimized, and counter-transference is more easily mastered. The realistic view of the marital problems presented and the opportunity to do individual psychotherapy are the unique advantages of concurrent psychotherapy. In our opinion it is often the most efficient method for the effective treatment of intra-marital and nonmarital neurotic problems of married couples, particularly if conjoint interviews are held at regular intervals. The following case is typical.

CASE 4   Mr. and Mrs. R. complained of difficulties in their marriage. An evaluation disclosed that Mrs. R. had had lifelong phobias, which kept her somewhat confined to the house. She was excessively dependent on her husband but could not deal with her anger toward him, except by sullen withdrawal. Mr. R., on the other hand, a man of violent temper, flew into a rage at the slightest provocation. He was particularly sensitive to his wife's emotional withdrawal, which he handled by excessive drinking. They were an intelligent, college-educated couple who had studied a great deal of psychology and who communicated well with each other. As they explained their difficulties, it appeared that both Mrs. R.'s phobias and Mr. R.'s temper tantrums, which had caused him to be fired from several jobs, were problems both within and outside the marriage. Both appeared to recognize that the problems had neurotic origins from their childhoods, and each was eager to work on these problems. The decision was made to see them concurrently since it did not appear that the problems were of recent origin but rather had existed for the duration of the marriage nor that they were willing and able to work in intensive psychotherapy. During the course of therapy, they were able to resolve their neurotic problems and improve their marriage greatly.

We have found that if married partners hold the other responsible for the problems, there will be difficulties using concurrent psychotherapy. We have become increasingly convinced that blaming the partner should be viewed as an indication for either joint interviews or group therapy. In such a case, the definition of the marital realities is the issue. Each member inevitably tries to convince the therapist or the group that he or she is not the patient or the problem. The difficulties of establishing responsibility are well illustrated in the discussion by Masters and Johnson of what is premature ejaculation, which they define as occurring if the man comes too soon to satisfy his wife 50 percent of the time. We may ask why 50 percent? Why not 40 percent or 60 percent? For the marital therapist, the question is not whether he comes too soon or she takes too long; rather, it is the failure of cooperation and collaboration. These are matters best dealt with by seeing the couple together, as indeed Masters and Johnson discovered. If the blaming is neurotic, sometimes this fact can be brought into the therapy and internalized. But often this cannot be done easily since frequently the allocation of responsibilities is in part justified. For example, a therapist may be hesitant to tell a wife that she was overreacting when she became depressed because her husband failed to express any enthusiasm over her graduation from college. The therapist may agree with the wife that her complaint is justified. How is he to deal with this problem when treating the husband? He cannot with impunity violate the confidences of the wife and say to the husband, "I hear you're not interested in your wife's graduation." Such direct use of material from one partner's therapy in the other partner's therapy tends to put the therapist in the position of taking sides and causes the statement to be experienced by the partner as an accusation. It also conflicts the feelings of most therapists about confidentiality.

In summary, it appears that concurrent psychotherapy is most useful when each spouse recognizes that his problems with his partner are a significant, but clearly not the sole, source of difficulties and when communication between them is adequate.

PARAMETER 3: ARE THE PROBLEMS ACUTE AND EGO-ALIEN OR CHRONIC AND EGO-SYNTONIC?

If the troubled marriage is one to which both partners are committed and the difficulties are acute, conjoint treatment is indicated. It seems to make little difference whether the precipitating stress stems from the entry of a child into the family, from the growing up and imminent departure of a child, or from a major decision (about a job, house, and so on). When couples come for treatment showing great anxiety, with a clear bilateral recognition that something has recently gone wrong in their marriage, and with a feeling of, "We need to get back to where we were," conjoint treatment is indicated. The diagnostician leaves the interview feeling that the marriage involves genuine caring and concern of the partners for each other. As indicated previously, some couples come to the diagnostic interview blaming each other. But what is vital is that the blame is of recent origin; that is, that the partners say something like, "Things were all right until you changed jobs," or ". . . until the baby was born." If the blame is chronic, conjoint treatment is rarely useful.

The following is an example of indications for, and successful use of, conjoint treatment.

CASE 5   Mr. D., a man many years older than his wife, had successfully completed psychoanalysis some years before their marriage. He was looking forward to accepting a new position out of state. Mrs. D. was graduating from college and had just stopped using contraceptives so that they might have a child. Both came to therapy because their sexual relationship, and their marriage in general, had deteriorated markedly since they had ceased birth control and both recognized that the fear of having a child was somehow involved in their difficulties. In a two-month series of interviews, they were treated together, with the entire focus on this recent problem. Mr. D. made numerous efforts to talk about his severe childhood deprivation, but these were dealt with as his way of asking to be mothered by his young wife and his inability to assume paternal responsibilities. Mrs. D. tended to have frequent fantasies of extramarital relationships, which her husband questioned her about endlessly. They were dealt with as her fear of growing up and assuming maternal responsibilities. In a series of ten interviews, the couple reported rapid improvement in their sexual relationship; and, although their difficulties could be understood as the outgrowth of patterns established in childhood and although each had certain symptoms outside the marriage, it was clear that they were committed to life with each other and that their problems were primarily inside the marriage and acute.

When the evaluation of a couple demonstrates that the problems are both chronic and ego-syntonic, that is, that the problem marriage is a way of life, group psychotherapy is most useful. It is common in our experience that couples who do well only in groups have problems that are experienced as primarily within the marriage and that blame for these problems is often put on the partner. Furthermore, it is usual that these couples do not have a period to look back on when the marriage itself was happier —

certainly not in the recent past, although occasionally such couples state that before they were married things were better.

Couples-group psychotherapy offers certain special advantages. First, the couple can gain some objective evaluations of their problem, since the problems are not only described but often are also enacted — and often with a new partner. It helps if everyone agrees that Mr. A. should not yell at his wife and should not beat her. However, it may be even more useful when the group points out that long-suffering Mrs. A. provokes the attacks. Secondly, the strong members can make interpretations of each other's problems that are accepted because of mutual respect. Thirdly, the weaker members are natural allies and the therapist leading the sessions does not have to defend them.

Jones [8] has noted that certain couples can gain perspective only in a group; in conjoint sessions they engage in "issue-rehashing," with attacks and defenses. He feels, as we do, that an indication for group treatment is "the chronic interlocking of the couple's mutual regressions," with "compromise adjustment." The couple stay together "not because they want to but because they must."

In our experience, groups often work most satisfactorily when the couples have problems at a similar developmental level. We have delineated a class of couple who do well in group psychotherapy. They are exemplified by the following.

CASE 6   Mr. and Mrs. X. had been married seven years and had two children, but since their courtship things had gotten steadily worse as Mr. X. became increasingly successful. He was a physicist who frequently took his work home. Mrs. X. complained of many psychosomatic ailments and resented her children, yelling at and hitting them more and more, which led Mr. X. to withdraw further into his work. In the group, Mr. X. was able to help Mr. V. a traveling salesman, and, in turn, learned from him. Mrs. X. gradually realized that a husband was not a mother and that with the help of babysitters she could do much more with her life on her own. They terminated treatment after two years with great improvement.

Couples such as this one tend to be fairly healthy; and, although some have neurotic traits, they have developed socially adaptive means of coping with their character problems. Both partners have had reasonably healthy premarital adaptations. Often the marital difficulties begin between the fifth and tenth year of the marriage, when the woman is confined to her home by her children and the man is led away from it by his success.

Some of these couples appear to fit the classification of the lovesick wife and the "cold-sick" husband; that is, the women complain of feelings of loneliness, isolation, and lack of fulfillment, and the men tend to substitute intellectual pursuits and intellectualization for emotional closeness. We have found these couples particularly suitable for group therapy: cross-couple interpretations carry weight since the members recognize each other as equals in intellectual level and insight.

Another group of couples do as poorly in group treatment as they do in general. These couples have been married much longer (usually more than 15 years), and they have chronic problems. Their interaction is pathological. Most have children who are adolescent or older, and many of the children have left home. It appears often that so long as the children were young or childish, gratification could be obtained from them, and thus the focus was kept off the partner. Because of their character disturbances, few of these persons have had much success in life. Frequently, they are addicted to food, alcohol, or gambling. Individual psychotherapy or casework has usually been of little avail, although it is often continued for years because of the gratification it provides. The stability of these marriages has depended on the maintenance of distance between the partners, and new demands for mutual involvement lead to anxiety and further distancing maneuvers.

CASE 7   Mr. S. said that his wife, to whom he had been married for 18 years, was leaving him. Both Mr. and Mrs. S. were asked to come for a joint interview when it became clear that although both said only the love of their children had held them together, they were bound together by chains of hostility and dependency. He was a gambler and an alcoholic. She was a long-suffering woman who had ignored her husband for the children, and she was frigid. A referral to a group was made, and after three years some progress was noted.

Couples such as the S.'s require prolonged, arduous group psychotherapy, and they often drop out when the dangers of change appear real. Mutual recrimination is especially prominent in these couples. There are, of course, couples who fall between the two general types exemplified in Cases 6 and 7. Although it is a continuum that is being described, we have been particularly impressed, nonetheless, with how often the two types are noted.

THE EMERGING OF ISSUES AS THERAPY EVOLVES

Thus far, we have discussed diagnostic assessment and the indications for
the choice of therapy in the treatment of troubled marriages. But the
impaired functioning of any given couple may be viewed in terms of a
hierarchy of issues that emerge sequentially. The resolution of these
issues may require different therapeutic settings and goals.

CASE 8   Mr. and Mrs. S. were seen in consultation. They had been quite happy until
she had graduated from nursing school and begun to support her husband and his
education. They began to argue, and he withdrew into his work, claiming that although he loved his wife, she had turned into a shrew. Discussion with her suggested
that since beginning work, which she knew was vital to their future, she had felt more
and more like a slave. This feeling was closely related to the fact that her mother had
always had to work to support her father. She felt degraded in her role as the family
support and in her role as a woman, since, in addition, her father had always wanted
her to be an accountant and work in business as he did, hoping she would be the son
he never had. In view of her immediate neurotic problems, exacerbated by the recent
change from student to worker, it was recommended that she be seen in individual
treatment and that the couple be seen together to evaluate his less available fears of
closeness. As predicted, as she recognized her difficulty, she became less unhappy
and began to make increasingly realistic and affectionate, rather than argumentative
and belligerent, demands, on her husband for closeness. When this occurred, the
reasons for his need to withdraw into his work and his difficulties in responding to
her closeness began to emerge. At this point, they were treated together and he was
also treated individually.

Thus, it must be recognized that the treatment of marriages requires
recognition of problems as they emerge hierarchically and that in this
endeavor the active and interested involvement of the couple in evaluating
the progress of work is of major importance.

SUMMARY

We have discussed a basic diagnostic framework and given case examples.
It has been suggested that the couple be seen separately when the partners
are uncommitted to work on their marriage or when marital problems
appear secondary to immaturity or severe pathology. When the couple
is committed to the marriage and the symptoms relate almost entirely to
the marriage, the partners should be treated together. If the problems are
acute and ego-alien, conjoint treatment is indicated; if the problems are
chronic and ego-syntonic, couples group psychotherapy is recommended.

REFERENCES

1. Bloch, S. L., Minker, B., and Grunebaum, H. The accompanier. *Psychiatric Quarterly Supplement* 42:508, 1968.
2. DuPont, R., Ryder, R., and Grunebaum, H. An unexpected result of psychosis in marriage. *American Journal of Psychiatry* 128:735, 1971.
3. Flint, A. A., and MacLennan, B. W. Some dynamic factors in marital group psychotherapy. *International Journal of Group Psychotherapy* 12(3):355, 1962.
4. Freud, S. The introductory lectures on psychoanalysis, Part III (1916–1917). In *The Standard Edition of the Complete Psychological Works of Sigmund Freud,* trans. and ed. by J. Strachey and others. London: Hogarth and Institute of Psycho-Analysis, 1963, Vol. 16, pp. 459–461.
5. Greene, B. L. Management of marital problems. *Diseases of the Nervous System* 27:204, 1966.
6. Grinker, Jr., R. R. Complementary psychotherapy: Treatment of "associated" pairs. *American Journal of Psychiatry* 123(6):633, 1966.
7. Haley, J. Marriage therapy. *Archives of General Psychiatry* 8(3):213, 1963.
8. Jones, W. L. The villain and the victim: Group therapy for married couples. *American Journal of Psychiatry* 124(3):107, 1967.
9. Kern, J. W. Conjoint marital psychotherapy: An interim measure in the treatment of psychosis. *Psychiatry* 30:283, 1967.
10. Leichter, E. Group psychotherapy of married couples' groups: Some characteristic treatment dynamics. *International Journal of Group Psychotherapy* 12(2):154, 1962.
11. Mann, A. M., and Lundell, F. W. Psychotherapy of marital partners: A critique and re-evaluation. *Canadian Psychiatric Association Journal* 9(4):313, 1964.
12. Martin, P., and Bird, H. W. An approach to the psychotherapy of marriage partners: The stereoscopic technique. *Psychiatry* 16:123, 1953.
13. Mittelman, B. The concurrent analysis of married couples. *Psychoanalytic Quarterly* 17:182, 1948.
14. Oberndorf, C. P. Psychoanalysis of married couples. *Psychoanalysis Review* 25:453, 1938.
15. Papanek, H. Group Psychotherapy with Married Couples. In J. Masserman (Ed.), *Current Psychiatric Therapies.* New York: Grune & Stratton, 1965.
16. Watson, A. S. The conjoint psychotherapy of marriage partners. *American Journal of Orthopsychiatry* 33:912, 1963.

15

The Therapeutic Alliance in Marital Therapy

James W. Smith
Henry Grunebaum

The skill involved in the therapeutic intervention in marital disorders requires at least two areas of competency on the part of the marital therapist: (1) the ability to assess and distinguish individual pathology from the disturbed marital interaction and (2) the ability to discern the meaning of the marital interaction in order to derive a workable diagnosis and plan of treatment.

The literature concerning conflicts in marriage and their resolution emphasizes the individual's object relations [1, 3], the couple's interactional approach to problem-solving [4], the importance of viewing the couple as a system [7], and treating the couple as a unit [9], as well as the importance of evaluating where the couple are currently in the family life cycle [8, 10].

It is our contention that for the therapist there are three issues that are basic to helping the unhappy marital unit:

1. The establishment of a psychological diagnosis of each partner in the marriage, as well as an assessment of the interactional patterns of the marital unit.

2. The development of a plan of treatment which is realistically derived from the diagnosis.
3. The establishment of a therapeutic relationship with the marital unit, which allows change to occur.

Emphasis should be placed on item 3. Probably it is the area in which the therapist fails most often. He or she may conceptualize a couple's problem clearly but never sufficiently operationalize insight with the couple to permit change to occur. We maintain that careful diagnostic work may elicit evidence that the possibilities of a therapeutic alliance are quite limited. This may be clarified by assessing the nature of object relations in each member of the couple and their individual and collective motivation for coming to therapy.

THE THERAPEUTIC ALLIANCE

The concept of the therapeutic alliance comes from psychoanalysis. It can be defined as the working relationship between the patient and the therapist [5, 6, 13], a definition that implies that the couple, as individuals and as a unit, have the ability to identify with the analytical approach of the marital therapist.

The therapist assesses ego functioning as a part of the diagnostic evaluation. The object relations of the ego of each partner in the marriage are of key importance.

Zetzel [13] points out that Freud described a well-developed rapport with the patient as the therapist's allying himself with the ego of the patient under treatment. Zetzel further describes the process:

During the course of analytic work, a split in the ego of the patient takes place. . . . This split allows the mature or observing part of the patient's ego to identify with the analyst in the task of modifying pathological defenses previously set up against internal danger situations. In addition, since two participants are inevitably involved, it is clear that analytic progress must in some respects depend on an object relationship.

Certainly marital therapy is not identical in technique or approach to psychoanalysis. However, there are some similarities which are important to effective work with the marital unit.

People come to professionals for help with their intrapsychic or interpersonal problems because they are feeling pressure from their own conflicts and/or pressure from others in important interpersonal situations. If an individual comes for help for himself, he usually is saying that he desires at some level to change his way of coping. If a couple seeks help, each partner may want to change himself or herself, but usually each seeks to change the other.

Furthermore, the fact that a marital unit seeks professional help does not necessarily presume some major psychopathology in either or both individuals. We have seen many relatively mature people seeking help of some kind with their marital relationship. The reasonably healthy person may even feel that the marital difficulty stems from the partner rather than from himself or herself.

However, the key to working with the marital unit is in helping them to ally with the observing ego of the therapist in order to bring some understanding to the conflicts they experience. The task of helping the unit to identify with the "reasonableness" of the therapist's ego may vary in difficulty.

For example, the couple may have established in their relationship such an unconscious coalition against change that any intervention may be fervently resisted. This is often seen in the classic descriptions of the sadomasochistic couple.

Another example is a couple that is embroiled in a conflict that each feels is caused by the other. Yet, because of their fairly mature ego development, they respond rapidly to the therapist as they are able to form an alliance.

CASE 1   Mr. and Mrs. A. were referred to marital therapy after Mrs. A. had seen a psychologist about her own wish to end the marriage. It was evident that she really was committed to the relationship and was advised that marital therapy would be more appropriate than individual therapy. Mr. and Mrs. A. had been married four years, and both were career-minded people who were fairly strong-willed. There was no evidence of any major psychopathology, even though during their first interview each of them heartily blamed the difficulties on the other. As they were able to let an alliance develop with the therapist, they began to see their distortions. Within six sessions they were comfortably working out problems at home without getting caught in the vicious cycles of previous times.

A working alliance between the patient and the therapist is established when the patient can sense a partnership with the therapist. Even when the patient is distorting the therapist's identity through a transference neurosis, he can ally himself with the "reasonableness" of the therapist ego sufficiently to begin to analyze what is happening.

Obviously, this requires that the patient be able to maintain some sense of the therapist as a separate individual. If the patient's ego is so weak that object relationships are difficult, the potentiality for forming such a therapeutic alliance is considerably lowered.

The therapist in such a situation must evaluate the ability of the marital partners to maintain object relationships. He further must be able to convince the couple of his own ability to participate and his willingness to form a partnership with them in order to establish the working alliance.

MOTIVATION FOR MARITAL THERAPY

What confronts the marital therapist initially in his contact with the unhappy couple is usually the subtle, though sometimes blatantly obvious, complex of motivations for seeking marital therapy. This complex may become evident in the very manner in which help is requested, such as when one mate calls for an initial appointment and requests that it be for himself or herself alone. Sometimes, when one partner calls for the appointment, he or she attempts to convey over the phone "what is really happening."

Our policy is to urge firmly that the first appointment be a conjoint interview. However, when the above type of request comes, one begins to get a picture of that partner's motivation: "You and I will ally against my mate to change him (her)." This request is contrary to the goal of establishing a working relationship between the couple and the therapist. It often exhibits the same wishes and fears which have been a part of the couple's relationship. If the therapist allows himself to become aligned with this type of request, he has removed from the unit the "reasonableness" of his own ego for a suitable alliance to be formed.

A patient may insist that the mate will refuse to come for an interview, and his seeking advice on how to get the partner to come for an appointment can be quite appropriate. The therapist needs to evaluate carefully if the patient's pushing the mate to come for an interview may be unconciously destructive. If it appears to be so, it may be wise for the therapist himself to call and ask the reluctant partner to come for an appointment.

CASE 2   A 34-year-old wife was encouraged strongly by her husband to consult the therapist. She was a tearful, anxious, attractive, seductive woman who said she felt that she and her husband were drifting apart and that she would collapse if he left. After the therapist and she had two interviews alone, her husband was persuaded to come. He made it clear that he found life with his wife intolerable, he had got into a pattern of permitting her to make all the small decisions and doing just as he pleased in larger matters. He saw her as unable to function on her own and so wanted her to be in individual therapy. When this was accomplished, he refused to explore his problems further and left her. She, on the other hand, was able to engage productively in psychotherapy for herself.

It is the task of the first interview to determine as accurately as possible why the person or persons are present. As the motives become clear, some sense of ego functioning can be determined as it relates to the working relationship in therapy.

Although we make the usual distinctions between evaluation and therapy, sometimes it may be necessary for the therapist to convey to the couple his understanding of their motives in order for the evaluation to proceed, for therapy to be undertaken, or for therapy to be decided against.

CASE 3   This example involves a 55-year-old man and his third wife, who was 45 and had herself had two marriages. Both were in individual therapy; the referral for marital therapy came from the husband's therapist at the husband's request. His wife had moved out of the house, and he urgently wanted her to return. She and her therapist were reluctant, feeling she had "suffered enough," and had postponed the evaluation while they sought still another consultant to confirm that her therapy was dealing with the salient issues. Early in the second evaluation interview, the husband's goals for the diagnostician became clear when he said, "Of course, you will agree with me that it is hard, if not impossible, for us to work on our marriage when we are not living together." The therapist then clarified that the wife's return was the husband's goal, but that it appeared equally clear that his wife had a quite different goal — namely, to decide for herself whether the marriage was one which she wished to continue. She was much relieved that the therapist did not take the position that they had to live together in order to study their marital difficulties. It was later learned from her therapist that a previous attempt at conjoint interviews had foundered when the therapist took the husband's side. The husband terminated the interviews soon after his attempt to get his wife back home failed.

The importance of analyzing the initial motivation cannot be stressed too much. If a couple cannot see that their resistance to forming a therapeutic alliance is within themselves, the therapy is at a standstill.

CASE 4   The court referred for possible marital therapy a couple who were seeking legal separation after a six-year marriage. They appeared to be a couple who could be helped; they were attractive, young, healthy, intelligent, and had status in their community. In the interview, neither partner was willing to make a self-examination — everything was projected and displaced onto the partner. Each communicated clearly to the therapist that all change had to come from the partner. They were not hostile, unreasonable, nor disruptive in any way, but they each held firm. They accepted the therapist's interpretations of their motivations and resistance to an alliance. Therapy for the marriage was not a possible alternative for them at that juncture.

An individual diagnosis of the partners in this example would clarify their resistance. There were many ego-syntonic patterns, and the motivation for reversal was lacking. Therapy would have been a wasted effort.

One of the diagnostic tasks is to evaluate to what extent each partner is able and willing to assume responsibility for his own contribution to the marital difficulties. Dr. Justin Weiss [12] has suggested the simple, direct approach of asking each partner to explain what some of the difficulties are and how he or she would like to change them. If necessary, he would remind each partner that the task is to discuss his or her own contribution rather than the partner's. He would then listen and assess the ability and willingness of each member to expose some of his own self-diagnosed traits that make for difficulty and to what extent the person can change. Therapeutic marital progress is limited to the extent that the partner responds to this task by blaming the other and insisting that he or she change.

MOTIVATIONAL CONSTELLATIONS

We wonder if many failures in marital therapy may not stem from un-analyzed motivation that precludes the development of a clear therapeutic alliance between the therapist and the marital unit. From our clinical experience we have identified various constellations of motives that are geared to the formation of a specific type of coalition with the therapist by one or both mates. The purpose of the coalition, however, may be detrimental to the forming of a therapeutic alliance.

We have summarized these constellations under six headings: (1) looking for the exit, (2) looking for an ally, (3) looking for reentry, (4) response to an ultimatum, (5) avoidance of self-observation, and (6) mutual recognition of need.

Looking for the Exit

A request for help can be a covert communication of the desire of one or both partners to bow out of the marital relationship with a minimum of guilt. The guilt may stem from having abandoned the mate and the children; it may follow an extramarital affair; or it may reflect feelings of shame about a broken marriage. Seeking help from a professional person may be a way of relieving the guilt feelings. After marital therapy fails, the partner can say "See, I did all I could to save the marriage. My mate would not change."

CASE 5   Mr. E., 35 years old, initiated the idea of marital therapy with his wife and made an appointment with a therapist. In the conjoint interview Mr. E. told a long story of sexual involvements with other women in his professional life and accused his wife of being unaccessible to him emotionally. He claimed no current affection for another woman but stated magnanimously that he thought it was his moral obligation to try to make his 17-year marriage work. In his unverbalized fantasies he had planned to use therapy as an acceptable way out of the union while having his wife continue to serve his dependent needs. Though he denied this in the initial interview, after several sessions his wife saw his plan. She was finally able to refuse to participate passively in his manipulation and to be the villain in the marriage. She requested individual help and was referred for psychotherapy.

Mr. E.'s attempt to form a coalition with the therapist to allow him a way out of the marriage was counter to the essential nature of the working alliance and detrimental to the marital unit. If a motive like Mr. E.'s is accepted and allowed to govern the relationship there is no opportunity for an alliance with the therapist's ego to take place. If Mr. E.'s motives had not been analyzed early, the therapy sessions would have gone on for a prolonged period of time, with the husband's hidden and destructive motive controlling the process. However, the resistance is not so strong in all such cases that the therapy ends in defeat.

CASE 6   Mr. and Mrs. F., in their late thirties, sought help for their tense marital relationship. The last six years of their 10-year marriage had been a time of gradual alienation. Mr. F. was most cooperative, but he was clearly role-playing in order to bow out of the marriage as guiltlessly as possible. His compliant posture was assumed to show he had done all he could and that thus separation was inevitable. The therapist interpreted his motivation for therapy. Mr. E.'s defense was to hide from himself his guilt over his anger at his wife, which he could not express directly to her, as well as his guilt about an affair. He soon quit therapy after he found himself unable to manipulate the therapeutic situation. However, in two months he was back, still strongly resistant but seeking insight into his resistance to the working alliance. Eventually he and his wife joined a couples therapy group and worked steadily to reestablish a relationship. This proved to be quite effective for them.

The key to progress was that the motive was brought to the surface early. The therapist asked the couple to look at the meaning of their joint resistance. This made it possible to discuss the fact that the therapy process was fantasied as a door to escape. It allowed the fleeing mate to see therapy as an opportunity to face and overcome his own destructive urges. It thus offered a place of help.

Looking for an Ally

In the constellation "looking for an ally," one partner or both are seeking to gain strength to stand up to the mate. The therapist is fantasied as a reinforcement for the patient's feelings of weakness and helplessness. The mate seeking the alliance has chosen to "fight" instead of "taking flight." Part of this motive to fight may be the subtle desire for control which he feels he has lost to the mate or perceives that he is in the process of losing.

CASE 7   Mrs. G. came to her first appointment saying that her husband had refused to come. She then told how horrible the marriage was and that her husband was the most insensitive beast one could imagine. She denied that she caused any marital disharmony, saying that all the blame rested with him. She became upset when the therapist refused to ally himself with her fantasies against her husband. She was instructed to have her husband come to the next session. The second interview was like the first; she maintained that her husband had refused to come. Later, a phone call to the husband revealed that she had never told him she was coming for help. She admitted this was true in a later conjoint interview.

The choice of fight instead of flight may reflect positive ego strength. However, Mrs. G. was actually choosing fight as a type of flight since she was acting from a distance and with what she considered to be strong assistance. Analysis of the marital unit revealed that she used her parents in the same way as she was attempting to use the therapist, which left her husband feeling castrated. His method of retaliating destructively would have appeared in the therapy process if the therapist had accepted the ally position.

The interpretation of the "ally syndrome" to a couple is most often quickly rejected by the mate who is seeking the alliance. But even though it is denied, the interpretation establishes that the therapist will not be a partner in an "ally wish." The secret, so to speak, is out.

Even though the mate with the ally wish may not publicly admit these feelings for some time, he or she can participate in forming a therapeutic alliance since the therapist has rendered the wish less effective.

CASE 8   Mr. and Mrs. H. were advised by the court to seek professional help as neither was sure he or she wanted a legal separation. When they came into the office, Mrs. H. handed the therapist a 10-page summary of their marriage. She said her lawyer had instructed her to write it out and present it to the therapist. The therapist took her summary, laid it on a table without reading it, and proceeded with the interview. Eventually it became clear that this subtle ploy with the paper expressed her feelings about being married to an alcoholic husband. She really wanted out of the marriage and had no interest in forming an alliance with the therapist for marital therapy. She wanted an alliance to give her the strength to carry through her decision to separate.

Looking for Reentry

The constellation "looking for reentry" is composed of persons who seek professional help for marriage problems in the hope that the therapist will declare them "sick" (neurotic) and thus enable them to get back into their marriages. This is a type of ally motive, except that instead of wanting an escape route out of the marriage, the person is looking for a painless way back into the marriage. The client fantasizes that being declared sick is a safer and more certain way of reentry than being declared a "sinner." Thus secular professionals — psychiatrists, psychologists, and marriage counselors — may see more couples in this category than the parish clergyman or other pastoral counselor.

It appears that the two bases on which most clients want to be declared sick are sexual acting out and excessive use of alcohol. The alcoholic wants to be declared sick not in order to get help but to secure a shield against the mate's anger and thus regain his source of supplies for his oral-dependent needs. This may be seen as a special form of the desire to gain an ally.

CASE 9   Mr. I., a 45-year-old alcoholic, had been thrown out of his home by his wife. He came to the therapist seeking help for his marriage. His wife had agreed to come after his first interview. Eventually it became clear that Mr. I. wanted to return home and that he was relying on the therapist to convince his wife of Mr. I.'s hopeless illness. He lacked motivation to change any of his basic dependent patterns or control his behavior patterns by joining A.A.; instead he sought to manipulate his wife and therapist to continue to supply his oral needs.

CASE 10 Mr. J., a very successful 40-year-old businessman from a lower-class background, brought his furious wife to a joint interview. She had just discovered that he was having an affair with his secretary. He felt guilty and was anxious to placate his wife, who stated that she never wanted him back and that she wouldn't be able to stand herself if she gave in and took him back (although she did). Over a series of interviews it became clear that she was the more rigid partner; she downgraded him and withheld affection when he transgressed her strict limits. On the other hand, while he was superficially compliant with the therapy, he made little effort to change. It was clear that he wanted the facade, but not the substance, of marriage; When charged issues were raised, rather than attempting to work them out, he terminated the therapy and had another affair.

CASE 11 Mrs. H. (Case 8) was looking for an ally in the therapist who would help her escape from her marriage. Mr. H. was an alcoholic. He repeated the slogans of A.A. to convince the therapist that he was an alcoholic and that he knew it. He wanted to maintain an excessive dependency on his mother, and he was willing to admit his alcoholism to get the therapist to help him keep his marriage also.

It has been our experience that patients whose motive is reentry do not often continue treatment when their goal is secured. And perhaps when infidelity is the issue for the couple, its recurrence during therapy is to be expected. Early interpretation of the motivation has had ambiguous results. When reentry motivation is seen, we advise a separated couple not to resume living together until they understand more clearly the dynamics that led to the conflict and separation.

Response to an Ultimatum

The request for help can arise out of an ultimatum that one partner issues to the other — an "or else." One partner has clearly placed the blame and has demanded action. Sometimes the ultimatum has arisen from a family crisis that has brought the couple to the therapist in a state of shock. They are not sure why they are seeking help, but they feel that the crisis demands that they seek some type of analysis and assistance. One such couple had resisted any intervention by their pastor in their chronically troubled marriage of 20 years. But when their son stole a valuable object belonging to a neighbor, the couple sought a consultation with the pastor. They saw in their son's action a symbol of their poor marital relationship. On the other hand, the "or else" issued by one partner may not be an ultimatum but an attempt to break the pattern of the disturbed marriage in order to bring about some type of intervention.

CASE 12 Mr. K. felt for several years that his home situation was more than he could tolerate. He had suggested to his wife several times that they seek professional help for their sexual problems. She had always refused because she was afraid to talk about sex in front of a stranger. His temptation to act out sexually at work became stronger. Finally, he told his wife that either they seek help or he was leaving home. She became actively concerned and agreed to see a marital therapist; however, she was resistant in therapy, saying that he was the one who was complaining and that she was happy with the marriage. Eventually she was able to work through her resistance, and she began to look at the marriage relationship from the standpoint of the therapeutic alliance. This came about after continual interpretation of her feelings about the ultimatum and of her responsibility to look at the marriage objectively.

Mr. K.'s "or else" forced Mrs. K. to act. Previously, conflicts had been avoided, denied, suppressed, and even retreated from through fantasy. Mr. K.'s action — unique to the K.'s marital interactional pattern — secured a different type of response from his wife.

The difficulty for the therapeutic alliance arises from the feelings of the mate who reacts to the ultimatum. One person has conquered, and one has been conquered. Dominance-submission and feelings of anger in the conquered mate are involved. However, the task is to interpret the feelings about conquering and being conquered as part of the analysis of the motivation which allows direct confrontation of the feelings. This also opens the possibilities of new approaches to the handling of feelings.

CASE 13 Mrs. L. continually refused therapeutic help by always saying that all the problems lay with her husband, who had been hospitalized twice for severe depression. The husband contacted a marital therapist and he, in turn, contacted Mrs. L. Her resistance was fierce; she was adamant in her verbalized reasons for not wanting help. The husband had delivered an ultimatum about getting help, and she had acquiesced. However, feelings were not resolved until her fear of therapy had been analyzed. Mrs. L. had been deeply afraid that during Mr. L.'s years of individual therapy, she had been blamed for his depression. Her guilt caused her to fantasize that all helping professionals would see her this way. An interpretation allowed this fear to become conscious in a way she could manage. She was able to make progress in forming an alliance for marital therapy and eventually she sought the individual therapy she had long needed.

Lederer and Jackson [7] classified "psychosomatic avoiders" as a subtype of the unstable-unsatisfactory marriage. They noted that often such couples "stick together because each partner hopes to collect unpaid emotional bills from the past." Often it appears that a crisis is unconsciously designed to lead to an ultimatum. The ultimatum upsets the equilibrium of the former patterns of interaction, thus allowing some form of intervention to occur within the marital patterns leading to the possibility of eventual change.

Avoidance of Self-Observation

The psychotherapist often sees the patient who complains excessively in the initial sessions about the mate, saying that much would improve if the mate would change. The therapist knows that this is a resistance to therapeutic work, but he also knows that since the patient has come for individual help the patient is aware that the problem is more than the partner.

It is not uncommon in an initial conjoint interview for one partner to complain about the marriage with such ardent passion that the defensive nature of the complaining is obvious. The partner, in a great expenditure of emotional energy, is avoiding looking at himself. He is resisting all individual help. Projecting the problem onto the marital relationship is a convenient defense that the marital therapist must deal with as quickly as possible so that proper therapeutic intervention can occur. Marital therapists who have little experience in individual diagnosis can be caught in a trap and become frustrated when little movement seems to occur in the marriage.

CASE 14   Mrs. M., 40 years old, made an appointment seeking help for what she described as a very unhappy marriage. She said that her husband was coming, but he did not arrive. He did come eventually for a series of interviews after the therapist called and invited him. The husband was resistant because he felt the problems in the marriage related to his wife's emotional problems. During the evaluative interviews Mrs. M. attempted to ally herself with the therapist in a way that would prevent him from evaluating her individually. The marriage did have problems, but many of the problems lay within Mrs. M.'s intrapsychic conflicts. It took careful work to deal with Mrs. M.'s resistance to observing herself and accepting a referral for individual psychotherapy.

Marital difficulties are not the inevitable concomitant of psychopathology. A psychotic break in one partner followed by treatment perceived as helpful tends to make the couple feel closer and stronger in their mutual bond. However, marital difficulties may be present when one partner is sick. Frequently the healthier member comes for marital counseling because he desires an ally to help him with the disturbed spouse.

CASE 15   Mr. N., a minister aged 65, sought help because of his inability to deal with a paranoid wife. They came to therapy together, but she was convinced that he was cheating on her and that the only solution for her was to leave him. The underlying problem appeared to be his impending retirement, which meant that they would be forced to live more closely than before, since he traveled a great deal. But dealing with this problem led nowhere because of her defenses.

It sometimes happens that when one or the other spouse refuses to consider individual help, the *couple* will come for treatment. The reluctant spouse may be the sicker one (although not necessarily), and involvement of the healthier mate may be a precondition to any therapy. Finally, it is well known that as the overtly psychotic or sicker spouse improves, the other mate may find the concomitant changes in the marriage intolerable and seek divorce or psychotherapy or forbid the spouse to continue in treatment. The changing member may well be sicker at the outset, but what is more crucial — the better functioning member is inflexible and unable to mature. In such cases, who is sicker and who is healthier becomes a question of semantics.

At times, the question of who needs individual treatment may be academic since one partner may refuse to be treated without the other, feeling that to become a patient is to be stigmatized as a sick or defective person. Sometimes the healthier partner can be helped to adapt to the sicker one, thus improving the relationship. Many ego-syntonic characteristics can be studied only when they are brought into treatment because of their maladaptive effect on the marriage.

CASE 16   After 16 years of marriage, Mr. and Mrs. O. were referred by their pastor for marital therapy. Their problems were long-standing ones, and eventually the couple were placed in marital group therapy. Mrs. O. was concurrently seen individually in psychotherapy because she had a particular emotional difficulty that could not be helped in the group. As a result of individual therapy she began to move out of a fantasy world and to stand up to her husband both at home and in the group. Using the excuse that money was short, Mr. O. convinced his wife to terminate individual therapy. He could not tolerate the changes he said he wanted in his wife. He eventually was able to discuss this in the group.

Mutual Recognition of Need

The therapist's utopia is to have a couple who agree that there are problems to which they both unwisely contribute. Often a couple will present themselves in a way that says they have both arrived at the decision to seek help, but closer investigation in the first interview reveals that they actually belong in another category. It is our experience that the overwhelming majority of cases that fall within the category "mutual recognition of need" come from professional referrals. This means that another caretaker has probably been involved, perhaps a clergyman, doctor, friend, or teacher. Rather than allowing them to continue their individual projections, this person has helped the couple see that there is a mutual problem.

CASE 17   Mr. and Mrs. P. had been married less than a year when they returned to the clergyman who performed the marriage ceremony. Mr. P. had been married once before, and Mrs. P. had had two previous marriages. The clergyman had had a brief premarital session with them in which he had urged them to seek professional help if they ever had marital difficulty. It had been his private judgment then that the marriage-to-be had little hope of success without professional help, but they were not open to any such suggestions before their marriage. They returned to him reporting that they were not able to work out conflicts and that they wanted help. He referred them to a marital therapist, with whom they were able to form a good therapeutic alliance early due to previous work with the pastor.

It is easy to be seduced by a couple who appear to be, but are not really, "mutually motivated." This could be an unfortunate aspect of their therapy if the therapist fails to confront their ambivalence and to interpret it for them. Partners who need some assistance with their marital relationship may not be severely disturbed emotionally, but more than likely there is ambivalence in their affectional-interactional processes. This ambivalence will be apparent first in their expectations of marital therapy.

CASE 18   Mr. and Mrs. Q., both professional persons in their fifties, had spent several years in individual analytically oriented psychotherapy. They came for marital therapy at the urging of their individual therapists basically to integrate some of their individual growth into their marriage. In the first session the separate motivations and the resistance to the establishment of a working alliance were quite clear.
  Mr. Q., a passive person, was asking the marital therapist to give him strength to overcome his assertive wife (to make her feminine); Mrs. Q. was asking the therapist to make the husband active (to make him masculine). The interpretations centered

around these requests, which they recognized and then moved toward forming an alliance.

Even when both partners are seeking growth, they will still express ambivalence and resistance. Usually they respond to the therapist's interpretations more quickly and will not ward them off defensively. This is particularly true, of course, if one or both mates have had individual psychotherapy.

AN OVERLAP: RETURN TO "BLISS"

A colleague of ours commented that there are couples who come to therapy seeking to achieve a former state of "bliss." They tend to see therapy only as a way "to bring us back to where we were happy before." In other words, the therapy alliance is limited to restoring equilibrium to the relationship.

Probably this type of couple overlaps with other constellations we have identified. Most couples have a tendency to avoid issues, and their concept of therapy may involve the fantasy of its bringing them to the point of being in love as they once were. Probably this desire for a former state of "bliss" is a resistance which occurs in work with all couples who want to avoid depth analysis and confrontation. Some couples clearly choose never to go beyond a certain point, although the therapist may know and interpret for them that they are biding time rather than resolving conflicts.

CASE 19   When Mr. and Mrs. R. arrived for their first appointment, Mr. R. appeared in dark glasses, which he wore throughout the interview. During the interview he turned continually in his chair, looked out the window, and pretended indifference to what was happening. He said that there was no marital problem except that his wife had been out late a couple of times and he had objected. He wanted the marriage as it was. He considered all aspects of it satisfactory. However, what he was looking for was the previous equilibrium of the marriage, in which he had asserted his maleness by going and coming as he pleased, with his wife at home, ready at all times to serve his needs. Unfortunately for Mr. R., his wife had been reading about women's liberation and had rejected the previous structure of their marriage. When the interpretation was made, the husband refused to see that what he saw as a former state of bliss had not been satisfactory to his wife and that her chronic sexual difficulties might be related to angry feelings about the old days.

It is the therapist's responsibility to help a couple go as far as they can in developing their relationship and enhancing affection for one another.

When a couple begins to demand the restoration of a former state, whether it is a "flight into health" or an actual return to a former romantic state, it is the therapist's responsibility to interpret the demand as resistance and to encourage the couple to utilize the therapeutic alliance to analyze their feelings.

CASE 20   Mr. and Mrs. S., members of a couples group, began to talk in group session of their wish to come to the group less frequently. They felt they had achieved a plateau in the marriage that was satisfactory and that the group was useless. Mr. and Mrs. S. were forced by the group to look at their flight from issues within the group itself, and they began to see that their satisfaction with the former state of "bliss" reflected deep-seated wishes to avoid the conflicts that made them feel inadequate.

Our culture tends to reinforce the idea of a state of blissfulness as seen in the wishes of couples who idealize a state of romantic love. Steiner [11] attacks romantic marriage as hedonistic. The therapist should see this wish for a return to a former state of blissfulness as a defense against establishing a workable marriage.

THE CRISIS COUPLE: A TYPE OF RESISTANCE

Studies of the processes of crisis experience have emphasized the centrality of the sense of being overwhelmed. As individual therapists know, often a patient who first comes into psychotherapy during a severe emotional crisis does not form a therapeutic alliance for some time. As Chessick [2] so aptly points out, supportive therapy (the "giving approach") may have to precede analytical therapy (the "investigative approach").

The same is true for married couples. It is not unusual to have a couple come who are in such a state of crisis that there is little chance for an investigative alliance to be established. Support may be needed immediately to help them deal with the overwhelming anxiety they are encountering. To help them establish control so that they will not act foolishly is often a demanding task for the therapist.

However, there does exist the "crisis couple," the couple who function to maintain a crisis and to resist analysis. Theirs is often an unconscious collaborative effort to avoid looking at their marriage and its interactive processes.

The clue to defense is often the timing of the crisis. Couples of this type have a crisis to report each session. Usually the crisis begins the day before the session or even as the couple is on the way to the therapist's office.

The crisis couple can usually be fitted into one of the other motivational categories, but the crisis is the basic defense blocking the analysis of the hidden resistance. Interpretation of crisis as a resistance usually is met with indignant cries about the ineffectiveness of therapy and the therapist. Another cry concerns the insensitivity of the therapist, who does not empathize with the agony the couple endures. Actually, the therapist is working on the unconscious collusion that the couple maintains in the marital relationship.

THE MOTIVE AND THE ALLIANCE

If the therapist is working from certain assumptions not shared by the patients, his probablity of success is drastically lowered. If he assumes that the patients are seeking help to stay in the marriage when in reality one partner wants to get out, then a therapeutic relationship does not exist.

In the case of Mr. M. (Case 14), the wife thought they both were there to save their marriage. It was the therapist's task to help them clarify their motives and to lead them toward insights concerning the difficulties. Unrealistic expectations cannot be fulfilled by marital therapy, and the couple should be brought to this realization as soon as possible. If an alliance is not formed or active steps are not being taken to form it, the potentiality of the work is very limited.

If a couple cannot form such an alliance, it is the task of the therapist to help them understand why. This alone may lead to a clearer understanding of the individual pathology and thus motivate them to individual treatment, if that is appropriate.

CASE 21   Mr. T. was a professional man, thirty-six years old, who had high aspirations for himself and a conviction that they were unattainable. Mrs. T., also thirty-six years old, was made out by her husband to be the "sick one." She did have her own neurotic problem; she was seeking a lost loved object in her husband and appeared to be holding on to him inappropriately. The husband used this to illustrate a point he had made about her instability. Therapy was difficult because each was fighting the treatment, attempting to counteract the other's motive for being in therapy while resisting exposure of his or her own motive. Active interpretations of their motivations, particularly Mr. T.'s, led them to see their needs. The results led to group therapy for the couple and long-term individual psychotherapy for Mr. T. It was interesting to hear Mr. T. ask for individual therapy when he began to realize that the defenses he used were really developed outside the marriage.

Resistance in individual psychotherapy is seen not simply as a blocking of the therapeutic task but also as an opportunity to carry out the therapeutic task. A patient's recognizing and eventually understanding his resistance is often the impetus to the eventual giving up of the neurotic behavior. The blocking of the therapeutic alliance through inappropriate or incompatible motives should be seen as a resistance. Its recognition and eventual understanding by the couple is just as essential to the work of marital therapy as is any building of insights about their interaction.

REFERENCES

1.   Blanck, R., and Blanck, G. *Marriage and Personal Development.* New York: Columbia University Press, 1968.
2.   Chessick, R. *How Psychotherapy Heals: The Process of Intensive Psychotherapy.* New York: Science, 1969.
3.   Dicks, H. *Marital Tensions: Clinical Studies toward a Psychological Theory of Interaction.* New York: Basic Books, 1967.
4.   Goodrich, D., and Boomer, D.   Experimental assessment of modes of conflict resolution. *Family Process* 2:15, 1963.
5.   Greenson, R. The working alliance and the transference neurosis. *Psychoanalytic Quarterly* 34:155, 1965.
6.   Greenson, R. *The Technique and Practice of Psychoanalysis,* Vol. 1. New York: International Universities Press, 1967.
7.   Leder, W., and Jackson, D. *The Mirages of Marriage.* New York: Norton, 1968.
8.   Luckey, E., and Bain, J. Children: A factor in marital satisfaction. *Journal of Marriage and the Family* 32:43, 1970.
9.   Masters, W., and Johnson, V. *Human Sexual Inadequacy.* Boston: Little, Brown, 1970.
10. Rollins, B., and Feldman, H. Marital satisfaction over the family life cycle. *Journal of Marriage and the Family* 32:20, 1970.
11. Steiner, L. *Romantic Marriage: The Twentieth Century Illusion.* Philadelphia: Chilton, 1963.
12. Weiss, J. L. Personal communication, 1972.
13. Zetzel, E. *The Capacity for Emotional Growth.* New York: International Universities Press, 1970.

16

Treatment of Marriage Disorders

Jacob Christ

The treatment of disorders perceived by clients as residing in their marital relationships requires that the therapist pay attention to a number of factors that are part of the marriage relationship itself, as well as individual factors relating to the partners. In each case the individuals, of course, bring with them their psychological and cultural histories, which may be quite disparate. Each of the partners may have individual problems, perhaps related to growth, development, and relationship to the primary family; but the coming together of two individual personalities creates a third unique entity, the marital relationship.

The marital relationship can be described by itself, and it can be viewed as an entity apart from the two individuals involved in it. The section in this chapter on the history of marital therapy and marital counseling takes this third force into consideration, and a number of other authors have made various suggestions as to where the true focus of therapeutic intervention should be, or what really needs to be changed in order to effectively treat marital disorders. At the present time, it is possible to classify the considerable variety of approaches to marital problems into a few broad categories:

1. Approaches that are centered on the individual and adhere to a

371

psychodynamic or psychoanalytic frame of reference. A section of this chapter is devoted to the psychotherapeutic approaches to marital problems based on the individual model.

2. Approaches that focus on the relationship between the spouses. Marriage counseling approaches are traditionally of this sort. Modern marital therapy adheres to models of social psychiatry or communications theory and considers the nature of the interaction between the two spouses in the "here and now" and brings some influence to bear on the relationship. Along with the conventional counseling or psychotherapeutic techniques, methods based on the model of Gestalt therapy or transactional analysis are being used widely.

3. Group therapy with married couples. This has become an important approach, particularly for long-term marital problems. It is described in Chapter 17.

4. Combinations of the individual approach and the relationship-oriented approach. These are frequently used in psychotherapy or counseling. They permit flexibility and thus allow the treatment to be fitted to the patient's needs. I prefer a setting with a co-therapist that permits individual and conjoint approaches.

BRIEF HISTORY AND REVIEW OF THE LITERATURE[1]

Historically, psychiatrists have focused on the individual partners in the marriage rather than on the dynamics of the marital system; in the psychiatric tradition quite often the problem is perceived as that of two separate people, each with his or her own symptoms. Lussheimer [17] feels that often people who request marriage consultation are in reality asking for help for their individual neurotic difficulties. But Balint [3] feels that it is of little value to try to understand the individual partners separately. By preference one should look at the marriage itself and make a "marital diagnosis." Mittelman [22] was one of the first psychoanalysts who called attention to the fact that the nature of the marital relationship has a strong influence

[1] I am grateful to four people affiliated with the Beth Israel Hospital in Boston for their help with this discussion: Carol C. Nadelson. M.D., Ellen L. Bassuk, M.D., Christopher R. Hopps, M.D., and William E. Boutelle, Jr., M.D. They are the authors of an article, Evaluation Procedures for Conjoint Marital Psychotherapy [24] and of a relevant paper that has not been published [25].

on the course of psychoanalytic treatment. He practiced and advocated
the concurrent psychoanalysis of marital couples by studying the complementary interaction of the mates. He described four typical patterns that
are regularly seen in current practice: (1) one partner dominant and aggressive, the other submissive and masochistic, (2) one partner emotionally
detached, the other craving affection, (3) rivalry between the partners
for aggressive dominance, (4) both partners helpless and craving care;
both wish for a strong mate but are disappointed that the other wants to
be dependent.

Ackerman [1, 2], viewing marital disorders through a therapeutic
approach to the family-as-a-whole, emphasizes the dynamic evolution of
the relationship through various phases of development, and we now
recognize that there is a history of every marriage through stages of a
family life-cycle.

Theoretically and ideologically, there are viewpoints that are psychoanalytically oriented and viewpoints based on communication theory.
They do not necessarily contradict one another and in many instances
are complementary.

Among those authors who subscribe to a psychodynamic frame of
reference, a number of differences of opinion exist. Main [18] emphasizes
the destructive effect of mutual projections of early internalized objects,
which cause the marriage to become a "repository for old conflicts."
Popularly expressed, a man who has "married his mother" or a woman
who has "married her father" is likely to experience difficulties in the
marriage. Main stresses the necessity of interpreting the individual's
transference projection onto the marital partner as well as onto the therapist. Greene and Solomon [6] pursue this matter further and state that
when the negative image is projected onto the spouse, he or she will respond
to these projections with continuous feedback. This will result in an unconscious collusive process [11, 12] leading ultimately to changes in both
spouses (see also pp. 452–454). Giovacchini [5] defends the classic
individual approach to marital problems and feels that couple therapy,
in which the same therapist forms a relationship with both spouses leads
to difficulties in the resolution of the transference neurosis. Sager [29,
31, 32] disagrees, feeling that the working through of neurotic difficulties
requires resolution of both dyadic and triadic transferences. He emphasizes
the value of the already established "transference situation" between the

two marital partners themselves, in which one might intervene skillfully. In individual treatment it may take a long time to develop a similarly intense transference situation. Sager observes the rapid symptomatic improvement in the early stages of conjoint treatment, which he attributes to the rapid clarification of the transference aspects of the couple's behavior. A similar observation on the effect of interpretations in marital therapy was made by Grunebaum and Christ in an article written in 1968 [9].

Haley [11, 12] and Satir [33, 34] are associated with the communications point of view in marital problems. Communication within the marriage may be direct and explicit on one level, while subtle and implicit communications on another level may contradict them. Discrepancies between verbal and nonverbal behavior may culminate in serious marital disturbance. Haley also emphasizes the importance of the establishment of rules (possibly unspoken rules) and the eventual development of "meta-rules," or rules for making rules. An established rule can be considered as defining an aspect of a relationship. A rule that a husband should comfort his wife when she is in distress relates to a complementary aspect of the relationship. An agreement that the wife has equal say about the budget is an example of a symmetrical aspect of a relationship. Each partner brings to the marriage rules or assumptions about how rules should be made. Often the partners replicate rules that prevailed in their primary families. To have a successful marriage, a couple must be capable of establishing both complementary and symmetrical relationships in various areas of their marriage. Communications analysis needs to consider, for instance, who speaks for whom and who attributes blame or credit for his actions to someone else. Such an analysis must consider how messages are transmitted or heard and how their transmitted and perceived meanings match, as expressed in language and through nonverbal expression. Rabkin [28] discusses marital conflicts that arise when partners come from families with different communication codes (which are largely unconscious). He points out that, even when husband and wife have similar class backgrounds, communication codes may differ, since they are indigenous to families. He made a study of uncoordinated communication between marriage partners and noted that happier couples are different from unhappily married ones in that they talk more to each other, they convey the feeling of what is being said by them, they have a wider range of subjects available to them, they have open communication channels even during arguments, and they have personalized language symbols. The unhappier couples tend to be impoverished in their modes of communication.

A variety of procedures for dealing with marital problems has been advocated, with indications and contraindications for many categories of people and conflicts. Haley [11, 12] suggests marriage therapy, particularly when individual psychotherapy had failed or could not be used, when the patient has a sudden onset of symptoms related to martial conflict, when marriage therapy is directly requested by a couple because of conflict and stress that they are unable to dissolve, or, finally, when it appears that improvement in a patient involved in individual therapy would result in a change of the equilibrium in the marriage and cause increased conflict. More specifically, Watson [35] recommends conjoint couples therapy when distortions are gross and when speed in halting family disintegration is a critical factor. He feels that conjoint couples therapy is indicated when the problems involve acting out and are due to character disturbances. It also can be useful when the partners are poorly motivated or not ready for individual treatment. A number of authors [6, 13, 27, 30, 31] stress the importance of including both partners in a treatment program if one is severely disturbed. A relationship in which the equilibrium is based on one partner's mental illness is unstable; as the sick partner improves, the healthy partner may develop difficulties. Brody [4] suggests a combined approach, in which conjoint sessions may be indicated at different times in the individual treatment process. He recommends that such sessions be held to "concretize" gains made in the individual therapy. He considers the patient's ability to utilize conjoint sessions as an indication of progress toward the achievement of a treatment goal.

The picture is confusing when one looks at the contraindications to couples therapy. The contraindications include: "inadequate couples," great anxiety, psychosis in one partner, fragility of defenses, use of therapeutic situations by patients for manipulation, or "individual" secrets, such as infidelity of which the other partner is unaware. According to Sager [29], severe disturbance of one partner is not a contraindication. In fact, he believes that the only valid contraindication may be the therapist's inability to prevent a spouse from utilizing the conjoint session for destructive purposes against his or her mate. He believes that there is cause for concern about premature exposure of privileged communication or secrets to the other spouse, but that, if sufficient trust of the therapist prevails, the fear can be overcome. Grunebaum, Christ, and Neiberg [10] have outlined some of the issues in treatment planning for marital disorders, covering the complicated issue of indications and contraindications.

Several types of treatment deserve mention. Mudd and Goodwin [23] discuss counseling couples in conflicted marriages, stressing that counseling is primarily concerned with the ordering of the environment. They advocate joint interviewing after some individual work with each partner. Couples group psychotherapy is discussed by Linden [16], Leichter [15], and others, and is reviewed more extensively in this book on pages 401–410.

Among the treatments oriented toward in-depth understanding of psychodynamics, classic psychoanalysis and psychoanalytically oriented therapy involving each partner separately have their place. Oberndorf [26], Mittelman [22] and Grotjahn [8] have investigated the marital relationship through the medium of the two individuals in treatment. Collaborative therapy, in which the marital partners are treated by different therapists who communicate with each other has been described by Martin and Bird [21]. The obvious advantage of this approach is that distortions about the partners can be identified and dealt with sooner. On the other hand, collaborative therapy poses a problem of advocacy, or partisanship, of the therapist with his own patient. Concurrent therapy, in which two spouses are seen by the same therapist but in separate sessions, has been used widely and has the same advantages as collaborative therapy because distortions can soon be identified. The problem here is in the countertransference of the therapist who may find himself taking sides. Conjoint therapy as described by Haley and Watson [11, 12, 35] has been widely used. According to Greene [6], indications for conjoint therapy include not only stalemated individual treatment but also the need for improved communications between spouses or for a speedy result in stabilizing the marriage. Satir [34] finds that the major indication for employing conjoint sessions is the desire of the couple to improve and to maintain their relationship, but she feels that conjoint therapy is not generally feasible if either member desires to dissolve the marriage. Finally, a combination of individual, concurrent, conjoint, and group sessions is discussed by Greene, Broadhurst, and Lustig [7], who feel that all technical variations are desirable because of the marked variation in marital patterns and the often unpredictable therapeutic course.

THE MARITAL RELATIONSHIP IN INDIVIDUAL PSYCHOTHERAPY

When one treats a married person in individual therapy, inevitably a topic of conversation is the marriage and the patient's relationship to the spouse. Not infrequently, the marital relationship is the problem or one of the main problems for which the patient has sought help from a psychiatrist or other mental health professional. The marital relationship thus becomes a problem for individual psychotherapy, or, in unfavorable cases, the marital relationship becomes an obstacle that will prevent the patient from making progress in psychotherapy. In order to understand this, a few remarks on the psychotherapeutic relationship are necessary.

By virtue of its specialized and confidential nature, the psychotherapeutic relationship quite regularly displays patients' ways of establishing personal relationships. Since the birth of psychoanalysis, it has been commonly accepted that the relationship between the therapist and the patient is of crucial importance and must be a constant subject for observation and, if necessary, interpretation by the therapist.

Commonly, two aspects of the psychotherapeutic relationship are distinguished: (1) the therapeutic alliance, which refers to the conscious and voluntary agreement that the patient makes to work with the therapist toward his own health. The therapeutic alliance is thought to be made between the healthy part of the patient that wants and accepts help and the therapist; (2) transference, the unconscious and often troublesome aspect of the patient-therapist relationship. Often, without the patient's knowing it, he will invest the therapist with characteristics that refer to important people in his past, for instance, one or both parents. Quite likely, in the course of treatment the patient will react to his transference distortions, and feel threatened, loved, supported, or attacked by the therapist much the same as he may have felt he was treated earlier by important persons in his life. It becomes important to test this unrealistic transference relationship against the reality of the therapeutic alliance, that is, the overt therapist-patient relationship. It is quite common that the distinction between the two types of relationships with the therapist gets lost in the process and that there is either exaggerated transference (such as when the patient "falls in love with the therapist", or sees the therapist only as a good "father" or "mother" figure) or too much therapeutic alliance and not enough transference. The patient will then work rationally with the therapist but not produce any of the more emotionally colored transference distortions that would give him access to his deeper and hidden feelings.

It is often extremely painful for a patient to find himself in the throes of painful emotions based on transference expectations. If a woman patient who has fallen in love with her male therapist realizes that the therapist is, in fact, only a helper and not a lover, she will have to suffer through the disappointment of rejected love. The nonfulfillment of transference expectations is a regular feature of psychotherapy, and awareness of it is a necessary milestone. Yet, there are patients who never accept the differences between the realistic helping-relationship and the unrealistic lover-relationship; in these cases the treatment suffers. Falling in love with the therapist may be a stage of treatment, but it should not be the end product.

Unfortunately, some therapists are not ready to acknowledge transference expectation, taking them instead for real expectations of themselves. They are unwilling or unable to help a patient live through the transference-love disappointment. Attempts at satisfying the patient's transference needs by shows of affection, handholding, hugging, and so on, often lead to a deeper dependence and unrealistic attachment of the patient and, consequently, a deeper frustration and disappointment later.

Problems in the Treatment of Married Persons

Unsatisfactory Balance of Transference and Therapeutic Relationship If a married person is involved in a treatment situation marked by an excessive transference, a painful situation can occur that may lead to a "triangle conflict" marked, at best, by jealousy on the part of the spouse and, in the more severe cases, by what might be called the *irate husband syndrome.* The psychiatrist might even be charged with alienation of affection.

CASE 1   A 30-year-old woman had sought help from a young male psychiatrist for a general dissatisfaction culminating in depression of a moderately serious nature. In the psychotherapeutic situation that followed, some improvement of the depression was evident, yet the patient increased her demands on the psychiatrist by repeatedly creating emergency situations. In time she insisted that the therapist was interested in her sexually and would shortly divorce his wife to marry her. The resulting stalemate in therapy could only be resolved when the patient discontinued treatment and, with the help of a female psychiatrist, realized that the therapist did not love her. The husband, while understandably angry, was wise enough not to act precipitiously.

The popular belief that psychotherapy involving a married psychiatrist and a married patient of the opposite sex leads to divorce, is based on a similar failure to distinguish between the real helping relationship and the unrealistic transference relationship. A female patient may lose perspective at one point and see the therapist as a real lover, and she may express this fantasy to her husband. The same situation may occur when the sexes are reversed — male patient and female therapist — although female therapists are usually better able to handle the situation. Regrettably, therapists themselves occasionally feed the jealousies in such triangle situations by gratifying the patient's transference needs.

Sometimes the therapeutic relationship enters into direct competition with the marriage as a relatively concrete distortion. This situation can often be remedied by clarification of everyone's purposes. Often the intervention of an additional person is needed, and, if the pathological transference is not curable, separation of the patient and therapist may be necessary. The presence of the spouse in therapy sessions often corrects such a situation. A demonstration of the reality of the marriage relationship will often sufficiently "dilute" the transference relationship to permit therapeutic work to continue undisturbed.

CASE 2   A psychotic woman was being treated by a male therapist. Regularly, after every two or three sessions, a transference psychosis would become apparent; the patient would act as though she were in love with the therapist, would make seductive comments, or would act amorously. It was possible to keep this situation within bounds and treatment progressing by having the husband attend about one out of five of the weekly therapy sessions. The psychotic patient usually recaptured herself and continued her work when the reality of her marriage was kept in front of her by the husband's physical presence.

Distortions of the Marital Relationship   A problem of a different order in the treatment of married people is that quite often the marital relationship is presented to the therapist in a distorted fashion. For reasons that usually become apparent sometime in the course of therapy, a spouse will often present a one-sided picture of the partner's assets and shortcomings. The therapist who does not see the spouse has little with which to verify his patient's accuracy and can be led to believe that his patient's distortions are true. If a patient paints a grim picture of the marriage, a therapist may be seduced into believing that a destructive reality situation exists and may advise steps of an irrevocable nature that the patient may later regret. Quite often a masochistic female patient will portray her husband as a raving maniac who is intent on harming and humiliating her. Although theoretically a therapist should not take sides, it is entirely understandable that after a barrage of such complaints he may begin to be swayed to the patient's point of view.

The most practical approach is to take a firsthand look at the person being maligned. A degree of assurance is gained by the therapist's ability to contrast his own perception of the spouse with the perception that his patient presents.

CASE 3   A woman who had been married approximately two years complained continuously to her therapist about her husband, whom she described as a very selfish, immature, and ungiving person. She repeatedly asserted her wish to divorce him, which was checked only by a great fear of loneliness. Although she had been advised that her husband would sooner or later have to have treatment, she discouraged him from seeking help. Instead, she continued to describe him in the most unflattering terms. When he was finally seen, he was not the monster that had been described, but a rather helpless man who was disturbed at his wife's continual despondency. It appeared later that her anger, which had been so evident in her projections onto her husband, had really been intended for her mother, who during childhood had given little attention to her and instead concentrated on taking care of a younger brother who was sickly and needed a great deal more care. The distortion in the marriage relationship, which at first sounded credible, had served to hide and overshadow the woman's severely disturbed relationship with her mother.

The distorted presentation of a marriage relationship may not in itself become a problem if it is properly studied and understood. But it may lead to the triangle situation described earlier in which the distortion remains unrecognized and the therapist erroneously feels called upon to treat a destructive reality situation. In clinical practice, whether in private practice or in a public outpatient clinic service, *distortions of this sort are so frequent that it is a legitimate policy to ask the spouse to come for consultation if treatment of a married person is contemplated and if marital issues play any role in the presenting problem.* The gains in objectivity almost always help the therapist and the patient in resolving the problem more expeditiously. It is usually well worth the additional time and effort to consult with the patient's spouse.

Acting Out of Earlier Conflicts Through the Marriage   Frequently, it
is possible to understand the specific dissatisfactions that spouses have
with each other in terms of the unfulfilled needs that spouses have brought
into the marriage from their earlier lives. It is quite common that a
neurotic person will expect from the marriage relationship all those
satisfactions he or she has not had from mother or father, or both. A
situation comparable to the transference situation occurs: the spouse
is expected to be all things that the father or mother was, or was supposed
to have been, and the other person is disappointed if these expectations are
not fulfilled, regardless of what the spouse does offer. It is in the nature
of falling in love that one becomes, to some extent, the victim of his
earlier life (as well as the beneficiary of the tremendous energy of which
the instinctual drives are capable). The fact that in marriage some expectations remain unfulfilled must be taken as a necessary accompaniment or
as the price to be paid for the benefits the relationship bestows.

CASE 4   The young woman in Case 3 had expected from her husband the care and
consideration that she had not been given by her mother. The disappointment was
severe and was resolved only with the recognition of the significance of her poor
relationship with her mother. After her recognition of her depression and after
becoming a mother herself, the marriage relationship improved greatly and she appreciated her husband for what he was.

THE RELATIONSHIP MODEL OF MARITAL THERAPY: AIMS AND TECHNIQUES

If the therapist is to help a couple whose difficulty seems to lie in the
marriage relationship, it is necessary that he pay attention to a number
of factors that are an integral part of the marriage or family relationship.

The Marriage System as a Whole

The therapist may, from the beginning, decide that a marital relationship needs
treatment rather than the person who presents himself as a patient. After
assessing the situation as a whole, it becomes possible to formulate a
treatment plan for both partners that may have better results. In crisis
intervention, the best approach is not necessarily to treat the sicker partner.
Often it is more effective to begin at a different point, possibly by finding
the stronger person and wielding some influence there.

CASE 5   An attractive 35-year-old mother of two young children came to a psychiatric facility for help. Her complaints were that since the time her husband formed his own engineering company two years ago, he was rarely at home, paid little attention to her, and that, as a consequence, their marriage had deteriorated. She had anxiety spells approximately every month or two, felt that she was no longer a good mother to her children, and wondered if perhaps some medication could help her recover her strength so that she could cope with the situation. The therapist might well have chosen to treat her anxieties and hope for the best. Instead, he arranged an interview with both spouses and later one with the husband alone. It was learned from these interviews that the husband was indeed spending more time away from home and that he was doing it primarily because, whenever he came home, his wife would chastise him for being unloving. She kept the children close to her, did not allow her husband to take them out, and engaged in long telephone conversations with her mother, who lived some 50 miles away. Her husband was in a position to change his life-style and schedule somewhat now that his business was established, but he was not coming home to be criticized in front of the children. The husband was told that he would need to come for a few weeks in weekly interviews. He reluctantly agreed. In a series of 10 interviews, the husband expressed his frustration at the wife's ungiving attitude and connected it in turn to his relationship with his mother, who had had no faith in his abilities. After two rather stormy sessions with his wife, he found ways of changing his schedule in order to spend more time at home. After two or three months, there was a noticeable change in their relationship, and the wife felt she did not need psychiatric treatment or medication.

Admittedly, not all such marital problems are so easily treated. But experience with a series of similar cases has convinced me and my collaborators that the method of choice in treating this fairly typical marital syndrome (of the depressed, frustrated wife and the aloof unfeeling husband) is not to treat the "weaker" or the "help-seeking" patient, but to look at the situation as a whole and try to exert influence where it can be most effective. In this case, it was with the rational, hard-working husband. Had the wife received treatment, the husband would probably have considered the treatment, with its financial and emotional costs as another burden he had to bear, one that would demand an even better job performance and more time away from home.

The rationale of this form of treatment is: (1) the marriage relationship is seen as a whole, as suffering from an imbalance or from a gradual, but severe dwindling of emotional satisfactions and (2) the treatment consists not of insight-oriented psychotherapy for the most frustrated part of the "system" (in this case, the wife), but of intervention at a point at which a restoration of the balance is possible. The therapist did not "treat" the patient; he intervened helpfully in the existing crisis situation.

Marriage as a Support System

Another technique stemming from the awareness of the situation as a whole has to do with the reestablishment of support systems when the breakdown of one spouse threatens. It has long been known that severe mental disorders do not occur in a vacuum but are closely related to family circumstances, sometimes past ones, but frequently present ones. The participation of family members in the treatment of severe mental disorder is essential, because the patient who is excluded from his family because of mental illness, is the one who is not likely to recover. A patient whose support systems are intact is much more likely to recover, and often in a rather short time. The following example illustrates the reestablishment of a support system for a man who threatened to become seriously and permanently disabled.

CASE 6   A 42-year-old small-businessman and father of three children presented with problems concerning his wife. He appeared to suffer from a paranoid-like conviction that she had been unfaithful to him. Statements of an "expert" on physiognomy to the effect that a certain configuration of the chin and lips reflected sensuality convinced him that his wife fit the pattern, and since that time, approximately five months before his admittance to the clinic, he was convinced that she had been unfaithful. In the meantime, his general work performance had declined and he had become moderately depressed and had caused considerable grief and hardship to his wife and himself. There was no reality basis whatsoever for his allegations, as he was occasionally able to admit.

At first, we did not give this man's difficulty a very favorable prognosis. It seemed as though he had little insight, was on a downhill course, and seemed an unlikely candidate for psychotherapy. We did, however, take the precaution of interviewing him with his wife, and, although that particular interview was far from being a success, it revealed certain pertinent diagnostic criteria. In the interview, we observed that the wife, an obese and dowdy lady, looked past her husband while he was explaining his difficulties. It was clear that she was thoroughly bored with him, had heard the same things many times before, and was thoroughly unhappy with the entire situation. She was unwilling in the interview to support her husband in any way, and it seemed fairly evident that any sort of continued joint interviewing with the two spouses would be fruitless. She was, however, willing to see a social worker on the husband's next visit to the clinic.

During the next four or five sessions, in which the husband engaged in a fruitless search for the source of his troubles with the evaluating psychiatrist, the wife began to relate meaningfully to her social worker. She revealed her life history, which reflected a masochistic pattern and could meaningfully acknowledge her disenchantment with her situation. A telltale change occurred at the third visit, when the two spouses no longer sat on opposite ends of a waiting room bench, looking away from each other, but sat next to each other and were talking. After approximately three more interviews, the husband's symptoms subsided, he put aside his previous concerns about his wife "for about 80 percent of the time," as he put it, and was once again able to function.

What had happened? How could we have achieved such a relatively satisfactory result in a comparatively short time. We had noted in the initial interview the wife's boredom with her husband and had seen the situation as a whole as one of alienation. Although we were not able to cure the paranoid disease, we were certainly able to intervene in the marital alienation through the social worker's treatment of the wife. At the end of a relatively few interviews, she was willing to resume the supportive role to her husband she had held for 19 years and had relinquished only recently. The husband's psychotic symptoms had yielded to a reestablishment of support from his wife.

Similar measures can be taken when the breakdown is not psychotic but behavioral. There are a number of circumstances in which it is difficult to treat the disturbed patient but helpful to treat the marital situation. In this regard, one might consider the problem of treating alcoholics on an individual basis or treating law breakers either with or without a court order. The therapist's typical experience is that the patient at first presents a picture of normality, seemingly making a strong effort to remain healthy or stay out of trouble, then all of a sudden — and to the therapist's surprise — a new catastrophe occurs. The patient had seemingly "gone along with the therapist," but after a while had fallen back into his former disturbed behavior. *If such a person is married and if the spouse is available, it is always preferable to have the patient treated in the relationship with the spouse.* There is often little a therapist can do when he is alone with such a patient, since an unsuitable phantasy relationship exists between a punishing authority figure and an inadequate or criminal personality. A one-to-one relationship leads to a need on the part of the offender to defy authority. The easiest way to defy a helping person is to commit another offense, which usually prevents the helper from continuing. A simultaneous relationship with a person to whom the offender is close permits support systems to come into play, and the delinquent or offender is then not alone with the frightening, and only possibly helpful, authority figure. It is this same principle of "dilution of authority" that has made group treatment much more effective than any individual approach in the rehabilitation of persons who suffer from alcoholism and drug addiction and in the rehabilitation of law breakers. In the group, one is not alone with the authority. There is recourse when one feels that one's own self is being threatened by the power of the therapist.

CASE 7   A 46-year-old man was apprehended for indecent exposure and sent for treatment. It appeared in an initial interview that over the years he had had a number of extramarital contacts, some of which had come to his wife's attention. He also had repeatedly indulged in both voyeurism and exhibitionism. His job record was mediocre, but he had maintained his marriage. When his wife was seen with him in conjoint therapy, she appeared to be a masochistic person, currently somewhat depressed, partially because she was menopausal. In the course of a series of 12 conjoint interviews, the wife increasingly vented anger at her husband, a feat that she had never been able to accomplish before. Her more assertive attitude set more concrete limits on her husband, reestablishing at the same time that she cared about him a great deal. Toward the end of the interviews, the husband once again was able to establish himself in the marital relationship, and it became clear that his arrest for indecent exposure had occurred at the point when the wife was at her most depressed state and had, emotionally speaking, left him. The treatment situation, which focused in part on the wife's depression, was never one in which the husband was the accused offender who had to justify himself in the therapist's eyes. Instead, the vulnerability of a rather unstable personality had come to the fore, and his wife took measures to reestablish security.

Closeness in Marriage

It is not only the support systems in the marriage relationship that can be mobilized for best therapeutic advantage. The closeness of the marital relationship provides an unusual opportunity for a therapist to help spouses toward a better understanding of themselves and of each other. Interpretations or explanations can become extraordinarily effective when both spouses are present, not because the therapist is so meaningful for either of the two, but because they have a close, and therefore a meaningful, relationship to one another. Comments pertaining to either of the spouses cannot be shoved away, forgotten or ignored, since the other spouse is a witness. Moreover, both spouses' perceptions of each other and themselves will always affect them at the deepest level of communication between them. Unlike an individual patient and his therapist, who talk to one another on a rational and emotional level, only spouses communicate with each other on all possible levels — rational and irrational, emotional and physical. Observations about the physical relationship between the two are likely to evoke a great deal of emotional reaction so that a discussion of sexual problems with both spouses present tends to stir up feeling and can be quite effective, even if neither spouse has particularly strong feelings about the therapist. The effectiveness of such an intervention stems from the intensity of the relationship that spouses have with one another. The modern sex therapists are the beneficiaries of the effects of closeness in marriage (see Chapter 18).

CASE 8   Mr. F., a 48-year-old man of considerable achievements, and his 46-year-old wife, were discussing in a joint interview the wife's tendency to suspect him of interest in younger girls. Although both knew that there was no real danger of extramarital involvement, the husband's surliness when criticized about this interest and his "guilt feelings" about sexual thoughts were a constant irritation. It appeared in the interview that Mrs. F. was raking her husband over the coals and that he was not only allowing it, but almost welcoming it. Instead of commenting on the pathological jealousy of the wife and the husband's fear of his own impulses, the therapist pointed to the husband's acceptance of his punishment at the hands of his wife. The effect of the interpretation became clear only later. The wife found it totally unacceptable that she might be seen as punishing her husband. She had always seen herself in the role of the victim who was penalized by her husband. The husband, in turn, realized that he did not have to "take the punishment" the way he had had to take it at home when he was a child and that he could easily protest or walk away when his wife treated him in this fashion. He subsequently did so, and the pressure on the wife to repeat her jealous concerns to him diminished considerably.

Developmental Stages in the Marriage

A last, but not unimportant, aspect of the marriage needs to be kept in mind. The marriage is not only a close relationship distinct from other human contacts; it is also a lifelong one, at least in the participants' expectations. It therefore shows development over the years; a marriage that is only one or two years old is different from one that has lasted over a number of years. The family life-cycle involves a number of marital stages. Treatment of a marriage of two people who barely know each other and treatment of the marriage of a couple who have been together 25 years are two different propositions. Treatment planning for a young couple in distress quite often involves looking at the relationships that both spouses still have with their primary families. Frequently, the marriage of such a couple suffers from the immaturity of one or both spouses; and often when help is sought for the marriage, the prospects for both to work together are not good. It is different with a couple who has a basis of closeness to draw on. A couple that has been married 12 years and has children will think twice before separating, over, for example, the issue of the husband's having had an affair. They may regain the closeness they once had and restore the equilibrium that had been disrupted by, perhaps, the husband's success or the wife's growing needs for autonomy. Another type is the couple whose children have grown up. At this stage of full success and performance for the husband, the wife may have reached menopause, and often a crisis in the marriage occurs, sometimes leading to divorce. Often a therapist is consulted, and issues of marital unhappiness are brought forth. The two spouses are once again alone with themselves, the children having left home. In a sense, they are back where they started as a young couple, once again face to face with one another. But this time they may not like as well what they see in one another. Issues of disappointed expectation are probably the most common ones at that stage; each spouse has not found in the other what he expected, and the hopes for change in the desired direction have been frustrated.

Overview of Techniques

The techniques of marital therapy can be summarized as follows:

1. It is always necessary to look at a complaint about a marriage as involving a total situation. Rather than treating the individual who presents as a patient, one should ascertain the interests of all parties involved and the nature of the relationship.

2. Interventions should take place not necessarily where expected, i.e., on the person who presents the complaints, but at the point where the most benefit can be derived. Often this may mean treating the other spouse rather than the one who presents himself or treating the two spouses together. In general, it may be said that the spouse who *appears to be the stronger one socially*, who "holds the high cards," may be the one to whom a therapist should address himself.

3. Marital closeness means that there is a great deal of support available from the spouse. It is important to realize that even severe mental disorders can often be helped greatly by reestablishing marital support systems.

4. When the problem is one of authority and defiance, as is often the case with behavior disorders, a spouse can fulfill a middle role in the treatment situation and thus prevent a fantasized situation of primitive authority and childlike defiance to develop between therapist and patient.

5. The stage of the marriage should be considered. Young spouses often have too many individual unresolved conflicts that need to be resolved before they make a suitable marital adjustment. Parents whose children are grown need to reestablish themselves as husband and wife. Couples in in-between stages may often experience difficulty related to the growth and development of their children, and they may need to improve their communication patterns and to establish or reestablish the depth of communication required for harmonious functioning.

CONJOINT THERAPY

The term *conjoint marital therapy* has become increasingly used to con-
note a treatment situation in which a therapist and the two spouses are
present at the same time. Conjoint marital treatment, therefore, is a
triangular situation and, as such, has some of the characteristics of any
other triad situation. It is a form of treatment quite distinct from concurrent treatment, also in which both spouses are seen but in separate
therapeutic situations, each one alone with the therapist; and it is obviously
different from cooperative therapy, in which the two spouses are seen by
two separate therapists.

Conjoint therapy is, of course, specifically designed to investigate not
only the individual problems of the two spouses, but more specifically the
relationship between the two spouses. Marriage counseling may always
have focused to some extent on the relationship between the two partners,
but perhaps the term *marital counseling* implies a bias in the direction of
"saving the marriage" or restoring peace between the two spouses. Conjoint marital therapy as a form of treatment does not have the bias of
"saving the marriage" built in, even though it addresses itself to the study,
and possibly the improvement, of the marital relationship. It is obvious
that the marriage that is about to break up is not likely to be a good one
for conjoint therapy, since spouses about to separate are rarely willing or
able to be open with each other and to work with each other toward constructive goals. Whenever an agreement to work together can be reached
with the two spouses and the therapist, marital therapy in one form or
another is possible; and conjoint therapy, by and large, works best when
such an agreement of the two spouses to work together toward a reasonable goal can be reached. It is not so much the severity of the pathology
in either one or both spouses that determines whether conjoint therapy
is possible as it is their willingness to work together. The therapist may
attend to both spouses and their individual problems, as well as to their
relationship. In fact, he usually has to address himself to the individuals
and to the relationship.

Conjoint marital therapy carries with it a peculiar intensity in the
interaction between the spouses that quite regularly involves the therapist
emotionally. The intensity is comparable to that experienced in family
therapy, in which the immediacy of the issues and the closeness that the
clients have to one another create a sense of the relevance and the importance

of matters transacted by all concerned. Quite usually, interaction in conjoint marital therapy is intense from the beginning; little time is wasted,
and the effects of such therapy are usually quick to show themselves.
Conjoint marital therapy therefore is a short-term therapy, ranging from
a few sessions to perhaps six months of work.

The Triangle as a Therapeutic Setting

Some particulars of the triangular setting deserve attention since they
tend to influence the conjoint marital therapy setting regardless of the
individual pathology of the partners involved. A triangle is, of necessity,
an unstable setting. The possibility that two will be united against one
is forever present. The two spouses may unite against the therapist (sometimes a favorable outcome), or, more commonly, each of the feuding
partners may at first solicit the therapist's help against the other, a situation
sometimes called *playing divorce court*. The therapist may become an
identification object for the spouse of the same sex and an object of sexual
attraction for the spouse of the opposite sex. Any number of interactions
can be easily explained by these few basics of the triangular relationship
alone. These general interactional dynamics of the triad are in themselves
neither good nor bad. They simply exist as a screen upon which the
specific features of the couple may project themselves.

Many positive features can arise from the elucidation of the triangular
situation. An individual may relive his earlier Oedipal situation in the
triangular relationship, or more commonly, he may realize how he has
projected the image of the parent of the opposite sex onto his spouse.
The triangular situation reminds him of the earlier triangular situation,
and the therapist is sometimes cast in a parental role. The triangular
therapeutic situation, furthermore, may become a stimulus to looking at
triangular situations in the family of the couple under treatment, such as
their relationship with their children.

Evaluation and Treatment Planning

When the request for a joint interview has been made and the preliminary
information points to a marital problem, it is often preferable to schedule
the conjoint interview first. This eliminates the odium of one spouse's
being assigned the primary-client-role, with the other one coming in as an
afterthought. The fact that both spouses appear at the same time focuses

the whole treatment on the marriage, even if, at a later point, only one spouse is seen intensively. The initial conjoint interview should investigate enough history of both spouses to arrive at some formulation of their individual situation and, at the same time, to reveal something about their interaction. If the crisis is clearly marital, or if one of the spouses is not likely to profit from an individual interview, one may continue seeing the couple only together. But if many complex issues feed into the problem, as is often the case, it is useful to schedule individual appointments with the spouses to explore each one's background and individual problems. Sometimes one is surprised by the confession of one of the spouses that he has already planned a separation and is ready to marry someone else when the divorce becomes final. Such a disclosure in an individual session will obviously impede further marital therapy. Without the individual session, much time might have been wasted, since the one spouse might not have had another opportunity to make his intentions clear. After the individual interviews with the spouses, one may discuss with the couple what their impressions were, and what has been accomplished so far.

The Role of a Co-therapist in Evaluation and Treatment Marriage therapy, like family therapy and group therapy, offers many challenges to the expert as well as to the beginning therapist. The idea of having a co-therapist present when evaluating or treating a marital problem is a natural one for the therapist, who appreciates all the help he can get. Most of the time, troubled couples will also quite readily accept the fact that understanding and dealing with their difficulties may require two people. Most frequently, the two professionals are of different sexes — sometimes they are a husband and wife team.

At times "modeling" has been stressed by a husband-wife therapy team treating a couple in trouble. While indeed an element of learning "how to do business with one another" may be present in such a situation, the therapeutic input per se — that is, the acquisition of an understanding of one's own actions and their effect — seem to me far more effective than setting an example. The effectiveness of co-therapy lies in the much enhanced availability of support or transference situation, as well as in the fact that two people can do more work than one can. A team approach is particularly effective and timesaving in the evaluation stage, when two people can obtain a fairly comprehensive picture of a marital problem with relatively little effort. The following is a scheme the proved valuable in the practice of marital therapy:

An evaluation appointment is scheduled from 90 minutes to 2 hours. At first, all four people — the co-therapists and the couple — meet. This setting permits both therapists to form ideas about the problem and about the interaction of the two spouses based on the observation of who tells the story, who dominates the scene, and who is withdrawn or depressed.

After approximately half an hour the therapists may suggest that the couple split up and that each partner talk to a therapist separately so that the therapist can obtain a fuller picture of each spouse. Sometimes "the men may go together" and "the women may go together"; sometimes the sexes may be crossed. In any case, an individual and private interview will permit the therapist to explore the personal history of each client and, if possible, to connect the present marital problems with problems related to childhood, adolescence, or the primary family in general. It is understood, however, that information obtained in the separate sessions can be brought back into the foursome setting, unless secrecy is specifically requested. Secrecy, will then, of course, be a problem of its own. After the individual sessions, all reassemble to conclude the session and to discuss plans for proceeding further. Any number of approaches are possible: conjoint interviewing only, if there is a recognition that most of the trouble lies in communicating; individual treatment for one or both spouses; or a repeat of the same procedure — first together, then separate, and then together again. The availability of a co-therapist permits treatment planning in a flexible fashion, as needs arise. Some clinical examples will illustrate this:

CASE 9   A woman who had been divorced but was currently married to an alcoholic husband, requested that a female co-therapist be present. She was frightened of her husband and did not trust a male therapist alone in the situation. Treatment was therefore conjoint with female support present. The woman came to the conclusion that, despite her tendency to depression and her fear of loneliness, she had to separate from her husband. He accepted this fact.

CASE 10   A young couple, married about six months, who had difficulties getting along, came for treatment. The husband was contemplating further treatment in a different location and therefore invested little in the therapeutic situation. The wife, however, was able to give herself to the treatment with a female co-therapist. In the initial evaluation with her, she identified a problem with her mother and her emotional deprivation, which had led her into an adolescent marriage and, more recently, into her present marriage, which was much better than the first. In six individual sessions, she came to terms with her own situation and brought the marriage back together by being able to take a more positive and more giving stance in regard to her husband. She had perceived the therapist as a giving, motherly person. There were only two conjoint interviews.

CASE 11   A couple married about 15 years presented with problems with their adolescent son. It soon appeared that they had little ability to communicate and felt much anger and resentment against each other. The conjoint part of the sessions was, at first, of little use, and the focus for both spouses rested for a long time on the individual therapy, in which each obtained some support, understanding, and clarification from a therapist of the same sex. As time went on, the individual sessions became shorter, and more work was done in the conjoint sessions. After four months of weekly treatment only conjoint sessions were held until treatment was terminated after about seven months of therapy.

CASE 12   A man who had been married five years and who had no children called for counseling for him and his wife. The conjoint setting revealed a great deal of anger between the two, but only in the individual setting did it emerge that the wife had already decided to move out. She, in essence, enlisted the help of one of the therapists to "let her husband down gently"; the husband, on the other hand, wanted the therapist to "keep his wife in the marriage." The clarifications could have been given by one person, except that the co-therapy situation in the beginning allowed the whole situation to be brought into the open in one two-hour session.

The Supportive Function of Conjoint Therapy   Many people tend to feel deeply ashamed about marital problems. Seeking a therapist and confessing one's inability to have a good marriage appears for many to be akin to treason. When one spouse is ready to "spill the beans" but the other refuses, usually there is already advanced alienation. When both spouses more or less agree that they have a marital problem and when they are allowed to appear together, the burden of revealing a shameful secret becomes lighter since it is shared. The frequency with which such joint appointments are requested today and the ease with which a suggestion to that effect is usually accepted, indicate that there is something in the conjoint situation that is easier on the patient. The presence of the spouse somehow makes each client only partially responsible for the difficulties. Secrets, when revealed, will also be evident to the spouse, and he has the option of contradicting any statements. Finally, one does not get as personally involved with a therapist if the spouse is there to provide an alternate and very close relationship. When one partner has difficulty in individual relationships, it is particularly evident that the conjoint situation facilitates a beginning of therapy. A person who is either afraid of or vulnerable in human relationships of the one-to-one variety, such as a borderline psychotic or schizoid patient, quite often participates effectively as long as the spouse is present, whereas a meaningful relationship with a therapist in a one-to-one situation would be much too threatening to this type of person. Reversing the picture, one can observe that in those cases in which the relationship with the spouse has become very painful, the presence of a third party, the therapist, often makes it possible to negotiate difficult issues, which, in the one-to-one marital relationship would be impossible to settle at home. The supportive character of the conjoint situation may, therefore, soften the stress of painful or potentially painful relations and facilitate the sharing of heavy burdens through communicating about intimate and difficult topics.

Horizontal and Vertical Approaches in Conjoint Therapy   A marital crisis or problem can be perceived in various ways. The more traditional, individual-oriented psychotherapist will search for the origins of the present malaise in the histories of the two spouses.

It may become evident from a review of the beginning stages of the marriage and from the relationship each individual has had with his parents, that the present situation represents a repetition of a conflict situation experienced in the primary family. In some instances, the unconscious motive for the choice of the particular spouse may become evident. The spouse may represent the parent of the opposite sex, occasionally of the same sex, or a combination of traits from father and mother that seem desirable to the person at the time of marital choice. Quite often in such instances, expectations that are unfulfillable are placed on the spouse, since they are descendants of infantile wishes for a perfect father or a perfect mother. It is often useful, when using the individual depth-oriented (or vertical) approach, to point out such parallels and to draw the spouse's attention to the similarities between his earlier relationships and the present marital situation. Theoretically and practically, such an approach can be carried out with one individual in the absence of the spouse, (pp. 376–381) and much individual psychotherapy or psychoanalysis is done in transacting exactly such issues. However, if such an in-depth exploration is undertaken in the presence of the spouse who has been the focus of unfulfilled wishes or demands, it can become much more directly meaningful and effective in leading to change. A husband and wife who have sexual problems may relate them to earlier situations. In a typical case, a wife, after mentioning that her father had always wanted her to be a tomboy, realized in the presence of her husband that she had been trying to be a boy for her father's sake and that this was a root of her sexual difficulty with her husband. Had the same realization taken place in the absence of her husband, the episode may have passed or become interpretable only much later, when transference to the therapist had been established. Moreover, in this example, the husband was able to bring a similar insight to the therapy session a week later so that the wife's discovery in his presence stimulated a discovery of his own. One may say that in-depth work with one partner in the presence of the other rarely leaves the other partner unaffected. It will force him to go into depth as well, because he realizes he is an accomplice.

One may also take a horizontal approach focusing on particular interactions between the spouses and describing not so much the individual origins of general attitudes as the immediate consequences that certain acts of one spouse have on the other. It is remarkable how frequently spouses are unaware of the consequences of their own actions to their partner. For example, it is often a surprise to a husband who has been accustomed to withdrawing into his own room or the basement when the wife discusses an increase in physical symptoms and relates this to the husband's "not caring"; and the wife may be surprised to hear that the husband withdraws because he cannot stand to listen to her recital of the bodily ills from which she suffers. The sequence of events — the demand for physical attention, the withdrawal, and then the increased demands — is rarely obvious to a couple who have been living in a moderate or severe state of alienation. Conjoint therapy almost always brings to light such fairly obvious sequences of cause and effect that have remained unknown to the spouses because of their lack of effective communication. One might say that this horizontal interactional approach tries first to uncover the disorders of communication. Furthermore, it tries to demonstrate to both spouses their particular behaviors toward each other and the consequences. An amelioration, or at least a toning down, of the pathogenic behavior rarely fails to materialize after such confrontation in conjoint therapy.

Conjoint therapy may combine horizontal and vertical approaches. A common technique, for instance, is to have one spouse comment on a biographical account given by the other. The nature of their cooperation or competition, whatever the case may be, is usually evident at an early

point, when a spouse may respond by telling a life story that is even better
than the one his partner just told. On the other hand, a husband may
address some supportive remarks to his wife and collaborate in solving
what is presented as her problem. It is necessary to keep a degree of equilibrium between the two spouses lest one dominate the situation to the
detriment of the other.

Conjoint marital therapy has, on occasion, the character of crisis intervention and works best when both spouses feel that their difficulties
have left them in a state of pain that they wish to relieve. Conjoint marital
therapy, therefore, requires an already relatively well-established marriage
and works best in a marital crisis of recent occurrence. Lifelong marital
problems are poor risks for conjoint therapy, but they may do better in a
couples' group. Poorly established marriages and marriages in the process
of breaking up are also poor risks for conjoint therapy. By contrast, a
marriage that has existed and been relatively satisfactory for some years
and has recently become the victim of alienation is a very good candidate
for conjoint therapy.

Special Situations and Techniques   Several types of classifications of
marital disorders have been attempted, some of which deserve to be considered classic syndromes. Dichotomies of stable-unstable, satisfactory-
unsatisfactory have yielded knowledge about the unsatisfactory but stable
marriage, the "gruesome twosome," a syndrome not infrequently encountered [14]. The picture of two people, usually advanced in age, who
fight with each other constantly but at the same time seem to be really
fond of one another and would never think of separating, does not fail
to impress even an inexperienced observer. Usually little can be done to
change the relationship. Quite often when a couple of this variety comes
for help, their request is not for a change in the marital relationship but
for something else — often support of a rather mundane nature. Their
actual need, which is often overlooked in the heat of ever-present arguments,
might well be for their children to pay more attention to them; the psychotherapist's help is enlisted not to remedy the marriage situation but to
call on the children to visit more often.

Syndromes involving an extreme marital imbalance (that is, in which
one partner is clearly dominant over the other) are frequently described.
Among these are the sadomasochistic marriage and the marriage best
described as the mother-son or father-daughter marriage, each with its

characteristic problems. These types of marriages have a common characteristic treatment hazard: the weaker partner always seems to invite the therapist to side with him or her against the stronger one. Since therapists are in the habit of serving the infirm, the danger for conjoint therapy is that the therapist might take sides and choose to treat the weaker one, resulting in the stronger partner sitting in the background feeling "healthy." If therapy is not to come to grief, it is vital that the dominant partner be considered and given attention and credit for his or her strengths as well as support for his weaknesses. It is often advisable when treating marriages with a pronounced social imbalance or sadomasochistic marriages to address oneself primarily to the more active, sadistic, or dominant partner, recognizing that the sadism may arise from a hidden depression or disappointment with the weaker partner. In these situations "changing the patient" may be the therapy of choice. In other words, the person who seeks treatment is usually the weaker of the two and is ready to complain about the spouse, who is described as strong and evil. The weaker partner can be dismissed, and the stronger partner invited to become the patient. After initial protestations, the dominant partner often comes to appreciate the attention inherent in patient status and may relax his sadistic pressure, which, in turn, will permit the weaker partner to grow. The technique of choosing one's patient has been described by Grotjahn [8]. Focusing on the dominant partner may, indeed, be accomplished within a conjoint therapy or, as described, by "switching the patient role." In any case, as a rule, the therapist might remember that in an imbalanced marital relation, he should resist the natural temptation to side with the weaker partner and try instead to deal with the stronger one.

Psychosis in one of the spouses has sometimes been considered a contraindication for conjoint therapy [10]. Indeed, the combination of a ruthless, perhaps obsessional, character disorder and a helplessly schizophrenic spouse, in which psychosis and marital alienation are present, would appear to be treatable only if the couple separates. However, when the dominant, nonpsychotic member of the marriage is willing to support the sick spouse and at the same time allow her or him some autonomy, much can be done to make conjoint therapy viable. Often it becomes the only method by which a psychotic patient can be successfully treated. In a psychotic state a conjoint situation may be perceived as safer than an individual relationship.

CASE 13   A masochistic woman repeatedly made suicidal attempts, even after becoming
established in treatment with a male psychiatrist. A conjoint therapy situation, led
by a female caseworker, permitted a change. The husband came to see what some of
his actions in dealing with daily realities meant to his wife. She had perceived him, in
analogy to her father, as depriving her of her identity and doing everything better than
she could. Guidance of the female patient by the caseworker and a diminishing of
the husband's compulsive defenses led to a workable situation, and both spouses could
once again attend to their tasks.

A syndrome of excessive disparity has been described by Martin and
Bird as "the lovesick wife and the coldsick husband" [21]. The authors
did not postulate this syndrome as a good indication for conjoint therapy
but rather advocated cooperative therapy with two therapists. The title
of the syndrome is descriptive and refers to a husband, perhaps involved
in technical or scientific work, with poor ability to relate to people and
emotions but with considerable skill with material things or figures, and
to a wife who depends heavily on emotions and people and finds herself
frequently disappointed by her husband's strongly contrasting attitudes.
The syndrome is related to what is described elsewhere as the *hysterical
marriage* (Chap. 19).

Conjoint marital therapy may prove its value in other situations which
are often resistant to individual treatment. The effect of marital stress
on alcoholism, for example, is too well known to require discussion at
length here. In suitable cases, conjoint marital treatment may lead to
better results than treatment of the alcoholic alone. In many of these cases
and similar ones, the supportive aspect of the marital relationship in therapy
is paramount. While a great deal of exploring in terms of past history is
sometimes not possible or necessary, improved communications and the
creation of mutual support in the marriage may go a long way in remedying
a crisis situation.

REFERENCES

1.   Ackerman, N. Disturbances of Marital Pairs. In *The Psychodynamics of Family
      Life* (1st ed.). New York: Basic Books, 1958. Chap. 10.
2.   Ackerman, N. The Family Approach to Marital Disorders. In B. Greene (Ed.),
      The Psychotherapies of Marital Disharmony. New York: Free Press, 1965.
3.   Balint, E. Marital conflicts and their therapy. *Comprehensive Psychiatry*
      7:403, 1966.

4.   Brody, S.   Simultaneous Psychotherapy of Married Couples.   In J. Masserman (Ed.), *Current Psychiatric Therapies*. New York: Grune & Stratton, 1961.

5.   Giovacchini, P. L.   Treatment of Marital Disharmonies: The Classical Approach. In B. Greene (Ed.), *The Psychotherapies of Marital Disharmony*. New York: Free Press, 1965.

6.   Greene, B., and Solomon, A.   Marital disharmony: Concurrent psychoanalytic therapy of husband and wife by the same psychiatrist. *American Journal of Psychotherapy* 17:443, 1963.

7.   Greene, B., Broadhurst, B., and Lustig, N.   Treatment of Marital Disharmony: The Use of Individual, Concurrent and Conjoint Sessions as a Combined Approach. In B. Greene (Ed.), *Psychotherapies of Marital Disharmony*. New York: Free Press, 1965.

8.   Grotjahn, M.   *Psychoanalysis and the Family Neurosis*. New York: Norton, 1960.

9.   Grunebaum, H., and Christ, J.   Interpretation and the task of the therapist with couples and families. *International Journal of Group Psychotherapy* 18:495, 1968.

10.   Grunebaum, H., Christ, J., and Neiberg, N.   Diagnosis and treatment planning for couples. *International Journal of Group Psychotherapy* 19:185, 1969.

11.   Haley, J.   Marriage therapy. *Archives of General Psychiatry* 8:213, 1963.

12.   Haley, J.   Marriage Therapy. In *Strategies of Psychotherapy*. New York: Grune & Stratton, 1963. Chap. 6.

13.   Kohl, P.   Pathological reactions of marital partners to improvement of patients. *American Journal of Psychiatry* 118:1036, 1962.

14.   Lederer, H., and Jackson, D.   *Mirages of Marriage*. New York: Norton, 1968.

15.   Leichter, E.   Group psychotherapy of married couples' groups: Some characteristic treatment dynamics. *International Journal of Group Psychotherapy* 12:154, 1962.

16.   Linden, M., Goodwin, H., and Resnik, H.   Group psychotherapy of couples in marriage counseling. *International Journal of Group Psychotherapy* 18:313, 1968.

17.   Lussheimer, P.   The diagnosis of marital conflict. *American Journal of Psychoanalysis* 27:127, 1967.

18.   Main, T. F.   Mutual projection in a marriage. *Comprehensive Psychiatry* 7:432, 1966.

19.   Mann, A. M., and Lundell, F. W.   Psychotherapy of marital partners: A critique and re-evaluation. *Canadian Psychiatric Association* 9:313, 1964.

20.   Martin, P.   Treatment of Marital Disharmony by Collaborative Therapy. In B. Greene (Ed.), *Psychotherapies of Marital Disharmony*. New York: Free Press, 1965.

21.   Martin, P., and Bird, H. W.   An approach to the psychotherapy of marriage partners: The stereoscopic technique. *Psychiatry* 16:123, 1953.

22.   Mittelman, B.   The concurrent analysis of married couples. *Psychoanalytic Quarterly* 17:182, 1948.

23. Mudd, E., and Goodwin, H. Counseling couples in conflicted marriages. In B. Greene (Ed.), *Psychotherapies of Marital Disharmony.* New York: Free Press, 1965.

24. Nadelson, C., Bassuk, E., Hopps, C., and Boutelle, W. Evaluation procedures for conjoint marital psychotherapy. *Social Casework* 56(2):91, 1975.

25. Nadelson, C., Bassuk, E., Hopps, C., and Boutelle, W. Conjoint Marital Psychotherapy. Unpublished paper, 1973.

26. Oberndorf, C. P. Psychoanalysis of married couples. *Psychoanalytic Review* 25:453, 1938.

27. Pollack, O. Sociological and Psychoanalytic Concepts in Family Diagnosis. In B. Greene (Ed.), *Psychotherapies of Marital Disharmony.* New York: Free Press, 1965.

28. Rabkin, R. Uncoordinated communication between marriage partners. *Family Process* 6:10, 1967.

29. Sager, C. The Treatment of Married Couples. In S. Arieti (Ed.), *American Handbook of Psychiatry*, Vol. 3. New York: Basic Books, 1966. Pp. 213–225.

30. Sager, C. The conjoint session in marriage therapy. *American Journal of Psychoanalysis* 27:139, 1967.

31. Sager, C. Transference in the conjoint therapy of married couples. *Archives of General Psychiatry* 16:185, 1967.

32, Sager, C. Marital Psychotherapy. In J. Masserman (Ed.), *Current Psychiatric Therapies.* New York: Grune & Stratton, 1967. Pp. 92–102.

33. Satir, V. *Conjoint Family Therapy.* Palo Alto, Calif.: Science and Behavior Books, 1964.

34. Satir, V. Conjoint Marital Therapy. In B. Greene (Ed.), *Psychotherapies of Marital Disharmony.* New York: Free Press, 1965.

35. Watson, A. S. The conjoint psychotherapy of marriage partners. *American Journal of Orthopsychiatry* 33:912, 1963.

17

The Group Psychotherapy of Married Couples

Norman A. Neiberg

Since the emergence, following World War II, of group psychotherapy as a viable therapeutic tool, there has been a gradual spreading of its application to the treatment of various kinds of problems. The specialized application of group psychotherapy to the treatment of marital couples is a logical development. The issues, the dynamics, and the potentialities of a group, which are the province of group psychotherapy, are available regardless of the population being treated. Each problem area, however, focuses and highlights specific aspects of group function as well as presents specific problems. In this context the group psychotherapy of married couples occupies a position somewhere between the treatment of totally separate persons, who meet only for their group psychotherapy and then go their separate ways, and the treatment of a family by a group technique where members all live together during an entire week. In spite of current controversy, it appears to be only a matter of semantics as to whether one views a married-couples group as closer to the family model or closer to the individual model. The crucial issue is how one takes into account the specific problems of this population and deals with them in the framework of the group.

Marriage is the coming together of two persons, each with a unique life history, under a legal contract that, in a more or less permanent way, binds them together for mutual need satisfaction and problem-solving. Usually, the initial bond is that of early love or infatuation. In many marriages the initial contract does not involve this stage of initial love, and thus much of the binding force necessary for adjustment is missing. Marriage will remain stable so long as mutual need satisfaction occurs. Marital disruptions will occur either from the beginning, if the contract is viewed frivolously, or later on in the relationship, when the initial issues of the contract are lost or when events occur that somehow upset the capacity of either partner to deal effectively with the other or himself. The simple fact is that marriages in equilibrium, regardless of how neurotic or psychotic they may appear to the observer, do not appear as candidates for treatment, so long as the partners perceive and experience a sense of mutual need satisfaction. It may thus be deduced that for any couple who present themselves for marital therapy, something has happened to upset the equilibrium. Chapter 14 delineates an outline for the diagnosis of couples that implies a series of relevant treatments, among which is group psychotherapy for the couple. Others, notably Ard [1], Couch [3], and Flint and MacLennan [5] have described their criteria for the inclusion of couples in group psychotherapy. Ard suggests selecting couples who display the following characteristics: (1) acting out, (2) unawareness of feelings, (3) sadomasochistic relationships or (in Ard's language, victim-offender styles), and (4) communication and cooperation. These last two criteria are central to my conception of the diagnostic process. While there are many formats for work with married couples, group psycho-therapy seems to be the treatment of choice when problems are chronic and ego-syntonic. This is not meant to preclude any concurrent indi-vidual treatment but to point out the treatment of choice.

REFERRAL

In the schema alluded to above, couples are referred to groups on the basis of, among other factors, the nature of the initial referral. Couples may be referred by other professionals, when, in the course of other psycho-therapeutic intervention, the marriage itself or its use as a resistance to change or its sudden imbalance caused by changes in one partner becomes the center of focus. Often the referral.is made for inclusion in a group.

In referrals by other professionals, much work has usually been done; many of the basic diagnostic issues are clear and decisions can be made relatively easily by the group therapist. When the couple comes with no prior referral, the case is more complicated, and the diagnostic evaluation must start from the beginning. Sometimes only one partner appears, and in the initial screening it is clear that the major sources of tension lie in the interaction between the marital partners. The problem is that of attempting to move the individual to consider treatment as a couple as a more efficient and economical way of resolving tensions.

Essentially, the diagnostic process attempts to ascertain whether the individuals are committed to their marriage, whether the symptoms arise only from the marriage, and whether the problems are acute and ego-alien or chronic and ego-syntonic. To the extent to which they are ego-syntonic, group therapy is the indicated treatment. It does seem possible that problems that are acute and ego-alien could be treated by group techniques, provided the therapist could compose a group of persons with similar problems. In the typical clinic or private practice this seems somewhat impractical, although it appears that the general techniques of crisis intervention with this pairing of acute and ego-alien problems are as applicable to small groups as they are to individuals. Often I must make a further decision as to which married-couples group suits which married couple. Two extreme categories of marriage are (1) those in which decompensation has occurred and (2) those in which it appears that the couples have never really known each other. Since the issues of ego development and narcissistic involvement are so different and the problems of technical management so challenging, it is more profitable not to mix couples from these two categories.

Yalom [10] refers to the ideal group balance between heterogeneity and homogeneity as being that mix which provides optimal diversity coupled with enough similarity so that cohesion can occur. This is as true for couples groups as it is for other types of groups. With the position of this mix, the previously mentioned psychological decision based on the capacity for object relatedness is only one of many possible dimensions. Another useful approach to group composition lies in the conceptualization of marriage as a developmental process, with an attempt to place couples with at least proximate developmental issues in the same groups. This approach tends to take care of age discrepancies and other relevant variables automatically.

The normative developmental crises of marriage are viewed in this discussion as distinct from individual psychopathology or individual crises of development. These factors may or may not be the same, and the attempt to strike a balance among them as a basis for forming groups is extremely difficult. Whether an individual is fixated or has regressed to any given stage of development — oral, anal, phallic — or instead, in Eriksonian [4] terms, has progressed to a level of basic trust (versus mistrust) or autonomy (versus shame and doubt) relates to the way the person copes with the developmental crisis of the marriage but does not define the marital crisis. The marital developmental stages may be categorized as follows: (1) dating, (2) courtship, (3) engagement, (4) marriage proper, (5) getting acquainted, (6) the first pregnancy, (7) first birth, (8) subsequent births and childbearing, (9) adolescence and letting go, (10) alone together, (11) grandparenting, (12) retirement, and (13) death of a spouse. Obviously, these stages are marked by some major crises and, perhaps, disasters. People build a solid marriage around successful coping, not around a crisis precipitated by entry into a new stage. In my experience, people always present one of the above as the specific issue that brings them to treatment. Often the problem is obscured, and the couple simply complains that they just can't seem to communicate. However, the precipitating event is more specific. It is my experience that couples who are reasonably well matched in regard to mental issues tend to do well together in groups. It appears that, when matching follows the above criteria, other so-called problems, such as differences in education, job success, and ethnic background, do not present major problems.

Other parameters that may be relevant in assigning persons to married-couples groups are individual ego development, capacity to communicate verbally, capacity to inhibit response, duration of symptoms, and so on. The problem is not one of defining parameters but of determining which parameters are most relevant.

THE AGREEMENT

In my experience, the explicit contract between patient (or couple) and therapist is central. It seems to me that deviant behavior and acting out can be interpreted only if there is an agreed on baseline; it is best that this baseline be clear and explicit. When, in an initial interview, it is felt that couples group therapy is the indicated treatment, the screening procedure and orientation proceed essentially as follows. Both partners agree to work on the problem together. If this contract cannot be made, either the initial diagnostic assessment is incorrect or continued exploration of resistances is indicated. The agreement is essentially similar to that in other therapeutic situations — the partners agree to be there, to be on time, to notify the therapist in advance when they cannot be there, to pay their bills promptly, refrain from physical violence, that termination is "group business," that when one partner cannot attend a session, the other partner is expected to be there, and, finally, that any contact between couples outside the group that affects how persons feel in the group is group business.

A distinction must be made between the couple's agreeing to work together and their having to stay together. From the beginning the therapist's stance must be one of disinterest as to whether the marriage continues or not. The focus is always on assisting two individuals to work out their destiny; whether they choose ultimately to do it alone or together is a free choice that they must make themselves. Often beginning therapists sound more like lawyers or judges trying to arbitrate than like psychotherapists trying to understand and lead individuals to an awareness of those problems that are hidden.

THE GROUP

Yalom [10] delineated 10 curative factors in groups: (1) imparting of information, (2) instillation of hope, (3) universality, (4) altruism, (5) the corrective recapitulation of the primary family group, (6) development of socializing techniques, (7) imitative behavior, (8) interpersonal learning, (9) group cohesiveness, and (10) catharsis. These factors are as relevant for married couples as they are for others. It might, however, be wise to delineate some specific aspects of married-couples groups that might make them preferable to conjoint or other forms of therapy. When couples arrive at the group, regardless of the feeling of emotional distance or closeness, they are usually so intertwined that they have lost their capacity for observation and distancing, which are aids to understanding. But when the new couple observes the group interactions, which inevitably are like their own, they come to feel that they are in a safe situation, a reaction that is so necessary for further observation and the establishment of patterns leading to exploration and understanding. This relatively rapid identification often contributes to the feelings of symptomatic relief that couples experience early in group psychotherapy. The change is a temporary one, and hard work is needed to solve their problems. A good rule is that the group therapist tries by his interventions to recreate the difficulties of a particular couple with a member or members of another couple, thereby breaking, or at least displacing, the pathological bond between partners. Thus one of the technical goals is to have Mr. A. begin to experience the same difficulties with Mrs. B. that he has with his own spouse. In attempting to accomplish this, the therapist can reinforce those responses that relate to interaction across couples rather than those remarks related to interaction within a couple. This technical maneuver varies, depending on what stage the group is at and what the issues are.

CASE 1   Mr. and Mrs. A. came to the group with a long history of fighting and arguing. It was clear quite early that her somewhat hysterical nature was chronically frustrated by his distant intellectual approach. These clashes were brought to the group, but all attempts by the peers or by the group leader to intervene in the patho-logical interaction were fruitless.

   Mr. and Mrs. B., members of the same group, had similar difficulties but with the roles reversed. Mr. B. was the warmer and more tender while Mrs. B. (in the same profession as her husband) was more distant and aloof.

   After several months the relationships between these couples intensified, with Mr. A. beginning to complain about and react strongly to Mrs. B.'s manner. This finally came to a head when he told her that she was unbearable and that he could see why her husband was so chronically upset.

   In keeping with the exploitation of cross-couple affect, the therapist turned to Mrs. A. and Mr. B and commented that the remark sounded like a billiard shot. The reaction was intense, prolonged and anxiety laden as the two couples began to look more clearly at what they had been doing to one another and to themselves.

CASE 2   Mr. C., a passive man, was married to an aggressive, domineering woman who continually cut him off and attempted to do his thinking for him. For many months, he attempted to be more assertive, both alone and with the group's help. Whether the focus was on his passivity or her aggressiveness, no progress in developing a more balanced relationship was being made.

   Mrs. D. in the group was very similar to Mrs. C. At one meeting she interrupted Mr. C. He exploded and vented what seemed like 10 years of pent-up frustration on Mrs. D., the displacement object. With the group's support and the leaders focusing on the here-and-now reality incident and hurt, Mr. C. began to deal effectively with Mrs. D. and in the next few meetings was openly asserting himself with his wife, who, by then, was beginning to be less defensive.

In this incident, the therapist exploited the here-and-now affect across the couples, and, because of Mr. C.'s hyperdefensiveness, made no attempt to bring the issue of Mr. C.'s feeling directly to her. After several weeks the group and the C. couple were able to talk and feel openly about being "cut off" and about the pent-up rage. In these latter exchanges, cross-couple conflict was spontaneously related by all to intramarital events and history.

While all groups and all psychotherapies are somewhat of a mix between intellect and emotions, my own orientation is that affective experience and affective learning are the vital ingredients and that intellectual comprehension, as distinct from intellectualization, is a natural outgrowth of the integrating experience of discovering new or hidden aspects of one's own personality. Therefore, it is expected in groups that, for many reasons, people will recreate their bedroom and kitchen arguments. Often, this is done as a way of saying hello to the group and letting people know what life is really like for them. When groups become locked in a contest of which couple can yell the loudest or which is the most woebegone, the group members are walking the same treadmill that brought them to the group. One must examine these contests, for perhaps there are more subtle conflicts which the fights protect the combatants against.

Often therapists are concerned that intimate sexual material cannot be dealt with effectively in groups. My own observation is that, to the extent to which the leader pursues issues as they arise, no subject is too difficult for a group to handle. Perhaps much of what is considered too difficult for groups represents the therapist's countertransference attitudes and inhibitions rather than inherent difficulties.

After persons or couples identify bits of themselves in others, they usually begin to attempt to resolve problems in other persons' marriages by giving advice. This attempt inevitably fails, and the members are confronted with the realizations that they need to change fundamentally if things are going to be different and that living together in a dynamic ongoing relationship requires more than playing the game. As the group progresses to middle phases of treatment, the major problems are those of closeness and distance, separation and togetherness, and how much each person is willing to surrender to the marriage or to the group in order to profit from the relationship. How can two such different beings as a man and a woman be close and yet separate, be apart yet together? Against this basic biological distinction, other differences seem to fade away.

As part of this ongoing middle phase, much historical material is introduced, usually as it relates to the peer or leadership transferences that develop. Historical material that arises from the here-and-now effect of the group seems especially relevant, whereas historical material of the story-telling type is sterile and unproductive. As persons in the group are able to work out with each other problems of belonging and closeness, with their partner or with someone else, there seem to be parallel changes within the various marital relationships.

As individuation and mutual respect proceed, there comes a time to terminate the therapy. In married-couples groups this is an especially sensitive point. In addition to what the group has recreated historically, the members have often socialized with one another and even entertained one another for the first time in a group context, and moving to a wider world is often poignant for all concerned. I have observed that many couples continue their relationships after termination of group therapy and have become lasting friends. While this may be interpreted as an incomplete resolution of the group transference, it appears to me much more a reflection of how real and integral a part of their lives the whole process of sharing and becoming closer has become.

While leadership styles may vary, it would appear that for any procedure to be successful a climate must be created within which it becomes possible to try what has been untried before, to experience what has been forbidden before, to be close when one has had to flee, and to be separate when one needs to be separate. In general, the environment of the group is one of freedom within boundaries defined by the contract. The capacity of the therapist to stay in the middle and to focus on the process allows him to facilitate change through his technical skill as well as to offer himself as a model for identification.

Other authors have slightly different views of the leader's task. Ard [1] focuses on the interaction between persons. Blinder [2] adopts an interpersonal approach based on the assumption that mate selection is highly specific and designed to gratify both mature and neurotic needs and that, when disappointment occurs, there is reciprocal dislocation, disturbed communication, frustrated dependency, and fears of the unfamiliar. Henderson [7] focuses on resistance to change and delineates three types of resistance: (1) classic psychoanalytic resistance, (2) avoidance that is motivated by fear of external control, and (3) fear of ridicule and reproach. Henker [8] focuses on the working of the marriage as a unit. This latter operation I tend to let occur more passively, while I focus on the needs and wants of the individuals and how they are inhibited or facilitated by others, specifically by the spouses. Linden [9] in a somewhat specific delineation of the efficacy of this approach to married couples notes that married-couples groups tend to (1) facilitate communication, (2) develop a group superego, (3) foster an acceptance of peer interpretation, (4) facilitate generalization, (5) reduce regressive behavior, (6) serve as a medium of socialization, (7) serve as a medium of stimulus and support, (8) dilute pathological defenses, (9) dilute transference,[1] and (10) permit reality testing.

LEADERSHIP

For heuristic reasons, it would appear that having couples lead a married-couples group makes eminent sense. My own experience is in single leadership. I have not found any obvious limitations in my practice using this technique. In groups that are co-led by either a couple or nonrelated co-leaders, complications of co-leadership may arise; to the extent to which co-leaders are unable to work through and face issues between themselves, the groups reflect the leadership conflict much as the patients in their childhoods reflected parental conflict. If these communication issues are of major importance, there are probably severe limitations as to what can be worked through in the group, although often couples groups have a very salutary effect on problems between the couples in the roles of leadership. Obviously, with single leadership, there are also intrinsic difficulties; specifically, (1) the leader does not have a co-leader to help him observe his own blind spots (although groups are usually all too ready to point them out anyway), and (2) since the single leader represents only one sex, members of the opposite sex may feel they are unequally represented. To the extent that this is a problem for the leader, it will be a problem for the group. Transference relationships seem to develop with a single leader much as they do with co-leaders, although transferences

---

[1]I believe that the transferences in groups are not diluted but are different. While the direct leader-patient transference appears more diminished, in fact, group support may make it stronger. In addition, the opportunity for multiple transference to present peer figures greatly complicates the transference issue in groups as opposed to that in one-to-one psychotherapy.

involving those of the same sex as the leader develop somewhat more slowly, because such transferences are more anxiety laden than those between men and women.

SUMMARY

The preceding discussion is an overview of group psychotherapy of married couples drawn primarily from my own clinical experience. I have attempted to highlight issues of referral, screening, problems of the group, issues of leadership, issues of contract, and, in addition, to delineate some typical behaviors in the development of the groups.

REFERENCES

1.   Ard, B., and Ard, C. *Handbook of Marriage Counseling.* Palo Alto, Calif.: Science and Behavior Books, 1969.
2.   Blinder, M. G.   The technique of married couple group therapy. *Archives of General Psychiatry* 17:44, 1967.
3.   Couch, E. H. *Joint and Family Interviews in the Treatment of Marital Problems.* Boston: Family Services, 1969.
4.   Erikson, E. H. *Childhood and Society.* New York: Norton, 1950.
5.   Flint, A. A., and MacLennan, B. W.   Some dynamic factors in marital group therapy. *International Journal of Group Psychotherapy* 12:355, 1962.
6.   Grunebaum, H., Christ, J., and Neiberg, N. A.   Diagnosis and treatment planning for couples. *International Journal of Group Psychotherapy* 12:185, 1969.
7.   Henderson, N. B.   Married group therapy: A setting for reducing resistances. *Psychological Reports* 16:347, 1965.
8.   Henker, F. O.   Married couples group in therapy of psychoneuroses. *Southern Medical Journal* 55:401, 1962.
9.   Linden, M. E., et al.   Group psychotherapy of couples in marriage counseling. *International Journal of Group Psychotherapy* 18:313, 1968.
10. Yalom, I. D. *The Theory and Practice of Group Psychotherapy.* New York: Basic Books, 1970.

18

Therapy of
Sexual Dysfunctions

Avodah K. Offit

This is a time in the history of psychotherapy when new methods are essential to progress. Although in-depth psychoanalysis is an important element of therapy for psychosexual problems, there is a great need for the rapid treatment of specific sexual dysfunctions.

The broad historical antecedents of sex therapy will be discussed in this chapter, which will also outline important principles and illustrate their application with reference to case histories. These are composites of the histories of couples I have treated in private practice, at the Lenox Hill Hospital Sexual Therapy and Consultation Center and at New York Hospital.

Many people have extraordinary misconceptions about sex therapy. Some people are suspicious; others are hostile. One of the most common misconceptions is that sex therapy consists of a set of stereotyped instructions to the couple, who then press the appropriate anatomical buttons and wait a prescribed length of time; a catalytic reaction takes place and orgasmic potency, sexual freedom, loss of inhibition, and a rapaciously lusty appetite follow. All this, however exciting, is not really good spiritually. Obviously, such therapy would take all the joy and spontaneity out of lovemaking. Besides, what about privacy and

poetry and love and philosophy? Patients and public alike are afraid they
will be treated like laboratory animals and will emerge as sexual zombies,
just as people feared in the early days of psychoanalysis that its products
would come off an assembly line as lifeless, guiltless psychopaths.

Sex therapy — fortunately or not, depending on one's viewpoint —
will not turn most people into sexual machines capable of performance
and conquest on all occasions, nor is it intended to.

BACKGROUND

Why has sex therapy emerged as a specific discipline in the second half
of the twentieth century? And why especially in America? The French
regard sex as love, the British consider it a sport, the Italians respect sex as
an art, to the Germans it is aggression, and to the Americans sex is a
science. Perhaps there is an answer in the idea that America is a leader
in technology — from the technology of selling detergents to how to find
peace of mind. These are superficial reflections on the complex evolution
of sexual change in response to economic and social change. The bans
on sexual expression are gradually being lifted simply because modern
society is less threatened by sexual freedom than previously. Sigmund
Freud believed that society curbed sexuality because it was afraid its very
fabric would be destroyed by free erotic expression. It may be that we
will yet see a return to sexual rigidity in America under certain predictable
conditions.

Sexual change, then, is responsive to economic and social influences,
but why? After all, have human beings not copulated in the same ways
throughout history? Yes, but modern civilization has been proceeding
in two paradoxical directions. One direction is toward increasing distribution of national wealth among more individuals. Along with this has
come codification of the laws of property possession, so that the owner
of material goods need not fear that they will be taken from him by
force during his lifetime. Therefore, there is freedom to expand the
population. There is also freedom to control that expansion through birth-
control devices and abortion. The result is, theoretically at least, the new
sexual freedom of which we are all aware.

Paradoxically, civilization has maintained its tradition of periodic war
between nations. War and stress invoke sexual repression at times when

battle is a testimony to belief. To be a warrior means to abstain from the fleshpots, to curb the desire for wine and lechery and the long sleep. America had to fight for her independence, conquer a wilderness, engage in civil strife, and fight two exhausting wars to preserve her status among nations, in addition to the conflicts of 1812, 1898, Korea, and Vietnam. Lust may be satisfied or love renewed in the moments after battle.

"Make love, not war" was a slogan reflecting disillusionment with our last war. While the battle that one believes in is being fought, however, love and sex are frequently considered preoccupations of the weak. They are immoral and wrong if indulged beyond a minimum necessary for emotional survival. Should America become involved in another grim war, the bans on sex may be established again.[1]

Not only does America have her own tradition of war, she has also inherited the British traditions. England, after all, was the most powerful and bellicose nation in the world a little less than a century ago. In the reign of Queen Victoria masturbation was considered sinful and un-healthy, and in both America and England it was the explicit duty of every good mother to defend her child against feeling or displaying signs of sexuality. The clitoridectomy — removal of the clitoris of a bad little girl — and burning the clitoris with a hot iron were medical procedures that are rarely recorded in medical history texts. Examples of the horrendous effects of other sexual practices are legion in the work of Krafft-Ebing.

Against this background, Freud and Havelock Ellis appear incredibly courageous. If public reaction today to sexual themes is only a fraction of what it was in the nineteenth century, Freud must have been a lion indeed.

Freud and Ellis brought science to sexuality. And the science of psychology and psychiatry has flourished in America as nowhere else. Sex had been investigated in Germany before Hitler by Magnus Hirshfeld and his institute, but the institute, together with all its documentation, was burned. Sexuality has always been more acceptable in the Scandinavian countries than in America, perhaps because of their less-pressured Lutheran heritage. The Russians proclaimed sexual freedom to be a state necessity in the early twentieth century. Europe at large has a tradition of sexual

---

[1]In 1973, the Supreme Court voted to create local options for censorship of sexual material. It seems meaningful that this removal of more liberal decisions came at a time when the nation was in the throes of the moral crisis provoked by Watergate.

sophistication which combines piety and lechery in a curious potpourri that reflects the enormous attempt and the enormous failure of Christianity to eradicate nonreproductive sexual pleasure. America was left to undertake as a national investigation what had formerly been the province of individual hypotheses.

In America the Puritan-Calvinist heritage has been the most influential repressive force, in war as in peace. The inhibiting effect of religious precepts on sexuality needs no emphasis. More interesting is the product of religious morality known as the work ethic. It is interesting to speculate that the modern scientific exploration of sexual behavior is an outgrowth of the work ethic applied to this new field. Our Calvinist-Puritan heritage has its good uses. Sex therapy may have emerged as a natural consequence of Kinsey's studies and of all those studies that preceded and followed.

Many of these factors have contributed to the modern interest in sex therapy. The original work ethic holds sexual pleasure in open contempt, although there is reason to believe that our Puritan ancestors were lustier than conventional histories tell us. Many people are still committed to the work ethic, and these people comprise the majority of sex patients. They have worked so hard and have been so good that they really do not know how to enjoy themselves. But that is not what brings them to the sex therapist. It may well be that they come to get a quick education in how to achieve another success. The emphasis is on *quick* because for these people anything related to sex that might take a long time would be guilt-provoking. The word *achievement* is used because enterprises involving pleasure as a goal are still frowned on in America. The fact that violence is acceptable in motion pictures goes virtually unchallenged, but overt sexual pleasure remains controversial. It is characteristic that one of the most critically accepted of the films dealing with lust — *The Last Tango in Paris* — is sexually sadistic and ends with a nice clean shooting.

People who seek sex therapy have relatively conventional values. Many are greatly repressed by religious convictions or a strong sense of the sinfulness of sex, which they have absorbed from the social milieu and the family. Parents, schools, the church, and the law have reinforced negative attitudes. These people have become more sensitive to the positive aspects of sexuality through the media. Those seeking sexual therapy have identified their problem. The majority of them have a fair degree of emotional sturdiness; it takes stamina to tell a stranger that one is impotent, or frigid, or suffers from premature ejaculation. These are not people who suffer sexual repression in the old psychoanalytic sense; they are concerned with the faulty expression of their sexuality. Once they have stated their problems, they are frequently inhibited about talking freely, but helping them do so is the therapist's job.

Sex therapy emerged against this background, but each person has a unique history in which religious, social, or familial restraints may dominate. The background of the sexually dysfunctional individual may also include an assortment of specific traumas: parental psychopathology, unusual sexual behavior within the family, the early loss of a parent through death or separation, and so on. These traumas may be reflected in the patient's sexual dysfunction, or additional interpersonal or intrapersonal difficulties may have arisen that have no specific relationship to early family experience: a harmful initial sexual episode, work problems, difficulties with children.

TRAINING OF THE SEX THERAPIST

Just as sex therapy is not a matter of giving a patient a collection of simple rules to follow, so the training of a sex therapist is not a quick and easy procedure. In the training program for sex therapists at Lenox Hill Hospital, modeled on that at the Payne Whitney Psychiatric Clinic of the New York Hospital—Cornell University Medical Center,[2] trainees must participate in the program a full year before they are qualified to enter private practice.

Although treatment is directed toward the sexual symptom, the therapist must have a background in analytic work and be competent in marital and couples therapy, group therapy, transactional work, and the various modalities of behavior therapy, such as assertive training and desensitization. Knowledge of organic disorders and pharmacologic agents affecting sexuality must be acquired or reviewed.

Training in the kind of sex therapy taught at these institutions takes time because it is important not only that the therapist have a number of

[2]The Sexual Treatment and Education Program of the Payne Whitney Psychiatric Clinic of the New York Hospital was founded by Helen S. Kaplan, M.D., Ph.D. For a fuller presentation of therapeutic techniques, the author recommends *The New Sex Therapy* by Helen S. Kaplan, Brunner-Mazel, New York, 1974.

techniques available for understanding and treating patients but also that
the therapist coordinate and develop an individual style. This style must
be creative within limits and should judiciously combine activity and
passivity. The therapist must be comfortable in an active role. Listening
and allowing patients to cure themselves is not effective. It also takes time
to know which cases to accept and which to reject. Most important, it
simply requires time to experience a number of cases of the same dysfunction, to appreciate the variety in each category, and to develop a
flexible approach.

Finally, each therapist must resolve his or her sexual anxieties, as these
will inevitably affect the therapy. No matter how free, open, and mature
one may think one is, there is often an appreciable hidden conflict,
anxiety, or guilt which must be resolved. For example, one staff member,
deeply influenced by Freudian analytic concepts, had to struggle with
herself to give up the idea that a "vaginal" orgasm was more psychosexually mature than one induced by clitoral manipulation.

METHODS AND GOALS OF THERAPY

The most familiar approach to sex therapy is that of Masters and Johnson.
Their landmark book, *Human Sexual Inadequacy* [1], has publicized the
two-week format, the physical exam, the extensive history, the round-
table discussion, the magic of the motel room, the dual-therapy team.
Imitations of the original method abound, but none seem to reproduce it
exactly. Particularly difficult has been getting patients to spend a block
of two weeks in sexual activity. The new therapy, therefore, has pioneered
techniques which adapt the conventional psychotherapeutic time structure
to the demands of this new discipline.

Sex therapy in the office of an individual practitioner may proceed on
the basis of once- or twice-weekly visits. The patients and the therapist
talk; there is no sexual activity in the treatment room. A complete medical
history is taken, a review of systems is done, and mental status is evaluated.
Medical or sexological examination is performed if indicated by, among
other things, progressive impotence, in which case the possibility of
diabetes, testosterone deficit, or other organic etiology must be investigated.
Anorgasmic women and patients with vaginismus must bring a gyne-
cologist's report. Men who ejaculate prematurely generally require no

medical exam, and women who are orgasmic in masturbation but not during coitus are usually not examined, although even the slightest suspicion of a physical disorder must be investigated.

Treatment may continue for several months, although the actual time spent in treatment may be less than in a two-week program, with its pretreatment screening activity. Between visits, telephone contact with the therapist is encouraged. (This usually entails middle-of-the-night calls.)

While office treatment may seem disadvantageous, it has specific benefit because therapy continues in a home setting. With office treatment, most of the resistances and defenses against sexuality have to be worked out in the difficult circumstances to which the patients are normally exposed. Even if the children are ill, and the dog has distemper, and grandma resents the nursing home, and the roof has a leak, and it is income tax time, somehow patients must acquire an enthusiasm for the notion that sex can still go on. The therapist should also confront the compulsive work habits of many patients, which permit only brief and furtive trips to a private place to relieve tension by masturbation, if such people allow themselves sexual indulgence at all.

If the obstacles described above are overcome, it may be said, in astronaut jargon, that reentry problems are minimized. With office treatment, people have to learn to rearrange their lives for the better, and many are grateful for a lessening of tension even when the sexual problem is not eventually improved.

Although a dual-team approach to therapy, with one male and one female co-therapist, has become popular recently, a single psychotherapist can treat the sexual problems of a couple; teams do not seem to be necessary or economical. Nearly a decade of results bear out the validity of the single-therapist method. Therapists are trained to handle a multiplicity of problems, including sexual ones, not only on an individual basis with members of the same or opposite sex but also with couples and in groups; and they have been doing so for years. If a member of a marital pair has such negative feelings toward a therapist, feelings based on the therapist's sex, that he or she cannot speak openly and with trust to the therapist, that person needs more intensive treatment than any rapid therapy can provide. Of course, if a dual-team member has not had long-term training and experience in psychotherapy, it is advisable for that person to collaborate with someone who has.

What is the goal of sex therapy? It cannot and should not be distinguished from the aim of psychiatry: to heal the mind. Certainly most sexual symptoms are psychological in origin. The approach is to reduce the therapeutic procedure to the barest essentials for clinical efficacy. The kinds of problems that can be treated are quite limited, although patients have been referred for exhibitionism, castration attempts, difficulties with gender identity — problems that are not the province of specific short-term sexual therapy.

Couples are selected for therapy as carefully as possible on the basis of their commitment to their relationship and the recognition that they have a sexual problem impairing the relationship. This problem may be premature or retarded ejaculation, impotence, orgasmic dysfunction, or vaginismus. These are sexual dysfunctions, not deviations (such as fetishism) or variations (such as homosexuality). Patients with the best possible prognosis are sought; those with severe mental pathology or intense marital discord must receive different initial treatment. If the sexual symptom is clearly a defense against the emergence of other threatening psychopathology, sex therapy may be contraindicated.

CASE 1   A recently married older man who was impotent with his young wife was referred for therapy after his release from an out-of-state hospital, where he had been treated for depression and a suicide attempt. During the history-taking, he confessed that he had seduced his daughter when she was a young child and that they had sexual relations for approximately ten years. The daughter eventually married, and, according to her father, she was living happily with her husband and three small children. In trying to suppress his desire for his daughter, the father could not become sexually aroused by his wife. When talking about the dilemma, he showed signs of moving into another agitated depression. He was certainly not an appropriate candidate for short-term therapy.

Although patients with organic components to their dysfunction, such as impotence associated with diabetes, may be treated, an organic disorder that rules out any possibility of sexual competence, rules out sex therapy. Cases in which improvement will trigger a psychic casualty in the spouse are also not acceptable, although this most common adverse effect of sex therapy is the most difficult to anticipate as the following case illustrates.

CASE 2   A diabetic social worker who came to me for treatment had been told by his internist in a well-known clinic that his impotence was related to his diabetes and that he could not anticipate a return of function. For eight years he had been impotent with his wife, who said she wanted very much to have children. During this time, he explained, he had morning erections. I decided to accept this case for treatment because of the obvious contradiction between the medical diagnosis and the man's sexual potential. The patient's wife had been in therapy for many years to resolve her feelings of neglect by her father. It was extraordinarily difficult to elicit the wife's cooperation in adjusting to her husband's potential for intercourse in the morning, but she finally did adjust, and, ultimately, he was able to function whenever he wanted to. The better he felt, the more unhappy and inadequate she felt, particularly in regard to raising the family she had said she wanted. The last follow-up revealed that he was well but that she was in therapy again, trying to resolve her fear of loss and of motherhood in some other way than by making her husband impotent.

Patients suffering from drug or alcohol abuse or who must take a drug that has been known to interfere with sexual functioning, are not presently candidates for sex therapy. People whose life-styles preclude sexual interaction, in spite of sincere motivation to change, may not be accepted into sex therapy until they have made provision to alter their modes of avoidance (among them, jobs involving long unexpected separations and schoolwork or jobs that involve an inordinately high level of stress).

Although persons with active psychoses are not suitable candidates for therapy, there are individual cases in which severe psychiatric difficulty, particularly latent schizophrenia, does not contraindicate treatment. The patient may be able to improve his sexual behavior without disorganizing other adaptations. Acceptance of patients with neuroses and personality disorders depends on the judgment of the therapist as to severity and prognosis.

TECHNIQUES AND PROCEDURES

Some of the major sex-therapy techniques have been outlined by Masters and Johnson [1]. Others used in office therapy constitute original variations. The behavioral aspects of both approaches have a common origin.

One of the most widely known techniques is *sensate focus*. In sensate focus, the partners come to each other naked, rested, and in good spirits. One partner is designated the giver, and one the receiver. The giver touches the receiver in different ways — massaging, fondling, and tracing outlines — but avoiding genital areas in the first experience. The purpose of this approach is to eliminate the pressure for achieving orgasm and thus allow the partners to experience simple, sensuous pleasure. (Some psychiatrists consider this a regression to pregenital levels of stimulation.) The major goal of the technique is reduction of anxiety about performance or achievement and appreciation of the sensual, pleasurable qualities of touching and being touched.

Impotence and Orgasmic Dysfunction

Treatment of impotence in the male and orgasmic dysfunction in the female is based on the adoption of a "nondemand" strategy. Eliminating fear of performance for the female and both fear and the "spectator role" for the male are major goals. When the man plays a spectator role, he sees himself as if from a distance, critically observing the capacity of his penis to become erect and perform satisfactorily. He becomes impotent because he fears he will not meet his own or his partner's demands. Treatment may begin with sensate focus to relieve the pressure for sexual stimulation and observable response.

The principal assumption on which sex therapy is based is that sexual dysfunction has many causes. The psychoanalytic model may be applicable, but one must also search the patient's history for other elements. Experiential trauma, clear parental and religious inhibitions, blocks to sexual development imposed by obvious sociocultural pressures, failures in interpersonal communication between spouses, the dampening effects of preoccupation with economic striving or childrearing — anything that appears related to the problem presented may be a causal factor.

In the newer therapy, there is no standard operating procedure, such as sensate focus followed by stereotyped instructions according to the dysfunction. Instead, specific experiences are designed by the therapist with attention to the patient's psychological patterns and his or her previous modes of functioning. These experiences, to be carried out at home, are designed to increase eroticism and decrease obstacles to sexual fulfillment. There are many techniques for sensitive manipulation, and their use depends on the case. For example, the therapist may permit sexual activity or give instructions for abstinence. Sometimes the therapist may promote self-esteem and give assertive training; at other times, the therapist may determine that self-aggrandizement should be reduced and that the patient must learn aggression control. The therapist may sensitize patients to their physical feelings or desensitize their fears. The therapist may bypass early traumas or confront the patients with their destructive patterns of Oedipal rivalry, their separation anxiety, or their other core problems and anxieties.

Assertive training in a sexualized form is of great value to orgasmically dysfunctional women and impotent men. Such people either are too insecure to tell their partners what pleases them sexually and therefore they become sexually dysfunctional, or they become insecure about making specific requests because they cannot will their own orgasm or ejaculation.

Usually, the orgasmically dysfunctional woman cannot ask her husband to do what pleases her sexually. If she does not already know how, treatment begins with teaching her to masturbate to orgasm. Generally, this involves teaching awareness of genital sensation. Conversely, depending on the patient, it may involve training in the use of sexual fantasy to distract from anxiety, a method long used in behavior therapy for patients with nonsexual problems. It is an interesting variation to use in the sexual situation itself.

If progress is slow, a vibrating massager with a small smooth disc attachment may be recommended for producing the initial orgasms. This device is superior to the insertable type because it offers a more comfortable method of stimulating the clitoris and surrounding areas, makes less noise, and is potentially less hazardous. General Electric and Oster manufacture satisfactory instruments, which are not manufactured nor advertised as sexual stimulators. The vibrator should be used gently, and it should not be used to stimulate the clitoris directly. Once the woman achieves facility in vibrator-induced and then manual stimulation, she can instruct her husband in the method. It requires assertiveness for the wife to let her husband's hand rest on hers to guide him, to move his hand if necessary, or to tell him to do it faster, or slower, or with less pressure, or up higher, and to change as the phase of excitement changes. Women generally want to be passive during sexual stimulation, yet they must be active when directing it. (It can be quite astonishing to watch the ripple effect of this new assertiveness on other aspects of a patient's life.)

Frequently, men are made impotent by a similar inability to express themselves to women. While the psychotherapeutic route may enable a man to cope with a demanding parent and, ultimately, to become potent, the sex therapy method enables him to refuse to be pressured by his partner's demands. It also teaches the partner not to be demanding. A man has intercourse only when he wishes to, not when he is worried about his spouse's needs. His penis becomes erect when he is not experiencing anxiety. Erection is governed by the parasympathetic system; therefore, the man must be in a state of physiological and psychological comfort in order to maintain an erection. Anxiety can be therapeutically reduced by distraction from worries about performance, either by a competing erotic stimulus (fantasy) or by thoughts that do not provoke anxiety, such as counting his partner's freckles. Most often impotence occurs when the man is confronted with his partner's demand for satisfaction and he is afraid he will not meet it. He cannot bring himself to the point of not accepting this pressure, real or imagined, without therapeutic intervention. It is sometimes helpful, if time and finances permit, to continue assertive training with men and women after their sex-therapy goals have been achieved in order to help them resolve other problems of self-expression.

Reducing self-aggrandizement and teaching aggression control is most often useful with the spouse of the sexually dysfunctional person. The husband who constantly criticizes his wife should be taught not to express his negative thoughts impulsively. Often he first has to be taught to recognize how damaging his criticism is, as must the wife who boasts of her sexual insatiability and thus diminishes her husband's sense of adequacy.

CASE 3   Wendy, 35 years old, and Bob, 38 years old, had been married for three years. It was a second marriage for both. Wendy was a housewife who had never had coital orgasms with either husband, although before her first marriage, frictional body contact with a boyfriend while both were clothed had produced orgasm. She masturbated rarely, and with great guilt; and Bob's manual stimulation only infrequently brought her to orgasm. Wendy was a submissive, yielding, but passive-aggressive person, who was tearful throughout the first interview and deferred to her husband when asked to describe their sexual behavior.

Bob, a tall, athletic executive, prided himself on his leadership qualities and on his forthrightness. "I believe in being honest and getting it all on the table," he said often. "When I think Wendy's out of bounds, I tell her." At one point during the interview, he turned angrily to his wife. "Frankly," he said, "not only is our sex life lousy, but I cooked and cleaned better for myself when I was a bachelor."

Wendy sighed unhappily and explained that somehow the dinner was always getting burned and she was oddly unable to be as enthusiastic about domestic order as she once was. She became tearful, and Bob reached over to squeeze her affectionately on the shoulder. "If I didn't let you know how I felt, we would really have to split up," he said. "Right, honey?" Wendy nodded and wiped her eyes with her handkerchief. "I've read enough psychology to know that saying what's on your mind is healthy, so I guess you're right," she agreed.

The couple had a dual problem. Wendy had never had coital orgasms, and Bob suffered from long-standing premature ejaculation. His efforts to control his ejaculations frequently led to the loss of erection. Although occasionally impotent, he could often masturbate himself to erection, insert, and ejaculate quickly.

The first week's prescription for the patients was total abstinence from sex and affection. Bob was not to touch his wife, and particularly not after he had just been "honest" with her. I confronted him with the idea that his openness was a form of rude criticism that his wife did not enjoy. One might hypothesize that he indulged his sadism to increase his feelings of power in the light of his sexual insecurity, but I did not make this point because it was unlikely the patient would accept it or profit by it. Whenever he had an "honest" thought, Bob was to think it and not say it.

In the second session, Wendy was tense and uncertain, but she was not tearful. Bob was sullen and depressed, but he had followed the prescription. I praised Bob for the strength it took to withhold his "honest" thoughts. Wendy was certain "it wouldn't last" and tried to provoke Bob to criticize her by citing her inadequacies. I made her aware of her action and prescribed for the second week that she refrain from verbalizing self-critical thoughts.

In the third session Wendy was still tense, Bob appeared ebullient. "For the first time in our married life," he explained, "she kissed me without my starting first."

"I felt so sorry for him," Wendy said. "He looked so blue, holding himself in and being so dishonest." She then apologized for disobeying the therapeutic instructions.

I pointed out that she was continuing to be self-critical and that when she had asserted herself by kissing Bob and disobeying my instructions, Bob responded very well. Sensate focus was prescribed for the fourth session, but only for Wendy. It was a special form of sensate focus, designed to accompany assertive sexual training. Wendy was to indicate, first nonverbally, then verbally, what she liked and did not like about Bob's nongenital touching. It was to be all for her, nothing for Bob.

On alternate nights, they were to begin treatment of Bob's premature ejaculation according to a method that will be described later.

Wendy did extremely well at helping Bob control his ejaculation; within a month he had mastered his problem. She was much less successful at giving Bob any indication of her preferences or pleasures in sensate focus but continually provoked him to criticize her performance. "I've got your number," Bob finally said, still pleased with his new prowess. "When you used to put yourself down, I never minded because I felt insecure, but now you're not going to ruin our sex life with all that self-hate stuff." He added quickly, "Not that I'm being critical."

I encouraged Wendy to read erotic literature to stimulate her fantasy, of which she had little. I also encouraged her to explore her genitalia, to touch each area: the vaginal lips, the vagina, the mons, the hood of the clitoris, the clitoris itself, and to see what touch felt best. She had masturbated only rarely since early childhood because of parental prohibition. Wendy was surprisingly responsive to erotic literature. She experienced orgasm during the second self-exploration, which took place after she read about a seduction reminiscent of a premarital episode with a boyfriend.

After 11 sessions, Wendy reached orgasm during coitus, was able to tell her husband what she liked, and was able to indulge her favorite fantasies during intercourse. Bob had achieved control after the first six sessions. When therapy was terminated the couple's spirits were high.

Training patients in the use of fantasy, either to increase eroticism or to decrease anxiety about performance, is important. Which erotic literature, art, photography, or films to recommend is controversial. Much depends on the patient. It is safe to start with the most sophisticated stimulation of which the patient is capable. Classics such as *Fanny Hill*, as well as the works of Frank Harris, Henry Miller, and D. H. Lawrence, are often recommended. Curiously, patients rarely read what the therapist recommends. They tend to select what appeals to them. Sometimes the choices are amusing. One devout young lady, to whom the Song of Songs, Michelangelo's *David*, and the paintings of Rubens had been suggested as a start, returned the following week with a copy of *The Happy Hooker*, stating that she wished that more material depicting the activity of prostitutes were available. Ultimately, her interest in such works was satiated, but they did serve to release and dilute her sadomasochistic fantasy. An often observed phenomenon is that masochistic fantasy, once it is accepted as sexually stimulating and is not prohibited, frequently becomes sadistic and then diminishes rapidly. The same is true, in reverse, of inhibited sadistic fantasy. The process is like encouraging a patient to express anger for the first time. Once the inhibited feeling is expressed, it turns out not to be so frightening or dangerous.

In this and other ways, guilt and shame can be relieved regarding homosexual impulses, masturbation, adulterous, Oedipal, and sadomasochistic fantasies, anal preoccupations, and other such variants; indeed, the therapist may actively encourage use of these variations in a nondestructive way to promote erotic feelings. Education is also therapeutic. The therapist and patient might discuss orgasmic response statistics, sexual anatomy, and sexual expectations at different ages. The therapist might also instruct the patient in effective modes of stimulation and in ways of creating a romantic or sexual ambiance at home.

During the once-weekly sessions, which are held for as long as necessary, the assignment that was performed is discussed and the therapist attempts to help remove any obstacles (unconscious, transactional, perceptual, and so on) by any of the methods described above. Further experiences are then assigned or suggested.

Techniques vary according to the patient's particular dysfunction. Perhaps a discussion of several specific cases will demonstrate the variety and flexibility of techniques. A nondemand strategy was adopted for the social worker discussed in Case 2 (p. 418). Sensate focus was recommended at the start, but it failed to give either partner pleasure. The wife said a number of times that all she wanted in life was a big firm erection inside her for an hour or more every day, a comment that made her husband cringe. I instructed her to stop saying such things, that it was in the best interests of her marriage to keep such remarks to herself. Then I instructed the husband that if he achieved a morning erection while his wife was asleep, he should wake her and tell her. Later, I suggested she touch his erect penis. The next few weeks were spent working through the wife's resistance to being awakened and to doing anything, no matter how trivial, before she had brushed her teeth. She provoked her husband to attempt intercourse at times other than the morning, but he would inevitably fail. The wife finally realized she was sabotaging treatment, and she began to cooperate. At long last, the husband was able to ask his wife to have intercourse in the morning. She refused, saying she could not do it because she was dry and had to be stimulated. She was persuaded to use a lubricant, and after some weeks, the couple had achieved a richer pattern of lovemaking. However, as already mentioned, the wife became increasingly depressed about her own inadequacies and went into therapy.

This case may be contrasted with another case in which the treatment was simpler. I suggested to one couple that they not have intercourse the initial week of treatment, because I first wanted to take their history. This suggestion relieved the husband. Knowing that he no longer had to produce an erection, he became aroused spontaneously. This reaction, in turn, led to his rebellion against my authority, which resulted in his cure. It is reassuring when a patient receives such immediate satisfaction, but the therapist has to select carefully the patient for whom such an approach is possible.

The treatment of anorgasmic women can be complex or relatively simple. My easiest case was that of a woman who, the weekend before the first session, found a vibrator in her sister-in-law's bathroom, tried it out, and had an orgasm. She had "cured" herself before her appointment. I had only to teach her how to masturbate to orgasm and how to persuade her husband to stimulate her properly for the carry-over to be made to their sexual relationship.

More complex are cases like the following:

CASE 4 Jeanne was mature and responsible in every way but sexually. She
was an executive in a department store, and her husband was a college professor.
The couple's sexual behavior was juvenile. Sometimes Jeanne and her husband would
take a bath together; they would have water fights in which she sprayed water at him
with her "rubber ducky." This childhood frolic would have been fine had it led to
sexual activity, but it never did. Jeanne could command her staff with aplomb, but
sexually she was incompetent. Sensate focus exercises were of no avail; nonsexual,
regressive pleasuring as a stimulus only made her more infantile. Teaching her husband
how to please her did not work either. What did work was confrontation. I said to
her, "You behave in every other way like a capable woman, but sexually you act like
a three-year-old."

Jeanne went through a week of hating me. She then confronted her sexual immaturity, and sexual treatment began. In her sixth week of treatment, she had her
first orgasm. Jeanne tolerated my directness. After recognizing her problem, she
was able to feel like an erotic woman instead of a playful child. Her passive husband,
who had not been able to convey his view of his wife to her, was grateful.

The method that I most frequently use to help women who are
orgasmic during manual stimulation but not during coitus is to teach
them to take responsibility for their own orgasms. This means that
they must learn to stimulate themselves to orgasm, first in their husbands'
presence and then during intercourse. They are instructed to have intercourse in whatever position it is most comfortable to masturbate. Once
the woman can bring herself to orgasm during intercourse, she is instructed
to stop stimulating herself just before orgasm, when penile stimulation
may complete the experience. She learns to stop stimulating herself
earlier and earlier, so that ultimately she may not need any direct manual
stimulation at all.

Some women cannot allow themselves to experience orgasm on coitus
although they can masturbate to climax. These women may be helped by
introduction of the penis at the very moment of a manually-induced
orgasm. This desensitizes them to the presence of a penis in their vagina
during orgasm.

Many variations of the manually-induced orgasm during intercourse
are possible. (1) Those who prefer, may have their husbands stimulate
them during coitus. (2) They may stimulate themselves or have their
partners stimulate them with a vibrator. (3) Instead of beginning self-
stimulation with the penis inside, the woman may wait until she is close
to orgasm and then signal for insertion. Or she can bring herself close
to orgasm three times, and signal for insertion at the fourth pre-orgasmic
moment. The method that is most suitable to a couple depends on the

therapist's judgment and on the couple's preference. A woman's masturbation patterns — how a woman brings herself to orgasm — have much to do
with the choice.

Psychodynamically, the factors inhibiting orgasms are so complex as
to preclude discussion in this brief chapter. Most therapists are, of course,
familiar with them: fear of abandonment, fear of losing control, of
expressing anger, and of rejection; failure of identification; all the ramifi-
cations of the Oedipus complex; and guilt and fear from a wide variety
of other causes.

Vaginismus

The precise remedy for vaginismus is to get the woman to introduce an
object into her vagina. All the tasks given her are designed to overcome,
in a gradual nontraumatic manner, her phobic resistance to doing this.
Behavior therapists describe the use of graduated wax bougies; Masters and
Johnson use Hegar dilators [1]. The fingers are a more natural set of tools,
being of several different widths and lengths. The importance of these new
treatments can only be realized in light of the old — in the past vaginismus
was treated by obstetrical surgeons by cutting and excising sphincteric
muscle, often extensively and without effect. Premature ejaculation is
still treated by some urologists with cautery.

Vaginismus is usually evidence of a phobic avoidance of penetration.
Sometimes vaginismus can be cured by telling the woman to imagine an
object such as a tampon penetrating her vagina, then a finger. This fantasy
should be followed with the gradual introduction of one, then two of the
husband's fingers. For some women, this "covert desensitization" is too
similar to actual intercourse, and a more systematic desensitization or
hypnosis may be used. One patient needed to take Stelazine before penetration. Another woman, afraid of the idea of having coitus, was therapeutically deceived by the doctor, who told her not to have intercourse
at all but rather to allow penile insertion. The husband was directed to
insert his penis repeatedly and pull it out most of the way. The woman
acknowledged that she had had an orgasm on the fourth insertion, but
dutifully reported that she had followed my instructions and they had
not had intercourse yet! She was confident, though, that the treatment
would soon be successful.

Premature Ejaculation

I make an important distinction between types of premature ejaculators, which I have not seen previously discussed in the literature. I define *primary prematurity* as a condition that a man has during the entire course of his sexual life; there is no evidence that anxiety induces it. I define *secondary prematurity* as a condition which, whenever it occurs, is stimulated by anxiety. It may occur after a period of good functioning and full ejaculatory control with the same person. It may occur with one person and not with another, in which case it may be called *situational prematurity*. Secondary prematurity is difficult to detect since it may occur simultaneously with primary prematurity. It occurs as an expression of anxiety, which stimulates a man's sympathetic nervous system. As such, it is a harbinger of impotence. Cases of impotence occuring during treatment of premature ejaculation probably have a component of secondary prematurity.

A high level of resistance to the change necessary for improvement is the most predictable feature of patient response that arises in the treatment of premature ejaculation. Though the treatment format is fairly standard, emotional responses to impending cure are often most difficult to handle. Either the patient or his spouse may experience anxiety, and during the third or fourth session the couple may elaborate an array of defenses. This is a crisis, and unless it is resolved successfully, treatment can fail. It is a challenge to the sex therapist.

Some definitions of premature ejaculation are in order. Masters and Johnson [1] consider a man a premature ejaculator if he cannot sufficiently control his ejaculation during intravaginal containment to satisfy his partner in at least half of their coital connections. Other definitions also derive from the duration of containment. The essential pathology, however, is not related to time, but rather to control in delaying the ejaculatory reflex. Prematurity can therefore be said to exist when orgasm occurs reflexly and is beyond the man's voluntary control once he is intensely aroused. Ejaculatory control is realized when the man tolerates high plateaus of excitement without ejaculating reflexly.

The therapy for curing premature ejaculation is most economical. The average case involves only six once-a-week sessions. The therapy is pared down to essentials. For example, sensate focus may be eliminated since it does not always relate to the alleviation of premature ejaculation.

The decision as to whether to prescribe sensate focus first in cases of premature ejaculation is based on a couple's previous relationship.

If they already have a warm, affectional bond characterized by kissing, caressing, and extensive foreplay, it is generally unnecessary. However, if they do not have such a relationship, or if it is interfered with by frustrations secondary to the symptom, sensate focus may come first. Sometimes, however, even if the affectional pleasuring is limited, I may decide to forgo sensate focus and simply to teach control. The intimacy of foreplay can be too threatening for some people; this is rare, but possible.

The simplest method of treating premature ejaculation is a refinement of that first published by James Semans [2]. It consists of manual or oral stimulation of the husband's penis by the wife until just before the point of ejaculation. During stimulation the husband focuses on the sensations in his penis. Just before he is about to ejaculate, the husband tells his wife to stop stimulating him long enough — 10 or 20 seconds — to let the urgency subside. This procedure is repeated three times, and then the man may ejaculate. If performed manually, the first exercise is done without lubrication. When that is successful, petroleum jelly is used both to simulate vaginal secretions and to make control somewhat more difficult. The couple may then proceed to coitus, with the wife in the superior position. The woman moves until her husband instructs her to stop (she uses her vagina to stimulate her husband). When the man has comfortable control while lying passively, he may begin to thrust; and when this is comfortable the couple may change to a lateral and then to male-superior position. As the man gains confidence, the time between stops tends to increase. Ultimately, he may choose when he wants to ejaculate.

CASE 5   Henry was 26 years old, a graduate student in humanities. He had long-standing premature ejaculation. He was a reticent, passive-aggressive person who presented as being pleasant, intelligent, and cooperative.

He and Martha had been married for three years. She was 24 years old and already well on her way to being a successful actress; she was attractive, outgoing, and emotionally expressive. She was able to experience orgasm on manual stimulation easily, but had only rarely done so during coitus, which usually lasted one or two minutes.

Martha and Henry at first described a warm and lively sensual life. They said they enjoyed touching each other, kissing, and caressing. They liked each other and each other's bodies, and Henry was always able to stimulate Martha to orgasm.

The relationship was quite different when intercourse became the focus. Henry then became disinterested in sexuality. Martha would have to initiate sensual exchanges, and Henry might refuse or agree half-heartedly. But he would become more involved as the foreplay progressed. Their warmth had decreased of late; Martha was tired of asking.

I did not prescribe sensate focus first because it would in no way change the pattern of the relationship. Martha would have to ask Henry to pleasure her, and he would reluctantly agree. He would resist being pleasured because of his insecurity about rapid ejaculation. If intercourse was not the goal, he would experience more freedom and pleasure, a fact that was already established and did not have to be proved again. I therefore proceeded directly to the first step of the delaying procedure. I was alert, however, to any sign of resistance, and when Henry said he had a lot of school pressures and thought he might not have time to do the exercises in the coming weeks, I confronted him: "We have an extremely limited time for work. I can't help you if you don't want to be helped. Either you rearrange your habits and put aside time for this, or we can't proceed with treatment." Henry thought it over and concluded he could manage the time.

The second session proceeded without difficulty. By the third meeting, however, the couple appeared somewhat depressed. They reported their activity: the prescription had been to continue manual stimulation, with lubrication, but Martha said she had been "carried away" and had requested intercourse. Henry had performed, in the male-superior position, without control.

It was necessary to stop and explore why Martha had been "carried away." The answer turned out to lie in Martha's fears about herself. In spite of her unusual attractiveness, she thought she was ugly. She had had plastic surgery on her nose, she had lost a lot of weight, and she had had voice and acting lessons; but her self-image was still poor. Secretly she feared that if Henry became a better lover, he would seek other women. I had to confront her with the possibility that her fears about herself were sabotaging treatment. She understood and became determined to follow instructions more closely after reassurance that Henry planned to stay with her.

The fourth session was no better than the third. Again, it seemed to be Martha who was resisting. "I just can't ask him for sex anymore," she complained. "If only he would come after me for once. And when I do go after him, if only he would be more enthusiastic."

We had already discussed Henry's unwillingness to initiate sex because of his fear of rapid ejaculation, but this had not helped to resolve the situation. It was necessary to look at the past and review Henry's history. His parents had been domineering. To free himself from domination, he had adopted a pattern of responding negatively to any kind of request. I pointed out that his reluctance and passivity were carryovers from his early years and served no current purpose. Although this observation did not change his behavior immediately, it did help Martha feel less personally rejected by his lack of response. She was able to continue to initiate sexual activity.

By the fifth session, intercourse began, in the female-superior position. After the first experience, in which Henry ejaculated too early, the couple stopped having relations and became distant from each other. Henry had a sudden return to his old compulsive work habits. In the next session, both were extremely depressed and convinced that treatment could never be successful for them. Henry thought he was a failure; Martha was tired of trying. Yet I knew that they were actually only a session or two away from their goal. I reiterated what they had forgotten: that their seeming failures were really learning experiences; without them Henry would not really be able to judge when to stop. I encouraged them to try again, this time being sure that Henry was lying still and not thrusting, and was concentrating on his penile sensations.

The following week was much better. In the last two weeks of treatment, as Henry began to gain confidence in his ability to delay ejaculation, he was also able to initiate sexual activity several times. He realized that his "automatic no" was a handicap, not only sexually but in all his relationships.

In this case, the major crisis came in the sixth session, when failure of belief in the therapy and many personal reasons kept it from being effective. Whether I should continue to offer insight at this point, or interpret, or explore dynamics of the past, or confront, or simply support and encourage was a major therapeutic decision. It is the handling of such moments that determines the success or failure of sex therapy. Anyone can give instructions, and knowing the techniques is only the beginning.

Retarded Ejaculation

Treatment of retarded ejaculation involves desensitizing the patient to ejaculating in his partner's vagina. First he must learn to ejaculate when she is aware of what he is doing. He must masturbate to orgasm while she is in another room, then in her presence, and eventually on her body. She may then place his penis inside her as he ejaculates, after which he may enter by his own decision just before ejaculation. Gradually he enters earlier and earlier. He may have to withdraw to masturbate until close to orgasm and insert his penis again. Gradually he becomes able to ejaculate without withdrawing and masturbating.

Treatment of retarded ejaculators is most often complicated by personality problems. These men tend to have more than ordinary difficulty in handling rage reactions.

SEX THERAPY FOR THE PERSON WITH A PARTNER AT HOME

Results have been remarkably encouraging for a mixture of insight therapy, assertive training, and specific sex therapy for the person who comes to the office without a partner present. Women may be taught to masturbate in preparation for doing so during intercourse. The initial treatment of totally anorgasmic women is the same whether they have a partner or not. A premature ejaculator may, himself, teach his partner to help him at home. Impotent men may be taught how to handle their fears in a variety of situations. They can be taught to assert that they do not plan to have intercourse unless it occurs spontaneously; they can learn fantasy and distraction techniques for use under a variety of circumstances. Retarded ejaculators can take charge of their own treatment by ejaculating closer and closer to their partner's vagina and finally entering just before ejaculation. Women with vaginismus may insert their own dilators or instruct a partner at home to do so, or use his fingers.

Time of treatment is usually longer than for couples therapy, since insight, assertive sexual training, and techniques for reducing stress in the partner who does not visit the office, must be acquired before sexual activity can begin. Of course, if there is no partner, sex therapy is limited to autoerotic techniques.

Sex therapy with unmarried couples, whether the partner is at home or comes to the office, would seem to be less effective than with married couples because of an absent or limited commitment to a specific partner. When a treatment crisis comes, the couple may separate. In addition, if a future marriage depends on the resolution of the sexual problem, the pressure may be too great for a successful outcome, especially in cases of impotence and orgasmic dysfunction. However, I have no doubt of the value of sex therapy for unmarried couples, even if it sometimes proves they cannot work things out together. A failure to respond to sexual therapy may be symptomatic of more fundamental conflict in the relationship.

THE EFFECTIVENESS OF SEX THERAPY

What are the "cure" rates? So far, there have not been enough patients treated to produce definitive statistics. However, the statistics that do exist are most encouraging, with close to 100 percent relief in premature ejaculation and vaginismus, and a high percentage in orgasmic dysfunction and impotence. Most anorgasmic women treated have achieved orgasms. If a woman can masturbate in a position that allows a man to enter, the possibility of orgasm on coitus is greatly increased.

SUMMARY

My approach to sex therapy is eclectic: it derives from whatever therapeutic discipline seems appropriate. (At times, one may even use love poetry.) It is committed to brevity: the average number of sessions is eight, and the range is one to twenty. The main features that differentiate it from other methods are (1) its unique synthesis of modalities drawn from a multi-disciplinary background, (2) the fact that only one therapist and not a dual team is required, (3) weekly office visits instead of a two- or three-week intensive period, and (4) a fee scale that makes sex therapy more widely available.

REFERENCES

1. Masters, W. H., and Johnson, V. E. *Human Sexual Inadequacy*. Boston: Little Brown, 1970.
2. Semans, J. H. Premature ejaculation: A new approach. *Southern Medical Journal* 49:353, 1956.

19

The Hysterical Marriage

Jurg Willi
Translated by Jacob Christ

Today we still lack to some extent a nosology or typology of marital
disturbances. This in a way is remarkable if one considers the frequency
and variety of marital problems encountered in psychotherapeutic practice.
Perhaps a major reason for this lack is the fact that the majority of modern
researchers who have worked with marital conflicts have put the major
focus on the interpersonal dynamics of the marriage. The definition of
individual sickness in this area has often been considered irrelevant because
there is such an overlap of neurotic syndromes. In my opinion, however,
it would be advantageous for a deeper understanding of marital psychology
and for outlining the basics of marital therapy to consider the ways in
which typical neurotic syndromes manifest themselves in the marriage.
In this, I am in agreement with H. E. Richter [20] who has proposed
several types of character neuroses that appear in the context of the
family. The marriages of those with anxiety neurosis or narcissistic
personalities, for instance, show a structure that is markedly different
from that of the hysterical marriage. These differences became particularly
clear in a study I carried out that used conjoint Rorschach testing of
married couples [22]. This tool has indicated important directions for
this chapter and has in many ways opened my eyes for better clinical

observation. I would like to try to tie together a clinically oriented, descriptive presentation of the hysterical marriage with a psychodynamic and psychogenetic, or depth-oriented, point of view.

But first the concept of the hysterical marriage should be defined more precisely. I understand it to be the long-lasting marriage of the severely hysterical woman, which continues in spite of all crises and which for her is the only possible form of marriage. I gained my insights in psychotherapeutic practice and refined them through a systematic study of the marriages of women with classic hysteria. The study involved hysterical symptom neuroses as well as patients with a hysterical character [23]. The term *hysteria* will be used in a clinical-descriptive sense and not in the psychodynamic sense that refers to all neuroses with phallic problems and the disturbances of love-life resulting therefrom.

THE HYSTERICAL WOMAN AND HER RELATIONSHIP TO HER PARTNER

There is a wealth of literature about the character structure of the hysterical woman. I need not refer to specific studies here. For this chapter, the writings of Freud (6–12), Abraham [1, 2], Reich [19], Kuiper [17], and Lempérière [18] were particularly important. In the early psychoanalytic literature the main emphasis in regard to hysterical neuroses was on disturbances of the instinctual drives. Freud saw the important cause of hysteria as the fixation of the libido or the regression of the libido to the phallic stage, caused by an unresolved father complex. Presently, the attention is more on the functions of the superego and the disturbances of ego functioning. The most typical clinical symptoms of the classic hysteria syndrome are conversion phenomena, disturbances in consciousness, frigidity (often accompanied by anxiety), phobic symptoms, inferiority feelings, addictive tendencies, and suicidal gestures. In this chapter the hysterical character will be considered, especially in regard to her own way of relating to her marital partner.

The hysterical woman often lives her emotional life on the surface. She suffers from an inner emptiness and tries to achieve a feeling of selfhood by dramatizing emotional expression. She cannot do anything alone and finds no inner resources to give her security. She has the tendency to repress or to project her conflicts. With her low self-esteem, she often lacks the ability for introspection and reacts with narcissistic injury if her behavior is pointed out to her. Often she has a depressive feeling of being annihilated, and so she lives almost always "on the outside." She busies herself with manipulation and intrigue and is often expert at both. This escape from her inner conflicts often comes naturally to her and with promise of success, particularly if she is physically attractive. An adept way of manipulating the environment is her demonstration of weakness through being sick, through crying helplessly, suicidal gestures, and so on. It can be said of her that her strength lies in her weakness. She entrusts other people close to her with the solution of her conflicts. She is particularly satisfied when she "has to" watch two rivals — "knights in shining armor" — do combat over her. She thus externalizes her intrapsychic conflict onto the people she relates to and participates as a spectator in the drama that takes place between them.

The hysterical woman appears high-strung and puts herself on the stage. She is coquettish, tries to please, shows off her personality, and must always play an important role. The attention of those in her environment must be on her, and she must remain stimulated by constantly new sensations. The hysterical woman often chooses to be eccentric and takes care to remain glamorous, glistening, and interesting. She is busy creating ever new surprise effects. Her lack of self-esteem is compensated for somewhat when she succeeds in making her environment tense or suspenseful. Her triumphs over her environment provide her with a degree of cohesion and self-affirmation. This increase in self-esteem is, however, only transient and evaporates with the decrease of the affective tension in the environment. Only as long as everything is in a state of commotion and excitement does she feel alive and secure. As soon as the attention of the environment lags, she falls into feelings of abandonment and anxiety about losing herself. In this fashion she remains overly dependent on her environment and is constantly driven by the fear that she might lose the attention of others.

The theatrical nature of her behavior often leads to her being despised and rejected by her environment. Those who reject her, however, often overlook the fact that she tries to influence her environment by dramatics only because she fears that otherwise she will not be taken seriously or accepted at all. Her dramatization and her rejection by the environment become a vicious cycle.

The hysterical woman is shy and afraid of intimate contact. She is afraid to surrender herself to another, and she fears being overpowered or exploited. She may not be sufficiently independent to distance herself from her environment. She is filled with a deep fear of trusting herself to the environment and of allowing someone to get close to her.

With her strong tendency to externalize all her conflicts and to live on the outside, she needs from her partner an auxiliary ego. With her ego weakness she needs someone to guide her, govern her, direct her, and apply "the brakes." In a quick identification with such an auxiliary ego, she can transiently bring structure to herself. She, therefore, needs a husband who is absolutely loyal and who will strengthen her self-esteem and substitute his ego for hers.

She accepts as a female prerogative her being courted and spoiled by a man. She turns all responsibility over to her husband. "Now I have finished struggling. Now *you* can continue to battle for me," said one such woman to her husband on her wedding day.

While the majority of hysterical women have premarital sexual experiences, later they are generally frigid, unless they are able to split off sexuality from the totality of a love relation. This splitting can lead to nymphomaniac behavior with, however, the inability to find satisfaction (as in borderline psychotic or schizoid individuals). The exhibitionistic type of hysterical woman has a special tendency to sexualize all her human relations. She may tell off-color jokes and flaunt her charms, but then take flight from concrete genital sexuality.

Her strong display of sexual interest is, among other things, a defensive maneuver in regard to the partner. The original genital impulse is utilized to explore the source of the danger and to assess the magnitude and proximity of the dreaded event [19]. In a sort of "flight straight ahead," she tries to intimidate the men with impudent directness. On occasion this maneuver misfires and she ends up being "raped against her wishes." The "disappointments" which she may have experienced in this regard from men who are strongly motivated sexually will lead her to seek unconsciously a sexually weak man as a partner.

Hysterical women who are more pregenitally fixated will behave somewhat differently, at least as seen from the outside. They are able to bring about situations in which they are taken care of by employing conversion symptoms, which have a particularly sexually seductive effect on men.

These women behave in a bashful, naive manner, appear almost childishly innocent, and are terribly surprised that the sexually excited man suddenly thinks of "other things."

Hysterical women suffer from an unmastered, positive father complex. They have a strongly affect-cathected and ambivalent relation to their fathers. Many were their father's favorite child, and the father often had expressed quite overtly and unabashedly his sexual desire for her. The father both created conflicts and was himself full of contradictions. On the one hand, he was strongly instinctually motivated, violent, impulsive and often alcoholic, and on the other hand, childish, helpless, soft and pity-seeking. Often such a father would come crying to his favorite daughter about his marital difficulties. This seductive situation, or course, made the little girl's mastery of the father complex difficult and makes her own later marriage a problem.

Many hysterical women have fathers who have overpowered and dominated their wives; and thus a fixation is enhanced by the miserable fate of the mother. Often, a reversed parental relationship exists: the mother is possessive and domineering, often with marked hysterical trends, and the father is treated as an ignoramus, shamed, despised, and continually humiliated. Mothers of hysterical women almost always appear to be strongly inhibited sexually. An ambivalent, sister-like intimacy often exists between these mothers and daughters, and sexuality is presented to the daughter as something dirty, undignified, or even annihilating.

The choice of a partner, as well as the entrance into marriage, is notably more difficult for the hysterical woman because of her unresolved father complex. Karl Abraham [1] has described two transformations of the "female castration complex": the "wish fulfillment type," and the "revenge type." In the wish-fulfillment type, the woman has a fantasy of possessing a penis; she wants to take over the male role and prove to the man her equality in every regard. In the revenge type, the woman unconsciously repudiates the feminine role and has a repressed desire for revenge against the husband, who has been assigned a father role and who has to do penance for the fact that her real father has left her deficient.

The hysterical woman who stays in a long-lasting and disturbed marriage represses all desires for masculine activity and accepts feminine passivity almost too well. Her thought may be, "O.K., so I am only an inferior woman. But then nobody can make any demands of me. The man will be

the man. He has to prove himself everywhere as a man and must always
be the stronger one. Let's see whether he really is as strong as all that."
She defiantly limits herself to the passive feminine attitude and exhibits
her feminine weakness to the man in an almost provocative fashion with
the secret, and usually unconscious, fantasy of taking revenge on him in
this fashion.

The hysterical woman must avoid a relationship with a masculine,
strong man because it would activate sexual fears to a dangerous extent.
While the hysterical woman may act sexually provocative, she despises
men who are strongly motivated sexually. She is particularly satisfied
when she can attract such a man and then abruptly turn him down when
he believes himself to be close to her. For a stable relationship, she can
choose only an "asexual" man who activates none of the childhood
complexes but rather softens these conflicts.

The regression toward passive needs will be enhanced further if a strong
pregenital fixation is present. As Freud has pointed out, the strong tie to
the father only covers the even stronger tie to the mother. With her
passive demands, which come from this fixation, the hysterical woman
wishes for a man who displays maternal activity in her regard, and therewith
confirms her in her infantile passive stance.

The "Hysterophile" Man

The husband of the hysterical woman is unremarkable, taciturn, soft,
shy, and almost overly well-adapted and thoughtful or respectful. In
contrast to his often extravagant wife, he is pedestrian, pale but sturdy,
the "good guy" type. He is chosen by the woman because as one such
woman said, "I feel safe with him, he will never get really mad. He
couldn't even kill a fly." Quite frequently this man is his wife's superior
intellectually and is a more sensitive and differentiated person. But because he is insecure about himself and his social inhibitions, he is often
an underperformer in his professional position or in his work circle.

The hysterophile man shows a rather clearly defined form of neurotic
character formation. In our studies we found a significantly higher number
to be only sons and youngest children. Related to this is a remarkable
tie to the mother, with much dependency. Most of the time they are
"Mama's boys" and a good many of them live with their mothers until
marriage. The mothers are consistently described as possessive, active,

and strong personalities. Contrasted to them, the fathers are usually unremarkable and bleak, and they have only a small role to play.

It was the special nature of the mother-son relationship that made the son's resolution of the Oedipus complex difficult. Open rivalry with the weak father would create guilt feelings, and an active search for the strong mother would be too dangerous. So the son rejects a conquering stance and accepts submission to his mother's authority. A negative Oedipus complex develops. The son accepts a passive feminine stance similar to that of his father. His heterosexuality takes on a passive character, and drives with passive goals take over — a desire for warmth, for stroking or touching, for being cared for, protected and cuddled. He regresses into this early infantile attitude to avoid the positive masculine strivings.

This passive feminine stance, however, is in contradiction to the demands of the ego ideal, that is, to the ideas that he has of his role as a grown-up. In his expectations of the future, he would like to become the incarnation of active love, nobility, and goodness. To this end, however, his passive needs, which would lead to infantile dependency on a mother or a substitute have to be defended against; overcompensating activity comes about as a reaction against the passive tie to his mother. He is, for instance, an enthusiastic sportsman, particularly in fields that prove masculinity. Mountain climbing, with daredevil exploits, or flying may be chosen in a counterphobic manner as a fantasy-attempt to overcome the tie to his mother. To replace the lost mother, as an adult the son identifies with her and needs a woman he will treat, in a displaced fashion, the same way as he would have liked to have been treated by his mother. He tries to sublimate his need to be taken care of by becoming a caretaker himself. From an anxious refutation of his need for mothering, he becomes a mother — a helper of others. His lack of assertiveness in society and in his work life leaves him with the strong wish to overcome his inferiority feelings by closeness to his family and by becoming its main support. He wants to be totally engaged in his marriage; he wants to be useful and adept; he will even sacrifice himself to earn the gratitude and high regard of an adoring wife. He would like to be quietly and indispensably in the center of the family. With his narcissistic problems of self-valuation he tries to consolidate his self-image by hard efforts in this job. Unconsciously, he believes that he will make the woman dependent on him if he puts himself totally at her service.

He is likely to deny his need for satisfaction of passive desires in the marriage: satisfaction of passive needs would represent renewed dependency on a mother figure and might be experienced as a sign of weakness and lack of self-reliance. Thus, this overcompensating, defensive stance is directed against the passive, feminine, submissive basic attitude. Submission, in turn, acts as a defense against unresolved competition and castration problems.

This type of man is shy toward young women and generally insecure and passive. In contrast to their wives, most husbands of hysterical women rarely dated because they feared rejection and rarely had premarital relations because they feared impotence. Sadistic, aggressive, and exhibitionistic tendencies are strongly suppressed. The man seems to adopt a submissive attitude toward women almost as if he had to excuse himself for his masculinity and give assurances that he would certainly gain no advantage from it and that there could be no question of male superiority. With the first glance he signals to the woman, "You will not have to fear me at all sexually; I will not harm you in any way, but if you take me as a helper and healer in your services, I will always be there."

His most remarkable outward difference from the hysterical woman is the inhibition of all exhibitionism. In gestures, facial expression, and language this type of man displays modesty and discretion. He does not want to inconvenience anyone and is disinclined toward all dramatic scenes. He practically never has conversion symptoms, suicidal gestures, or other directly engaging symptoms. And yet, he has a particular need to prove himself, but this is blocked by altruistic attitudes. He has an urge to dramatize only the situations of other people, especially that of the beloved woman. He would like to see himself as a totally unique and absolutely incomparable creature who stands above and beyond all normal requirements. He has a need to report dramatically the scenes played by his wife, in particular suicidal threats. He tends to enhance the general excitement and creates great turmoil around her because he can best display his functions as a helper and rescuer when things are the most dramatic.

The male partner of the marriage then stands in an understandable relation to the hysterical woman, as will be explained more fully in the discussion that follows. It is possible to define the man's neurotic attitudes as *hysterophile,* since he has a tendency to invest in a partner relation with a hysterical woman.

THE COURSE OF THE HYSTERICAL MARRIAGE

Phase I — Choice of the Partner

At the time of meeting, the woman is frequently in a life situation in which she feels powerless in the face of unhappy external events. She urgently needs the rescuing support of a man. This may be because of an unresolved relationship with overpowering parents; most often, however, she is involved in an unhappy love affair.

The prehistory of this situation is that the hysterical woman has seen time and again how her love for a man has ceased at the moment she had to commit herself. As soon as the man was "conquered," a strange phenomenon had occurred: the man who, until now, had been the goal of her longing, suddenly had become less interesting, and the woman had asked herself, "Is he really the right one for me?" [17]. Now, in the presence of a new relationship, she is desperate about this regular disappearance of her feelings of love. Under the pressure of the environment toward marriage or in an attempt to end this neurotic repetitiveness, she makes a forced attempt to put a finish to her excuses and "compromise with reality." Although she is never really in love with her husband-to-be, she chooses a hysterophile man with the vain expectation that love will come "by itself" later. At least, living with him will not lead her into any particular dangers. At times these women may be flirtatious toward other men, even on the wedding day. The relationship with a former lover is frequently relived with sentimental and tragic feelings, as if she were saying to him, "I am a very complicated person, but I assure you that you will have a special place in my heart as long as we live. It will never be with my husband the way it was with you, but I simply feel more secure with him." Very often the former lover was a sexually inconsiderate and brutal man by whom she had been "raped."

The hysterophile man feels himself especially qualified to rescue such a woman from her entanglements. He is desirous of proving himself in a difficult task [17]. The woman's hints that she cannot be in love with him and that she cannot kill all her feelings for the earlier lover increase his anxieties at first. He may not feel adequate sexually for this attractive woman. But he feels assured by her remark that the sexual aspects of their relationship are not particularly important to her and that she has chosen him because he radiates assurance and confidence.

In this fashion a good number of hysterical marriages become *marriages of rescue.* The husband senses a chance to prove himself, not through his own qualities but through his rescue function. He decides that this woman will need protection and firmness all her life, and he thus feels urgently needed. It is a great narcissistic gain for him to know that his wife will be bound to him with ties of gratefulness, and this is for him the safest guarantee that she will continue to be tender and loving toward him. With hints on her part, ("You are really a good man . . . , if you really loved me . . . ,") without becoming aware of it, he allows himself to be directed by her whims. He wants to be solely responsible for the marriage and sees his marriage as his life's work.

Phase II — The Phase of Idealization

This stage, which usually begins premaritally and continues during the first part of the marriage, is frequently a very happy one, or, at any rate, it will be idealized as very happy. The wife denies her own wishes toward masculinity and the weakness of the man she has chosen. She wants to see the man as strong, and she projects onto him the satisfaction of her passive needs. The idealized expectations of the man, however, lead to her manipulating and subtly disparaging him, "You're so nice with me, so thoughtful, so totally unegotistical that I feel very safe with you and very sheltered. I have peace with you and I know that I can always rely upon you." These projective reinforcements of the husband are not empty words — women in this phase do feel much better and are doing much better. Conversion symptoms that existed before disappear, and phobic symptoms remain in the background. The women are emotionally better balanced, more content, and happier.

What does this strongly projective behavior mean for the hysterophile man? He identifies himself with the maternally caring image his wife projects on him, and endeavors to assume it. It is an image that coincides with his own ego ideal. He can be a protector and perhaps even "a knight in shining armor," and he is needed in this role. When there is somebody who trusts him in this function and thinks him capable of the tasks it involves, he finds the force in himself to grow beyond himself. He had been shy and reticent, but in the rescuing of his wife, he becomes forward and adventuresome, gains in self-assurance, self-affirmation, and power to see things through. The positive projections coming from his hysterical wife

fulfill a narcissistic need for self-affirmation. To use a simile: the hysterical
woman uses her projections to "pump up" her husband. However, she
holds the valve always in her own hands so that she can regulate, at all
times, his "size" and scope. If needed, she will let him "shrink and shrivel"
again. The inflated man, as the bearer of the projections, feels elated.

Phase III — Decompensation

Most of the time this state of happiness in the hysterical marriage turns
into a phase of disappointment. The husband has gained some self-esteem
through the supportive expectations of his wife. Yet this self-esteem is
overplayed or inflated. He suddenly becomes fearful about his own
courage. He has the impression that he has gone too far or has committed
himself far too much. His former doubts about himself return, and they
are stronger than ever. He is not all that his wife has expected of him.
His former passive needs for childlike security with a giving and uncondi-
tionally loving mother return with force. But such needs for regression
are repressed by him and are moreover refused decisively by his hysterical
wife. She will not become a mother to her husband. She cannot give up
her own privilege of being childlike, weak, and in need of consideration.
But as soon as the husband collapses in his pretense of chivalrous grandeur,
he becomes a laughingstock to her and an object of her angry contempt.
She is disappointed and berates him continuously. But he does not fight
her; rather he supports and confirms her in her reproaches. He is ashamed
of his weakness and accepts the contempt of his wife as just punishment
for his failure. He even hopes to be stimulated toward new and better
performance by her contempt. His ambivalent needs, on the one hand,
to be an inexhaustible, undemanding "mother," and, on the other, to be
mothered passively, often result in clumsy behavior. He may buy flowers
for his wife but leave them at his office. Or he may put them on the
newly upholstered couch and make spots on the costly material. Or he
may do the cooking but spill the food. All his actions demonstrate his
readiness to continue to be noble and helpful, but he does things in such
a manner as to force his wife to supervise him as if he were a child and to
chastise him to satisfy his need for punishment. His behavior becomes
pointedly helpless. The wife is partially angry about the husband's
clumsy exploits but still experiences a degree of satisfaction and self-
validation in chiding and correcting him, particularly so if she is his rival.

After a while, the husband exhausts himself in his ambivalent sacrifices. His wife's emotional life-style begins to deplete him and destroy completely the few resources he feels he still has. Finally he has nothing left to give to her or with which to oppose her. He is physically present with his wife but not really with her. He falls into increasing lethargy and passivity. All his actions seem to be aimed at avoiding arguments, to escape conflict, and to stay out of any involvement. He tries to find refuge in his work. He may protect himself behind a newspaper or a book or take flight into drinking. This avoidance behavior of the husband is, however, the worst thing that the hysterical woman could encounter. Her own self-esteem demands unceasing contact with the environment. She lives only for the attention of those around her and experiences herself only in the eyes of other people. She can bear hatred or refutation more easily than the absence of attention or reaction to her. "If only he would fight me, but this routinized boredom is totally unbearable." She finally nags and chastises her husband in an attempt to bring him back into motion. She may embarrass him publicly, try to arouse others against him, or try to gain his jealousy by extramarital flirtations and coquettishness.

The husband may well become jealous but not more active. Rather he becomes paralyzed. Constantly defensive, he insists that he is right and tries to explain his point of view in longwinded lectures. His righteousness sometimes arouses his wife's fury and hatred. He tortures her with his unending tolerance and generates guilt feelings. His attitude toward himself, his wife, and the environment is, "Look at all the suffering I have to go through." The environment (including many physicians and psychotherapists) will side with the husband. They admire his endurance and pity him for the fate that he suffers at the hands of his wife. Her affirmations that her husband is a common, hypocritical sadist are rarely acknowledged. A closer look into circumstances, however, will reveal the overt masochism and the hidden sadism of such passive, feminine, long-suffering husbands.

The hysterical woman's inability to keep her husband interested in her leads her to become confused about herself. She experiences her husband's behavior as an insult and a sign of contempt. If she, however, succeeds in making him react emotionally, she can relax momentarily, since "something is happening." The husband will occasionally allow himself to be goaded into short-lived temper tantrums. He will, however, stage a scene ineptly, so that later he feels full of guilt and asks for forgiveness. This brings him back into the arms of his wife.

Sexually, such couples live almost like siblings. The wife expresses outspoken disgust over her husband's inexpert sexual approaches. Often she cringes at his touch. If she accedes to sexual relations she feels like a whore because she does not experience any love for her husband. She complains about her husband's lack of sexual aggressiveness, yet the fear of sex has played the most important part in her choice of a partner. The hysterophile man suffers the often total sexual frustration without complaint. He begins to have secondary impotency or more commonly, premature ejaculation. His frigid wife will often laugh at him for this, and her derision may ruin his confidence in his potency. More and more overtly, the woman falls into the pattern of the revenge type described by Abraham [1]. Such a woman may try to prove her own strength by rendering her partner impotent.

For the hysterophile man the immediate sexual satisfaction is secondary to his relationship with his wife. A precondition for successful intimacy for him is her message that she will accept him and receive him willingly. His potency is entirely subject to her goodwill. His past personal problem is fear of castration emanating from his relationship with his mother. The present anxiety he feels about intercourse is enhanced by a castrating and contemptuous wife who classifies him as a failure. In particular, he cannot allow himself genital satisfaction because it might serve his underlying sadism. He tries not to hurt his wife during intercourse, yet, in his clumsiness, sadistic aggressive instincts often break through the repression barrier, and he does hurt her, "totally unintentionally." His wife, coincidentally, is beset with fear of being injured through sexual intercourse and reacts in an exaggerated manner. And so the man is happy to accept his impotency rather than expose himself to the dangers of sexual aggressiveness. His message to his wife is always, "I will encounter you much more tenderly than all those instinctual, sexually reckless ruffians." If she challenged him to "rape" her, he would become impotent, as he would if she gave the slightest hint of a sexual refusal.

The exaggeratedly thoughtful behavior of the husband and his need for a hint from his wife to start intimate relations is particularly difficult for the hysterical woman. She has her own ambivalence in regard to sexual relations and could enjoy them without guilt only if she were raped by her husband. She cannot tolerate the thought that she has to offer an invitation. In her ambivalence she behaves alternately demandingly and frustratingly when approached sexually. She always asks from the partner the opposite of what he is trying to do according to her instructions. When he has no sexual desire, she demands intercourse. If he expresses a need for sex, she turns him down. If he presses for sexual union, she commands him to be patient, tender, and thoughtful. If he waits tenderly and feelingly, she blames him for lacking masculine temperament and the will to power. This complicated courting of a capricious woman becomes too tiresome for the husband. He no longer has the resources to follow her every whim. So impotency becomes an expression of "staying out of the way" or even retiring with pique. The husband seems to indicate reproachfully that he is "no longer a part of this."

Phase IV — Character Formation in the Hysterical Marriage

Through the long-lasting violent battles in the marriage both partners are exhausted. They try to reduce the involvement in the marriage. A more stable equilibrium becomes established, and each one tries not to disturb it. They attempt to retreat to their own positions and no longer react to conflicts and arguments. Seen from the outside, the marriage has become more quiet and more peaceful. There are no more altercations, but there is also less emotional communication. Sometimes the fighting goes on loudly and dramatically, but without affective involvement and in a routinized fashion. And so the marriage becomes a skeleton of its former self.

But this is not good enough for the hysterical woman. She must experience the reaction of her environment toward her to avoid a feeling of disillusion and so that she will not experience inner chaos. She eventually relents in her demands on the husband, but then she must find structure, affect, and attention outside her marriage.

Sickness in the form of conversion symptoms is one way in which she may try to attract attention. She may suffer from real physical diseases, with hospitalization, dramatic operations, or chronic overuse of sedatives or pain killers. It is usually only these advanced symptoms that lead to psychiatric treatment. Sickness is often a "way out" for both partners, especially for the "nonsick" husband, since he need no longer bear the marital conflicts alone. Other people, potential rescuers, have to deal with the wife and give her security. The husband once again has clearly defined tasks through which he can prove himself: visits to the hospital, care of the household and children, care of the wife under medical direction, financial sacrifices, and so on. All these are carried out with great zest and good sportsmanship.

A second road to security and affection is open for the wife after her disappointment by the husband. She may attempt to engage the children as allies in the marital arguments and to make them judges between the two factions. Through her beratings of the father, such a woman initiates her children into almost all the couple's intimacies. The helpless father, in his turn, comes to "cry" with them and solicit their pity. The children are overburdened by this situation, but they soon learn that it is possible to turn the conflicted situation to their own advantage by playing the two parties against each other. Such children do not experience any firmness from their parents and, therefore, do not learn to build solid interpersonal relations. In their experience, everything can be manipulated, and because of this, relationships are false and insecure. In particular, the daughters often show an all-too-wise and pretentious behavior. Many will show behavior problems. The unhealthy and contradictory intimacy with both parents often becomes the base for a hysterical relation with a partner in later years.

The hysterical woman experiences feelings of inadequacy and guilt in regard to her children. She complains also that she is not able to love her children enough. An orally fixated hysterical woman especially shows a marked jealousy toward her child, who, she feels, has displaced her from a child's role in regard to the husband, who should act as a mother toward her.

Social activity is a third path that the wife may choose in looking for sufficient cohesion after the marital altercations have ceased. She may make fun of her husband in front of others, hoping to be consoled or to find self-affirmation by proving her superiority and letting the husband appear as a pitiful weakling. The manner in which a hysterical woman treats her husband in public may appeal to a male bystander and present him with the temptation to rescue a lovesick woman from her husband. If she takes a lover, she once again projects onto him the fulfillment of all of her fantasies: the beloved is masculine, strong, and understanding,

in contrast to the lame and weak husband. He knows how to tame her
and contain her. She feels requited and structured with him. She exults
that only with the beloved has she found out what living and loving are
all about. She will emphasize, especially in the presence of the husband,
that with the lover she has orgasms and can submit to him in truly feminine
manner. But looking more closely at this infidelity, one finds that the
beloved is usually a caricature of the husband. The hysterical woman
repeats the same game with her lover that she played in the beginning
with her husband: she chooses a partner whom, consciously, she expects
to guide her, but she decides when, where, and to what extent. She
refuses to allow the marital reality to spoil the projected relation with
the "strong" lover. By bragging about her relationship with her lover, the
woman sometimes succeeds in "castrating" the husband. He retires from
genital sexuality without battling the lover, and instead he identifies with
him in part and participates vicariously in sexual relations.

Frequently, hysterical women have extramarital relations and lovers
for years. This is in great contrast to their husbands, who remain forever
faithful to the unhappy marriage.

Threats of divorce are often used to pressure the husband. Although
these women broadcast complaints about their marriage everywhere,
they rarely take serious steps toward divorce. They remain with the
husband, as they see it, "out of pity." The husband, however, is against
all thoughts of divorce. Even though he appears unhappy and slighted in
every regard, he wants to remain with his wife. Many of these husbands
assert that they feel abandoned, lost, and unhappy without their wives.
Almost all emphasize that they would marry the same woman again if
they could start over. If one asks them directly, most of them will deny
that they have been exploited or oppressed or that too much has been
demanded of them. However, in contrast to these expressions are the
findings of the projective psychological tests: one finds a multiplicity of
evidence of being crushed, deadened, and transformed into a skeleton, as
well as many hints of strong needs for tenderness and nourishing security.
One man brought in a very descriptive dream: a fox was leaping at him,
biting at his throat to suck the blood out of him. Suddenly the fox had
the face of his wife. Another man mentioned that he felt like a burned-out
candle, another one like a battery with no charge left in it. Others fall
victim to a chronic depression with generalized fatigue and a feeling of

weakness. Neurasthenic complaints of various sorts, decreases in work capacity or professional performance, and general despondency are common. All these husbands accept this state of affairs, this fate, as the only way they can live with their wives. One man who was being treated by an internist for psychosomatic hypertension and multiple neurasthenic complaints expressed it this way: "If I am trying to criticize only the smallest of things, my wife reacts so violently that I prefer to be silent. I don't say anything any more, and I allow her to walk all over me. So the both of us will get along best. I prefer to have my present complaints than to go through once again what we went through last year."

The painful aspect for the hysterical wife is that she lives in an insolvable ambiguity. She would like a potent man, and yet she cannot tolerate a potent man. If the man is impotent she triumphs in revenge but remains sexually unrequited. If he is potent, her inferiority feelings are activated.

Her passivity demands that her husband be active. Yet because of her sexual problems, she cannot tolerate masculine activity. If she makes the man passive she can develop activity of her own, but in doing so she loses the gratification of her own passive needs. And if she limits herself to a passive existence, she must fear masculine "superiority."

In this severe ambiguity she finds the possibility of compromise with the hysterophile husband. The compromise is unsatisfactory, yet possibly the only bearable solution. The hysterophile man has the same problem: his own unsolvable ambiguity makes him seek a woman with such ambiguous wishes. He would like to be rendered potent by his wife, yet he fears that he might become aggressive in the process. He would like to become an active man if only to counter his passive needs, yet because of his castration anxiety, he does not dare display masculine activity.

Consciously, both partners choose each other with the hope of overcoming through each other their neurotic disturbances. Unconsciously, they choose each other to remain fixated in their neuroses. Thus, the marital relationship freezes into character formation. The interaction takes a schematized form and becomes a ritual. The couples reproach each other over the years with the same complaint — the behavior of one is only a reaction to the behavior of the other. The one can change only when the other changes. If, however, one of the two tries to change, he is immediately sabotaged by the other, because the other fears being returned

to his or her own inner conflict. If one then weakens in his desires for
sex or love, he is immediately stimulated by the other. If the other weakens
in his defense, or relaxes, he will be provoked anew. In this way, well-
regulated systems of interaction are created, and all behavioral variables
have a tendency to remain within defined boundaries. Each change in
behavior in one partner leads to a neutralizing reaction in the other. A
marital homeostasis comes about, a balance that both partners strive to
leave unchanged. "A marital couple in difficulty tends to perpetuate their
distress by attempting to resolve conflict in such a way that it continues"
[14]. Each one of the partners can use the other as an excuse for not
changing.

TREATMENT OF THE HYSTERICAL MARRIAGE

In the psychotherapy of hysterical marriages it has become necessary
to create new therapeutic concepts. Dealing with the thoughts, emotions,
and behavior of one partner at a time most often proves to be therapeutically unrewarding, and therefore concepts applying to the marriage
as a whole are needed. I have found the notion of *collusion* particularly
useful. H. Dicks [5] has used this concept, meaning by it an internal
object that is common to both partners. To collusion, one might add the
concept of the common defense arrangement. A fruitful hypothesis might
be that choice of the partner, as well as marital conflict, is explained by a
pattern similar to the neurotic conflict structure. Both partners in interaction try to master the neurosis. They attempt to act out their disturbances with each other in an effort to potentiate their own defenses.
Collusion then means a collaborative play put into effect by both partners.
The rules of the game are secret, often unconscious, but definitely agreed
on. Each one needs the defensive structures of the other to obtain substitute satisfaction for his own repressed needs. One of the partners may
allow himself a vehement presentation of an otherwise repressed need as
long as he feels sure that the partner will vicariously take care of matters
through his own defenses. He might also use his injuries at the hands of
the partner for his own defensive needs or to justify and legitimize his
neurotic positions. So the partners both participate in their needs for
satisfaction and for defense formations. Need and defense against need
in a similar neurotic conflict can be divided between two partners as
polarized roles. Each one will hold the partner to his role to justify his

own posture as merely a reaction to the neurosis of the other. This explains why these partners need each other urgently in spite of all their difficulties. There is an interdependence of the partners; the substitute satisfaction of one and the defenses of the other are intertwined. There may be symptom formation in one partner and reaction formation in the other. Such collusions play themselves out in verbalized interaction, usually in the form of *interaction circles* [21]. It is most important in psychotherapy to find the common neurotic denominator of such interaction circles, which usually appear in polarization. It is easily demonstrable that with these apparent opposites the conflict is often only the positive and the negative side of the same thing.

CASE 1   The therapy of a young oral-hysterical marriage showed that both partners had a disturbance in the earliest human experience, that is, a disturbance in the fulfillment of the elementary needs of the very small child for care, food, and warmth. Both of them had had mothers who had rendered them insecure and were possessive and domineering. Both had entered the marriage having been greatly deprived of genuine maternal tenderness and caring. In the beginning, the following polarized roles were accepted by both: she was allowed to be weak and in need of help and to lean on him; he saw a life-fulfilling task in the guidance and care of his wife. The wife, through her repetition compulsion, soon led the husband to an absurd point in the fulfillment of the mothering role and demanded too much from him, and he began to reject her harshly. He had denied his own dependency needs and passive expectations for care and tenderness. In her disappointment, the woman tried to reverse the situation. She allowed herself to become pregnant, she interrupted her work and began to devote herself totally to a mother role. As soon as the child was born, a change of roles took place. The wife, now a mother in her own right, did not seem to need her husband anymore, and the husband assumed a childish role, became openly dependent, and felt neglected by his wife. He demanded intercourse regularly at the same time that the child demanded feeding. The woman rejected him, stating that she could not starve the child because of his sexual needs, therein indicating how much in her fantasy, as well as in her husband's, the sexual act was merely an equivalent for being taken care of. The husband's situation presented itself beautifully in a dream: "There are a lot of fat market women in a big square. Each one of the women has an over-sized baby carriage with her. An older man appears and bargains with one of these matrons and is allowed to get into one of these big carriages for payment of money to be pushed around." The man's dream was a search for infantile gratification for neglected spouses.

The example shows how both partners have strong dependency needs and how both defend themselves, with each other's help, against the satisfaction of those needs for fear of being disappointed once again as they had been in childhood. The common ambiguity can be seen as a constant interaction cycle, with the formula: "I am so dependent because you are so rejecting — I am so rejecting because you are so dependent." Both are so dependent on each other and both reject the satisfaction of this need because of their own anxieties. The collusion — that is, the conflict about dependency — is split into two parts: at first the woman is in the frustrated and dependent role and the husband in the rejecting role. Later, the roles change, and the husband assumes the dependent side of the conflict, with the wife in the rejecting role. The total conflict situation can be understood as a symbiotic disturbance and forms the basis of a long-lasting marital conflict on the oral level.

Similar interaction cycles may be found in different types of conflicts, such as a conflict on the exhibitionist level. A woman who tended to show herself off in sometimes outlandish clothing complained about her frigidity and justified it by the fact that her husband was not considerate enough and was too greedy sexually. The husband, in turn, was disappointed with his wife, whom he perceived as threatening, overemotional, making impossible demands, and requiring sexual satisfaction incessantly. He became impotent. Neither was satisfied with his partner or his own role. The woman covered her own sexual defensiveness by finding fault with the husband and in this way denied her own problems. She was totally engrossed in her forcible demands for sexual satisfaction. The man, on the other hand, displayed a symptom of sexual inhibition, impotence, and he assigned all sexual needs to his wife since he could not take an active sexual role himself. The interaction formula in this instance is: the wife is so demanding sexually because the husband is impotent — the husband is impotent because the wife is so demanding sexually.

It is of crucial importance to interpret to the couple the interaction cycle in its totality. If the behavior of one partner only is interpreted, the attitudes of the spouse can always be presented as a defense, which does seem valid, because the spouse's behavior does adapt itself to maintain the accepted collusion in homeostasis. If, however, both partners are present when the essential interactions are observed, it is possible to begin to make changes.

SUMMARY

The chapter describes the hysterical marriage as the only possible kind of marriage which a woman with marked clinical hysterical traits can live in. The term *hysteria* is used in a wide clinical sense principally referring to hysterical character formation.

The hysterical woman in her marital relation is described as needing a great deal of self-confirmation from the outside to compensate for what she feels to be an inner weakness or emptiness. In this effort she engages in dramatic behavior and involves her husband in activities centering around her. By contrast, the husband she chooses, the hysterophile man, appears to be an inconspicuous person who may see in the marriage to his complicated wife a challenge that will justify him to himself. A characteristic of the hysterophile man is the inhibition of his own phallic exhibitionist needs, which, however, may be satisfied through grandiose fantasies of heroic deeds.

The phases of the hysteric marriage include an early idealization phase, a phase of disappointment, and, ultimately, a state where the hysterical marriage has become a way of life and has profoundly affected the character of both partners. Dynamically, the hysterical marriage is a bond into which both partners, the hysterical woman and the hysterophile man, enter, hoping to be cured of their respective neurotic disturbances. Yet this unconscious arrangement results in their becoming fixated in their neuroses; the typical course of a hysterical marriage eventuates in an interactive cycle in which each partner depends on the defenses of the other for the maintenance of his or her own defensive structure. Any effort by one partner to disrupt the interactive ritual is immediately neutralized by the other. For a psychotherapy to be successful, it is decisive that the common denominator of the dovetailing neuroses (the "collusion") be found and worked through.

REFERENCES

1. Abraham, K. Ejaculatio Praecox. In E. Jones (Ed.), *Selected Papers of Karl Abraham, M.D.*, Vol. 1. London: Hogarth, 1949.
2. Abraham, K. Manifestations of the Female Castration Complex. In E. Jones (Ed.), *Selected Papers of Karl Abraham, M.D.*, Vol. 10. London: Hogarth, 1949.
3. Arkonac, O., and Guze, S. B. A familial study of hysteria. *New England Journal of Medicine* 268:239, 1963.
4. De Boor, C. Hysterie: Konversionsneurotisches Symptom oder Charakterstruktur? *Psyche* 20:588, 1966.
5. Dicks, H. *Marital Tensions.* New York: Basic Books, 1967.

6. Freud, S. The disposition to obsessional neurosis (1913). In *The Standard Edition of the Complete Psychological Works of Sigmund Freud,* transl. and ed. by James Strachey with others. London: Hogarth and Institute of Psychoanalysis, 1958. Vol. 12, pp. 311–326.
7. Freud, S. The introductory lectures on psychoanalysis (1916–1917). *Standard Edition,* 1963. Vol. 16, pp. 243–476.
8. Freud, S. Group psychology and the analysis of the ego (1921). *Standard Edition,* 1955. Vol. 18, pp. 65–143.
9. Freud, S. The dissolution of the Oedipus complex (1924). *Standard Edition,* 1961. Vol. 19, pp. 173–179.
10. Freud, S. Inhibitions symptoms and anxiety (1926). *Standard Edition,* 1959. Vol. 20, pp. 77–174.
11. Freud, S. Female sexuality (1931). *Standard Edition,* 1961. Vol. 21, pp. 223–243.
12. Freud, S. New introductory lectures (1932). *Standard Edition,* 1964. Vol. 22, pp. 5–182.
13. Gastets, E. Eléments pour une systématique de l'hystérie. *Annales Medico-Psychologiques* 118:245, 1960.
14. Haley, J. Marriage therapy. *Archives of General Psychiatry* 8:213, 1963.
15. Ingham, J. G., and Robinson, J. O. Personality in the diagnosis of hysteria. *British Journal of Psychology* 55:276, 1964.
16. Johnston, M. L. Features of orality in an hysterical character. *Psychoanalytic Review* 50:663, 1963.
17. Kuiper, P. C. *Die seelischen Krankheiten des Menschen.* Stuttgart and Bern: Klett/Huber, 1968.
18. Lempérière, T. La personalité hystérique. Confrontations psychiatriques. *Specia* 1:53, 1968.
19. Reich, W. *Character-Analysis,* transl. by Theodore P. Wolfe. New York: Orgone, 1949.
20. Richter, H. E. *Patient Familie.* Hamburg: Rowohlt, 1970.
21. Watzlawick, P., Beavin, J. H., and Jackson, D. D. *Pragmatics of Human Communication: A Study of Interactional Patterns, Pathologies, and Paradoxes.* New York: Norton, 1967.
22. Willi, J. Joint Rorschach testing of partner relationships. *Family Process* 8:64, 1969.
23. Willi, J. Zur Psychopathologie der hysterischen Ehe. *Nervenarzt* 41:157, 1970.
24. Willi, J. Die Hysterische Ehe. *Psyche* 5:326, 1972.
25. Woerner, P. I., and Guze, S. B. A family and marital study of hysteria. *British Journal of Psychiatry* 114:161, 1968.

20

Learning to Work
With Couples

Lynn Parker Wahle

The treatment of marriage problems is complicated. The therapist not
only has to learn about marriage and the family and develop treatment
techniques, but has to develop a treatment style and philosophy that involves her[1] as a person. Learning to treat married couples involves a
process that takes time and experience and requires that the therapist
develop insight into her feelings, behavior, and role within her own family.
When she treats a marriage, she treats a system; and that system can
exert pressure on the therapist. If the therapist unwittingly joins the
system of the couple or family in treatment, it can seriously hamper
her effectiveness. In the process of treating married couples, the
therapist most often reexperiences feelings about her own primary family
and her current family, if she has one; she may be directly confronted
with issues related to her own family or marriage. Unless the therapist
is able to recognize and come to terms with these issues, they can
seriously interfere with her treatment of married couples.

[1]"She," "her," etc. are used throughout this chapter in reference to the therapist to avoid
repetition of "he and she," "him and her," etc. and because it is written from the perspective
of a female therapist. This device is not intended to exclude the many male therapists nor does
the information in this chapter only apply to female therapists.

A THEORETICAL FRAMEWORK

In focusing on marriage, it is important to examine the way in which the married couple is related to the family group of which they are a part. I view the family as a system, with the married couple as the focal point and the directors of the family. The couple sets the stage for the psychopathology existing in the family. Whether the presenting complaint centers around a child or a marital difficulty, the couple together needs to be actively involved in treatment.

The family functions as a system in which each family member affects and is affected by the other. When dealing with either a family or marital system, the therapist is dealing with more than the sum total of the parts. For example, the family has a history that significantly influences its course. This consists of both the history of the immediate family and the histories of both husband and wife, what they bring with them to their own family's stage. Families develop certain operating principles, or rules that allow for constancy and predictability. These rules are inherited from the spouses' own primary families, frequently having been passed along from generation to generation. They can be conditioned by the other growth experiences of family members, but they operate largely outside conscious awareness.

In a similar way, families also develop a mythology that governs the behavior of family members. (A myth differs from a rule in that the myth predicts the outcome as well as prescribes behavior.) A certain myth is often seen in a family in which there is difficulty acknowledging and expressing angry feelings. The myth goes something like this: "If I get angry, I will hurt somebody." A family's mythology exerts a strong influence on the family members and, again, usually operates outside of conscious awareness. The family's rules and myths reflect the need of the family members for constancy — the need to be able to make predications about their environment and relationships. The more functional a family unit, the greater its flexibility. In a closed family system, the ground rules are rigid and do not permit new experiences and growth. It becomes the therapist's task to help family members, or spouses, to begin to identify dysfunctional rules and myths and the ways in which they hamper the family's functioning and limit the ability of the family members to see all of the behavioral and emotional options open to them.

Because a marital unit or a family functions as a system, its potential for growth is greater than the sum of the individuals who comprise it. Treatment of the marital or family system can be a powerful vehicle for change, because even the smallest shift allows for greater flexibility in the system and will have an immediate and dramatic impact on the family members. The corollary also holds true — a change in any individual, in turn, feeds back into and has an impact on the system.

Just as it is important to examine the identified patient or spouse in the context of his family system, so it is important to view the therapist in the context of those systems of which she is a part. One of the reasons why treating marital disorders is such a difficult process is because the therapist, too, is a member of a family group. In the process of treating marital couples and families and in assimilating system theory, the therapist can be put into conflict with aspects of her own family system. Until the relatively recent advent of family system and communication theory, the system aspects governing behavior were largely unrecognized and frequently operated outside the therapist's conscious awareness. Simply recognizing the existence of systems and the way they work cannot help but have an impact on the therapist and the systems of which she is a part. Recognizing the existence of systems puts the therapist in touch with influential systems in her own life. As she begins to treat systems, the therapist is required to recognize and experience certain things about her own systems and the rules which bind her. If, for example, in the therapist's background there have been such unspoken rules as "Issues are best kept under wraps" and "Don't rock the boat," then treating a family system, in which it is necessary to deal directly with the rules and issues, immediately puts her in conflict with one of her own family rules. This can also occur in a more concrete manner when some of the therapist's rules or myths concur with those of the family or marital couple being treated.

A second, frequently overlooked, group that forms an important part of the therapist's context is the psychotherapeutic community. The psychotherapeutic community is composed both of the immediate work situation in which the therapist functions and of the broader professional community with which she comes in contact. Given the degree of controversy in the field over treatment approaches, this community may offer the therapist who views marital difficulties from a systems point of view more or less support for her position. Depending on the situation, this can either help or deter the neophyte therapist in the struggles of learning how to treat married couples. On a more subtle level, the psychotherapeutic community can also promulgate rules and myths that will affect the therapist to the degree that the community is an important reference point. When a group of professionals[2] representing the major disciplines in the mental health field, was given the task of identifying some of these rules and myths, they quickly produced the following list:

1. The therapist should make everything better.
2. Confrontation is not nice.
3. Being "human" is bad — we must be strong.
4. There is a right way to do it.
5. The answer is outside of me.
6. I have to have the answer.
7. Spontaneity is unprofessional.
8. Don't try anything unless you know it works.
9. I have to be liked.
10. Negative feedback means that you don't like me.
11. Being perfect is good.
12. Craziness is bad.
13. The emperor is wearing clothes.

Although the subject is beyond the scope of this chapter, it is important to acknowledge in a discussion of systems that married couples and families fall into ethnic and societal groups. These groups also have rules and myths that can have an important impact on the families and couples that the therapist treats, and the therapist should be cognizant of this fact. A simple but pertinent example for the therapist who is treating marriages is the impact on married couples of the greater acceptability and ease in recent years of obtaining a divorce due to the shift in societal norms.

THE NEED TO BE AWARE OF PROCESS

In learning how to treat married couples and to deal with marital systems,

[2]Students at The Family Institute of Chicago's intermediate course *On Becoming a Family Therapist* given during the summer of 1973 and led by the author of this chapter.

the therapist must become aware of the process of how family members relate to one another, as well as of the content of what is being communicated between family members. In treating a married couple, it is easy to get caught up in the content of what they are saying (or arguing about) rather than recognize the significance of the process occurring between them. Communication can be broken down into two parts. First, there is the content, or informational, part of the message. Second, there is the interpersonal intent[3] of the communication, usually a non-verbal indication of the speaker's relationship to the person receiving the message.

The therapist needs to become sensitive to process. The fact that this requires sensitization goes back to the way in which the therapist was socialized in her own family. Most therapists, as children, were trained to deal with people on a content level. An example of this kind of family mythology is seen in such dicta as, "All that is, shows" or "What people say is what they feel (mean, think)," or, stated slightly differently "If you are a polite (good, courteous) person, you ignore or do not respond to the other messages" (primarily the nonverbal ones that qualify communication). An exaggerated illustration is that of one person's pretending to like another. The person receiving such a communication does not respond by pointing out that the speaker's facial expression is contemptuous, that the speaker, in fact, cannot quite look him in the eye and that the speaker even turns his body away slightly as they converse.

THE ALLOCATION OF RESPONSIBILITY

It is important for the therapist to be aware of the process by which responsibility becomes divided between her and the married couple. This provides a valuable way for the therapist who has become "jammed" in the treatment to identify why it happened and how to correct it. When treatment has reached a stalemate, it is frequently because the allocation of responsibility has been mismanaged or has not been successfully completed.

The manner in which a treatment contract is established with a marital couple sets the stage for the treatment process. For this reason, it is of critical importance how the responsibility is initially divided between the

[3]This notion was suggested by Bernard Liebowitz.

therapist and the married couple. The allocation of responsibility is an
active dynamic issue, one of the key points around which growth and
change occur, and it needs to be examined throughout the treatment process.
One of the most common mistakes that neophyte therapists make in treating
marital problems is to begin dealing with the content of what is upsetting the
spouses without having established a treatment contract. By treatment
contract, I mean negotiations about how the spouse or family members
define the problem, what they expect from the treatment, what the
therapist feels she realistically is able to do, and the therapist's expectations of the couple. The treatment contract can be either explicit or
implicit, depending on the therapist's particular style and the couple's
needs.

The treatment contract is not static; it represents the agreement between the therapist and the couple around which the entire treatment
process revolves, and it may be renegotiated or changed. It provides a
valuable means of allocating responsibility. The term *responsibility*
as used in this chapter refers to an individual's being accountable for his
behavior, acknowledging his feelings, and actively working on the tasks
that he or she has defined for himself or herself in treatment. Conflict
over issues of responsibility can occur between the therapist and couple,
as well as between spouses and family members.

Responsibility has been appropriately divided between the therapist
and couple being treated if the therapist is in charge of the treatment and
each spouse is actively engaged in doing the work necessary to grow and
change. The therapist is in charge of the treatment when she sets appropriate limits on her responsibility. Being in charge of the treatment means
that the therapist functions with integrity, has a sense of her own identity,
as apart from the married couple, and is able to move freely in and out of
the marital or family system. When in charge, the therapist feels comfortable with herself and what she is doing, not as if she is compromising
herself out of deference to a spouse or a marital or family system. This
does not necessarily mean that the therapist removes herself from the
system, but that she examines how the system impinges on her and she
on the system.

Each spouse is responsible for his growth and progress in treatment,
and if the therapist assumes a patient's responsibility, it interferes with
the spouse's growth, and the treatment cannot progress. The therapist

becomes trapped when she starts doing the work for the spouse or couple. If this happens, the therapist is in a position of being responsible for her patient's work in the treatment and the patient takes charge of the treatment process. If the patient is in charge, the therapist loses her ability to direct the treatment and to have an impact on the patient or married couple. At such a point, the therapist frequently feels burdened and overworked in relation to the couple — a feeling that should be a clue to the therapist that it is time to review and reconsider the allocation of responsibility.

CASE 1   Paul called, requesting treatment for himself and his wife Joanne. Paul was 38 years old and Joanne was 31. They were recently married and had been having chronic serious arguments. Paul was highly anxious in the first session, defensive, suspicious, and angry. Underneath his aggressive facade was much fear, to which the therapist attempted to relate.

At the end of the first session, Paul angrily turned to the therapist, and asked her what made her think that she could be of help. The therapist avoided getting caught in the trap of making promises, but rather spoke of her past experience working with marital couples in a manner that gave hope but not a guarantee. The therapist explained that Paul's situation with his wife needed to be explored further, and she clarified the diagnostic process.

Paul's concern about the therapy was further manifested when he consulted another therapist. He reported to the therapist in the following session that he had seen someone else to check out the validity of the therapist's impressions and skill. The therapist responded by explaining again to Paul and Joanne how she worked, and she summarized the observations she had made about their difficulties. She asked Paul to clarify his intentions about treatment and whether or not he wished to work further with her. The decision about whether the couple felt the therapist could be helpful and whether or not they wanted to continue in therapy with her was left to them.

This example illustrates negotiations for setting up a treatment contract. The therapist clearly indicated what she felt able to do, giving the couple the responsibility of defining what it was they wanted and of deciding whether they wished to work with her. The therapist made the decision-making process explicit, so that a decision about remaining in treatment with her was clearly their responsibility. It would therefore be difficult for the couple to make the therapist feel responsible and guilty later for any lack of progress, to compare her unfavorably with the other therapist, and so on. The therapist could have been trapped into assuming too much responsibility had she felt the need to compete with the other therapist for this couple. Had she competed, the couple would have gained control of the treatment situation.

THE USE OF PROJECTION IN MARRIAGE AND THE FAMILY

No discussion about marriage and family systems is complete without examining the concept of projection (see also pp. 293–307). In evaluating how well a family system operates, a helpful index is the degree of projection occurring within the family or between the spouses. Another way of measuring this is the degree to which family members are able to take responsibility for themselves, that is, for their feelings and behavior. Focusing on the degree and ways in which families and marital couples utilize projection offers the therapist a way to organize the data presented to her and something on which to base her interventions. It becomes an important guiding therapeutic task to help each family member or spouse become responsible for himself. This includes issues like the family member's responsibility for communicating his or her feelings and where he or she stands in respect to other people. It means that the family member takes personal responsibility rather than worrying about somebody else in either a protective or controlling manner.

Other ways family members avoid taking responsibility for themselves is by blaming other people or by behaving, in response to an outside authority, as a sole motivator; here again, everything is seen as outside the self. In addition to the projections that occur within the family, the family or married couple can project responsibility outside the family system, for example, by blaming the community, school, or police for the difficulty, whatever it may be. The therapeutic task for the therapist is to reverse the projections and to work toward the individual.

TYPES OF MARITAL PROJECTION SYSTEMS

It is possible to classify marital couples according to the ways that they utilize projection. Marital projection systems can be divided into three different types as defined by Kramer [7]: (1) conflictual, (2) overadequate-underadequate, and (3) united front. A marriage is rarely of one pure type, but the divisions are presented here as distinct types to underscore the projection process that occurs in each one. Frequently, marriages contain elements of more than one marital type. Sometimes one pattern is more prominent than another, and a marital couple can appear superficially to be utilizing one projection system, but as treatment progresses, the more basic pattern emerges. The therapist needs to be aware that in attempting to intervene in the marital projection system, there is always the danger of the couple's shifting to another projection pattern rather than each spouse's assuming responsibility for himself in a real way.

The following sections examine each marital type in relation to its definition and function and to the therapeutic task and risks for the therapist. A case example will be given to highlight each marital type.

The Conflictual System

The conflictual pattern of marital interaction is one in which the interaction between the spouses is marked with much conflict. Of the three marital projective types, it tends to encapsulate psychopathology the most, with children the least involved in the projection system. The conflict centers around "who is to blame," with each spouse attempting to project blame and feelings of inadequacy onto the other. The function of the conflictual pattern of interaction is to allow for displacement of feelings to the area of conflict in order that the central issues and intrapsychic and interpersonal conflicts can be avoided. In this instance, neither spouse takes personal responsibility but blames the other. In this type of marital projection system, the fact that there are marital problems is openly acknowledged by both spouses.

The therapeutic task with the conflictual couple is to interrupt the conflict to help each spouse experience and deal with the feelings that have been projected so that he can become responsible for himself as a person. In giving up the conflict, a compensating factor for the couple is that it allows each spouse to feel a greater sense of security and less of the nagging feeling that he is avoiding something that is too threatening. The therapist helps break into the system by implying, through her therapeutic interventions, that it is safe to look at one's self and take responsibility for one's actions and feelings.

One helpful therapeutic tactic to take the focus away from the conflict is to help the couple find areas of agreement. With this interactional pattern, it is important that the married couple feel that the therapist is strong and able to take charge. The family unit is often chaotic. There frequently seems to be nobody in charge, and it is not unusual for a child to assume, or attempt to assume, some parental functions. Another approach to the conflictual marital type is to engage the children in the treatment process in order to get some clues as to what some of the family issues are.

The risk for the therapist in treating the conflictual couple is that of being pulled into the family system by becoming a referee or the family's "parent." This can be a necessary and helpful step, in the process of engaging the couple, but the danger is that the treatment may reach a stalemate there. If that happens, the therapist is stuck with all the responsibility, and the spouses are off the hook, rather than gradually relieving the therapist of the responsibility that is properly theirs. In such a family constellation, the children often fear divorce and are usually able to talk about their fears.

CASE 2   Dick and Tina H., a young couple in their twenties, applied for treatment because their marriage was marked with continual conflict. They had been married for about a year and had no children. Both Dick and Tina were fearful of their dependent feelings and utilized the conflict between them as a way to distance each other.

The marriage of Tina's parents was also marked with much conflict. Tina felt closest to her mother, whom she tended to idealize because she was the only person she perceived as "coming through" for her. Her father was portrayed as hostile, distant, and aloof. The underlying fear in Tina's family was that the father was "weak," that he could not handle emotions, and the myth was that, given too much pressure, he would "break." Therefore, the hostility and aloofness of Tina's father was interpreted by other family members as an indication of his strength and independence.

In contrast, Dick's family was very fearful of conflict. His mother was overprotective and domineering, although Dick denied this for a long time. Dick's relationship with his father was also a distant one; his father denied feelings and would avoid conflict either by giving in or tuning his mother out.

Dick and Tina unconsciously chose one another because of the "parental fit," where each of them was able to re-create with their spouse a relationship similar to the one that existed with their parent of the opposite sex. Tina was fearful of Dick's "weakness," as she was of her father's, and their arguments would center around Dick's being gone all the time. Tina would attempt to control Dick because of her fear of abandonment, but her behavior actually functioned to provoke his being gone more, which, in turn, allowed her to idealize his independence of her, and thus his strength. This neatly fit with Dick's experience with a controlling mother, a tie that was difficult for him to recognize and break.

This example shows how the conflict between Dick and Tina masked their underlying concerns about their feelings of dependency. As Tina was able to recognize her concern about depending on Dick, her earlier fears of abandonment, and her fears of Dick's weakness, the conflict between them gradually eased. Dick became more responsive, became involved in activities around the house, and was finally able to recognize some of the feelings he had about his own family. If the therapist had focused on the content of the conflict rather than on the purpose it served for Dick and Tina and on their respective investments in maintaining the system, the treatment most likely would have failed.

The Overadequate-Underadequate System

The overadequate-underadequate pattern (a term derived from Bowen [1]) of marital interaction is marked by one spouse's playing the overadequate, or "healthy," role and the other, the underadequate, or "sick," one. The overadequate spouse tries to "treat" or take care of the underadequate one. It is seldom this simple, however, because each spouse can be over-adequate and underadequate in different areas. And, to add to the con-fusion, this can become layered — while one spouse may *appear* over-adequate, the other one really is, but on a covert level. Another way of stating this is that, although the underadequate spouse is perceived as weak, he holds a great deal of power in his "weakness."

The overadequate-underadequate pattern of interaction functions to help both spouses handle their feelings of inadequacy. The overadequate spouse projects his feeling of inadequacy onto the underadequate spouse, who is willing to accept the projection. The overadequate spouse can then feel a pseudo-adequacy through taking care of the underadequate spouse. The overadequate spouse experiences the underadequate spouse's dependency as reassuring. The underadequate spouse, on the other hand, gains a sense of pseudo-adequacy through recognizing the overadequate spouse's more subtle dependence on him for his sense of adequacy. In this interactional pattern, the underadequate spouse is willing to accept the whole responsibility for marital and family difficulties. Children in a family with an overadequate-underadequate parental arrangement tend to accept their parent's definition of where the strength lies and frequently will side with the overadequate spouse against the underadequate one.

In a family in which there is an overadequate-underadequate projection system, it is not unusual to find that neither parent has resolved issues concerning dependency and autonomy and that these issues are often perceived by the spouses to be mutually exclusive. One spouse functions in a totally "dependent" fashion, while the other is "independent," and the issue of dependency and autonomy becomes split between the spouses in its expression rather than resolved. This split can also manifest itself with the children, with a child's appearing either totally dependent or totally independent. In marital situations in which there is an over-adequate-underadequate projection system, the identified patient[4] may be either the underadequate spouse or a child. When the child is the identified patient, the underadequate spouse is quickly identified as the parent who is having the difficulty managing the child or is in some way responsible for the child's difficulties.

The therapeutic task in treating the overadequate-underadequate marital projection system is to change the system so that each spouse takes responsibility for his own sense of inadequacy. This allows the spouses to develop an understanding of those inadequate feelings, and, by coming to terms with them, to develop a real, rather than a pseudo, sense of adequacy. Another way of stating the task is that each spouse must deal with the unresolved aspects of the conflict over dependency and autonomy in himself and achieve a working balance in their expression.

One way for the therapist to begin to shift the system is to reinforce the underadequate spouse's strengths, begin to question the assumed weaknesses, and so on. This has to be done in such a way that the under-adequate spouse is given enough support, without the therapist's assuming an overadequate stance in relation to the underadequate spouse and, inadvertently, reinforcing the same pattern. At this point there is the real danger of alienating and threatening the overadequate spouse and competing with him for his position in the family. A way to deal with this is by beginning to engage the overadequate spouse's dependency and offer him some relief from playing the "independent role," stressing "how lonely it is out there," and so on. The support of the overadequate spouse is an important transitional step, because it helps stabilize the family system.

Another way of stating the therapeutic task is not to take the spouses'

---

[4]The identified patient, or scapegoat, is the person designated by other family members as "sick" or having the problem. He frequently is "presented" as the problem when treatment is requested.

role definitions seriously, not to "buy" the underadequate spouse's inadequacy or the overadequate spouse's strength. In treating a marriage with an overadequate-underadequate projection system, one of the risks for the therapist is that she might accept the family's definition of where the strengths and weaknesses lie and thus reinforce the projection system. It is important to remember that even the therapist's own mental set in this regard can have quite an impact on the marital or family system. Frequently, in a family with this type of marital projection system, the concern is that the overadequate spouse will "break." His overadequacy is set up as a reassurance against this fear. Case 2 (p. 466) contains an example of this. In the overadequate-underadequate pattern that underlay the conflict in the couple's marriage, the overadequacy of the husband was used to protect the wife against her fear that he would fall apart.

When the overadequate-underadequate structure begins to break down and spouses have to own up to their own feelings and take responsibility for their own behavior, it can be painful and threatening. It is at this point that many couples attempt to withdraw from treatment. Therefore, it is important that both spouses feel able to depend on the therapist so that they do not feel left in the lurch when they are making this transition.

CASE 3   The J. family presented with their oldest son Randy, age 7, as the identified patient. The parents' complaints included Randy's distracting behavior in the classroom, his inability to concentrate, and his "independent" behavior at home to the extent that they felt unable to discipline him. There were two other children in the family, Sandy, age 5, and Tony, age 2. Although Sandy was not described as presenting problems, when the family unit was seen, manifested in her behavior were signs of marked dependency, chronic thumb-sucking, constant clinging behavior, and so on. Tony, also described as problem-free, was hyperactive, threw temper tantrums, and manifested behavior directed at getting him into the center of family activities.

Evelyn and Daniel J. were both in their late thirties, and their overadequate-underadequate relationship quickly became apparent. Evelyn was underadequate and Daniel overadequate, and, as the treatment unfolded, Daniel's need of Evelyn's underadequacy became very clear. This illustrates how, although Evelyn overtly was in the underadequate position, on a more covert level she functioned in the overadequate role. Both Daniel and Evelyn had many unresolved conflicts in relation to dependency and autonomy. Evelyn's parents had an overadequate-underadequate relationship, in which her mother was overadequate and her father underadequate, while Daniel's mother was underadequate and his father overadequate. In both of their families the overadequate parent was the "like-sexed" parent. Daniel and

Evelyn had each been a threat to their overadequate parent; this parent responded by continually undermining their sense of adequacy, in order for the parent to protect his overadequacy.

Neither Daniel nor Evelyn had felt able to depend on either parent; the underadequate parents were perceived as weak and unavailable as well. The J.'s own overadequate-underadequate relationship was an attempt to deal with this, and the way in which the overadequacy and underadequacy became layered was a reflection of Daniel and Evelyn's conflictual feelings toward their parents and the roles their parents played. As they were able to deal with their feelings about not having their dependency needs met as children and as they experienced in a corrective way the support of the therapist, they each were more able to acknowledge both dependent and autonomous feelings. Evelyn began to assert herself and do more for herself, and Daniel was more open about his feelings, although this was still hard for him and he continued to depend on overadequacy to some extent. It appeared, however, as though Daniel did not take his overadequacy as seriously and was more aware of how he would adopt this at times as a facade to the outside world. Randy was reported to be showing his needs more openly and Sandy to be functioning in a more independent fashion.

This example shows clearly how unresolved issues about dependency and autonomy were reflected in the parent's establishment of an overadequate-underadequate projection system and how these issues were repeated in the family unit as a whole. Because the presenting problem was Randy, it was necessary to see the entire family in order to focus away from Randy and onto the marital system. In engaging this couple in treatment, one of the early techniques used was to point out how the parents were encouraging Randy to be independent while allowing Sandy to remain dependent, making few demands on Sandy.

The parents' investment in and contribution to the children's behavior was most graphically illustrated during a treatment session with the whole family. Tony and Sandy had been having a good time switching chairs in the office, some of which were more padded (and so more appealing) than others. Randy was indicating through his facial expression that he was eager to play this game as well, but he sat quietly in his chair. When this was pointed out, Evelyn doubted that Randy really felt like playing. It was suggested to Evelyn that she ask Randy if he would like to sit in the padded chair, which was free at that time. Evelyn did so, Randy leaped with joy to the chair, and both parents were astonished at his response. They were helped to see the ways in which they were subtly encouraging his "independent" behavior, which they complained about, and this led to an examination of themselves and their marital relationship.

The United Front System

The united front projection system [13] is the most difficult family interactional pattern to treat. There is usually no acknowledgment of marital difficulties because the spouses project all blame and underlying feelings of inadequacy onto a child, who becomes the identified patient. The spouses unite against this child, utilizing his difficulties as the issue around which to communicate and experience some pseudo-closeness. The child identified as the patient is always the presenting problem. The united front projection system creates a feeling of relatedness because of the two-against-one phenomenon. It allows both spouses to project their painful feelings and responsibility for their own behavior onto an outside source — the child. There is a strong fear of conflict and little tolerance for disagreement. Denial is a strong factor, and the child identified as the patient plays a central role in this form of marital interaction. The identified patient often feels responsible for holding the marriage together and frequently is able to verbalize this.

The task for the therapist in dealing with a united front projection system is to focus the treatment away from the child who has been identified as the patient onto the marital pair. This is difficult to do, and there are many risks for the therapist. One common danger is that the couple then forms a united front against the therapist. When this happens, the therapist can function to "stand in" for the identified patient and take some of the pressure off him, with resultant symptom relief. If the treatment does not become stalemated at this point or if the marital couple do not withdraw from treatment, it is possible to begin to focus more on the marital couple.

The timing of the "defocusing" process and of the setting up of the treatment contract is important; frequently, the harder the therapist pushes to get into the system, the more united the couple becomes. It can be helpful to permit the child to be the focus of the treatment for awhile to allow the marital couple to begin to develop a rapport with the therapist. A beginning treatment alliance can be formed by focusing on the parents' difficulties in handling the identified patient — the frustrations and real feelings they experience in relation to the child. This beginning focus on the parents is less threatening because it is approached through the child. The therapist needs to keep clearly in mind the goal of engaging the parents. Otherwise, the danger is that rather than utilizing the focus on the identified patient in a temporary way as a method to involve the parents, the therapist instead joins the system by making the child the focal point.

Another method of breaking into the united front system is for the therapist to identify areas of disagreement and to help the spouses to confront each other. The therapist may need to be provocative in stirring up the conflict in the here-and-now of the interview situation so that it can be highlighted and identified. Again, it takes skill and timing on the part of the therapist to evaluate each spouse's readiness for this and to provide the necessary support. Spouses who have a united front frequently present their feelings with the preface "we feel." It can be therapeutic for the therapist to point this out and insist that the spouses begin to go through the verbal mechanics of presenting their ideas as separate people. The therapist who actively intervenes in the couple's verbal united front has more opportunity and leverage to help the couple express their differences.

CASE 4   Fred and Elizabeth B. applied for treatment on the recommendation of their child's school. The identified patient, Joseph, age 8, was having difficulty reading and concentrating, had problems in his peer relationships, and was reported to be hyperactive. Joseph was in a special class at school. Fred and Elizabeth were both in their early forties, and Joseph was an only child; the parents decided not to have any more children because of the difficulty they had had with Joseph.

Both Fred and Elizabeth came into treatment viewing Joseph as the problem, and at points in the treatment when they felt uncomfortable, they would revert back to him as a focus. It was possible to begin to focus away from Joseph as the problem by talking about the parents' own sense of frustration and sense of helplessness in relation to Joseph. Both Fred and Elizabeth initially spoke about their situation in "we" terms, but with the therapist's guidance and constant reminders, they were able to learn to speak in "I" terms.

As this was worked with in the therapy situation, it quickly became apparent that Elizabeth relied heavily on her husband, constantly checking him visually for approval of her ideas and feelings. This was pointed out to her and the etiology of her insecurity explored. Elizabeth's mother had been highly critical of her, and her parents were divorced when she was an adolescent. This left Elizabeth with a fear of not being able to trust and depend on a man. Elizabeth was able to reexperience and deal with her fears and feelings, actively working in the interview situation on trusting her husband more and taking risks to present her own thinking and opinions.

As the result of Elizabeth's beginning to confront and disagree with her husband, Fred began to experience and be able to verbalize his own distrust, insecurity, and fear of being wrong. Fred had dealt with this by adopting a stern facade, which, it was revealed in therapy, had intimidated both his wife and son. Fred was able to get in touch with feelings about his childhood only in a vague way, experiencing a massive sense of insecurity and recalling that he could never do things right for his father. Fred's relationship with Joseph improved, and Joseph was more comfortable asking his father for help.

Both Elizabeth and Fred projected their concerns about their own adequacy onto Joseph by being highly critical of him, and this was demonstrated to them in the interaction of the treatment interview. Elizabeth and Fred used therapy to learn how to relate together as two separate people, how to express differences, and how to share their real feelings and concerns. Joseph was reported to be responsive in class and more involved with other children. Joseph was never completely "defocused" because the parents made constant reference to him throughout the two years of their treatment, and, although they were able to actively deal with some of their own problems, they became very threatened at any implication that they had a problem, labeled as such.

This example illustrates well the care needed to engage the united front couple. The therapist was able to develop a rapport with Fred and Elizabeth by engaging them over their concerns about Joseph and by offering them the hope of relief from the helplessness they both felt. Relating to this sense of helplessness, although it was manifested in regard to Joseph, permitted the therapist to begin to delve into both Fred and Elizabeth's more basic sense of insecurity in themselves. By using the couple's interaction in the interview situation, the therapist gained valuable clues to some of the central issues for the family. The therapist went ahead and dealt with the issues in such a way that Fred and Elizabeth never had to lose face by acknowledging that they were the problem as such, and the therapist was able to effect some change in the system.

CASE 5   Jack and Mary T., a couple in their forties, applied for treatment because of Roberta, their 16-year-old daughter. Jack was a successful attorney and Mary was a housewife. They were concerned because Roberta was withdrawn and restricted her social activities to an undesirable circle of friends. They verbalized immediately the situation as a "family difficulty" and superfically manifested an overadequate-underadequate relationship, with the husband "treating" his wife. The therapist only realized after she was totally left out of their interaction and communication in the interview that she had been substituted for the daughter in the service of their united front. Jack and Mary were both given to intellectualizing and frequently talked on such an abstract level that the therapist could not understand them. At times the therapist would find herself feeling like the "crazy" one, not an uncommon feeling for the identified patient in a united front family. Roberta experienced some relief from parental pressure as the therapist came to occupy the identified patient position. However, when the therapist recognized what was happening and attempted to pull herself out of the scapegoat position and focus more on the spouses in a direct feeling way, they withdrew from treatment.

This example illustrates how the therapist did not recognize, at first, aspects of the united front projection system with a couple who utilized another projective pattern of interaction, the overadequate-underadequate type. In this instance, the therapist was subtly shut out by the couple's communication pattern and prevented from effectively intervening in the system. It was impossible for the therapist to have an impact, except perhaps indirectly by taking some of the pressure off the identified patient, unless she detached herself from the system. This was intolerable for Jack and Mary, and they withdrew from treatment. To illustrate further how the marital projective types can overlap, termination of the treatment occurred at a point when Jack's overadequacy was being the most threatened, because Mary was beginning to act in a more assertive manner.

DEPENDENCY AND AUTONOMY

Dependency and autonomy are central dynamics underlying all three marital types and can be utilized as bases from which to work with both families and marital couples. Dependency is defined as the normal, natural need which individuals have for other people for support, feedback, and approval. In successfully meeting his dependency needs, the individual is given the feeling that there is somebody available to him, and he is able to revitalize his energies within the relationship. When the individual's dependent striving are met, he is able to establish a sense of security. Autonomy is defined as the freedom to step away from relationships, to allow distance, and to tolerate and enjoy being alone. Although the two can sound like opposites, one balances out and reinforces the other. For example, it is only when a person's dependency needs are successfully met that he has the kind of security and energy that allows him to reach out actively in an autonomous fashion. In turn, an individual is only able to be comfortably dependent when he has experienced enough autonomy to allow him the necessary distance and sense of self to turn to others without the fear of losing his sense of individuality and freedom. In these simplified statements, the interdependence between dependency and autonomy is obvious.

It is important to view the reciprocal and dynamic nature of dependency and autonomy as it operates within the context of a relationship. When these issues have not been successfully resolved by the individual, a likely place for their expression is in the marital interaction. This has been illustrated in the preceding case examples. Both spouses and family members experience difficulty when they are unable to shift flexibly and responsively from the dependent and autonomous positions. Also, this can affect what happens developmentally between parent and child; the child becomes unable to deal successfully with his dependent and autonomous needs, and the pattern is repeated when the child forms his own family.

There is a widespread myth in today's society that dependency and autonomy are mutually exclusive, that dependency is "weakness" and autonomy "strength." The result is that dependent feelings frequently are labeled as "childish" and "selfish," and people strive for a pseudo-independence, in which there is a denial of their needs rather than a true autonomy that allows for dependency. As a result, a cycle begins in which dependency needs are considered selfish and unacceptable and are not expressed or met. The individual becomes frustrated, angry, and feels deprived. He is unable to feel truly autonomous because of the hidden needs of which he feels ashamed, is therefore unable to give of himself freely, feels resentful of the demands made on him, and so on.

It can be helpful to uncover these issues and work with them in the here-and-now interaction between the marital partners, as well as to explore the ways in which the spouses' families of origin dealt with these issues. Seemingly simple issues, such as a spouse's inability to ask for anything for himself or feel that he has anything to offer his spouse, become, in fact, very critical and complex. Another common belief associated with dependency and autonomy is that one spouse should be able to please the other spouse automatically, without either having to ask. This can be viewed as an attempt to bypass the entire issue, and it can be dramatic to see the impact on the couple when the therapist begins to focus on how they communicate their needs, and what happens when spouses make their needs more explicit. The spouse who is able to ask for himself and receive, begins to experience greater self-worth. The spouse who gives and can appreciate his spouse's response begins to feel that he has more to offer. It is this type of working with the marital interaction in the here-and-now that is critical for change. The degree of attention given to historical factors, depends on the marital couple, how bound the spouses are to their families of origin, and the degree of freedom that they have to try new roles and responses.

Another related reciprocal process is that of risk and trust. Inherent in the growth process and necessary in creating the therapeutic milieu, is the freedom to take risks, where ongoing growth is dependent on continued risk-taking. To take risks implies trust, and, as one successfully takes interpersonal risks, this permits the growth of more trust. When patient and therapist engage in the treatment process, they are involved in a process whereby they mutually attempt to develop a reciprocal relationship within which there are opportunities to develop trust and take risks. It is not an uncommon psychotherapeutic tenet that the patient needs to develop a sense of trust in the therapist. However, the other side of the issue has been paid much less attention. That is, for the therapist to be real and effective in her interactions with the patient, she too needs to develop a corresponding trust in and ability to take risks with her patients. As the therapist is free to take risks with her patients, this will support and encourage patients to take risks with her, within their families, and in other relationships. This faces the therapist with the task of becoming comfortable with her humanness in her role as therapist.

The risk and trust factors can be worked into the fabric of the treatment itself, in dealing directly with family members' ability to trust in and take risks with one another. The therapist can take an active role in promoting the family members to take risks with one another and with her, and to use her own behavior as a model. What occurs between the therapist and family members can be used as a way of exploring what occurs between family members and between spouses. The therapist should let each spouse's and each family's way of relating wash over her so that she can experience what it is like to be the receiver of their messages. It is a way of putting herself in the family members' "shoes." Too much is lost when there is an attempt to screen out feelings of empathy in the service of being impartial.

TREATING MARRIAGES: ITS IMPACT ON THE THERAPIST AND THE THERAPIST'S FAMILY

So far this chapter has focused on ways in which the therapist can become trapped in the marriage or family system she is treating, and it has examined techniques which the therapist can use to be more effective in the impact which she has on the systems. However, since treatment is an interactional process between therapist and patient, it is of critical importance to examine the ways in which the therapist's experience with the marital couple she treats and her movement in and out of their family system has an impact on the therapist and on her own family and marriage. In the process of treating marriages and family systems, the therapist is affected by her direct experience with the family, her development of theoretical constructs, and her attempts to integrate the two in the course of her work with the family.

It is not uncommon that, when the therapist becomes stalemated in her work with a marital couple, she is struggling with personal issues similar to those being dealt with in the treatment of the couple and that she is experiencing much discomfort. Her exposure to these issues with the families she treats, may force her to struggle with issues she might have been avoiding in her own family. The therapist's work with a patient's family might contribute to a change in her own behavior — for example, her having a talk with her husband about a particular issue of concern, a full-blown marital crisis, where the marital contract is either renegotiated or dissolved, or the therapist and her spouse seeking treatment for themselves. The fact that the process of treating a marital couple also affects the therapist and her own marriage explains, at least in part, why there is frequently so much anxiety on the part of the therapist when treating a marital or family system.

The therapist is affected both by the similarities and differences between her family system and those of the marital couples she treats. There are aspects of the marital couple's family system, rules, myths, projection patterns, and so on, that are shared by the therapist and overlap with those of her family system. It is in this overlap that much interaction occurs between the therapist and couple she is treating. The therapist might be unable to deal with aspects of the couple's family system similar to her own and she may deny them. But pressure is continually being exerted on the therapist, because these aspects of the family system she is treating are operating dysfunctionally, and they may provide enough stimulation to help upset the equilibrium in her own family concerning a given issue. The therapist is not a formal member of the family she treats, but she moves in and out of their system. This may give her the objective advantage, therefore, to recognize an issue in the family she treats that she can later acknowledge in her own family. This is similar to what happens in a treatment group, in which a patient first recognizes something in another group member, which permits her to recognize it later in herself.

The overlap in the therapist's and the marital couple's family systems may not be accidental. As in marital choice, where the spouse's decision may be partially based on unfulfilled neurotic needs, there can be a similar process operative between the therapist and family with whom she chooses to work. It is my belief that although a neurotic choice reflects an individual's need for constancy, it also can represent an attempt to get into a workable reciprocal relationship, in which individuals within a familiar structure can grow in response to one another. This is seen frequently in the treatment of marital couples, when each spouse behaves and responds in certain ways that are helpful to his own growth and trigger new behavior in his spouse. The therapist, too, makes the choice of which marital couple she is going to treat. This is most obvious with the independent practitioner, who decides whom she will or will not treat. On a more subtle level, there is a natural selection process, in which certain couples stay in treatment with certain therapists. Even in an agency setting, in which cases are assigned, therapists engage certain couples in treatment, other couples drop out, and therapists and patients make the choice whether or not to work together.

This suggests that a factor in the therapist's and couple's choice to work together may be a similarity between their family systems and issues with which they are struggling. As in a marriage, patient-therapist choice can be based, in part, on a need for both parties to grow in response to each other. If therapists make an honest appraisal of the trends in their caseloads, it becomes apparent that patient choice — that is, the families with which the therapist is able to work — depends on "where" the therapist is as a person and within her own family system. Over a period of time, a therapist's caseload will reflect the personal progress and changes she has made and the changes in relation to her marriage and family. It is possible for a therapist to treat a particular family at one time in her life that she could not treat at another time. Also, the therapist's caseload itself forms its own system, which can promote an impetus for growth, as different family systems balance one another through the therapist.

In treating married couples and families, the therapist is exposed to family systems that are different from her own. She can be exposed to feelings, behavior, and rules that are directly opposed to those in her own family and that can invalidate her own family myths. This can have a direct effect on how she will then behave with her own family or spouse; the exposure may not even operate on a conscious level. Here again, the therapist's unique position, which allows her to join the family system of the marital couple she treats, further intensifies the impact of these differences. The experience that the therapist has "surviving" an issue with a patient family affects the way she deals with the same issue at home. Patient families can provide the therapist with opportunities to experiment with issues that she would not dare to risk with her own family; and after discovering that a certain approach is safe, she may try it with her own spouse or family.

What does it mean to the therapist to be able to include in her role definition the ability to treat a marriage? Difficulties in her own marriage immediately set up a paradox: by definition she is a person who can help marriages, but she cannot help her own. Frequently, students learning about the treatment of marital couples and families ask, "How can I help troubled couples if I cannot help my own marriage?" The dilemma this poses for the successful therapist is, "How can I not change, if I can be effective with others?" This dilemma can contribute to the therapist's difficulty in taking charge of the treatment session because it may interfere with her ability to project responsibility for herself within her own family and marriage. The development of a theoretical framework for understanding marital systems can also have an impact on how the therapist views her own marriage and family, can challenge her own family's rules and myths, and can expose her to different behavioral options. For example, a therapist might play the overadequate role in her own marriage, a fact she may never have recognized or was unable to conceptualize before learning about the overadequate-underadequate marital projection system. However, confrontation with this theoretical construct can create anxiety about her role in her own family, make it difficult for her to project onto her spouse, and help her begin to develop some insight into her own defense patterns. When this same therapist treats an overadequate-underadequate marital relationship, the process becomes intensified as she has to deal with the issue in the here-and-now of the treatment session. The treatment session represents for the therapist an arena where her own conflicts are reenacted in front of her. She cannot watch passively but must actively intervene and respond to be effective therapeutically. The therapist may either be able to grow from the experience and "take it home" with her, or she may become anxious, overwhelmed, and stalemated in the treatment.

CASE 6   David and Marilyn R. originally applied for treatment because of difficulties they were having with their 17-year-old-son John. As a result of John's treatment, they became aware of some marital dissatisfaction and subsequently sought out marital therapy for themselves. The therapist was an experienced male therapist, who had recently begun to treat families and work with marital couples on a conjoint basis.

Marilyn's presenting complaint was that she wanted more closeness with her husband and needed somebody to talk to. She complained a lot about her husband's unavailability and would frequently burst into tears. David's response was that he had allowed himself to get as close to his wife as he had allowed himself to get to anybody. When his wife would cry during the treatment session, he would not respond to her, but rather looked down and away from her. Furthermore, when David felt that his wife was being too demanding at home, he would shut her out, avoid coming home, watch TV, or drink too much.

In the interview session, Marilyn would plead with her husband to open up to her. The therapist believed that David was closing Marilyn out and found himself being sympathetic to Marilyn and angry with David. Also, the therapist began to recognize that he himself was feeling uncomfortable and emotionally blocked when dealing with this couple. The therapist was aware that he was having difficulty treating this couple and presented an audio tape recording of a treatment session with the couple for supervision. It quickly became apparent that the therapist was not in charge of the treatment session, his interventions were weak and ineffective, and although the therapist spoke of a rapport with the wife, the recording reflected periods of warm exchange with David, while his relationship with Marilyn seemed more remote.

During this period of time, the therapist had experienced discomfort with a number of other families and couples with whom he was working. He identified his investment in helping these family members achieve closeness and break down barriers, and as a result of the extreme discomfort he felt with them, began to recognize that he was struggling with issues of closeness within his own marriage and family, and that at times he felt safer taking risks with the families he was treating than at home.

The therapist began to recognize similarities between some of the interactional patterns between himself and his wife and those that were occurring between David and Marilyn in the treatment sessions. The therapist felt that when he was threatened by a relationship, his response was to get out of touch with his own feelings, deny his need for the other person, and withdraw. The therapist felt guilty for being unable to respond to his wife, and therefore became overly sympathetic with Marilyn in the treatment session and identified in a negative way with David. The therapist had misperceived some of the real qualities in his relationship with David, had overestimated the quality of his relationship with Marilyn, and did not see the ways in which Marilyn contributed to her husband's withdrawal from her.

The therapist was aware that his withdrawal from his own wife and denial of dependency on her gave him much more of a feeling of control in their relationship. He made the initial decision to seek out therapy for his marriage. The therapist he contacted suggested a weekend group experience for them both, which would allow both him and his wife to evaluate whether they wished to proceed further in treatment. When the therapist's wife decided that she wanted marital treatment, the therapist became more ambivalent about it, since this was counter to their usual experience of his wife following his lead.

In his own treatment, the therapist began to recognize that his wife had not really been pushing hard for him to change because of her need to see him as strong. They both began to recognize their investment in maintaining their pattern of interaction and the ways in which each manipulated the other to be dependent out of fear of losing each other. The therapist's own parents had divorced when he was very young, and he had lived with a number of relatives when he was growing up and had trained himself to be self-sufficient. He was unable to ask directly for himself, fearing that he would not get it, and was left with the feeling that he had to get what he wanted by manipulation. The therapist's wife was from an intact family, in which there was much control through guilt and threats that important family members would leave.

In the therapist's treatment session with the R.'s following supervision and his own initial treatment session, he was able to help Marilyn begin to see her investment in and contributions to the way in which her husband was responding to her. The therapist, in the past, in relating to his own wife, had to feel that she was vulnerable before he felt it was safe for him to be warm and open with her. Therefore, it is significant that the therapist no longer needed to relate to Marilyn in such a way that would perpetuate her vulnerability. The therapist was able to take charge of the treatment session and reported that he no longer felt bound up emotionally. The therapist and his own wife started to renegotiate their marital contract and to work on changing those aspects of their relationship which were based on desperation rather than choice.

THE IMPORTANCE OF TRAINING

Some type of formal training in marital and family therapy is important, if not imperative, for the therapist who seriously wants to invest in treating marital couples. The process is a difficult one, and, especially in the early stages of the therapist's work with couples and families, it is valuable for the therapist to have a resource outside herself to provide much needed support. Training can vary, from the more traditional one-to-one supervisory model, to in-service training programs, to more formalized training programs independent of an agency or institutional setting. Since the theoretical framework deals with system elements, it can be helpful to provide a group experience in which the examination of the group process provides additional learning opportunities. Family interviewing, co-therapy, role playing, and audio and video tape recordings can be helpful teaching tools. Including the spouse or family of the therapist in the training process can also be helpful.

The element of formalized training offers yet another dimension to the learning process and the therapist's experience. It provides her with membership in yet another system, which can support her in her movement in and out of the family systems she is treating, as well as in her struggles with her own family. A training program within an agency setting, offers yet another opportunity for the teaching and examination of family systems, of what is occurring within the "agency family," and of the way in which the therapist relates to that family. It is not uncommon for the beginning marital or family therapist to project her sense of helplessness about this undertaking within her "agency family." An example of this occurred in an in-service training program in a public institution. The training program was set up on a group basis, and early discussion reflected the therapists' sense of helplessness and feeling of impotency in the agency structure. Related issues concerning a sense of helplessness with the "agency family" were mentioned repeatedly until the therapists were helped to see that although their concerns were realistic on one level, their concern with this topic was also a projection of their feelings about doing family treatment and a way to avoid dealing with treatment issues. A parallel process emerged, in which therapists both learned to be more effective in their interventions with the families with which they worked, as well as to take more responsibility for changes they wanted on the job and to be more assertive.

THE PROCESS OF BECOMING A MARITAL THERAPIST

Although the process of learning how to treat a marital or family system is a highly individualized one, there are three overall stages that the therapist goes through. These are (1) initiation, (2) struggle, and (3) integration. It is helpful for the therapist who is attempting to learn how to treat marriages and family systems, to be aware of the fact that she herself is involved in a process. This process is an evolving one that takes time, that can stimulate or enhance her own personal struggle within her family system, and that will bring painful and uncomfortable times as well as opportunities for personal growth. Where the therapist is in her

own developmental growth and in her marriage and family, will influence
how she goes through these different learning stages. They will have different meanings for a therapist who is struggling to establish her own
personal identity than for one who has achieved a clear sense of self and
a good balance in her marriage.

In the initiation stage, the therapist first begins her work with married
couples and families. At this point, she has only some rudimentary
theoretical exposure, which she is just beginning to test out in direct
work with marital couples. This stage is marked by feelings of confusion
and anxiety, with the therapist frequently feeling helpless in treatment
sessions with the family or married couple. The therapist finds it hard
to take charge of the treatment sessions. She has little or no operational
framework from which to operate. An additional pressure is that the
therapist's initiation into family and marital treatment may stir up her
own unresolved family issues or touch current ones with which she is
struggling. The beginning therapist commonly feels "stuck," and her work
often reflects the fact that she is experiencing difficulty having an impact
on the family system and identifying relevant issues on which to work;
she feels that the family or marital couple is frequently in charge of the
treatment. It is in this stage that the therapist often looks for training or
supervision in marital and family treatment if she does not already have it.

The second stage is one in which the therapist is in the process of
developing a base, learning a theoretical framework to guide her in her
approach with married couples and families, and applying and actively
testing these principles directly in treatment. It is important that the
therapist test these concepts for herself and develop a framework which
is comfortable for her. The process of assimilating the theory requires
that she also test and question some of her own family rules and myths.
This is an actively engaging period for the therapist, which is often difficult and painful and which may precipitate a need for therapeutic
intervention for the therapist and her family. This phase can have a
powerful impact on the therapist and her own family that forces a variety
of issues to the surface.

The integration stage occurs when the therapist is well on her way to the
development of her own treatment style. Treatment style can be described
as the therapist's "identity as a therapist," and, when put in these terms,
has its parallel in the developmental process an individual goes through

in identity formation. The therapist's treatment style emerges from her integration of theory and its application and from her own personal struggles. At this point, the therapist as a person becomes integrated with her treatment style. There is a noticeable decrease in the therapist's anxiety level. The reciprocal process between the therapist, her family, and the families and married couples she treats always continues, but the therapist, hopefully, is at a point where she has developed her own warning system when becoming "stuck" with a family, her methods of becoming unhooked from a family system, and her ability to recognize the need for and obtain help when she needs it.

ACKNOWLEDGMENTS

I would like to thank my teachers and colleagues at The Family Institute of Chicago for the ideas, stimulation, and opportunities for experience that they contributed to the development of my theoretical framework and therapeutic and teaching style. A special thanks goes to my husband Kurt for helping me crystallize some of my thoughts, but most of all for his patience and support.

REFERENCES

1. Bowen, M. The family as a unit of study and treatment. *American Journal of Orthopsychiatry* 31:40, 1961.
2. Bowen, M. Family Psychotherapy with Schizophrenia in the Hospital and in Private Practice. In I. Boszormenyi-Nagy and J. L. Framo (Eds.), *Intensive Family Therapy*. New York: Harper & Row, 1965. Pp. 213.
3. Bowen, M. The use of family theory in clinical practice. *Comprehensive Psychiatry* 7:345, 1966.
4. Ferriera, A. J. Family myth and homeostasis. *Archives of General Psychiatry* 9:457, 1963.
5. Ferriera, A. J. Family myth: The covert rules of the relationship. *Confinia Psychiatrica* 8:15, 1965.
6. Jackson, D. D. (Ed.). *Communication, Family, and Marriage: Human Communication*, Vols. 1 and 2. Palo Alto, Calif.: Science and Behavior Books, 1968.
7. Kramer, C. H. The Theoretical Position: Diagnostic and Therapeutic Implications. In C. H. Kramer, B. Liebowitz, R. L. Phillips, S. A. Schmidt, and J. Gibson, *Beginning Phase of Family Treatment*. Chicago: The Family Institute of Chicago, 1968. Pp. 1–15.
8. Lidz, T., et al. Intrafamilial environment of schizophrenic patients; II. Marital schism and marital skew. *American Journal of Psychiatry* 114:241, 1957.

9. Liebowitz, B.   Diagnostic Interviews as Preparation for Family Therapy. In C. H. Kramer, B. Liebowitz, R. L. Phillips, S. A. Schmidt, and J. Gibson, *Beginning Phase of Family Treatment.* Chicago: The Family Institute of Chicago, 1968. Pp. 16–29.

10. Liebowitz, B., and Schmidt, S. The Adolescent's Family and Group in Therapy. Paper presented at the American Group Psychotherapy Association Annual Meeting, New Orleans, January, 1970.

11. Phillips, R. L.   Disengagement, Responsibility, and Defining a Self. In C. H. Kramer, B. Liebowitz, R. L. Phillips, S. A. Schmidt, and J. Gibson, *Beginning Phase of Family Treatment.* Chicago: The Family Institite of Chicago, 1968. Pp. 30–38.

12. Satir, V.   Conjoint Family Therapy. Palo Alto, Calif.: Science and Behavior Books, 1967.

13. Schmidt, S. A.   Special Treatment Applications: United Front, Acting-Out Adolescent, and Only-Adopted-Child Families. In C. H. Kramer, B. Liebowitz, R. L. Phillips, S. A. Schmidt, and J. Gibson, *Beginning Phase of Family Treatment.* Chicago: The Family Institute of Chicago, 1968. Pp. 39–51.

14. Schmidt, S. A., and Liebowitz, B.   Adolescents and Their Families. Paper presented at the American Orthopsychiatry Association Annual Meeting, New York, 1969.

15. Stein, J. W.   The Family as a Unit of Study and Treatment (monograph). Seattle: The Pacific Region Rehabilitation Research Institute of the University of Washington School of Social Work, 1973.

16. Vogel, E. F., and Bell, N. W.   The Emotionally Disturbed Child as a Family Scapegoat. In N. W. Bell and E. F. Vogel (Eds.)., *A Modern Introduction to the Family.* New York: Free Press, 1960. Pp. 382–397.

17. Watzlawick, P., et al.   Pragmatics of Human Communication: A Study of Interactional Patterns, Pathologies and Paradoxes, New York: Norton, 1967.

18. Wynne, L. C.   The Study of Intrafamilial Alignments and Splits in Exploratory Family Therapy. In N. W. Ackerman (Ed.), *Exploring the Base for Family Therapy.* New York: Family Service Association of America, 1962. Pp. 95–115.

19. Wynne, L. C., et al.   Pseudomutuality in the family relations of schizophrenia. *Psychiatry* 21(2):205, 1958.

Index

Index